Teacher Evaluation That Works!!

Second Edition

The Educational, Legal, Public Relations (Political) & Social-Emotional (E.L.P.S.) Standards & Processes of Effective Supervision & Evaluation

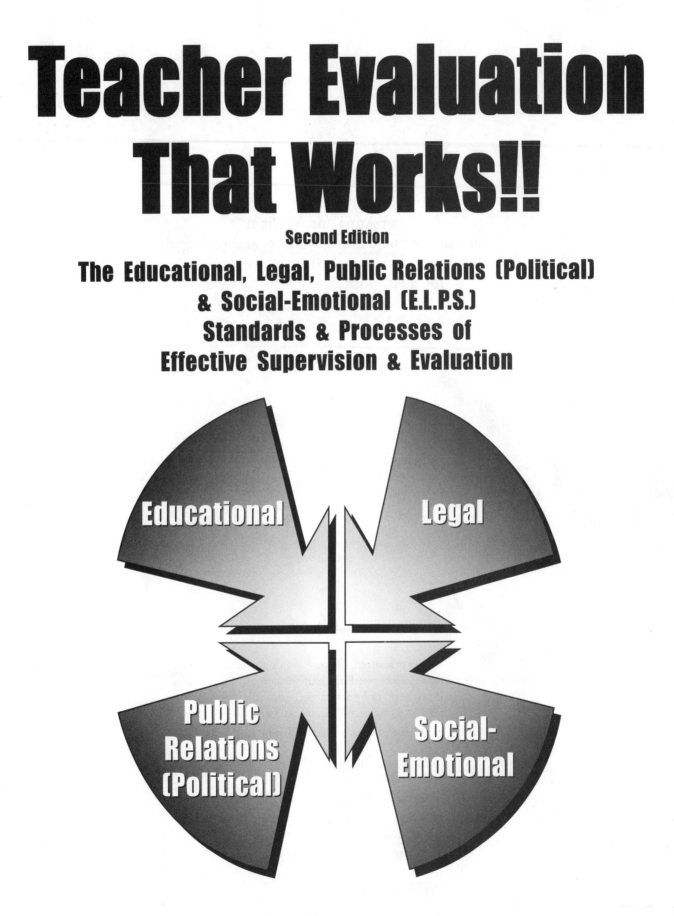

by William B. Ribas

For Anna and William,
and all the outstanding teachers and principals
who have touched their lives and
for their mother, my wife, Debbie.

William B. Ribas
Ribas Publications
9 Sherman Way, Westwood, MA 02090
Fax: 781-551-9120
Email: billribas2@aol.com
Web site: ribasassociates.com

ISBN 0-9715089-2-5

THANK YOU

My thanks to the following people for their help with various sections of this book.

James Walsh, Superintendent of Schools in Brookline, MA, and Associate Professor of Educational Administration at Simmons College, and the Brookline School Committee for supporting the development of the E.L.P.S. program.

Philip Katz, Brookline Educators Association President, and David Weinstein, Gretchen Albertini and Bill Hibert, Brookline Educators Association Grievance Committee Chairs for Brookline, MA, for their suggestions on various documents and procedures.

Dorine Levasseur, Massachusetts Teachers Association Consultant, for her descriptions of "Duty of Fair Representation" and the "Weingarten Right."

Martin Sleeper and Susan Moran, Retired Principals in Brookline, MA; Mike Frantz, Assistant Headmaster in Brookline, MA; Mark Springer, Principal of the Mason-Rice School in Newton, MA, and Robin Welch, Principal of the Woodrow Wilson School in Framingham, MA; Ina Hart Thompson, Brookline Educators Association Grievance Team; Sandra Spooner, Executive Director of Research for Better Teaching; Bill Simmons, Principal in the Oneida, NY, Public Schools; Eileen Kieser, Assistant Principal at Norton, MA High School; Kelly McCausland, Director of Human Resources for the Lexington, MA, Public Schools and Vice President of the Massachusetts Association of School Personnel Administrators; and Don McCallion, Director of Human Resources for the Framingham, MA, Public Schools and past President of the Massachusetts Association for Personnel Administrators, for reading various parts of the book and providing helpful editorial comments.

Robert Fraser, Attorney at the law firm of Stoneman, Chandler and Miller, for the initial translations from "legalese" into lay terms which are the basis for the sections of the book on *due process, just cause* and *progressive discipline*. Meg Maccini, Boston Public Schools and Catherine Reidy, attorney with law firm Deutch, Williams, Derensis and Holland for assistance with the do's and don'ts of investigations.

Claire Jackson, Superintendent of the Sharon, MA, Public Schools, for assisting with the connections between supervision and evaluation and curriculum implementation.

A special thanks to Jonathon Saphier who has been very generous with sharing his substantial expertise as a published author when reading drafts of the book.

Gretchen Underwood and Charles Webb, Deans at Brookline High School; Emily Ostrower, Principal, Cambridge, MA, Public Schools; Mary Matthews and Chris Whitbeck, K–8 Curriculum Coordinators, and Carol Schraft, Barbara Shea, John Dempsey and Milly Katzman, Elementary and Middle School Principals in Brookline, MA, for their assistance with case studies and sample documents.

Jennifer Dopazo, Assistant Town Counsel, Brookline, MA, for her help in writing "An Evaluator's Guide to Gathering and Verifying Evidence."

The Lexington and Brookline, MA, Public Schools for permission to use their excellent supervision and evaluation documents as samples for the readers.

Diane Pollard, Coordinator and Administrator of Development and Support for Statewide Initiatives, and the State of Texas for permission to use the Texas Professional Appraisal System (PDAS).

Audrey Anderson and Joshua Faigen of Folio Publishing Services, Inc., for copyediting and typesetting the second edition of this book.

Bill Ribas
January 2005

TABLE OF CONTENTS

INTRODUCTION 1

The Educational, Legal, Public Relations (Political) and Social–Emotional
Processes and Standards of Supervision and Evaluation 5

    Sources 6

CHAPTER 1

Ascending the E.L.P.S. (Educational, Legal, Public Relations [Political] and
Social–Emotional) Toward Excellent Supervision and Evaluation 7

E-The Educational Process and Standards 7

L-The Legal Process and Standards 8

P-The Public Relations (Political) Process and Standards 9

S-The Social–Emotional Process and Standards 10

Teacher Social–Emotional Processes and Standards 10

Evaluator Social–Emotional Processes and Standards 11

    Figure 1: Social–Emotional Components and Processes—Teacher 12

    Figure 2: Social–Emotional Components and Processes—Evaluator 13

Conquering the E.L.P.S. 13

    Figure 3: Supervision and Evaluation 14

    Sources 15

CHAPTER 2

District-Level Systems for Training, Coaching and Assessing
an Effective Program of Supervision and Evaluation 17

Training the Evaluators in Your District in
Supervision and Evaluation 21

The Archaeological Dig 25

    Figure 4: Evaluator Training and Support Cycle 26

The Role of Superintendents and Senior Administrators Beyond
Providing Evaluators With Training (Teaching) and Coaching
in Supervision and Evaluation 27

Figure 5: Identifying the Role the Various Central Office Administrators
Play in Supporting Building-Level Administrators. 28

Who Dropped the Ball? 29

Make Your Senior Administration User Friendly
for the Evaluators 30

Assessing and Reteaching the Implementation of
Supervision and Evaluation in Your District 32

Teacher's Assessment of His/Her Evaluator's
Performance as a Supervisor and Evaluator 35

One District's Experience With Teaching, Coaching, Assessing and
Reteaching the Concepts of Effective Supervision and Evaluation 37

Evaluator Survey of Potential Areas for Training and Support for
Your District's Teacher Supervisors and Evaluators 39

Criteria for Effective Observation Write-Ups 43

General Comments, Notes and Reminders for Improving
Supervision and Evaluation Practices 46

Sample Needs Assessment Report 48

Sources 59

CHAPTER 3

The Educational Skills and Knowledge Needed to
Be an Effective Supervisor and Evaluator

The Educational Skills and Knowledge Needed to
Be an Effective Supervisor and Evaluator 61

Analyzing Observations in Terms of Claims, Judgments, Evidence,
and Impact Statements and the District's Performance Standards 61

Excerpts From Sample Write-ups That Include Subjective
Conclusions Supported by Observable and/or Verifiable Data 68

Sample Observation Write-up That Includes Subjective Conclusions
(Claims, Interpretations and Judgments) Supported by
Observable and/or Verifiable Data 70

Data Sources 73

Developing Your Note-Taking Skills 83

Peer Support With Writing Observation Write-ups and
End-of-Year Evaluation Reports 95

Common Language and Standards 96

Time-Saving Tips for Supervisors and Evaluators 98

　　Time Study Survey 100

Sample Minimum Contract Compliance Observation Write-Up for a
High-Performing Teacher by a Principal With a Large Evaluation Load 110

Peer Review/Evaluation/Supervision/Coaching (All of the Above)? 112

　　　Figure 6: The Role of Peers in Supervision, Evaluation
　　　　　　and Staff Development 114

Example 1 115

Example 2 117

Example 3 118

Example 4 118

Conclusions 120

Sample End-of-Year Report That Includes Subjective Conclusions
(Claims, Interpretations [Impact Statements] and Judgments) Supported
by Observable and/or Verifiable Data 121

　　　Sources 129

CHAPTER 4

Sources of Observable and/or Verifiable Evidence
Other Than Classroom Observations

Sources of Observable and/or Verifiable Evidence
Other Than Classroom Observations 131

Conferencing to Create Change: What You Ask a Teacher
and Hear From a Teacher Is Often More Important Than
What You Tell a Teacher 137

　　Converting Performance Standards to Conference Questions 139

　　Pre-Conference Form 140

　　Post-Observation Conference 141

　　　Figure 7: Response to Teacher Performance 142

Post-Conference Preparation Sheet 143

Final Evaluation Conference 146

Six Stages of Listening and Questioning to Promote Behavioral Change . . . 146

Questions an Evaluator May Ask a Teacher About the
Following Performance Standards on Assessment 149

Questions an Evaluator Asks a Teacher about
Professional Development Portfolios 149

Sources 150

CHAPTER 5

The Public Relations (Political) Skills and Knowledge Needed to Work Effectively With Teachers' Associations/Unions and Other Constituencies . . 151

Many Teachers' Associations/Union Leaders Are Leading the Way 153

Figure 8   The Pressures on Teachers' Associations/Union Leaders as They
Balance Their Role in Supervision and Evaluation Between
Advocating for *More Teacher Performance Accountability*
and Advocating for *Job Protections:* Prior to 1995 155

Figure 9   The Pressures on Teachers' Associations/Union Leaders as They
Balance Their Role in Supervision and Evaluation Between
Advocating for *More Teacher Performance Accountability*
and Advocating for *Job Protections:* After 1995 156

Supervision and Evaluation: Quality Control for Public Education 156

The Public Relations (Political) Solution 157
The 33rd Annual *Phi Delta Kappan*/Gallup Poll
of the Public's Attitudes Toward the Public Schools 157

Each Party Must Own Its Part of the Problem!
A Case of Institutional Finger Pointing 160

Sources 163

CHAPTER 6

The Legal Processes and Standards as They Relate to Supervising and Evaluating Low-Performing Teachers 165

What Do Due Process and Just Cause Mean? 168

The Duty of Fair Representation 170

Legal Standards for Determining if the Union/Association
Has Violated Its Duty of Fair Representation for a Member 171

Weingarten Right 172

An Evaluator's Guide to Gathering and Verifying Evidence 173

Case Study: Using the Various Types of Evidence 176

Harassment? 179

Decision Tree for Administrators Responding to Indirect Claims 180

Figure 10: Indirect Data Decision Tree 181

The Team Approach to Supporting and Coaching Evaluators Involved in
Difficult Evaluations or Reducing the "Ghost Town" and "Goldilocks" Effects. . 182

Difficult Evaluation/Progressive Discipline Support and Coaching Seminars . . 183

Peer Conferencing to Help Your Peers With Write-Ups of
Low-Performing Teachers (Evaluations, Memos, Observations, etc.) 185

Case Study of a Difficult Seventh and Eighth Grade
Science Teacher Evaluation (Sample of a Four-Year Cycle) 186

Case Study of a Difficult Third Grade Evaluation
(Sample of a Two-Year Cycle) 188

Case Study of a Difficult High School Evaluation
(Sample of a Three-Year Cycle) 189

Case Study Activity 191

A Second Evaluator–Supervisor Model 192

Questions to Ask Yourself When You Are Supervising and/or Evaluating a
Teacher You Suspect Is Unsatisfactory (or Barely Satisfactory) 193

Reasons Contributing to Teachers and Teachers' Associations
Not Believing Just Cause Has Been Demonstrated in an Evaluation 195

Format for an Improvement Plan 196

Sample Improvement Plans 198

Open Book Assessment on Improvement Plans 213

Sources 214

CHAPTER 7

Progressive Discipline 215

What Is Progressive Discipline? 215

    Steps in Progressive Discipline 216

    The Exceptional Situation 218

Do's and Don'ts Related to Investigating an Employee Discipline Situation . . . 218

Knowing How to Use Progressive Discipline
Is Often Easier Than Actually Doing It 221

Documenting Your Progressive Discipline Actions 222

Components of a Written Reprimand
(and Memo Following an Oral Reprimand) 222

Peer Conferencing to Help Your Peers With Memos After
Oral Reprimands and/or Written Reprimands 223

Study Guide on Progressive Discipline 226

Progressive Discipline and Evaluation 226

       Sources 233

CHAPTER 8

**Creating a Culture of Openness to Change and
Receiving Feedback About Areas for Improvement** 235

Sample File Cabinet Assessments of Observation and Evaluation Write-Ups . . 238

Evaluators Teaching Sample Lessons as a Method of
Modeling a Culture That Is Open to Change and
Receiving Feedback About Areas for Improvement 268

CHAPTER 9

**Supervision and Evaluation Documents
and Contract Language** 271

The Problem With a Poorly Functioning
Evaluation Program Is Usually Not the Document! 272

Developing a Supervision and Evaluation Document 274

Tale of Two Documents 281

    The Brookline Document 282

    The Lexington Document 282

    Analyzing the Documents 283

Brookline Contract Language on Supervision and Evaluation 285

    Article 6 – Evaluation and Supervision 285

The Public Schools of Brookline, Massachusetts
Evaluation Criteria and Format 291

Annual Report of Teacher Effectiveness 291

Principles of Effective Teaching (Massachusetts Department of Education) . . . 294

    Brookline High School Student Comment Sheet 303

Evaluation Assignments for Integrated Services Staff. 308

    Timelines for Teacher Evaluations 310

Lexington Public Schools 312

    Article 10 – Evaluation and Supervision 312

    Chart of Evaluative Responsibilities 313

Professional Growth Plan 322

Final Report on Professional Growth Plan 323

Suggestions for a Professional Growth Plan. 324

Teacher Performance Standards 326

School Nurse Performance Standards 329

Special Education Teacher Performance Standards 332

Language Arts/Reading Specialist Performance Standards 335

Psychologist Performance Standards 339

Speech and Language Pathologist Performance Standards 342

Library Media Specialist Performance Standards 346

Counselor/Social Worker Performance Standards 349

Occupational Therapist Performance Standards 352

Elementary Consulting Specialist 356

Curriculum Leader Performance Standards 358

Lexington Public Schools Observation Form 362

Lexington Public Schools Final Evaluation Form 363

So What Are the Correct Answers? 365

Brookline Document 365

Lexington Document 366

Texas Professional Development and Appraisal System 369

Summary 426

       Sources 427

CHAPTER 10

Ensuring Inter-rater Reliability and Permanent, Positive Change in Your District's Supervision and Evaluation System 429

Please Don't Make Me Train the Administrators! 431

  Keep Them Interested 432

  Creating Training Groups 432

  Changing the Groups When Confronted With a Negative Dynamic 433

  Assigning Tasks to Group Members 434

  Getting Started 435

  Why Am I Here? (Think, Pair, Share) 435

  Sample Introductory Activity 436

  Procedures 436

  Handouts 437

  Inter-rater Reliability Activity 1: Climbing the E.L.P.S. 438

  Steps of the Lesson 438

Increasing Inter-rater Reliability Using Your
District's Performance and Curriculum Standards 439

  Inter-rater Reliability Activity 2: High-Performing Teachers and
  the District's Teacher Performance Standards 440

Inter-rater Reliability Activity 3: Recommendations for Improvement Are Hard to Hear! or Saying the "Hard-to-Say Stuff" Verbally and in Writing! . . . 440

Assigning Homework 441

Inter-rater Reliability Activity 4: Low-Performing Teachers and the District's Teacher Performance Standards 443

Inter-rater Reliability Activity 5: The Way We Want Supervision and Evaluation to Happen Versus the Way It Really Happens 444

Inter-rater Reliability Activity 6: Learning From Our Mistakes and Our Successes 446

Inter-rater Reliability Activity 7: Developing an Improvement Plan 446

Inter-rater Reliability Activity 8: The Social–Emotional Components of Stone Soup 447

Extension Activities 448

Checking for Competency and Understanding 451

"Hot Seat" Open Book Assessment 451

Study Guide for Open Book Test 1 451

Conclusion 454

Sources 455

Index 457

Introduction

One of the most important tools districts possess for improving the quality of education for all students is the supervision and evaluation process. It is a district's primary method of quality control and educational improvement. It is one of the few processes that impacts every teacher, thereby affecting the education of every student in the district.

Creating a system for successfully supervising and evaluating the entire teaching staff of a school district is a daunting task. The reason for this is that an effective system-wide program can be achieved only if the administrators, teachers and the teachers' association understand and attend to the educational, legal, public relations (political) and social–emotional dimensions (E.L.P.S.) of supervision and evaluation. Historically, the expertise, time and money needed to provide adequate training for such a program has forced most districts to focus at best on only one or two of these dimensions. Consequently, evaluators are often frustrated with the supervision and evaluation process because they lack the understanding, training and support in the dimensions not addressed.

This book provides districts with the tools to systematically *and cost effectively* assess and revise their supervision and evaluation programs so they successfully address the E.L.P.S. The book incorporates my own experiences and those of my colleagues during my twenty-five years as a teacher association officer, administrator association officer, teacher, guidance counselor, curriculum coordinator, vice-principal, principal, director of pupil services, assistant superintendent for personnel (a.k.a. human resources) and as a consultant to school districts assisting with the development of effective supervision and evaluation. During the years in which I worked as vice principal, principal and director of pupil personnel services, I personally conducted over 150 evaluations of teachers, guidance counselors, school psychologists, speech and language therapists and a myriad of support staff. In my years as an assistant superintendent for personnel, I directly supervised over 75 supervisors and evaluators who were responsible for evaluating over 1400 teachers and other school professionals. In my years as a consultant, I have trained over 600 administrators in dozens of districts in seven different states.

> Every example in this book is taken from an actual teacher's evaluation. The evaluation documents, the sample evaluations, the case studies and all the examples are from teachers' evaluations completed by administrators I trained or supervised.

I wrote this book as a practical guide that focuses primarily on proven techniques that are used effectively in school districts. Every example in this book is taken from an actual teacher's evaluation. The evaluation documents, the sample evaluations, the case studies and all the examples are from teachers' evaluations completed by administrators I trained or supervised. The book relies on theory and research, with the support of proven successful practice.

SUPERVISION VERSUS EVALUATION

There is a great deal of confusion among practicing administrators and teachers as to the definitions and parameters of the terms *supervision* and *evaluation*. This confusion leads teachers to think of the evaluation process solely as it is defined in recent textbooks that describe the various theoretic supervision structures.

In his book, *Approaches to Clinical Supervision: Alternatives for Improving Instruction,* Edward Pajak (2000) articulately describes the distinguishing features of the supervision models described by Robert Goldhammer (pp. 21–43), Ralph Mosher and David Purpel (pp. 45–62), Morris Cogan (pp. 63–85), Arthur Blumberg (pp. 91–110), Elliot Eisener (pp. 111–129), Keith Acheson and Meredith Gall (pp. 135–160), Madeline Hunter (pp.161–181), Bruce Joyce and Beverly Showers (pp. 183–201), Carl Glickman (pp. 207–227) and Arthur Costa and Robert Garmston (pp. 229–247). Each of the supervision models that Pajak discusses describes the administrator as someone who uses data, questioning and coaching in a collegial rather than hierarchical relationship.

In the book, *Supervision and Institutional Leadership: A Developmental Approach,* (Glickman, C., Gordon, S., & Ross-Gordon, J., 2001, p. 7) the authors discuss a paradigm shift toward a collegial model of supervision that includes the following:

1. A collegial rather than a hierarchical relationship between teachers and formally designated supervisors

2. Supervision as the province of teachers as well as that of formally designated supervisors

3. A focus on teacher growth rather than teacher compliance

4. Facilitation of teachers collaborating with each other to improve instruction

5. Teacher involvement in ongoing reflective inquiry

After reading these texts, one understands the confusion of teachers and administrators about the purpose of evaluation systems. Teachers take from these theoretic descriptions the belief that the teacher evaluation process is intended to be solely a collegial facilitation and is not intended to make judgments that differentiate among the levels of teachers' performance and inform decisions about their employment. Administrators who read these descriptions often dismiss them as unrealistic in terms of the demands on their time and the public demand for judgments. Administrators operate in an environment that is pressured by demands for accountability from parents, school boards, state boards of education and federal laws such as No Child Left Behind. They operate in a daily environment with demands such as keeping the lights on, keeping the furnace running, moving classrooms when the roof leaks, locating missing students who don't arrive on their scheduled busses, breaking up fights between students, dealing with clocks that tell a different time in each classroom, covering classrooms when substitutes don't show up and many other crisis management situations that pull them away from thoughtful yet time-intensive supervision with teachers. These factors seriously curtail the administrators ability to coach teacher performance.

In his book, *How to Make Supervision and Evaluation Really Work,* Jonathan Saphier (1993, p. 9) defines the terms **supervision** and **evaluation** as follows:

> Supervision means the four (administrator) outcomes: cheerleading, facilitating, stimulating, and problem solving. Evaluation means the four (administrator) outcomes: monitoring, directing, making decisions and remediating and dismissing.

These descriptions more accurately reflect the balance administrators must maintain between supervision and evaluation systems as coaching and facilitation and as means for identifying varying levels of performance and making employment decisions. Teachers often read these distinctions, however, and believe that the work of the administrator as a supervisor and his/her work as an evaluator are separate activities that do not inform one another. Teachers believe that the information shared during supervisory activities (as described by Saphier) is not supposed to be part of the data used to make evaluative judgments. Administrators often find themselves confused about these roles as well, and pursue stressful and unsuccessful efforts to categorize the data they obtain as supervisory and not as part of the written evaluation, or as evaluative and as part of the written evaluation.

Charlotte Danielson's and Thomas McGreal's book, *Teacher Evaluation: To Enhance Professional Practice* (2000, p. 8), quotes the work of Donald Hafele (1993) in describing the functions of a teacher evaluation system:

… a system should

• screen out unqualified persons from certification and selection;

• provide constructive feedback to individual educators;

• recognize and help reinforce outstanding service;

• provide evidence that will withstand professional and judicial scrutiny;

• aid institutions in terminating incompetent or unproductive personnel

• unify teachers and administrators in their collective efforts to educate students

The competencies evaluators need to perform these functions are described in subsequent chapters in this book.

Danielson's model of supervision and evaluation takes Saphier's definitions a step further by indicating that the collegial coaching and professional development functions (or the supervisory functions as described in the three texts noted above) are best performed by other teachers. Danielson makes the point that many (or most) teachers know more about teaching than the administrators who complete the evaluations. Peer feedback as a form of professional growth is addressed in this book with significant depth in chapter 3.

Most teachers derive greater teaching competency, therefore, through self-reflection and peer interaction rather than from the interactions they have with their evaluators.

Most teachers derive greater teaching competency, therefore, through self-reflection and peer interaction rather than from the interactions they have with their evaluators. The evaluators, on the other hand, have the primary function of quality assurance and a secondary function as professional developers.

An example of the inclusion of practical experience is that most authors on this topic draw a clear distinction between supervision and evaluation. The authors treat these concepts as connected but exclusive activities. I believe this separation has some value as an academic framework. For the evaluator in the *real world* of educational leadership, when it comes to data gathering, supervision and evaluation are virtually inseparable. For example, every evaluator in the course of his/her career will make decisions about whether an observed ineffective teacher behavior is indicative of the teacher's performance or just an aberration. If the evaluator concludes, based on his/her comprehensive knowledge of this teacher, that the activity is a distinct, one-time error, the evaluator may discuss the issue in a supervisory or even collegial manner without formally documenting the activity. If the future shows the issue is indeed a one-time error then the discussion concludes the supervision–evaluation interaction related to this incident. However, if the future shows that the teacher's behavior was an early incident indicative of a change in the teacher's pattern of behavior a yet undetected pattern of behavior, the evaluator will have to reach back to the first incident and the discussion and make it part of the teacher's evaluation history. Every supervisory, collegial or other piece of information the evaluator possesses about the teacher is part of the total body of information the evaluator uses, either consciously or subconsciously, to make his/her final judgments about the teacher's performance.

I agree with the theoreticians that in most evaluator–evaluatee relationships there are (or should be) innumerable interactions aimed at improving teacher performance but are not formally documented. I also agree with the theoreticians that there are specific interactions such as classroom observations, evaluation conferences and the review of professional development plans that are formally documented. In the final analysis, however, if the evaluator is to truly give a 360-degree assessment of a teacher's performance, everything the evaluator sees, hears, tastes and feels must impact the judgments the evaluator makes about the teacher's performance when it comes time to write a summative evaluation. Therefore, throughout this book, I speak of supervision and evaluation as a single activity that is divided into formative and summative activities.

The Educational, Legal, Public Relations (Political) and Social–Emotional Processes and Standards of Supervision and Evaluation

Districts with successful supervision and evaluation programs recognize that each of the four dimensions has processes and standards that must be adhered to. *Webster's New Riverside University Dictionary* defines a process as "a series of actions or functions that achieves a result." (Soukhanov, 1988, p. 938) It defines a standard as "an accepted measure of comparison for quantitative or qualitative value." (Soukhanov, p. 1113) Chapter 1 gives a brief overview of the processes and standards involved in supervision and evaluation.

SOURCES

Danielson, C. & McGreal, T. (2000). *Teacher evaluation: To enhance professional practice.* Princeton, NJ: Educational Testing Service.

Glickman, C., Gordon, S., & Ross-Gordon, J. (2001). *Supervision and instructional leadership.* Needham Heights, MA: Allyn and Bacon.

Haefele, D.L. (1993). Evaluating teachers: A call for change. *Journal of Personnel Evaluation in Education, 7,* 21–31.

Pajak, E. (2000). *Approaches to clinical supervision: Alternatives for improving instruction.* Norwood, MA: Christopher-Gordon Publishers, Inc.

Saphier, J. (1993). *How to make supervision and evaluation really work.* Acton, MA: Research for Better Teaching, Inc.

Soukhanov, A.H. (Ed.). (1988) *New Riverside university dictionary.* Boston: Houghton Mifflin Company.

CHAPTER

1

Ascending the E.L.P.S. (Educational, Legal, Public Relations [Political] and Social–Emotional) Toward Excellent Supervision and Evaluation

E-The Educational Process and Standards

The primary goal of supervision and evaluation is educational improvement. Most districts' supervision and evaluation systems are designed to improve students' achievement and attitudes by enhancing teachers' professional performance and fulfillment. Recent education reform initiatives throughout the United States and Canada have focused on the development of standards for teachers' and students' performance that can be used as the objective basis for evaluating teaching. In many states the Department of Education has developed standards for instruction, curriculum and assessment of student achievement that are consistent with the standards recommended by the various national organizations in each curriculum area (e.g., National

Council for the Teaching of Mathematics, National Board for Professional Teaching Standards). Other states have required individual districts to develop standards of instruction, curriculum and assessment. Public education's move toward articulated written standards has significantly enhanced districts' ability to objectively evaluate teaching. Examples of performance standards for teachers, guidance counselors, speech and language therapists, occupational therapists, library media specialists and other education professionals are found in chapter 9.

> Historically, the problem with most training programs in supervision and evaluation is that they enhance the evaluator's skills only in the educational component and ignore all or most of the other three dimensions.

The supervision and evaluation process works with teachers **formatively** to improve their performance on the standards of instruction, with the goal of improving students' performance on the district's curriculum standards. It also **summatively** assesses each teacher's performance as measured against the district's articulated standards for curriculum and instruction. The educational process and standards are the most important of the four E.L.P.S. dimensions. However, the educational dimension of supervision and evaluation can be successfully implemented only if evaluators effectively attend to the legal, public relations (political) and social–emotional processes and standards as well. Historically, the problem with most training programs in supervision and evaluation is that they enhance the evaluator's skills only in the educational component and ignore all or most of the other three dimensions.

L-THE LEGAL PROCESS AND STANDARDS

Every state has laws that require the evaluation of all public school teachers. The labor laws and contracts governing teacher and administrator evaluation in most states and districts use the legal standard *just cause* to indicate the level of *due process* required for personnel actions that impact teachers who have tenure (*professional or permanent status* in Massachusetts). The procedures set forth in districts' teacher evaluation documents are designed to be consistent with the just cause standard for due process. Fortunately, in most of the relationships between evaluators and teachers, the primary focus is on the educational and at times the social–emotional processes. However, one evaluation of a low-performing teacher can take as much of the evaluator's time as six to ten evaluations of high-performing teachers. Therefore, it is important that evaluators understand the legal standards for the procedures they use. If evaluators wait to learn about just cause until one of their evaluations is challenged for due process flaws, it will be too late to effectively use that knowledge. A procedurally flawed evaluation can legally negate hundreds of hours of an evaluator's effective and educationally sound work. Chapter 6 includes further explanation of the due process standard of just cause as it impacts teacher supervision and evaluation.

Another legal standard related to the evaluation of a low-performing teacher is the *duty of fair representation*. Teachers' associations are legally bound to provide a *reasonable level* of representation to their members. An association that does not provide this level of representation leaves itself open to being sued by the teacher for failure to meet its duty of fair representation. The key words related to the test of fair representation are *reasonable level* of representation. Most associations provide a reasonable level to protect themselves and their members, but will not provide representation beyond that point for a poorly performing teacher who has received reasonable notice, support and time to improve, and yet has still failed to be consistently successful in meeting the district's standards. Many teachers' associations in the new millennium are committed to quality teaching and understand the political advantage in avoiding a reputation for "protecting bad teachers." (See the following discussion and that in chapter 5.) Chapter 6 contains an explanation of duty of fair representation written in part by a teacher's association field representative well versed in matters of labor law. Chapter 6 also looks at the legal concepts of gathering direct and indirect evidence, harassment (gender, sexual, racial, disability or personal) of teachers and other labor law concepts that impact the supervision and evaluation process. Chapter 7 gives an in-depth discussion of the concept of progressive discipline.

P-THE PUBLIC RELATIONS (POLITICAL) PROCESS AND STANDARDS

Increasingly, administrators, school committee members, teachers and teachers' associations are becoming aware that performance evaluation contributes significantly to the public's perception of schools. Quality performance evaluation is an important part of the evidence public schools can use to demonstrate to the lay public that we have quality control in public education. It is one of the strongest defenses against the movement toward voucher programs, for-profit schools and charter schools. If the public believes schools can effectively maintain a high level of instruction and student achievement, they will have the confidence that public schools can successfully complete their mission. When the public feels an institution like public education cannot monitor itself, it tends to abandon the institution. It instructs its legislators to change it dramatically or to create alternative options for students, such as voucher programs and charter schools. A growing number of states have enacted just such legislation over the last six years.

School boards, administrators, teachers and teachers' associations are sure to understand the danger to public education indicated by polls that show this unsettling new trend. For the first time, *the majority of adults* in America (51%) and *public school* parents in America (56%) favor the use of public money to pay all or part of a school-age child's tuition to any public, private or church related school (Gallup & Rose, 1999). It is incumbent upon those who understand this connection to educate those who do not yet understand it. All educators must recognize that the future of public schools is dependent upon demonstrating to the public our joint commitment to ensuring that all children receive teaching that is competitive in quality and cost with the other options. Chapter 5 takes an in-depth look at the effect that supervision and evaluation has on the public relations and political processes and standards that impact the long term viability of public schools.

S-The Social–Emotional Process and Standards

To quote Dr. James Walsh, retired superintendent of the public schools of Brookline, Massachusetts, and a former deputy superintendent of the Boston Public Schools, "Leadership is more psychology than anything else." Of course, this quotation overly simplifies leadership, which is in reality a series of complex processes that can be assessed by measurable standards. However, it does underscore how important it is for leaders to pay careful attention to the emotional impact of their interactions on a subordinate's performance. The process of being evaluated is a significant social–emotional event for many people. Our career persona is an important component of our self-image and integral to our ability to provide for ourselves and the people we care about. A threat to our career, real or perceived, often sends us into the fight-or-flight response, thereby making evaluation an extremely emotional activity. The emotions intensify exponentially when the message to the teacher is, "Your performance is less than satisfactory." One need only recall Psychology 101 and Abraham Maslow's hierarchy of needs (Maslow, 1943, pp. 370–396) to understand why job performance evaluation is such an emotionally-charged issue.

Teacher Social–Emotional Processes and Standards

In the majority of the interactions between evaluators and teachers, the primary E.L.P.S. dimension in play is the educational. In the cases of teachers with performance issues, their personal support network and ownership of the problem (components of the social–emotional dimension) become essential for the teachers' ultimate success. In chapters 6 and 7, this book takes a more in-depth look at the social–emotional impact on low-performing teachers and the role of evaluators and the teachers' association in dealing with that impact. Figure 1 on page 12 illustrates the various people and processes that impact the social–emotional state of a teacher during the supervision and evaluation process.

EVALUATOR SOCIAL–EMOTIONAL PROCESSES AND STANDARDS

Evaluators also experience difficult social–emotional situations and stress related to their work with teachers during the supervision and evaluation process. Most schools and departments are designed so the evaluator (e.g., principal or department head) is the sole evaluator of a group of professionals in a department or school. This isolation can lead to loneliness and self-doubt for evaluators. Asking teachers to change their behavior is difficult for them to hear. This makes it hard for the evaluator to explain the required change in a way the teacher can accept. When the request is put in the form of an observation write-up or final evaluation report, this interaction becomes significantly more difficult for the teacher to accept and the evaluator to deliver. Evaluators spend a great deal of time (often awake in the middle of the night) trying to find the right words for delivering the message that change is needed. Chapters 2–8 provide guidance for evaluators to assist them with the delivery of these difficult oral and written messages.

> When an administrator is working intensely with a low-performing teacher, loneliness and self-doubt increase exponentially.

Figure 2 on page 13 illustrates the various people and processes that support the social–emotional state of an evaluator during the supervision and evaluation process.

When an administrator is working intensely with a low-performing teacher, loneliness and self-doubt increase exponentially. It is a typical human reaction for the teacher's colleagues to be emotionally supportive of their colleague. Even when staff members privately support the administrator's work with the teacher, very few ever indicate this position to the teacher, other teachers or the administrator. In some instances the low-performing teacher publicly berates the administrator to other staff members. Some colleagues join the administrator bashing, but most respond with silence or active listening. These responses are taken by the teacher as concurrence with his/her complaints about the evaluator. In this lonely and stressful situation, the evaluator can be prone to second guessing whether he/she is being too direct or not direct enough with the teacher.

Dr. Arturo Delgado, conducted research in 250 school districts in California which identified the top ten roadblocks to administrators giving constructive written and oral recommendations about performances that needed improvement. Nine of those roadblocks were social–emotional (Delgado, 1999).

Social–Emotional Components and Processes
Teacher

Figure 1

This book is designed to address these social–emotional issues in several ways. First, it enables a district to develop and maintain a high level of consistency (inter-rater reliability) among evaluators. Raising inter-rater reliability in the implementation of processes and standards decreases the feeling among some staff that performance evaluations are subjective rather than objective assessment, thereby increasing morale in general. Second, it increases the sense of support evaluators feel when all the evaluators in a district adhere to similar standards.

Third, trained evaluators and an effectively-monitored evaluation system create an environment where most teachers trust the validity of the process and trust their evaluators' ability to objectively evaluate their performance. It enhances administrators' trust in the teachers' association to work with them on addressing issues of low performance. An effective system helps eliminate the dynamic in which low-performing teachers feel "bullied" by the evaluation process (or evaluator), causing them to make negative statements about the evaluator to other teachers and community members. It also removes the tendency for evaluators to feel "bullied" by the teachers' association and make statements to teachers, other administrators and the public about the association's role in blocking administrators' ability to require high standards of performance.

Social–Emotional Components and Processes
Evaluator

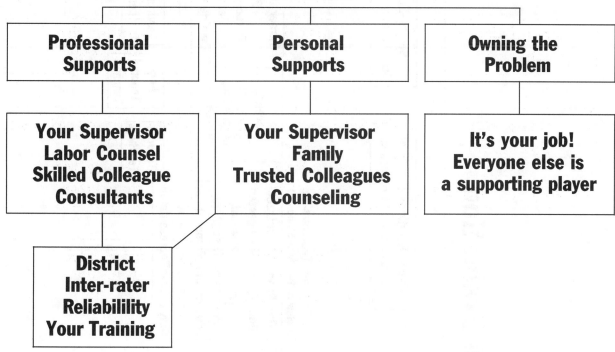

Figure 2

CONQUERING THE E.L.P.S.

An evaluation system that effectively attends to all of the E.L.P.S. helps administrators to be more effective instructional leaders, decreases litigation related to addressing low performance, improves staff morale and increases the public's belief that the entire school district (school board, administrators, teachers and the teachers' association/union) is committed to ensuring that every student receives a quality education.

This book provides teachers, school board members, district administrators, university faculty who train teachers and administrators and the lay public with an understanding of the complex, multifaceted supervision and evaluation process.

Figure 3 (page 14) illustrates the various components of the E.L.P.S. It at first appears more daunting than climbing the Alps. However, as you read on, you will see that this book breaks each dimension into its components. The E.L.P.S. enables districts to develop successful programs of professional development for evaluators.

Supervision and Evaluation

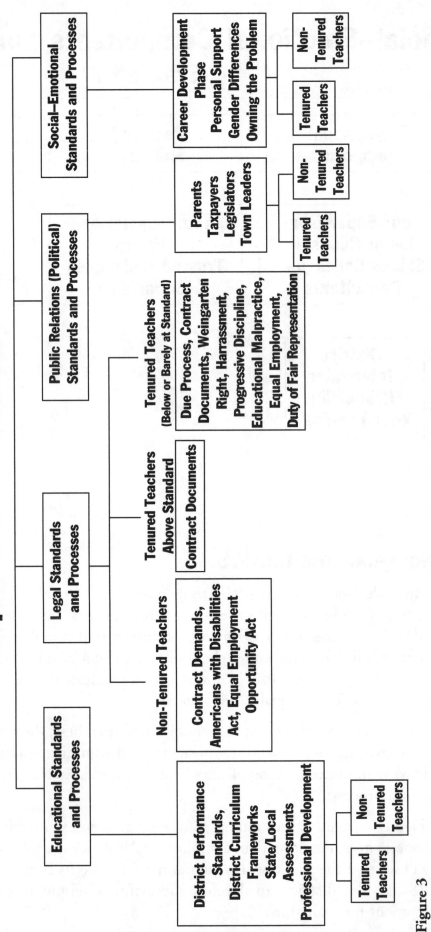

Figure 3

SOURCES

Delgado, A. (1999, October). *Factors that lead to internal conflict that influence elementary school principals when rating less than satisfactory teachers on formal teacher evaluations.* Dissertation research presented at the American Association of School Personnel Administrators Annual Conference, Ann Arbor, MI.

Gallup, A. & Rose, L. (1999, September). The 30th annual *Phi Delta Kappan*/Gallup Poll of the public's attitudes toward the public schools. *Phi Delta Kappan,* 41–56.

CHAPTER

2

District-Level Systems for Training, Coaching and Assessing an Effective Program of Supervision and Evaluation

This chapter focuses on the district-level systems that must be in place to support a successful program of supervision and evaluation. Such a program can be implemented only when supervisors and evaluators have been adequately trained in the E.L.P.S. standards and processes of this important education improvement activity. It is the interaction of these four standards and processes that makes supervision and evaluation inseparable activities in the real world.

The *educational standards* are primarily supervised and evaluated using a process that includes observing a teacher while he/she is teaching, conferencing with that teacher and writing about the teaching that was observed. This process is often referred to as **clinical supervision and evaluation.** In early years of clinical supervision and evaluation, teaching was often viewed as a set of rote skills that can be implemented successfully with a minimal amount of professional judgment by the teachers. The evaluator, in theory, could observe a lesson and make judgments solely on whether the teacher demonstrated certain skills. In recent years, educators' recognition of the complexity of classroom and out-of-classroom interactions has focused importance on a teacher's judgment in deciding when, how and to what extent to utilize specific teaching techniques. The work of Jonathon Saphier, Arthur Costa, Robert Garmston, Carl Glickman and others has focused our attention on the importance of teacher judgment and the need for evaluators to coach teachers in ways that improve teachers' ability to make these judgments.

Most states have laws that require the clinical supervision and evaluation of all teachers and administrators. A number of states also require that districts provide ongoing training in this area for their administrators. In addition, university graduate programs in administration and state certification regulations for administrators require training in clinical supervision and evaluation. This leads many administrators to receive preliminary training as part of their pre-service preparation. Unfortunately, this training is rarely comprehensive enough and is never sufficiently specific to an individual district's needs to enable evaluators to be effective. This chapter provides a framework that districts can use to provide the training and support needed for effective district-wide supervision and evaluation.

> Effective evaluators must know the *educational standards and processes* and be able to analyze a teacher's ability to use them, talk effectively with teachers about their implementation of them and write clearly and concisely about them. Evaluators must also be able to use a wide variety of data sources in addition to classroom observations to make accurate assessments.

The first step in improving a district's supervision and evaluation program is to require that all the supervisors and evaluators in the district attend refresher training in effective classroom instructional practices and the clinical supervision and evaluation of these practices (whether or not they have been trained prior to their employment in the district). This training should be designed to teach and/or refresh evaluators' understanding of the following five components of clinical supervision and evaluation. Effective evaluators must know the *educational standards and processes* and be able to analyze a teacher's ability to use them, talk effectively with teachers about their implementation of them and write clearly and concisely about them. Evaluators must also be able to use a wide variety of data sources in addition to classroom observations to make accurate assessments.

Component 1—Knowing the Educational Standards and Processes: Supervision and evaluation training should provide evaluators with an understanding of the components of successful classroom instruction. As in medicine, law and other professions, the knowledge base related to successful classroom teaching is constantly growing and improving. The evaluator need not be an expert on all classroom instructional techniques, but must possess sufficient knowledge about classroom teaching to be an effective supervisor and evaluator. Chapter 9 contains examples of the teaching knowledge base as it is articulated in several states and Canadian provinces.

Component 2—Analyzing the Implementation of the Educational Standards and Processes: The second concept evaluators need to master is the ability to recognize and then analyze the components of successful instruction through classroom observation. The variety of techniques used in successful classroom instruction can vary depending upon grade and subject. The observer needs to understand and be able to detect and label a large repertoire of teaching techniques. This is essential if the evaluator is to assess whether or not the techniques used by the teacher are appropriate for the situation to which they have been applied and to detect missed opportunities. Knowing how to teach and knowing how to observe and analyze teaching are two different skills.

The type of classroom observation can vary as well. Evaluators must build their comfort and competence with all types of observation. The most well known is the single class period observation. This continues to be an effective and important means of observation. However, it is also imperative that evaluators use other types of observations as well. These can include a series of short (five to ten minute) observations,[1] extended observations that can last a couple of hours or more and clustered observations that observe the same subject area or same instructional technique over two or more consecutive days. Chapter 3 looks at the various skills evaluators need to be effective classroom observers.

Component 3—Talking With Teachers About the Educational Standards and Processes: The third supervision and evaluation concept evaluators need to master is the ability to effectively conference with the teacher about the classroom observation in a way that causes serious reflection by the teacher and causes positive change in his/her teaching. Knowing effective teaching and knowing how to analyze teaching is only helpful to students if the supervisor/evaluator knows how to discuss observations with the teacher in an effective manner. These conversations should also include the core practices that are expected of all the district's administrators and those practices specific to the district's standards and procedures. Effective supervision and evaluation conferences require that the evaluator understand the *social–emotional* dynamics that exist between a supervisee and supervisor during the evaluation interaction. Chapter 4 takes an in-depth look at techniques for successfully conferencing with teachers about their performance.

[1] For more information on conducting multiple brief observations the reader will want to read the article written by Boston Public Schools principal and Harvard presenter Kim Marshall noted in the sources at the end of this chapter.

Component 4—Documenting a Teacher's Implementation of the Educational Standards and Processes: The training should clearly explain and frequently reinforce to administrators the message that supervision and evaluation in a standards-based program must be summative as well as formative.

Summative supervision and evaluation is a process designed to measure the level of success of teachers as compared to their district's curriculum and performance standards.

Formative supervision and evaluation is a positive, supportive and collaborative process designed to improve student performance and attitude by increasing the effectiveness and attitudes of a district's teachers.

Effective formative and summative evaluation requires that the evaluator document all the evidence and judgments made about a teacher's performance on the *educational standards and processes*. Clear and concise documentation is the only way to ensure that all parties have a common understanding of the evaluator's summative judgments about the teacher's performance. To the novice evaluator, this seems like common sense. Experienced evaluators know that people can often respond very differently to recommendations and admonishments once they are put in writing. Writing what we say and saying what we write is easier said then done. The written word raises far more *emotions* than the spoken word when it becomes a permanent record of a teacher's performance. Chapter 3 provides an explanation of the various strategies for writing clearly and concisely about teacher performance.

> Writing what we say and saying what we write is easier said then done. The written word raises far more *emotions* than the spoken word when it becomes a permanent record of a teacher's performance.

Component 5—Using Sources of Information in Addition to Classroom Observations: A common misperception among many evaluators is the belief that the only source of data they can use in summative evaluations is that gathered in classroom observations. Chapter 4 provides a comprehensive (but not all-inclusive) list of data sources other than classroom observations.

Chapters 2–4 contain documents which help evaluators use the common language, instruction standards, curriculum standards and procedures required to effectively recognize, analyze, discuss and write about the *educational standards and processes* that affect the majority of teachers evaluated. Chapter 9 contains examples of the supervision and evaluation documents used in two districts in two states to achieve this goal. Those documents and the documents in this chapter were originally developed for use in Massachusetts and Texas. However, since the documents' standards are similar to those used in most states and those used by the National Board for Professional Teaching Standards as published in *What Teachers Should Be Able to Do* (National Board for Professional Teaching Standards, 1994), the documents can be easily adapted for use in any state or with any district's curriculum and evaluation standards and procedures.

The next section of this chapter provides guidelines for selecting (or developing) a training program and a trainer.

TRAINING THE EVALUATORS IN YOUR DISTRICT IN SUPERVISION AND EVALUATION

A few districts have qualified staff to train their own administrators, however, most districts find they need outside expertise to develop effective training for their administrators in the area of supervision and evaluation. Rarely do districts have a person on staff with the time or expertise to develop a comprehensive program that incorporates the four E.L.P.S. dimensions of supervision and evaluation.

Specialists in the area of supervision are often used to either train administrators directly or to develop a training program that is carried out by a local administrator. Districts can obtain supervision and evaluation training from several sources. There are regional and national professional development companies that will provide on-site training for individual districts or training at a regional site for groups of administrators from several districts. All colleges and universities offering graduate programs in educational administration have faculty with backgrounds in clinical supervision and evaluation. These faculty will often provide training. Administrators who specialize in supervision and evaluation (often from larger school districts) may teach these skills in other districts. The Department of Education in your state or your state affiliates of the national professional organizations for school board members, superintendents, secondary school principals, elementary school principals, curriculum administrators and human resources administrators may provide the names of qualified trainers.

It is important that districts carefully research and interview any trainer or organization that is under consideration. The quality of training varies greatly among programs and presenters.

Districts may use the following questions to determine the quality and breadth of the service an outside expert offers.

1. **What are the trainer's qualifications in supervision and evaluation?** Does the trainer have practical as well as academic and theoretical knowledge and experience about supervision and evaluation?

2. What do the trainer's other clients think about his/her work?

3. **Can the trainer adapt his/her presentation to your district's language, standards and processes for curriculum, instruction and student assessment?** I have reviewed dozens of district supervision and evaluation processes and standards over the past twelve years. All districts have written procedures with a core of similar components. However, all have written procedures which have been used in a context of past practice that is unique to that district. Therefore no generic supervision and evaluation training program can be effective as a "one size fits all." Some of the generic practices must be adjusted to account for the procedures, past practices and the evaluation loads that differ from one district to another. The trainer must project a sense of confidence among the administrators being trained that he/she understands the complexities of this difficult process when it is applied within the context of running a particular school or department.

> All districts have written procedures with a core of similar components. However, all have written procedures which have been used in a context of past practice that is unique to that district. Therefore no generic supervision and evaluation training program can be effective as a "one size fits all."

4. **Does the trainer know how to maximize the evaluators' use of the district's present evaluation processes and standards?** Activities that contain written assessment and oral discussion with the district's evaluators of the following questions are one way to achieve this.

   a. What information in your evaluation documents and contract language do evaluators need to know?

   b. Why is it important for evaluators to know the information you identified?

   c. What other questions or comments do you have about your district's evaluation procedures (processes) and performance standards?

   d. What problems have you encountered when using your district's evaluation procedures (processes) and standards?

   e. What solutions have you found that resolved (partially or completely) the issues identified by your colleagues related to using your district's evaluation documents?

5. **Is the trainer's presentation sufficiently motivational so that the administrators being trained will be interested to learn the information?** We all have attended workshops and courses taught by brilliant people who practically put us to sleep or set us off thinking about issues back at the office which are totally unrelated to their topics. Supervisors and evaluators are busy people with many pressing personal and professional demands on their attention. Like a classroom teacher, the presenter needs excellent instructional skills to capture and keep the participants' interest. There are also some additional techniques a trainer of administrators should use in addition to those used by a classroom teacher. The following is a list of "should do's" for trainers of your administrators.

   a. Have a clear understanding of the information and skills he/she wishes the participants to master by the end of the program.

   b. Be realistic about how much the participants can absorb in the time available. It is better to teach a few techniques comprehensively than to give a great deal of information that cannot be readily implemented after the workshop.

   c. Have as much background information as possible about the participants, their level of knowledge about teacher supervision and evaluation and the contract procedures and standards they use in their districts. Later in this chapter, you will find a needs assessment for gathering much of this information.

   d. Teach participants at least one practice in each session that they can apply immediately in their jobs, without a significant amount of preparation work.

   e. Present the information in a way that maximizes retention of the learning by teaching to all four learning styles. In her book *The 4 MAT System: Teaching to Learning Styles and Right/Left Mode Techniques,* Bernice McCarthy (1981) describes the dominant learning styles of people who are primarily motivated by personal meaning, facts, how things work or self-discovery.

   f. Create training activities that enable the participants to practice the new techniques in a variety of scenarios. These activities will enable the participant to use the information learned in the training to solve problems when they arise in the future even if the situations are not similar to those presented in the training.

   g. When you give homework between sessions, make sure the assignment has direct application to their jobs. The best assignments are those that ask the participant to do something he/she normally does anyway, but also apply a new skill(s) taught by the trainer.

   h. Use the Evaluator's Survey of Potential Areas for Training and Support for Your District's Teacher Supervisors and Evaluators self-assessment, found later in this chapter, and the file cabinet assessments in chapter 8 to assess how much of the information and how many of the techniques taught in the training are applied over time in the participants' daily operation of their buildings/departments.

i.   Structure reteaching as needed, based on the assessment program described later in this chapter and in chapter 8.

6. **Does the program provide administrators with a solid foundation in current instructional practices, assessment practices and a common language for discussing these practices?** (See examples in the sample documents in chapter 9.)

7. **Does the program teach administrators techniques for observing and/or verifying and analyzing classroom observations and evidence collected by other means?**

8. **Does the program teach administrators to effectively conference with teachers about their practices in ways that create positive change in those practices?**

9. **Does the program teach administrators to write clearly and concisely about performance by supporting conclusions with a variety of types of observed and/or verified evidence?** (See the explanation of claims, judgments, evidence and impact statements in chapter 3 and the explanation of evidence in chapter 6.)

10. **Does the training program teach and coach the evaluators in the legal, public relations (political) and social–emotional standards and processes that dominate the supervision and evaluation process when working with a low-performing teacher?** These standards and processes are subordinate during the supervision and evaluation of good and excellent teachers. They can become dominant during the supervision and evaluation of low-performing teachers. The complex and unique nature of evaluating low-performing teachers has led to my devoting all of chapter 6 to the standards and processes for working with low performing teachers. Chapter 10 contains a sample of a lesson I use when training administrators to assess their knowledge of these four dimensions (pages 438–439).

11. **Does the program teach administrators the difference between formative and summative supervision and evaluation and how to teach this difference to their staffs?**

12. **Can and will the trainer teach the superintendent or other appropriate central administrator to establish systems to coach, assess and support the continued effective implementation of supervision and evaluation skills by the district's evaluators and central staff after the training period has passed?**

The next section of this chapter discusses the role of the central administration (superintendents, assistant superintendents, curriculum directors) in monitoring and supporting supervision and evaluation in their districts.

As you read on you will see that maintaining an effective program of supervision and evaluation requires a continuous process of teaching, coaching, assessing evaluator performance and reteaching the E.L.P.S. processes and standards? (See figure 4 on page 26.) Because effective supervision and evaluation requires this cyclical process, it is best if districts have someone available in-house to coach, assess and reteach. Or they should schedule the trainer to work with an in-house senior administrator to coach, assess and reteach the evaluators and to coordinate the central office functions such as labor relations, staff development, new teacher induction, etc. Many districts have invested a great deal of time and expense into a period of effective training by outside consultants only to see its impact diminish and even disappear over time because of the lack of continuous coaching, assessing and reteaching. The following case study is an actual example of this dynamic.

THE ARCHAEOLOGICAL DIG

Two districts in which I consulted (I will call them Districts A and B) exemplify the problem that arises when there is not a system within the district to support the supervision and evaluation program after the training consultant leaves the district. During the late 70s and early 80s, the districts trained all of their administrators and a large percentage of their teachers in a very effective model of supervision and evaluation and effective instructional practices. By the mid 80s both districts had trained all of their staff. District A changed to a maintenance training model that trained administrators and teachers new to the district in off-site courses taught by the consultant in other districts that were adopting the model. District B also sent its new administrators to off-site training sessions. However, District B had a teacher trained by the consultant to instruct new and experienced teachers on-site. Financial issues and senior administrative changes in the early 90s caused both districts to stop sending new staff to the off-site training. As a result, District A provided no training in the program for new teachers and administrators for five years. District B provided no training for administrators, but its specially trained teacher maintained the course for teachers each year.

I was hired by District A in 1996 and by District B in 1998 to reactivate training for administrators. Knowing the history of these two districts, I mistakenly assumed I could refresh the administrators' skills in the supervision and evaluation of classroom practice and build upon the previous years of training in which the two districts had already invested significant time and money. I soon learned that virtually none of the previous administrator training was operating in either district. It took an archaeological dig to find the remnants of the program in documents that were practically unused, although they were required by contract, and in the practices of a couple of the administrators who had maintained the skills on their own. In District A the teacher practices also were no longer in effect. However, in District B, the in-district trainer model established in the early 90s was still effectively training all second year teachers. (It was determined that first year teachers had too much on their plates to receive the training in that year.)

I was able to reteach the training for both districts in the skills of evaluating classroom practice. I now am able to focus the administrator training on other skills, such as working effectively with low-performing teachers and using sources of information other than classroom observations. I work actively with the senior administrators creating an "in district trainer" model to ensure that the model in Figure 4 continues to flourish after I leave the district.

Evaluator Training and Support Cycle

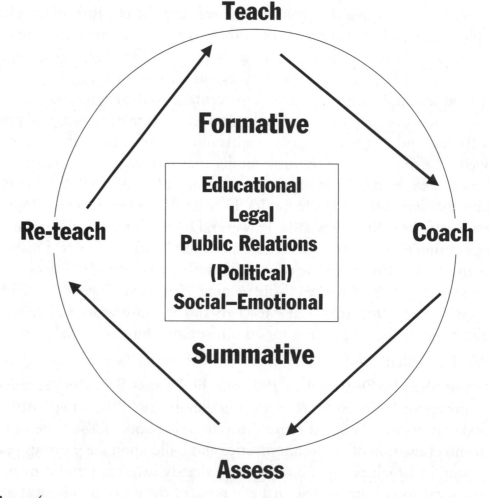

Figure 4

THE ROLE OF SUPERINTENDENTS AND SENIOR ADMINISTRATORS BEYOND PROVIDING EVALUATORS WITH TRAINING (TEACHING) AND COACHING IN SUPERVISION AND EVALUATION?

In the previous section, I alluded to the fact that many districts make the mistake of assuming that the school board and senior administration's job is completed once they have provided the funding and time for the evaluators to receive training in the skills of classroom supervision and evaluation. However, effective supervision and evaluation requires continuous planning, monitoring and support on the part of the superintendent and other senior level administrators. Figure 5 (on the next page) shows the responsibilities of the eight senior level administrators in one district. The lines between the boxes represent the lines of communication needed for an effective program of supervision and evaluation. As you can see, the

> A building-level evaluator involved in a difficult evaluation situation will usually make one call for help. If the only response received is that he/she is then directed to call another person, the evaluator might not make the second call. If directed to call a third person, it is unlikely the third call will ever be made.

larger the district, the more complicated and challenging it is to maintain an adequate flow of communication. In this district the grid below is sent to all administrators at the start of each school year. In so doing, senior administrators are reminded of their roles, and evaluators are reminded where to go for the coaching and support they need.

A building-level evaluator involved in a difficult evaluation situation will usually make one call for help. If the only response received is that he/she is then directed to call another person, the evaluator might not make the second call. If directed to call a third person, it is unlikely the third call will ever be made. As you will see on page 31, there is a long list of roadblocks that keep evaluators from addressing difficult evaluation issues. Senior administration should not add *"frustration with getting assistance for difficult evaluation situations"* to the list.

As a consultant and trainer to districts, I often find that developing clear lines of support, such as the ones developed in the district shown in figure 5, one of the most important ways of improving district-wide performance of supervision and evaluation.

It is a rare building-level evaluator who possesses all the *E.L.P.S. expertise* required to work effectively with a difficult evaluation.

Identifying the Role the Various Central Office Administrators Play in Supporting Building-Level Administrators

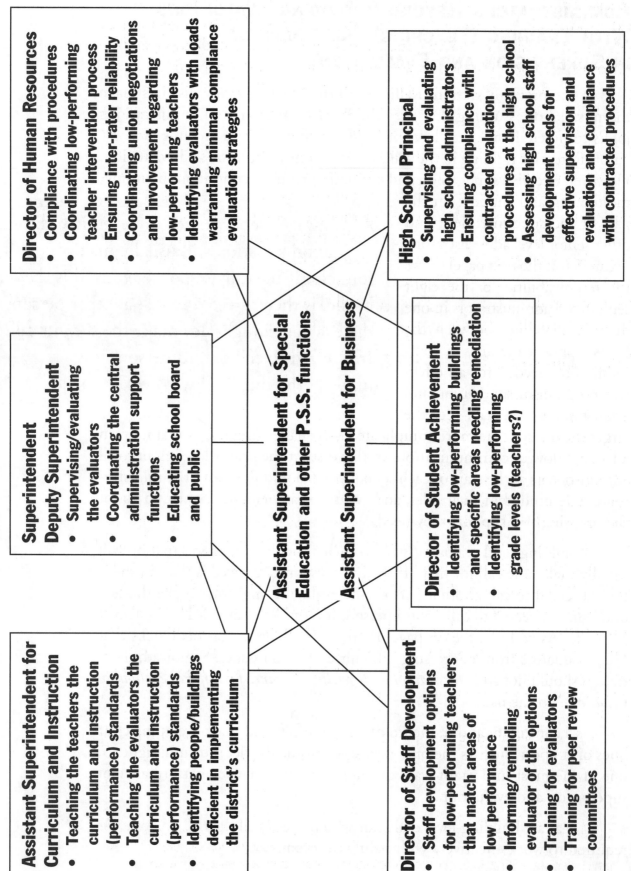

Director of Human Resources
- Compliance with procedures
- Coordinating low-performing teacher intervention process
- Ensuring inter-rater reliability
- Coordinating union negotiations and involvement regarding low-performing teachers
- Identifying evaluators with loads warranting minimal compliance evaluation strategies

High School Principal
- Supervising and evaluating high school administrators
- Ensuring compliance with contracted evaluation procedures at the high school
- Assessing high school staff development needs for effective supervision and evaluation and compliance with contracted procedures

Superintendent
Deputy Superintendent
- Supervising/evaluating the evaluators
- Coordinating the central administration support functions
- Educating school board and public

Assistant Superintendent for Special Education and other P.S.S. functions

Assistant Superintendent for Business

Director of Student Achievement
- Identifying low-performing buildings and specific areas needing remediation
- Identifying low-performing grade levels (teachers?)

Assistant Superintendent for Curriculum and Instruction
- Teaching the teachers the curriculum and instruction (performance) standards
- Teaching the evaluators the curriculum and instruction (performance) standards
- Identifying people/buildings deficient in implementing the district's curriculum

Director of Staff Development
- Staff development options for low-performing teachers that match areas of low performance
- Informing/reminding evaluator of the options
- Training for evaluators
- Training for peer review committees

Figure 5

You will note in Figure 5 that that the role of special education and other special services is not specifically stated. In many districts, the unique and varied responsibilities of these positions results in the need for as many as three sets of administrators having shared responsibility for evaluating and/or supervising these professionals. Often the evaluator and supervisor are clearly defined on paper. (See the document in chapter 9 for an example of clearly defined evaluation responsibilities for special services professionals starting on page 308.) However, in practice, the complex communications needed between and among the system-wide special services department administrators, the building administrators and the system-wide regular education administrators breaks down. This communications failure often leads to three different notions of the identity and methods of the supervisor and evaluators of special services practitioners. The result is that professionals such as physical therapists, occupational therapists, vision specialists, hearing specialists, psychologists and, even at times, special education teachers are ineffectively supervised and evaluated[2] or not evaluated at all. This problem is illustrated in the following case from a district in which I worked.

WHO DROPPED THE BALL?

In this district the assistant superintendent for special services retired. The district hired a consultant to conduct a yearlong evaluation of the department prior to hiring a new assistant superintendent. Among the recommendations, the consultant suggested that the evaluation responsibility for special education teachers in the elementary schools be moved from the special education administrators to the building principals. The consultant left when he completed his report and a new assistant superintendent for special services was hired. The special education administrators immediately followed the recommendation of the consultant and stopped evaluating the special education teachers. In addition, since the report did not mention speech therapists, occupational therapists or physical therapists, the special education administrators assumed they should no longer evaluate these people as well. The special education administrators were very happy to give up the *legal, public relations (political) and social–emotional* issues that summative evaluators face but continue to function solely as formative supervisors. The intention of the consultant, it was later clarified (though not written in the report), was that the special education administrators should continue to evaluate the speech, occupational therapy and physical therapy staff.

---

2 Starting on page 329 of chapter 9, is an excellent example of a district's performance standards designed for non-classroom teaching positions such as school nurses, psychologists, counselors, speech therapists, librarians and occupational therapists.

The principals, on the other hand, either didn't know they were responsible for picking up the special education teachers' evaluations or they "forgot." As a result, no special education teacher, speech therapist, occupational therapist or physical therapist was evaluated *for four years!*

Even in districts with a clear understanding of who evaluates whom, conflicts arise when there is more than one supervisor and/or evaluator. These conflicts can only be resolved with the assistance of the central administrator responsible for system-wide supervision and evaluation. Some of the longest and most contentious (and personally the most *emotional*) evaluation meetings I've run have involved neither the teacher who was being evaluated nor the union. The purpose of these meetings was to get two administrators to acknowledge and understand their differing responsibilities and perceptions of a single teacher's evaluation. This understanding is an essential step before the two or three administrators are able to work effectively with this teacher. Below are some guidelines for ensuring two supervisors/evaluators work effectively with a single teacher.

1. Discuss the evaluation with the teacher's other supervisor(s) before the start of the evaluation and periodically during the course of the evaluation so you send the same message to the teacher. This regular communication among supervisors will avoid confusing and overwhelming the teacher.

2. Come to agreement with the other supervisor(s) on the priorities and goals of the evaluation.

3. Use your partner(s)'s areas of strength.

4. Support each other through the periods of *aggression* often connected when giving a teacher summative areas for improvement. There will be times when the teacher will lash out at the person giving these recommendations.

Make Your Senior Administration User Friendly for the Evaluators

Evaluations are time-consuming for teacher evaluators. They are also socially and emotionally difficult, particularly when it comes to giving summative standards-based feedback in your conferences and write-ups. Dr. Arturo Delgado, superintendent of the San Bernardino Unified School District in California, researched the reasons why evaluators have a difficult time giving honest, summative feedback to teachers about areas that need improvement. Having surveyed evaluators in 250 California school districts, Dr. Delgado identified the top ten roadblocks to honest feedback, ordered below by the frequency stated by the respondents (Delgado, 1997, p. 64). The first is the most frequently cited roadblock.

1. I don't have a whole lot of confidence in the employee evaluation process.

2. I'm afraid of losing the employee's trust.

3. I'm afraid of hurting employee morale.

4. I don't like dealing with difficult people.

5. I've had too many negative experiences with employees when it comes to evaluations.

6. The employee has shown recent improvement.

7. I don't want a confrontation with the union over this.

8. I just don't have the time.

9. I hate to post a bad evaluation on the employee's permanent file.

10. I don't want to call the attention of the district office to my problems.

Most of the top ten concerns expressed by the administrators were about the *social–emotional* impacts on the evaluator, the teacher being evaluated and/or the staff that result from giving summative, standards-based feedback. When you couple these concerns with the frustrations that can occur as a result of the complex communications and multiple functions noted in figure 5, it is easy to see why many building-level administrators avoid tackling tough evaluation issues in their buildings or departments unless they have a senior administration that is "user-friendly." It is important that the senior administration streamline the building administrators' access to the functions noted in figure 5, making it easy for administrators to receive technical and emotional support when involved in difficult evaluation situations.

There should be a clearly articulated explanation of to whom the building or department administrator goes for the various supports he/she may need. Few districts have defined this line of support clearly for its evaluators. As a result, the evaluators feel they must deal with difficult evaluations alone, or the evaluators are quickly frustrated when they call someone in the senior administration for support and are shuffled to another office because neither central administrator sees the support requested as part of his/her job or resource allocation.

ASSESSING AND RETEACHING THE IMPLEMENTATION OF SUPERVISION AND EVALUATION IN YOUR DISTRICT

Someone in the district *must be responsible* to see that there is teaching, coaching, assessment and reteaching of evaluation work *by the evaluators*. Effective district-wide supervision and evaluation requires that someone ensure district-wide compliance, effective formative and summative work and consistent implementation of standards and processes by the evaluators. Depending on the size of the district, this responsibility is carried out by the superintendent or an assistant superintendent. Below are seven steps this person can take to ensure effective supervision and evaluation.

> Effective district-wide supervision and evaluation requires that someone ensure district wide compliance, effective formative and summative work and consistent implementation of standards and processes by the evaluators.

Step 1: The Evaluator Survey of Potential Areas for Training and Support for Your District's Teacher Supervisors and Evaluators (on page 39) should be given to all evaluators at the beginning of each year. A second copy should be sent to evaluators at the midpoint of the school year, when they are beginning to write their final evaluation reports for the year as a reminder of the competencies. Throughout the year, the central administrator responsible for supervision and evaluation needs to check in with evaluators to assess their progress on the standards addressed in this document.

The Evaluator Survey of Potential Areas for Training and Support for Your District's Teacher Supervisors and Evaluators contains criteria that superintendents can use to assess and evaluate the evaluators' implementation of the skills they need to be effective. It is a set of standards against which an evaluator's work can be measured. Chapter 8 contains an in-depth explanation of how these assessments are completed. The sample district evaluation documents in chapter 9 use the Massachusetts and Texas standards. However, since these standards were based on the work in other states and the standards set by national professional organizations (e.g., The National Council for the Teaching of Mathematics Standards, the National Board for Professional Teacher Standards) the evaluator competencies in the survey can be adapted easily for use with the standards for curriculum and instruction in most states and districts in the United States.

Step 2: The written observations and evaluations completed by teacher evaluators need to be reviewed for compliance with the Evaluator Survey of Potential Areas for Training and Support for Your District's Teacher Supervisors and Evaluators and the district's administrator performance criteria on supervision and evaluation and also to maintain inter-rater reliability. All the evaluations need not be read, however, an adequate sample should be reviewed. In one district with 50 evaluators and over 700 teachers, about 25% of all the evaluations (90 out of 360) are reviewed by the assistant superintendent for personnel and the superintendent each year to determine the extent to which the criteria in the Evaluator Survey of Potential Areas for Training and Support for Your District's Teacher Supervisors and Evaluators have been met. Individual evaluators receive written and/or oral feedback with recommendations and commendations. The written feedback comes in the form of evaluation memos using claims, value judgments, evidence and impact statements (see chapter 3 for more on claims, value judgements, evidence and impact statements) that connect the performance on the specific "characteristic" to its impact on the teacher evaluated and the evidence. Attached to each memo is the criteria sheet with the criteria from the survey, so the evaluator can easily refer to the standards. The attachment of this document also serves as one more reminder to the evaluators to review these standards.

In another much larger district with 200 schools we found that the volume of evaluations made it logistically impossible to evaluate 25% of the evaluations. In that district, we reduced the percentage to 10–15% per year. The logistical realities of time and money often cause movement away from the ideal. It is important to remember, however, that assessing even a low percentage of observations is significantly better than assessing none at all.

We call this process a file cabinet assessment. Samples of file cabinet assessments can be found in chapter 8.

Step 3: Evaluators should be observed in conferences with teachers and, where appropriate, with teachers' association representatives and second evaluators. Chapter 4 discusses the skills evaluators need to conduct effective conferences.

Step 4: Each year, evaluators should be surveyed to determine what supports will assist them in better meeting the standards in the upcoming year. The type of survey can vary depending on the size of the district. In some districts where I consult, the entire administrative staff is less than ten people. In those districts, we administer the Evaluator Survey of Potential Areas for Training and Support for Your District's Teacher Supervisors and Evaluators at a meeting of all evaluators. We collate the results on a chart paper and develop recommendations for future training topics.

In mid size districts (approximately twenty to sixty administrators and evaluators) and in large districts, the Evaluator Survey of Potential Areas for Training and Support for Your District's Teacher Supervisors and Evaluators is given to all administrators and evaluators and returned to the administrator responsible for supervision and evaluation in the district. The survey is designed so the results can be easily tallied by a clerical employee or by using computer scan answer sheets and the results given to a senior administrator. The clerical person need only sum up the numbers circled for each item. The higher the sum of the numbers, the greater the need for training in that area. Additional blank items are included so the evaluators can add skills that may not be included in the survey. This information enables senior administrators to maintain a user friendly support system for evaluators by providing the training and information evaluators want and need to be effective. It also provides senior administrators with useful information about which evaluators are accessing which resources and how well those resource people and programs are supporting the building-level evaluators. At the end of this chapter (Appendix A) is a sample of a report based on the needs assessment conducted in one district.

Step 5: The teachers' association should be informed about current research in effective supervision and evaluation, the school committee's and superintendent's philosophies of supervision and evaluation and the training evaluators are receiving to ensure effective supervision and evaluation. Inviting the association leadership to complete the Survey of Areas for Evaluator Training is often a good ice-breaker around which to structure the discussion about research, philosophy and training related to supervision and evaluation. This of course assumes the district's teachers' association has a commitment to high teacher performance as well as a commitment to meeting its duty to ensure teachers' rights are not violated. (See chapter 5 for more discussion on this topic.)

Step 6: Once the teachers' association has sufficient information from step 5 to give informed feedback, it should be asked to make recommendations for improvements in the implementation of the evaluation process. Most teachers' associations hear a different perspective on the performance of evaluators and the evaluation process from their members than the one that is usually available to the senior administration. Asking the association to frame its feedback with the same objectivity it expects in teachers' evaluations will increase the validity of that feedback.

Step 7: Ask teachers how well supervision and evaluation works in their schools or departments. One school district asks all teachers to fill out a twenty-nine question evaluation checklist with comments on all aspects of the performance of their direct supervisors. The Teacher's Assessment of His/Her Evaluator's Performance as a Supervisor/Evaluator (p. 35) instrument addresses skills specific to supervision and evaluation.

A sample survey related directly to the supervisors' work as supervisors and evaluators can be found below.

TEACHER'S ASSESSMENT OF HIS/HER EVALUATOR'S PERFORMANCE AS A SUPERVISOR AND EVALUATOR

Teacher's name: _____ Date: _____

Supervisor assessed below: _____

This survey is designed to help assess your supervisor's work as a supervisor and evaluator. It is based on research related to the practices used by effective supervisors and evaluators. Please fill out one survey for your evaluator. If you wish, you may also fill one out for any other person who functions as your supervisor.

Please circle the number that best matches your response to the comments below.

1= Always   **2**=Often   **3**=Rarely   **4**=Never

A) 1 2 3 4   My supervisor compliments me for good work with specific praise that enables me to understand the impact of my successful actions on students, other staff, parents and/or the community.

B) 1 2 3 4   My supervisor provides me with suggestions for improvement related to my performance.

C) 1 2 3 4   My supervisor's suggestions are connected to the district's performance standards.

D) 1 2 3 4   My supervisor's suggestions are stated in a way that helps me understand the impact on students, other staff, parents and/or the community.

E) 1 2 3 4   My supervisor assists me in developing the skills to consistently evaluate my own performance.

F) 1 2 3 4   When I talk with my supervisor, I feel I can have an honest exchange of ideas.

G) 1 2 3 4   My supervisor makes his/her expectations clear.

H) 1 2 3 4   When I am dealing with a problem, my supervisor asks questions that help me understand the issues and assess options.

I) 1 2 3 4   My supervisor gives me frequent and useful data so I can assess how he/she believes I'm doing as a teacher.

J) 1 2 3 4   My supervisor encourages my initiative and innovation within the parameters of the district's and school's expectations.

K) 1   2   3   4   My supervisor assists me in solving difficulties in interpersonal relationships with colleagues.

L) 1   2   3   4   My supervisor assists me in solving difficulties in interpersonal relationships with students.

M) 1   2   3   4   My supervisor assists me in solving difficulties in interpersonal relationships with parents.

N) 1   2   3   4   My supervisor assists me with interpersonal relationships as described in K, L and M in a way that helps me improve the skills I need to better solve difficulties in the future.

O) 1   2   3   4   I find my supervisor easy to approach and talk with.

Please make any additional comments related to the statements above in the space below.

Comments: _____

_____

_____

_____

Describe one skill your supervisor demonstrates particularly well as a supervisor and evaluator and the impact it has on your performance as a teacher.

Skill: _____

_____

_____

_____

Describe one skill your supervisor should improve in his/her practice as a supervisor and evaluator and the impact it would have on your performance as a teacher.

Skill: _____

_____

_____

_____

All of the *evidence* obtained in steps 1–7 is reviewed and used to plan evaluators' training. This evidence will determine which concepts need to be taught, coached, retaught and/or if new concepts need to be taught during the subsequent year.

ONE DISTRICT'S EXPERIENCE WITH TEACHING, COACHING, ASSESSING AND RETEACHING THE CONCEPTS OF EFFECTIVE SUPERVISION AND EVALUATION

The case below is an example of a district in which the senior administration used step 2 of the preceding section and the evaluator change cycle noted earlier in the chapter to ensure the evaluators used the supervision and evaluation process to assess district-wide implementation of a change in the curriculum.

A district implemented a new set of curriculum standards. Although the district's first teacher performance standard was Currency in the Curriculum, a review of the evaluations for that year indicated that very few of the evaluators assessed teachers' implementation of the Currency in the Curriculum standard. Interviews with several evaluators indicated they were having difficulty incorporating statements about the teachers' use of the standard into their evaluations.

To address this issue, the superintendent, assistant superintendent for curriculum and instruction (who was responsible for developing and implementing the curriculum) and the assistant superintendent for personnel (who was responsible for the training and assessing of administrators in the area of supervision and evaluation) met during the following summer. They planned a workshop for principals and other evaluators that taught the evaluators strategies for incorporating the curriculum standards into their evaluations using the Currency in the Curriculum standard. In chapter 3 you will find examples of evaluations that successfully incorporate this district's curriculum standards (called learning expectations in the district's documents) into evaluations. These examples were part of the workshop given to evaluators at the start of the second school year.

The assistant superintendent for curriculum and instruction and the assistant superintendent for personnel made themselves available throughout the year to coach and reteach evaluators in this new skill. During the following year, the superintendent and assistant superintendent for personnel's review of evaluations indicated a significant improvement in these areas. The number of evaluations incorporating the curriculum standards *increased* from 10% during the first year to over 70% in the second year. This assessment led to reteaching those administrators who had not yet incorporated the assessment of the curriculum standards in their evaluations and to the additional coaching of others.

In the fall of the third year, evaluators and the assistant superintendent for personnel were taught by the assistant superintendent for curriculum and instruction to evaluate teachers' lesson planning using the backward design model advocated by McTighe and Wiggins in their book, *Understanding by*

37

Design (1999). Both assistant superintendents made themselves available through the fall to coach evaluators in the implementation of the new model. Evaluations were again read in the spring to assess compliance and effectiveness. The column with references to the performance standards (see the examples in chapter 9) was revised to include connections to McTighe and Wiggin's book. As you can see, continued improvement required that the teaching, coaching, assessment and reteaching cycle shown earlier in this chapter continued on a regular basis.

As mentioned earlier, the following assessments should be used by the individual evaluator as a self-assessment tool. They should also be used by the senior administration to assess the performance of individual evaluators and provide evaluators with feedback on their performance. The Criteria for Effective Observation Write-ups, the Evaluator Survey of Potential Areas for Training and Support for Your District's Teacher Supervisors and Evaluators, the teacher survey and the file cabinet assessment described in chapter 8 can provide an administrator with a substantial amount of information about his/her performance as a supervisor and evaluator. Following each assessment, I have included some examples of comments made by a senior administrator who used the Criteria for Effective Observation Write-Ups.

EVALUATOR SURVEY OF POTENTIAL AREAS FOR TRAINING AND SUPPORT FOR YOUR DISTRICT'S TEACHER SUPERVISORS AND EVALUATORS

District: _____

Respondent: _____

Position: _____

Below are listed a number of areas related to the effective implementation of supervision and evaluation in your district. Please circle the number of the statement that best represents how you would rate your present knowledge and your need for additional information and training in each of these areas.

1 = I have sufficient knowledge and training in this area to do what is indicated and have little or no need for further information or training on this topic.

2 = I want to know more about this area and would benefit from more information and training on this topic.

3 = I need to know more about this area to effectively complete this competency. This is one of my priority topics for training.

A)   1 2 3   Write **classroom observations** that clearly identify the teaching "moves" you observed (a.k.a. make claims) in language that is used consistently throughout your district

B)   1 2 3   Write **classroom observations** that make clear value judgments about the claims

C)   1 2 3   Write **classroom observations** with impact statements (a.k.a. interpretations) that connect teachers' behavior to its impact on student learning, student development and the school's and/or department's culture

D)   1 2 3   Write **classroom observations** that contain objective evidence to support the claims, impact statements and judgments made by the evaluator

E)   1 2 3   Write **classroom observations** that begin with basic information, including the time and date of the observation, the teacher's name, the observer's name, the grade and/or subject, whether the observation is announced or unannounced, the school's name and any other information required by your district

F)   1 2 3   Write **classroom observations** that use the language of your district's performance standards wherever appropriate

G)   1 2 3   Write **final evaluation reports** that contain clear claims and judgments about each of the performance standards in language consistent with your district's performance standards

H)   1 2 3   Write **final evaluation reports** with impact statements that connect teacher performance on each of the standards to its impact on student learning, student development and the school's and/or department's culture

I)   1 2 3   Write **final evaluation reports** that contain objective evidence to support the claims, impact statements and judgments

J)   1 2 3   Write **final evaluation reports** that use the language of your district's performance standards wherever appropriate

K)   1 2 3   Pre- and post-conference in ways that effectively create positive change in teacher performance

L)   1 2 3   Explain the differences between peer review, peer evaluation, peer supervision and peer coaching in improving teacher performance

M)   1 2 3   Use time-saving tips

N)   1 2 3   Work constructively with the teachers' association/union on issues related to supervision and evaluation

O)   1 2 3   Explain to a colleague the most effective way to implement your district's supervision and evaluation documents and contract language

P)   1 2 3   Self-edit observations, memos and evaluations to ensure continuous improvement in the quality of your evaluation documents

Q)   1 2 3   Work with a partner to peer-edit observations, memos and evaluations to ensure continuous improvement of the quality of your evaluation documents

R)   1 2 3   Use effective techniques and time-efficient methods for teaching sample lessons

S)   1 2 3   Explain the ongoing interaction of the educational, legal, public relations (political) and social-emotional standards and processes of supervision and evaluation

T)   1 2 3   Use a standards-based approach in your district's supervision and evaluation

U)   1 2 3   Explain the numerous types of evidence that are available to evaluators in addition to formal observations

V)   1 2 3   Explain to a colleague which of your supervisors you should consult for information, coaching and/or support with your district's **standards for curriculum and instruction**

W)   1 2 3   Explain to a colleague which of your supervisors you should consult for information, coaching and/or support concerning **the legal standards and processes** of teacher evaluation

X)   1 2 3   _____

_____

_____

SUPERVISING/EVALUATING LOW-PERFORMING TEACHERS AND USING PROGRESSIVE DISCIPLINE

Y)   1 2 3   Explain the difference between a mediocre (barely satisfactory) teacher and an unsatisfactory teacher

Z)   1 2 3   Explain the impact of the law and work within the law during low-performing teacher evaluations. Include the legal concepts of *due process, just cause, duty of fair representation, rules of evidence, harassment, inefficiency, incompetency* and *the Weingarten right*

AA)   1 2 3   Explain the impact of the law and work within the law during low-performing teacher evaluations as it relates to classes of people with legal protections from discrimination for gender, race, religion, age and sexual orientation

BB)   1 2 3   Effectively observe, verify, document and record direct and indirect forms of evidence other than classroom observations

CC)   1 2 3   Use the team approach to support evaluators and reduce the roadblocks to effective evaluations of low-performing teachers

DD)   1 2 3   Effectively work with a second evaluator and/or supervisor during low-performing teachers' evaluations

EE)   1 2 3   Write and implement improvement plans for low-performing teachers

Go back and review your answers to "U" and "V" above in the context of your work with a low-performing teacher to be sure your answers have not changed.

FF)   1   2   3   Explain to a colleague the steps of *progressive discipline* used to discipline staff members

GG)   1   2   3   Correctly investigate claims of misconduct by staff

HH)   1   2   3   Correctly document each step in progressive discipline using your district's performance standards, policies and universally accepted appropriate practices

II)   1   2   3   Write progressive discipline notes and documents such as expectation clarification memos, memos after oral reprimands and written reprimands that contain clear claims and judgments about teacher performance, objective evidence to support the claims and interpretations that connect teacher behavior to its impact on students and the building and/or department

JJ)   1   2   3   Explain the impact of the law and work within the law during progressive discipline situations, including the legal concepts *due process, just cause, duty of fair representation, rules of evidence, harassment, insubordination* and *the Weingarten right*

KK)   1   2   3   Explain the impact of the law and work within the law during *progressive discipline* situations as it relates to classes of people with legal protections from discrimination for gender, race, religion, age and sexual orientation

LL)   1   2   3   Effectively conference with teachers about low performance and discipline issues

MM)   1   2   3   Explain to a colleague who to consult for specific supports (legal and otherwise) and coaching during a progressive discipline situation

NN)   1   2   3

_____

_____

_____

Comments:

SAMPLE DISTRICT PUBLIC SCHOOLS

CRITERIA FOR EFFECTIVE OBSERVATION WRITE-UPS

Evaluator: _____

NA= not applicable to this assignment

1= does not meet the standard

2= barely meets the standard

3= meets the standard

4= exceeds the standard

The evaluator

A) NA 1 2 3 4   began the observation with the grade level (or subject), number of students, time, teacher's name and any other relevant demographic data

B) NA 1 2 3 4   ensured that all "hard-to-hear" news (e.g., areas for improvement, recommendations) is delivered in person to the teacher prior to giving it to the teacher in writing in an observation report

C) NA 1 2 3 4   identified the teaching moves (made **claims**) using the language of the Sample District performance standards or language used by education professionals to describe effective teaching

D) NA 1 2 3 4   limited each **claim** to a single teaching move

E) NA 1 2 3 4   wrote value **judgments** based on the evidence about the teaching moves (claims) identified or missing from the class

F) NA 1 2 3 4   made value **judgments** that recognized and commended examples of successful practice where appropriate

G) NA 1 2 3 4   made value **judgments** that identified areas for improvement and offered recommendations within the text and/or in the summary of the observation write-up, after having discussed them in person with the teacher as noted in B above

H) NA 1 2 3 4   made value **judgments** using words that leave the teacher with a clear understanding of the evaluator's meaning. In districts that require it, the evaluator used language consistent with the district performance standards. For example, if the district requires the final evaluation be marked with the judgment statements (e.g., **unsatisfactory, satisfactory or exemplary**) the evaluator should use these statements whenever appropriate in the judgments made in the observation write-ups.

I) NA 1 2 3 4   wrote **evidence** about claims, impact statements and judgments in language that is observable, verifiable and/or measurable in observation write-ups

J) NA 1 2 3 4   wrote **evidence** in the language of the Sample District performance standards or in the language of effective instructional practices when describing teacher behaviors

K) NA 1 2 3 4   used a variety of forms of direct and indirect **evidence** in addition to classroom observations as needed to support claims, interpretations and judgments

L) NA 1 2 3 4   where appropriate, connected examples of successful practice, examples of unsuccessful practice and recommendations for improvement with a description of the impact they will have on student performance, development and/or school culture in all observation write-ups

M) NA 1 2 3 4   wrote narratives in a way that enables a third party reading the observation write-ups to determine the varying level of success of the class observed in relation to other observations in the school and/or district

N) NA 1 2 3 4   applied the Sample District performance standards at levels consistent with system-wide standards (inter-rater reliability)

O) NA 1 2 3 4   made **claims** about changes in the teacher's practice that are consistent with the school and/or district goals and initiatives where appropriate

P) NA 1 2 3 4   followed the contracted evaluation procedure regarding teachers' signatures or initials on written documents used in the observation cycle

Q) NA 1 2 3 4   followed the contracted evaluation procedure regarding number of days between each activity conducted in the observation cycle (e.g., time from observation to post-conference, time from post-conference to write-up)

R) NA 1 2 3 4   is clear about whom to consult for information, coaching and/or support with questions that may arise when completing an observation write-up

S) NA 1 2 3 4   goes to appropriate people for information, coaching and/or support with questions that may arise when completing an observation write-up

GENERAL COMMENTS, NOTES AND REMINDERS FOR IMPROVING SUPERVISION AND EVALUATION PRACTICES

In the example below, the wording of several items in the Criteria for Effective Observation Write-ups has been slightly revised for use by those central administrators in charge of evaluation programs as an instrument to provide feedback to the evaluators. I have included three items as an example from an assistant superintendent who used the previous document to evaluate the work of the district's evaluators. The wording in italics is the central administrators' feedback to the evaluator.

In those districts in which the document is used to assess the work of evaluators, the directions are modified as in the example on page 46.[3]

SAMPLE DISTRICT PUBLIC SCHOOLS

CRITERIA FOR EFFECTIVE OBSERVATION WRITE-UPS

Evaluator_____

Date this assessment was completed _____

Administrator completing this assessment _____

The following criteria are used as an annual assessment of an administrator's work as a supervisor and evaluator. Circle the number before each statement that best describes the administrator's performance on the criteria. There is space after each item for any claims, judgments, evidence and impact statements you may wish to make.

NA= not applicable to this assignment

1= does not meet the standard

2= barely meets the standard

3= meets the standard

4= exceeds the standard

The evaluator:

I) NA 1 2 3 4   wrote **evidence** about claims, judgments and impact statements in language that is observable, verifiable and/or measurable in observation write-ups.

You have included very good claims with judgments that clearly state the value you placed on the identified move. Your interpretations do a fine job of identifying for us the impact on the students. In those judgments that indicated a need for improvement, it would be good to give more evidence.

[3] Chapter 8 contains a complete district-wide file cabinet assessment and samples of individual observations assessed with this instrument.

In the next to last paragraph you support a judgment of poor pacing with one student's question about the assignment. I'm sure there was other evidence (e.g., puzzled looks on students' faces, failure of students to write the assignments in their assignment notebooks or failure to check the next day to see how many completed the assignment correctly) that would support this judgment.

J) NA 1 2 3 4   wrote evidence in the language of the Sample District performance standards or in the language of effective instructional practices when describing teacher behaviors

You frequently used the language of effective instructional practices such as time on task, appropriate questioning techniques, purpose of the lesson and others. This is the language used to describe these moves in the Sample Public Schools performance standards. Using the language of the performance standards reinforces a common language for successful teaching in the building and the district. Great job on this criterion!

L) NA 1 2 3 4   where appropriate, connected examples of successful practice, examples of unsuccessful practice and recommendations for improvement with a description of the impact they will have on student performance, development and/or school culture in all observation write-ups

After your recommendation about eating the Kiwi fruit, you go on to describe very well the impact on students. "If you allowed the students to eat the Kiwi at that moment they could have described how it tasted in addition to what it looked like and how it felt." You state in the third paragraph, "As students entered their classrooms . . . This is an example of Ms. Smith maximizing the time allotted to this activity. We know that more time for learning means more learning so we know the impact on the students.

I suggest you also make these connections to student learning in the other areas you commend. For example on page 2 you state, "This is an example of Ms. Smith using good questioning techniques." It would be helpful for you to add a sentence or two about the impact of good questioning techniques on increasing students' ability to use deductive and inductive thinking, etc.

SAMPLE NEEDS ASSESSMENT REPORT

9 Sherman Way
Westwood, MA 02090
Phone/Fax: 781-551-9120
Email: billribas2@aol.com
Web Site: www.ribasassociates.com
William B. Ribas, Ph.D., President

September 3, 2004

Dr. Mary Doe, Superintendent of Schools
Somewhere Public Schools
Somewhere Jr. High School
1 Main Street
Somewhere, NY 01030

Dear Dr. Doe,

The attached report contains the information obtained during the needs assessment sessions held in Somewhere on July 30, 2004. It has been updated based on the additional information acquired at the August 29, 2004 meeting. The report is divided into the following parts:

- Part 1: Information and questions about the Somewhere evaluation document gathered from the administrative staff and from my own review of the document

- Part 2: Information gathered with the Evaluator Survey of Areas for Training and Support form and from the Superintendent and Assistant Superintendent on the district's training needs in the area of supervision and evaluation. Recommendations for training in the areas identified as areas of need.

- Appendix A: The survey

- Appendix B: The collated results of the survey

Please do not hesitate to call me if you have any questions.

Sincerely,

William B. Ribas, President
Ribas Associates

cc: William Moe, Assistant Superintendent of Schools

Part 1: Information and questions about the Somewhere evaluation document gathered from the administrative staff and from my own review of the document.

The Somewhere document in its present state can be used effectively to complete supervision and evaluation in the district. Two specific strengths of the document in comparison to many I read are the following:

1. The document includes performance standards for positions other than classroom teacher that recognize the unique nature of those positions. I understand that there are other positions that still need similar standards; however, the district is to be commended for its work thus far in meeting that need.

2. The teacher self-evaluation form requires teachers to read and reflect on their performance in each of the performance areas. Self-reflection and assessment applied to the district performance standards is an important tool for improving professional performance.

The following clarifications and/or decisions related to the document were made during the session.

1. The Director of Special Services evaluates adapted physical education, psychologists, occupational therapists, behavior interventionists, inclusion specialists, vision and hearing specialists, adjustment counselors, evaluation team facilitators and speech and language specialists.

2. The principals evaluate permanent substitutes.

3. The contract allows for a minimum of one announced and one unannounced observation. This was clarified in the following ways.

    a. The number of observations stated in the contract is a minimum, and evaluators may do more observations than the minimum.

    b. The evaluator must announce at least one of the observations.

    c. Teachers may waive their right to the announced observation and have two unannounced observations.

    d. Pre-conferences are not required. There is varying practice around the district that ranges from formal pre-conference meetings prior to the observation to no meetings at all.

4. Teachers need to be informed about the evaluation procedures and performance standards through workshops and/or meetings.

5. The final date for all evaluations (professional teacher status and prior to professional teacher status) is now May 15.

The following questions were not yet resolved.

1. May someone other than the principal fill out the Staff Assessment Form found on page A6 of the evaluation document?

2. Who should evaluate the software specialist and library assistants?

3. What is the tool used to evaluate each of these positions?

4. What is the district expectation for the meaning of the Needs Improvement judgement in relation to a teacher meeting the standard? Does it mean that the teacher's performance is below standard or does it mean that the teacher's performance meets the standard with more area for growth?

5. Do the *Needs Improvement* and *Satisfactory* judgements mean the same thing for all teachers, regardless of their teaching experience or years in the district?

Comments

1. As stated above, pre-conferences are not required and there is varying practice around the district that ranges from formal pre-conference meetings prior to observations to no meetings at all. There is a need for more common understanding of the range of options for gathering pre-observation data and what the present practice is in each building. These options include 1) pre-observation form only, 2) brief informal pre-conference, or 3) full twenty- to forty-minute pre-conference, pre-conference form and formal pre-conference combined. There is also a need for the district to decide if it wishes to have more consistent implementation of these practices.

2. Above, I have articulated the understandings related to unannounced observations. There is a need for the district to decide if it wishes to have more consistent implementation of this provision.

3. The scope of this needs assessment only included teacher level positions. I would note, however, that there is need for further discussion and clarification by the district about the evaluation of teacher assistants. This process should begin with all administrators reviewing the evaluation explanation found on pages 11 and 12 and the evaluation form found on page 25 of the Contract Between the Somewhere School Committee and the Somewhere Education Association Teacher Assistants Association. The contract specifies that principals are responsible for the evaluation of teacher assistants, however, questions were raised in the assessment meeting about the ability of principals to complete these evaluations, given the proliferation of teacher assistant positions in recent years.

4. The scope of this needs assessment only included teacher level positions. I do wish to make some comments, however, based on the discussion of evaluating permanent substitute teachers. As stated above, the permanent substitutes are evaluated by the principals or their assistants. The evaluators do not have a specific process or standards for completing these evaluations. This is something the district will want to consider at some point in the future. Any work in this area should be cognizant of the evaluation loads and other time constraints already placed upon the principals and their assistants.

5. As mentioned above, the district needs to make a decision about the definition of the judgement, Needs Improvement. It is important that the definition be applied consistently throughout the district. If the district decides NI does not mean that the teacher's performance is below standard, then the district needs to devise a consistent way for communicating to a teacher when his/her performance does not meet the standard.

Part 2: Information gathered with the Evaluator Survey of Potential Areas for Training and Support form and from the Superintendent and Assistant Superintendent on the district's training needs in the area of supervision and evaluation.

1. The curriculum coordinators were not at the meeting. It was agreed, however, that they have not been trained in conferencing, note taking and writing reports related to classroom observations. The note taking and report writing training is typically done with the following steps. Further descriptions of these steps can be found in the document in the red folder given to Dr. Doe or posted on our web site, *www.ribasassociates.com.*

   a. at least 2 days of classroom training

   b. a day for every six to nine people taking the training for joint observations with Bill Ribas. The number of days depends on whether the teachers being observed will allow two or three observers to accompany Bill on the observation. We typically can complete three observations during a school day.

   c. The participants complete an observation write-up of the class and send this to Bill for review and comment. This review typically requires one consulting day for every eight observation write-ups.

2. The training survey results for each item are added together and divided by the number of respondents. This yields an average score ranging from 0 to 3. Please see the copy of the survey in appendix A to understand the definitions for a response of 1, 2 or 3. The higher the score, the greater

the need for training in the area indicated. The following items received a score of 2 or higher.

					Average
G	4	6	4	28	2.00
H	4	4	6	30	2.14
J	3	8	3	28	2.00
K	2	9	3	29	2.07
L	1	4	9	36	2.57
M	2	9	3	29	2.07
N	4	4	5	27	2.08
O	2	10	2	28	2.00
Q	0	9	5	33	2.36
R	4	5	5	29	2.07
S	0	8	6	34	2.43
T	3	7	4	29	2.07
Y	2	7	5	31	2.21
Z	1	4	9	36	2.57
AA	0	4	10	38	2.71
BB	4	4	6	30	2.14
CC	0	8	6	34	2.43
DD	0	7	7	35	2.50
EE	0	7	7	35	2.50
FF	2	7	5	31	2.21
GG	2	8	4	30	2.14
HH	0	8	6	34	2.43
II	0	5	9	37	2.64
JJ	0	6	7	33	2.54
KK	0	7	6	32	2.46
LL	0	9	4	30	2.31
MM	2	7	4	28	2.15

These results indicate that training in the following areas would be beneficial to the administrators surveyed. I would also assume that since these people have received more training than the curriculum liaisons, the following programs would be beneficial to the liaisons as well. Please note that descriptions of these modules can be found in the red folder given to Dr. Doe or posted on our web site *www.ribasassociates.com*. The following areas can be taught as separate modules or grouped together into a three credit graduate course with credits awarded by Fitchburg State College.

Day 1 (addresses G, H, J and Q)

a. use of the language of the Somewhere performance standards in the writing of observation and evaluation write-ups

b. writing observation and evaluation write-ups that connect the teacher's behavior to the impact on students

Day 2 Conferencing to Create Change (addresses K)

Day 3 Understand peer coaching, use time saving techniques and working constructively with the teacher's association (addresses L, M, N and O)

Day 4 Teaching sample lessons, supervising and evaluating in a standards-based (mastery-based) environment (addresses R and T)

Days 5-7 Supervising and evaluating the unsatisfactory or barely satisfactory teacher and progressive discipline (addresses S, Y, Z, AA, BB, CC, DD, EE, FF, GG, HH, II, JJ, KK, LL and MM)

APPENDIX A

District: _____

Respondent: _____

Position: _____ Date: _____

Below are listed a number of areas related to the effective implementation of supervision and evaluation in your district. Please circle the number of the statement that best represents how you would rate your present knowledge and your need for additional information and training in each of these areas.

1. I have sufficient knowledge and training in this area to do what is indicated and have little or no need for further information or training on this topic.

2. I want to know more about this area and would benefit from more information and training on this topic.

3. I need to know more about this area to effectively complete this competency. This is one of my priority topics for training.

A)   1 2 3 Write **classroom observations** that clearly identify the teaching "moves" you observed (a.k.a. make claims) in language that is used consistently throughout your district

B)   1 2 3 Write **classroom observations** that make clear value judgments about the claims

C)   1 2 3 Write **classroom observations** with impact statements (a.k.a interpretations) that connect teachers' behavior to its impact on student learning, student development and the school's and/or department's culture

D)   1 2 3 Write **classroom observations** that contain objective evidence to support the claims, impact statements and judgments made by the evaluator

E)   1 2 3 Write **classroom observations** that begin with basic information, including the time and date of the observation, the teacher's name, the observer's name, the grade and/or subject, whether the observation is announced or unannounced, the school's name and any other information required by your district.

F)   1 2 3 Write **classroom observations** that use the language of your district's performance standards wherever appropriate

G) 1 2 3   Write **final evaluation reports** that contain clear claims and judgments about each of the performance standards in language consistent with your district's performance standards

H) 1 2 3   Write **final evaluation reports** with impact statements that connect teacher performance on each of the standards to its impact on student learning, student development and the school's and/or department's culture

I) 1 2 3   Write **final evaluation reports** that contain objective evidence to support the claims, impact statements and judgments

J) 1 2 3   Write **final evaluation reports** that use the language of your district's performance standards wherever appropriate

K) 1 2 3   Pre- and post-conference in ways that effectively create positive change in teacher performance

L) 1 2 3   Explain the differences between peer review, peer evaluation, peer supervision, and peer coaching in improving teacher performance

M) 1 2 3   Use time-saving tips

N) 1 2 3   Work constructively with the teachers' association/union on issues related to supervision and evaluation

O) 1 2 3   Explain to a colleague the most effective way to implement your district's supervision and evaluation documents and contract language

P) 1 2 3   Self-edit observations, memos and evaluations to ensure continuous improvement in the quality of your evaluation documents

Q) 1 2 3   Work with a partner to peer-edit observations, memos and evaluations to ensure continuous improvement of the quality of your evaluation documents

R) 1 2 3   Use effective techniques and time-efficient methods for teaching sample lessons

S) 1 2 3   Explain the ongoing interaction of the educational, legal, public relations (political) and social-emotional standards and processes of supervision and evaluation

T)   1 2 3   Use a standards-based approach in your district's supervision and evaluation

U)   1 2 3   Explain the numerous types of evidence that are available to evaluators in addition to formal observations

V)   1   2   3   Explain to a colleague which of your supervisors you should consult for information, coaching and/or support with your district's **standards for curriculum and instruction**

W)   1   2   3   Explain to a colleague which of your supervisors you should consult for information, coaching and/or support concerning **the legal standards and processes** of teacher evaluation

X)   1   2   3

_____

_____

_____

SUPERVISING/EVALUATING LOW-PERFORMING TEACHERS AND USING PROGRESSIVE DISCIPLINE

Y)   1   2   3   Explain the difference between a mediocre (barely satisfactory) teacher and an unsatisfactory teacher

Z)   1   2   3   Explain the impact of the law and work within the law during low-performing teacher evaluations. Include the legal concepts of *due process, just cause, duty of fair representation, rules of evidence, harassment, incompetency* and *the Weingarten right*

AA)   1   2   3   Explain the impact of the law and work within the law during low-performing teacher evaluations as it relates to classes of people with legal protections from discrimination for gender, race, religion, age and sexual orientation

BB)   1   2   3   Effectively observe, verify, document and record direct and indirect forms of evidence other than classroom observations

CC)   1   2   3   Use the team approach to support evaluators and reduce the roadblocks to effective evaluations of low-performing teachers

DD)   1   2   3   Effectively work with a second evaluator and/or supervisor during a low-performing teachers' evaluations

EE)   1   2   3   Write and implement improvement plans for low-performing teachers

Go back and review your answers to "U" and "V" above in the context of your work with a low-performing teacher to be sure your answers have not changed.

FF) 1 2 3 Explain to a colleague the steps of *progressive discipline* used to discipline staff members

GG) 1 2 3 Correctly investigate claims of misconduct by staff

HH) 1 2 3 Correctly document each step in progressive discipline using your district's performance standards, policies, and universally accepted appropriate practices

II) 1 2 3 Write progressive discipline notes and documents such as expectation clarification memos, memos after oral reprimands and written reprimands that contain clear claims and judgments about teacher performance, objective evidence to support the claims, and interpretations that connect teacher behavior to its impact on students and the building and/or department

JJ) 1 2 3 Explain the impact of the law and work within the law during progressive discipline situations: including the legal concepts *due process, just cause, duty of fair representation, rules of evidence, harassment, insubordination* and *the Weingarten right*

KK) 1 2 3 Explain the impact of the law and work within the law during *progressive discipline* situations as it relates to classes of people with legal protections from discrimination for gender, race, religion, age and sexual orientation

LL) 1 2 3 Effectively conference with teachers about low performance and discipline issues

MM) 1 2 3 Explain to a colleague whom to consult for specific supports (legal and otherwise) and coaching during a progressive discipline situation

NN) 1 2 3

_____

_____

_____

Comments:

APPENDIX B

Somewhere results by item letter

	1	2	3	Total	Average
A	6	6	2	24	1.71
B	5	7	2	25	1.79
C	6	5	3	25	1.79
D	5	7	2	25	1.79
E	10	3	1	19	1.36
F	5	7	2	25	1.79
G	4	6	4	28	2.00
H	4	4	6	30	2.14
I	4	7	3	27	1.93
J	3	8	3	28	2.00
K	2	9	3	29	2.07
L	1	4	9	36	2.57
M	2	9	3	29	2.07
N*	4	4	5	27	2.08
O	2	10	2	28	2.00
P	2	11	1	27	1.93
Q	0	9	5	33	2.36
R	4	5	5	29	2.07
S	0	8	6	34	2.43
T	3	7	4	29	2.07
U	5	8	1	24	1.71
V	4	10	0	24	1.71
W	4	8	2	26	1.86
X**					
Y	2	7	5	31	2.21
Z	1	4	9	36	2.57
AA	0	4	10	38	2.71
BB	4	4	6	30	2.14
CC	0	8	6	34	2.43
DD	0	7	7	35	2.50
EE	0	7	7	35	2.50
FF	2	7	5	31	2.21
GG	2	8	4	30	2.14
HH	0	8	6	34	2.43
II	0	5	9	37	2.64
JJ*	0	6	7	33	2.54
KK*	0	7	6	32	2.46
LL*	0	9	4	30	2.31
MM*	2	7	4	28	2.15
NN***					

*one less respondent

**one comment asking for specific words that represent what was observed

***one comment asking for constant law updates and protocols

SOURCES

Curriculum frameworks. (1995). Malden, MA: Massachusetts Department of Education.

Delgado, A. (1999, October). *Factors that lead to internal conflict that influence elementary school principals when rating less than satisfactory teachers on formal teacher evaluation.* Dissertation research presented at the American Association of School Personnel Administrators Annual Conference, Ann Arbor, MI.

Marshall, K. (1996, January). How I confronted HSPS (Hyperactive Superficial Principal Syndrome) and began to deal with the heart of the matter. *Phi Delta Kappan,* 336–345.

Maslow. A. (1943). A theory of human motivation. *Psychological Review,* 370–396.

McCarthy, B. (1981). *The 4 MAT system: Teaching to learning styles and right/left mode techniques,* (2nd ed.) Excel Inc.

McTighe, J. & Wiggins, G. (1999). *Understanding by design.* Alexandria, VA: Association of Supervision and Curriculum Development.

Principles of effective teaching. (1995). Malden, MA: Massachusetts Department of Education.

Ribas, W. (2000, April). Ascending the ELPS to excellence in your district's teacher evaluation. *Phi Delta Kappan,* 585–589.

Rutherford, P. (1998). *Instruction for all students.* Alexandria, VA: Just ASK Publications.

Saphier, J. (1993). *How to make supervision and evaluation really work.* Acton, MA: Research for Better Teaching, Inc.

Saphier, J. & Gower, R. (1997). *The skillful teacher: Building your teaching skills.* Acton, MA: Research for Better Teaching, Inc.

What teachers should be able to do. (1994). Washington, DC: National Board for Professional Teaching Standards.

CHAPTER 3

The Educational Skills and Knowledge Needed to Be an Effective Supervisor and Evaluator

ANALYZING OBSERVATIONS IN TERMS OF CLAIMS, JUDGMENTS, EVIDENCE AND IMPACT STATEMENTS AND THE DISTRICT'S PERFORMANCE STANDARDS

This chapter looks closely at the process of observing and documenting classroom teaching. The first section of this chapter examines the component parts of observation and evaluation write-ups, *claims, judgments, evidence and impact statements (interpretations)* (C.J.E.I.) as they apply to classroom observations. Jonathon Saphier, a noted author and teacher on the subject of supervision and evaluation, describes the component parts of an observation write-up and evaluation as claims, evidence, interpretations and judgments (C.E.I.J.). (Saphier, 1993). This section expands upon that work by incorporating the most current practice related to the writing of observation and evaluation write-ups.

A **claim** is the identification of the areas of performance from the district's performance standards.

It is important that districts use a common language to discuss teaching. A claim is a label placed by the evaluator on a particular teaching move. Districts need to adopt a common language and train their evaluators to use it in their evaluation write-ups and conferences. The language used by evaluators should be consistent with that used in their district's performance and curriculum standards.

The following are examples of claims that correspond with the performance standards found in chapter 9.

Mr. Morales did an excellent job of clearly stating the objectives at the outset of the lesson.

Ms. Parmenter effectively used comprehension questions to formatively gauge the students' levels of understanding.

Mr. Burrows failed to use adequate wait time after asking questions.

Judgments are the value the evaluator places on the teacher's choice of teaching move and the teacher's level of expertise in executing the move. Judgments contain words such as satisfactory, exemplary, unsatisfactory, successful, unsuccessful, good, excellent, effective and outstanding. It is important in a standards-based evaluation system that, wherever possible, evaluators use the same terms that are used in the final year-end evaluation report. This is particularly important in the evaluation of a low-performing teacher. In example 3 on page 69, you will note that the final statement tells the teacher whether the evaluator judged the activity as satisfactory or less than satisfactory. This language is consistent with the final evaluation report language in the Massachusetts document in chapter 9.

I have placed in italics the words that indicate the evaluator's judgment from our three examples of claims noted earlier.

Mr. Morales *did an excellent job of* clearly stating the objectives at the outset of the lesson.

Ms. Parmenter *effectively* used comprehension questions to formatively gauge the students' levels of understanding.

Mr. Burrows *failed to use adequate* wait time after asking questions.

Implicit Judgment

With **implicit judgments**, like implicit impact statements, the claim, evidence and/or impact statements clearly convey the value judgment the evaluator placed on an observed teaching move. The example below is of an implicit judgment in an observation of a high school yoga class.

Example of a Paragraph with an Implicit Judgment

> Marcia was able to maintain momentum throughout the class session. She began promptly at 7:35, after students took their places around the circle. The students arrived with the 3 apparatuses (sponge ball, circle and sponge stick) that they know to pick up from the storage closet before taking a place in the circle. The apparatuses were in their correct locations in the closet.
>
> "Are we ready?" Marcia asked as she glanced to see that the students were indeed ready to begin. Marcia handled an intrusion when two girls entered the class at 7:39 and quietly joined the circle. At 7:42, a boy entered and took a place outside of the circle. Between the first and second posture, Marcia motioned to the class to enlarge the circle and to the boy to move forward into the circle. All three students were included without any break to momentum. In the post-conference meeting, Marcia explained that the late students' bus was a few minutes late. Just prior to the class, Marcia sent a girl who was not feeling well to the clinic. When that girl returned, Marcia whispered to her, "Lie down in the back" of the room. Marcia continued to lead the class from the front, and, when the class was engaged in the next posture, she moved to the back to check in with the sick girl and cover her with a coat. As a result, 100% of the students were able to remain on task for the entire forty-five minute period.

It is commonly accepted that a class on task without breaks to momentum is a positive situation. Therefore, the evaluator did not need to restate his/her implicit judgement with an explicit judgment.

Again, one must always remember that the implicit judgment must be obvious to both the teacher and to a third party reader. If the evaluator is uncertain if the implicit judgment will be clear, it is best to err on the side of writing an explicit judgment. I would further caution that it is rarely advisable to use an implicit judgment when the performance is poor. Human beings all have psychological defenses that help us put a "positive spin" on our actions. We also don't purposely teach in ways that we know are not effective. Therefore, without an explicit judgment in the case of a poor performance, the teacher may not understand that the evaluator has judged the performance as poor.

"Evidence is a literal description of something the observer heard or saw to support the claim."[1] (Saphier & Gower)

[1] Chapter 6 contains a comprehensive explanation of the types of evidence, including hearsay, circumstantial and direct.

Impact Statements (a.k.a. **interpretations**) explain the impact on the students or others. Impact statements typically start with "thus," "as a result of," "therefore" or other words and phrases that connect the teaching behavior to the impact on students.

Whenever possible, the impact statement should indicate the impact on students' behavior, performance and/or attitude. For some standards, such as standard VII in the Massachusetts document and Domains V and VII in the Texas document in chapter 9, the impact statement should be worded in terms of its impact on other staff, parents or the school culture. Over the last decade, we have increasingly become aware that there is more than one way to teach something well. This makes the impact statement a particularly important part of the evaluation. The impact remains constant no matter what strategy the teacher uses to obtain the desired student learning behavior. The students have either mastered the material or they have not mastered the material. The students have either exhibited the desired behavior or they have not exhibited the desired behavior. The impact statement enables us to evaluate the student outcomes that result from the teacher inputs, thereby limiting the impact of teacher style on the evaluator's objectivity.

> The impact remains constant no matter what strategy the teacher uses to obtain the desired student learning or behavior.

Explicit Impact Statements

Most impact statements are explicitly stated, such as in the following examples.

> As a result, the students were able to work throughout the lab period without a behavior disruption and using the appropriate safety procedures.

> As a result, the confused students better understood their task and were able to work productively.

Implicit Impact Statements

> In some cases, the impact is obvious based on what is written in the claim, judgment and/or evidence. In those cases, we refer to the impact statement as **implicit**.

In some cases, the impact is obvious based on what is written in the claim, judgment and/or evidence. In those cases, we refer to the impact statement as implicit. In these circumstances, it could sound condescending to the teacher or sound like excess verbiage if the evaluator makes an explicit impact statement. For example:

> Mr. Wheeler effectively used checking for understanding techniques to determine which students had mastered the concept and which had not.

"Give me a thumbs up if you think you are ready to try an example (two digit multiplication) yourself. Give me a thumbs sideways if you are not sure. Give me a thumbs down if you are not ready to try an example." All but three of the 24 students gave a thumbs up. These three students gave a thumbs sideways. "Here are two examples to try. Do one on each side of your white board. If you finish them both put your green cup up. Then find another student with a green cup and check your answers. If you agree, work either separately or together on the problem of the day. If you don't agree on both of the problems, work together to settle any disagreements. Put up your red cup if you need help." While the students worked, Mr. Wheeler had the three students with their thumbs sideways sit together while he retaught them the concept. All three of these students completed the first problem with Mr. Wheeler. They then went back to their tables to complete the second problem. Mr. Wheeler then circulated around the room, checking the progress of each student.

"Hold up your white board and show me example 1. Now turn over your white board and show me example 2."

In the post-conference, Mr. Wheeler indicated that all the students had completed the problems correctly.

"Miguel, explain to us how you do number one."

"Robert (one of the boys who worked with the teacher on the first problem), explain to us how you did number 2."

"What questions do you have about these problems?"

No one asks a question.

"For homework you have five problems on the worksheet on your desk. There is a bonus mind bender on the back of the sheet that I'd like you all to try. Remember, you should work for a minimum of 20 minutes at home. You may stop at that point even if you don't have all the problems and the mind bender finished. You have five minutes to start your homework and I will come around if anyone needs help."

All of the students worked on the problems, and Mr. Wheeler went first to the three who had indicated uncertainty earlier in the lesson.

Mr. Wheeler brought the corrected homework papers to the post-conference. Twenty-two students (including two of the three who received the reteaching) had four or five correct. Two students (including one of the three who had received the reteaching) had three correct.

In the example above, the evaluator indicated in the first sentence that Mr. Wheeler had checked effectively. The evidence also shows the high level of student mastery and Mr. Wheeler's knowledge of each student's level of mastery. Therefore, it might sound condescending to restate this in an interpretation.

One must always remember, however, that the implicit impact statement must be obvious to both the observed teacher and to a third party reader. If the evaluator is uncertain if the implicit interpretation will be clear, it is best to err on the side of writing an explicit impact statement.

Objective and Subjective Components

The order of presenting the four concepts above in a classroom observation write-up is less important than making the evaluation clear to the teacher and others who need to read it. It is also not important that the components be clearly delineated in separate statements, provided all the concepts are covered.

What is most important is that the write-up shows the two major components. The first being the **subjective** components. Claims, impact statements and judgments are based on the evaluator's conclusions of what he/she actually observes, verifies or, in cases of indirect evidence, can reasonably infer from the accumulated data or the observation.

The second of the major components is the evidence. This is the **objective** description of the actual behavior or information observed or verified by the evaluator. In the early years of clinical supervision and evaluation, we focused almost solely on the teacher during classroom observations. We now know that there is a great deal of data that can be derived from watching and analyzing the students' actions as well as the teacher's actions. Early childhood educators have known this for years. More recently, evaluators of elementary, middle school and high school teachers are increasing their observation of students during classroom observations as a way of analyzing the teacher's year-long impact on the students.

Evidence supports the claims and judgments and, perhaps more importantly, shows the teacher that the supervisor–evaluator cares enough to take the time to learn the specifics of what the teacher is doing. We draw a distinction between evidence and information. Both are data that is used to help the evaluator better understand the teacher's performance. They differ, however, in their ability to enable an evaluator to make a judgment.

Evidence is data that is sufficiently verified to make a judgment. For example, in the sample observation write-up paragraphs above, the behaviors observed by the evaluators, coupled with the data learned in the post-conferences, are sufficient enough to make a judgment. For those who are interested in learning more about how to determine when data is sufficient to make a judgment, chapter six contains a comprehensive explanation of the legal standards related to evidence.

> *Evidence* is data that is sufficiently verified to make a judgement . . . *Information* is data that leads us to decide that we need more data before we can make a judgement.

Information is data that leads us to make the decision that we need more data before we can make a judgment. For example, three high school math students ask to leave a teacher's class for placement in the same class with a different teacher because the teacher is "too easy" and "the class does not have the appropriate level of challenge." The supervisor's review of the teacher's first quarter grades, however, shows that two of the students had a B+ and one had an A. A conversation with the teacher indicates that the second quarter grades for each student show that two are continuing to work at a B to B+ level and that the one with the A is continuing at that level. Two classroom walk throughs and a formal observation indicate that the content being taught is at the level of challenge prescribed in the curriculum. In this circumstance, the information initially received was not sufficient to make a judgment. The additional data collected by observation and from reviewing class grades provide sufficient data to make the judgment that the class is not "too easy" for at least two of the students. In the case of the third student, the supervisor concludes that providing some extension of the learning is appropriate.

Both information and evidence come to the evaluator through two types of sources. The first source is **direct data.** This is the data that the evaluator experiences through his/her own senses. The evaluator sees, touches, hears or smells the data. The second form of data is **indirect data.** This data is experienced by someone else and reported to the evaluator by the other person. This chapter focuses primarily on the direct form of data known as the classroom observation. Chapter 4 looks at nineteen alternate sources of data other than the classroom observation.

Chapter 6 contains a comprehensive explanation about the differences between observed and verified evidence (direct) and indirect evidence (circumstantial and hearsay) in the data-gathering process. For most teacher evaluations, the majority of the data cited is gathered in classroom observations. Examples of sources for data other than classroom observations are discussed in chapter 4.

EXCERPTS FROM SAMPLE WRITE-UPS THAT INCLUDE SUBJECTIVE CONCLUSIONS SUPPORTED BY OBSERVABLE AND/OR VERIFIABLE DATA

Below are actual examples from teacher evaluation reports that use evidence in classroom observations to support the evaluators' subjective conclusions (claims, impact statements, judgments). The names have been changed to maintain confidentiality. The performance standard (principle of effective teaching or PET) and curriculum standard (learning expectation) are noted in italics. The claim/judgment and the evidence is marked in the margin.

Example 1

Claim/Judgment

Mr. Morgan used effective questioning techniques (PET IV C) to activate the students' prior learning and promote higher level thinking.

Evidence

He asked, "What questions do you have about the density of water based on what we've learned so far?"

The students brainstormed all the questions they had about density. Mr. Morgan wrote these questions on a chart paper.

"What does a rowboat do when it gets swamped with water in a lake? Explain why."

"What happens when a stick falls in the water? Explain why."

"What happens when a nail falls in the water? Explain why."

When the list was completed, Mr. Morgan worked with the students to determine which questions could be answered only with experimentation and which questions could be answered without experimentation.

Impact Statement

As a result, students learned to use inductive and deductive reasoning to synthesize the information they had learned at the beginning of the unit. They learned to delineate between that information which could be found through background reading and the information that could only be obtained through experimentation.

Example 2

Claim/Judgment

Mr. Morgan's lesson ensured that students maintained appropriate standards of behavior, mutual respect and safety (*PET III B*).

Evidence

The classroom procedures were clearly posted on a chart at the front of the room. These included the safety procedures for lab time. Mr. Morgan reviewed the procedures at the start of the class. "We will be using Bunsen burners and chemicals today. It is important that no one leaves their seat without permission when the burners are lit. Goggles must be used at all times and the test tubes should only be handled with the test tube holders. Who can review for me the emergency fire procedures if there is an accident?" John reviewed the fire expectations. Mr. M. asked if there were any questions on the expectations.

As a result, the students were able to work throughout the lab period without a behavior incident and using the appropriate safety procedures (*Eighth Grade Science Learning Expectation I B*).

Impact Statement

Chunking vs. Chronological

It is usually recommended that evaluators arrange their write-ups by area of performance rather than in chronological order. This is known as **chunking by claim**. However, there certainly are times when a write-up is better done in chronological order. You will note in example 3 below that the evaluator has carefully noted the time throughout the lesson and recorded the lesson chronologically. This was done to highlight the **efficiency** or **inefficiency**[2] of the teaching. Example 3 is a write-up for a low-performing teacher who had significant issues related to incompetency and inefficiency. She refused to acknowledge these issues. Chronological write-ups such as this one objectively demonstrated the inefficiency in her teaching and forced her to recognize its existence.

Example 3

The start of this lesson was unsatisfactory. The room was not physically ready: you were not present and ready to teach: and it did not begin within an appropriate time (*PET IIIA*).

Claim/ Judgement

The period began at 9:00. Four students came into the classroom through the double doors by 9:01 and took their bags to the lab area instead of leaving them in the lobby area. You came in seconds later as the four of them left your classroom without permission. As others began to arrive, the lollipop-selling controversy became an issue. A student said that Mr. (the evaluator) gave her permission to sell the lollipops. That was not true, but you took four minutes checking it out and making sure students wrapped up the lollipops.

The room was in disarray. Some of it was from the day before (salt on a lab table). Some of it was from homeroom. Students' chairs were helter-skelter or, in one case, on top of the lab table. Lab tables were not orderly. The counters near the windows were in disarray with papers and materials from the astronomy unit, which has been over for at least three weeks.

Evidence

---

2   Inefficiency has been defined by arbitrators as "not producing the effect intended or desired within a reasonable amount of time, whether or not a teacher has the knowledge or capability." (Lexington, Massachusetts, Public Schools, American Arbitration Association, 1995), and as "students not on task, teacher not monitoring work, not following lesson plans, inaccurate and incomplete record keeping have all been accepted as evidence of inefficiency in teaching . . . " (Little Rock, Arkansas, School District, American Arbitration Association, 1994)

Evidence, continued

At 9:05 things were beginning to calm down. You began to address the class at 9:07. Your first comments were "John, get in your seat. You have a seat." Jarmal interrupted with "How come there is salt on the table?" John chimed in with "Mrs. E., what is the stuff on the table?" "Why do you put stuff on the table?"

At 9:08 you began to explain, "What I have today is a short . . . At least you and a partner should have a pencil. I will pass out this sheet . . . Then go on to complete it for homework . . . So you have to do this whole packet." Jarmal interrupted again, "How come you didn't clean up the salt?" You responded, "I left it up to students." Jarmal made another comment, "Oh, so I have to clean it up?"

Meanwhile, David was walking around the room cleaning the tables.

At 9:10 you said, "Okay, the first activity . . . " and began the explanation of the first activity.

Impact Statement

The physical condition of the class, the students' interruptions and your late arrival in the room resulted in the loss of ten minutes of valuable instructional time and a less than satisfactory learning environment at the start of the lesson.

SAMPLE OBSERVATION WRITE-UP THAT INCLUDES SUBJECTIVE CONCLUSIONS (CLAIMS, JUDGMENTS AND IMPACT STATEMENTS) SUPPORTED BY OBSERVABLE AND/OR VERIFIABLE DATA

The following observation write-up integrates subjective conclusions with the evidence used to support these conclusions. *This write-up is longer than necessary for a high-performing teacher. It was chosen to provide multiple examples for the reader to see and try.* To test your skills at identifying C, J, E and I, read this write-up and answer the following questions.

1. Identify claims (C), judgments (J), evidence (E) and/or impact statements (I).

2. Can you determine the impact of the various teaching moves on the students' performance?

3. As a third party reader, did you find this write-up easy to read and understand? If yes, why? If not, why not?

4. Connie is a very good teacher and the evaluator frequently affirms her good work. However, please list those places in the evaluation in which the evaluator provided suggestions and/or questions designed to foster Connie's further growth.

Sample Observation Write-up of a High-Performing Teacher

Sample School Classroom Observation: Ms. Connie L. – Level 1 Trigonometry

Date and time: 12/12/01, Long Block

Observer: Joan Switt, Assistant Principal

Connie conveys a message to her students that her classroom is a safe, respectful learning environment where each individual is important. She liberally used the students' names and often called upon students to assist other students even as she was teaching: "Joe, Lynn wants some answers," "Todd, Vance needs help with the calculator," and later, "Lynn is going to help us again." Each student was called upon repeatedly during the class. When it appeared that every student had participated in the class, Connie looked around the room and asked, "Who haven't I talked to today?" Noticing a young man who had not contributed often during the class, she realized, "Greg, you weren't here yesterday." She went on to engage him more deeply in the conversation. As a result of this personal approach to her class, Ms. L. ensures that each student is attentive and has a feeling of genuine involvement and importance.

Beyond the use of names, Ms. L. sends other powerful expectation messages. Students are obviously aware that they are expected to participate in class, will be given time to formulate answers and may then speak without fear of ridicule or embarrassment. At one point, Connie called upon an individual to answer a question and waited a full ten seconds for the young woman to reply. Remarkably, during that time no one else attempted to volunteer an answer or made any gesture of impatience. Ultimately the chosen student answered correctly. During our conference, I asked Connie what she had done to ensure that individuals would not speak out of turn while a classmate was thinking. Connie noted that she had "established a rule with all my classes that every student has a right to his or her time and no other student has a right to encroach upon that time—and then made sure everyone stuck to it." As a result of Connie's expectation that learners can think/respond when given adequate time, students both take risks with difficult material and show a high degree of individual resourcefulness and mutual support when they encounter new challenges.

Ms. L. used a full array of clarity techniques during the class. To begin, she anticipated confusion among her students as evidenced by her warning to the class when she discovered a calculator error a student had made: "Check your calculator to be sure you are in degree mode." She later indicated to a student that she was aware of potential future errors he might make and announced, "That's why I want to show you this way." As a result of these cautionary steps, students were aware of potential problem areas and able to go on with their work with renewed confidence.

Throughout the class, Connie used a variety of explanatory devices. When students encountered difficulty finding the sides of the triangles, Connie immediately referred to the diagrams depicting the problem situations. Conversely, when a diagram confused one student because it was not drawn to scale, she reverted to a chart format for organizing the material. Rather than simply describe keystrokes on the calculator, Connie moved to a picture of the calculator prominently displayed on the wall and indicated the appropriate keys to use verbally while pointing them out on the picture. As a result, students were able to correct their own errors, either written or in their calculator usage, and continue immediately to master the skills they were reviewing.

(write-up continues)

Ms. L. returned and persevered with students who could not, or would not, answer her questions. Of particular note, a young man in the class refused to respond to Connie when she questioned him about labeling a diagram which was on the board. His replies ranged from a simple "no" to "I don't know" or "put them anywhere." Connie stuck with this young man: "Todd, back to you. What does c always mean?" "Todd, when you learned the Pythagorean Theorem, did you learn it with little letters?" "Todd, do you see why angle C is the right angle?" Later in the period, Connie went to Todd to check his calculator and show him that he had an incorrect setting. This one instance, coupled with all the other clarity techniques Connie employed, indicated that students can enter Connie's classroom knowing that she feels they are important, believes the material is important, and has the skills to help students gain mastery of trigonometry. Ultimately, that may be the most important lesson they learn.

Connie can capitalize on both her capacity for conveying high positive messages and her skill in explaining concepts by fine-tuning the way in which she focuses students on their learning goals. At the outset, she gave an itinerary and the reason for doing the activities in a particular order: "First we'll go over the homework; second, the law of cosines Case 4, and then the quiz on right triangles. I want to teach the new material so that when you finish the quiz you can go on to solve problems." She did not, however, explicitly convey what students would be expected to know or be able to do at the end of the 90 minutes—or why the material covered was important. There were several points at which she might have "nailed down" the objective:

1. when Kara made an interesting comment and Connie said "We have just discovered! Ah, we answered your question." and then repeated Kara's insight but did not say whether or not arriving at this conclusion was one of the goals for the class – or something everyone should know.

2. when a student asked a question about rounding and Connie responded, "That's a very important question. How important is rounding?" but then went on to another topic and did not follow up on her own focusing question.

At the end of class, 8 of the 9 students I sampled were not sure of what they were to have mastered and gave a wide range of procedural or activity based responses (e.g., pass the quiz, do some triangle problems, etc.) This lack of a clear objective limits their ability to assess their own progress and understanding and to use the challenging climate and Connie's skills to help themselves learn.

In our conference, Connie and I had a lively discussion about lesson plans vs. activity lists and activities vs. objectives during which I shared my own—and the students'—confusion about what the learning outcome was supposed to be. Connie then realized that she had not been fully aware herself of what she wanted students to know and be able to do. She has decided to focus on clearly conveying objectives both in her own work and in the next strategy sharing session at the department level.

_____   _____
Teacher's signature   date

_____   _____
Observer's signature   date

Teacher's signature indicates the teacher received the observation. It does not indicate agreement.
Teacher's comments: _____

_____

DATA SOURCES

Full Length Classroom Observation

There are a large number of data sources that evaluators use to obtain a comprehensive view of a teacher's performance on all of the district's teacher performance standards. The most commonly used, and arguably the most important, is the full-length classroom observation. This is typically an observation that lasts from thirty minutes to an entire block scheduling period. During this time the evaluator sits in the classroom and takes copious literal notes of what the teacher is saying and doing and of what the students are saying and doing. The evaluator's notes also may contain a description of the room arrangement and the displays that are on the walls and/or ceiling. Sometimes these observations are scheduled with the teacher (announced) and sometimes the evaluator shows up unannounced.

Literal Note-Taking

One of the more difficult skills for novice evaluators is the ability to take copious literal notes. These notes are important because they contain the evidence and information on which the observer will base his/her claims, judgments and interpretations. Evaluators typically take their notes on a pad of paper or on a laptop computer. Some evaluators prefer to use a system of two-column note taking, while others prefer three-column note taking.

In two-column note-taking, the first column is smaller than the second. In the first column, the evaluator jots down the time, notes to him/herself and questions that he/she wants to ask the teacher to obtain additional data in the post-conference. (See the sample on p. 74.) The stages of note-taking are typically as follows:

Step 1: While Observing

    a.   In the right column, take copious notes on what the teacher says and does and on what the students say and do.

    b.   In the left column, record the time, questions you want to ask the teacher in the post-conference and other notes to yourself.

Step 2: As Soon After the Observation as Possible

    a.   In the right column, fill in any literal notes you did not write down in the class that you remember.

    b.   In the left column, write down any additional questions for the teacher that come to mind and/or any notes to yourself.

    c.   Reread your notes, questions and comments. In the left column, identify the teaching strategy the notes represent. We call this stage analysis of the notes.

> In the left column, identify the teaching strategy the notes represent. We call this stage analysis of the notes.

Many observers like to use a different color when writing the names of the strategies.

Step 3:

During the post-conference, add any additional data that increases the comprehensiveness of the data in your notes.

The following notes are from the observation of a seventh grade technology teacher. The first set of notes appears as they were at the completion of step 1, above. The second set appears as they were at the completion of step 2. The third set appears as they were at the completion of step 3.

SET 1—LITERAL NOTES

	K is a computer teacher with a seventh grade class 8:05 to 8:35
8:05 7th grade class	Class has just completed the first quarter and took a test yesterday. They are working on a Tom Snyder game about geography. This is an interim activity because it is the day before Thanksgiving. A new unit will begin on Monday. This is first period on a snowy day and the students are filtering in. K is setting up the LCD. It is first period and the students are wandering in.
	Four students are sent to the get ibooks. The class is meeting in a foreign language room. The entire school has been temporarily relocated to this building during construction. There is no computer lab in this location. K's office is on the first floor and the classroom is on the third. K had to hold her classes in rooms that are free at the time she has a class scheduled.
Is this your homeroom? 8:12	K Ok you guys have a seat. Because you just had your test, it is the day before vacation and it is snowing we are going to do this game. I think it is best for us to dive into it (the game) rather than have me explain it ahead of time. You will work with partners today. Get with a partner.
Were the partners random? What are the expectations for working with partners and when were they taught? Why not have a student pass out the materials	K get with a partner S can we do three partners. K you can do three if you can play nice together K I am going to pass you out a map of the US. K passes out the maps. K Does everyone have at least one map? ??? (I missed some of K's instructions here) K Why do you think there are numbers next to those pictures of cattle (on the map) K explains that the numbers represent the state's rank in that product K the computer has given us a random starting point. It is Washington (state) today. We need to drive through all the states that produce cattle. We need to drive through as many of the cattle producing states as we can and gather points . You gather points as you go. For example you get 10 points if you get to Texas because it is the largest cattle producing state.

	S Could we drive in straight line across the United States? K Ah Mike just had a good point. You could go Michael's way. You want get the most points. That is what is great about this game there is no right or wrong way.
	S how do you count the points. K the computer will count the points for you Students start and there are three hands up. K goes to the first group of students. She then chooses to do one example on a sheet she is holding on the front board. The students in the front can see the paper. Most students cannot see it because it is too small.
8:22 What is your objective.	Aaron you asked about keeping track of your points. You may want to keep track of your own points so you can try different ways to find the ways that give you the most points. K demonstrates on the LCD the route she had made on the map on the board. People asked if you can go through the same state twice. You can but you cannot get the points a second time. K Now it is quiz time. Once you get to 10 steps the computer will ask you a quiz. K A quiz pops up and they do the quiz together. Students shout out the answers. The students who answer the ones on the left side of the room which is where the projector is located. The right side of the room (all boys) does not answer the questions. (15 students in the class: 7 boys on the right side of the room: six girls and two boys on the left side of the room near the screen)
8:27 Have you ever taught this before? (why are the numbers on the computers important)	What are the numbers on each of these computers. K checks the numbers and sends one students back to return a computer and return with number 17. Student returns to say computer 17 is gone but not signed out. Students are asked to plan in their groups.
Are the partners random or were they predetermined? 8:34 How did you know the students understood the direction prior to having them start working independently in their groups? 8:35 end of observa	Each group has a different product to map. They are given a new map and a second sheet that indicates the product they are to map and where the different products exist in each state. Students are working while K circulates around the room. S Ms A how do we (get the computer ready) K that is my job. You need to plan on you sheet of paper. K (to another group) You don't go to your computer until your plot is on your sheet. K works with one pair of boys walking them through the first few steps.

SET 2—LITERAL NOTES WITH ANALYSIS IN ITALICS

	K is a computer teacher with a seventh grade class 8:05 to 8:35
8:05 7th grade class	Class has just completed the first quarter and took a test yesterday. They are working on a Tom Snyder game about geography. This is an interim activity because it is the day before Thanksgiving. A new unit will begin on Monday. This is first period on a snowy day and the students are filtering in. K is setting up the LCD. It is first period and the students are wandering in.
Students know the routine for getting the I books:	Four students are sent to the get ibooks. The class is meeting in a foreign language room. The entire school has been temporarily relocated to this building during construction. There is no computer lab in this location. K's office is on the first floor and the classroom is on the third. K had to hold her classes in rooms that are free at the time she has a class scheduled.
Is this your homeroom? 8:12 *Gives a verbal overview of the big picture.* *Students quickly get into partners without any break to momentum* Were the partners random? What are the expectations for working with partners and when were they taught? Why not have a student pass out the materials *Questioning with open ended questions/ the word "think" also makes it more invitational* *No students answer. Wait time and scaffolding may be helpful prior to giving the answer.*	K Ok you guys have a seat. Because you just had your test, it is the day before vacation and it is snowing we are going to do this game. I think it is best for us to dive into it (the game) rather than have me explain it ahead of time. You will work with partners today. Get with a partner. K get with a partner S can we do three partners. K you can do three if you can play nice together K I am going to pass you out a map of the US. K passes out the maps. K Does everyone have at least one map? ??? (I missed some of K's instructions here) K Why do you think there are numbers next to those pictures of cattle (on the map) K explains that the numbers represent the state's rank in that product K the computer has given us a random starting point. It is Washington (state) today. We need to drive through all the states that produce cattle. We need to drive through as many of the cattle producing states as we can and gather points. You gather points as you go. For example you get 10 points if you get to Texas because it is the largest cattle producing state.
	S Could we drive in straight line across the United States? K Ah Mike just had a good point. You could go Michael's way. You want to get the most points. That is what is great about this game there is no right or wrong way. S how do you count the points? K the computer will count the points for you Students start and there are three hands up. K goes to the first group of students. She then chooses to do one example on a sheet she is holding on the front board. The students in the front can see the paper. Most students cannot see it because it is too small.

8:22 What is your objective. I think it is: By the end of class students will be able to: 1. Correctly start and use the software 2. make decisions about the stages of their trip that will enable them to gather the greatest number of points in the 10 moves. 3. name at least ? products produced in the U.S. and the top ? states for producing those products. *K did not appear to state the objective. Did you tell the students the objective for the class?* *Space needs to be better considered in terms of seating and where she focuses her teaching so the boys on the right side are more involved.*	Aaron you asked about keeping track of your points. You may want to keep track of your own points so you can try different ways to find the ways that give you the most points. K demonstrates on the LCD the route she had made on the map on the board. People asked if you can go through the same state twice. You can but you cannot get the points a second time. K Now it is quiz time. Once you get to 10 steps the computer will ask you a quiz. K A quiz pops up and they do the quiz together. Students shout out the answers. The students who answer the ones on the left side of the room which is where the projector is located. The right side of the room (all boys) does not answer the questions. (15 students in the class: 7 boys on the right side of the room: six girls and two boys on the left side of the room near the screen)
8:27 Have you ever taught this before? *No checking for understanding at this point. As a result at least five students (and maybe more) are confused about how to begin when they are allowed to work independently.*	What are the numbers on each of these computers. K checks the numbers and sends one students back to return a computer and return with number 17. Student returns to say computer 17 is gone but not signed out. Students are asked to plan in their groups.
Are the partners random or were they predetermined? 8:34 proximity How did you know the students understood the direction prior to having them start working independently in their groups? 8:35 *There were no disruptive behaviors. There is no need for desisting moves. It would be good to use some enlisting.* *This is again evidence of the students understanding the work and behavior expectations.*	Each group has a different product to map. They are given a new map and a second sheet that indicates the product they are to map and where the different products exist in each state. Students are working while K circulates around the room. S Ms A how do we (get the computer ready) K that is my job. You need to plan on you sheet of paper. K (to another group) You don't go to your computer until your plot is on your sheet. K works with one pair of boys walking them through the first few steps.

SET 3—LITERAL NOTES WITH ANALYSIS IN ITALICS AND TEACHER'S ANSWERS FROM THE POST-CONFERENCE IN BOLD

	K is a computer teacher with a seventh grade class 8:05 to 8:35
8:05 7th grade class *Students know the routine for getting the I books:*	Class has just completed the first quarter and took a test yesterday. They are working on a Tom Snyder game about geography. This is an interim activity because it is the day before Thanksgiving. A new unit will begin on Monday. This is first period on a snowy day and the students are filtering in. K is setting up the LCD. It is first period and the students are wandering in. Four students are sent to the get ibooks. The class is meeting in a foreign language room. The entire school has been temporarily relocated to this building during construction. There is no computer lab in this location. K's office is on the first floor and the classroom is on the third. K had to hold her classes in rooms that are free at the time she has a class scheduled.
Is this your homeroom? 8:12 *Gives a verbal overview of the big picture.* *Students quickly get into partners without any break to momentum* Were the partners random? What are the expectations for working with partners and when were they taught? Why not have a student pass out the materials *Questioning with open ended questions/ the work "think" also makes it more invitational* *No students answer. Wait time and scaffolding may be helpful prior to giving the answer.*	K Ok you guys have a seat. Because you just had your test, it is the day before vacation and it is snowing we are going to do this game. I think it is best for us to dive into it (the game) rather than have me explain it ahead of time. You will work with partners today. Get with a partner. K get with a partner S can we do three partners. K you can do three if you can play nice together **They are allowed to choose their own partners. I believe as long as they are productive they should get to choose their own partner.** **Early in the year I teach them my expectations for working in partners. They must work quietly, stay on task, and raise their hand if they have a question.** K I am going to pass you out a map of the US. K passes out the maps. K Does everyone have at least one map? **I never thought of that. I will try it next time.** ??? (I missed some of K's instructions here) K Why do you think there are numbers next to those pictures of cattle (on the map) K explains that the numbers represent the state's rank in that product K the computer has given us a random starting point. It is Washington (state) today. We need to drive through all the states that produce cattle. We need to drive through as many of the cattle producing states as we can and gather points. You gather points as you go. For example you get 10 points if you get to Texas because it is the largest cattle producing state.
	S Could we drive in straight line across the United States? K Ah Mike just had a good point. You could go Michael's way. You want get the most points. That is what is great about this game there is no right or wrong way. S how do you count the points. K the computer will count the points for you Students start and there are three hands up. K goes to the first group of students. She then chooses to do one example on a sheet she is holding on the front board. The students in the front can see the paper. Most students cannot see it because it is too small.

8:22 What is your objective. I think it is: By the end of class students will be able to: 4. Correctly start and use the software 5. make decisions about the stages of their trip that will enable them to gather the greatest number of points in the 10 moves. 6. name at least ? products produced in the U.S. and the top ? states for producing those products. *K did not appear to state the objective. Did you tell the students the objective for the class?* *Space needs to be better considered in terms of seating and where she focuses her teaching so the boys on the right side are more involved.*	Aaron you asked about keeping track of your points. You may want to keep track of your own points so you can try different ways to find the ways that give you the most points. **I want the students to problem solve with a partner the best method gathering points while crossing the country. I wanted to do something productive that could be a "one shot" lesson since it was the day before Thanksgiving and we had just finished a unit. I also wanted to have a lesson that incorporated some of they have been learning in social studies. The software helps them learn the states and their locations.** K demonstrates on the LCD the route she had made on the map on the board. People asked if you can go through the same state twice. You can but you cannot get the points a second time. K Now it is quiz time. Once you get to 10 steps the computer will ask you a quiz. **I explained the steps they were to take to complete the task.** K A quiz pops up and they do the quiz together. Students shout out the answers. The students who answer the ones on the left side of the room which is where the projector is located. The right side of the room (all boys) does not answer the questions. (15 students in the class: 7 boys on the right side of the room: six girls and two boys on the left side of the room near the screen)
8:27 Have you ever taught this before? *No checking for understanding at this point. As a result at least five students (and maybe more) are confused about how to begin when they are allowed to work independently. (why are the numbers on the computers important)*	What are the numbers on each of these computers. K checks the numbers and sends one students back to return a computer and return with number 17. Student returns to say computer 17 is gone but not signed out. Students are asked to plan in their groups.
Are the partners random or were they predetermined? 8:34 proximity How did you know the students understood the direction prior to having them start working independently in their groups? 8:35 There were no disruptive behaviors. There is no need for desisting moves. It would be good to use some enlisting. This is again evidence of the students undesrtanding the work and behavior expectations.	Each group has a different product to map. They are given a new map and a second sheet that indicates the product they are to map and where the different products exist in each state. Students are working while K circulates around the room. S Ms A how do we (get the computer ready) **No one raised their hand to say they did not understand. I also noticed that some of them seemed to have trouble starting after I had them start to work in their pairs. When that happens I go around and help those groups that need help.** K that is my job. You need to plan on you sheet of paper. K (to another group) You don't go to your computer until your plot is on your sheet. K works with one pair of boys walking them through the first few steps.

The following observation write-up was based on the previous set of notes. You will see that the observation write-up only includes a select number of the teaching strategies that can be discussed. In a perfect world, it would be best for an observer to address all of the observed strategies in the observation write-up. Most evaluators' heavy workloads make it impossible to write about every teaching strategy they see in every observation. Therefore, for their more qualified teachers they must decide which observed strategies are most important to discuss in the write-up. The observer may make a different decision for the evaluation of unsatisfactory or barely satisfactory teachers. The evaluation of unsatisfactory and barely satisfactory teachers is addressed more thoroughly in chapter 6.

Teacher: K   Date: 11/23/0000

Class: 7th Grade Instructional Technology   Number of students: 21

Time: 8:05 to 8:35 (first period)

The class just completed a unit of study and took a test on the previous day. I would also note that it snowed this morning and many students were arriving at school late due to the road conditions.

You made a very thoughtful decision on what concepts to teach in this lesson. In your pre-conference, you explained that, on the day before this observation, the class took a test on a recently completed unit. The lesson is taking place on the day before Thanksgiving and you have decided to work with a piece of software that is a curriculum connection to what they are learning in social studies. You further explained that you chose this lesson for the following reasons:

a. You did not want to introduce new concepts on the day before the Thanksgiving break.

b. The lesson would only last a single period and would enable you to introduce a new unit on Monday.

c. The lesson reinforced concepts that the students are presently learning in social studies.

d. The lesson is engaging and this is a day on which it is often difficult to keep students engaged.

As a result, the students learned the concepts and were actively engaged throughout the lesson.

The activity directly supported your objectives for what you wanted the students to know and be able to do by the end of the lesson. In the post-conference you explained that your learning objectives. were as follows:

(write-up continues)

I want the students to problem solve with a partner the best method for gathering points while crossing the country… I also wanted to have a lesson that incorporated some of what they have been learning in social studies. It provided practice in problem solving, reinforced the names and locations of the 50 states, taught students to identify various products produced in different states and enabled students to differentiate among states that were large producers, small producers and not producers of the products.

A review of the 7th grade social studies curriculum indicates that these objectives are contained in that curriculum. A result of your thoughtful consideration of the objectives and choice of activity is that the entire period served to increase the students' mastery of the objectives.

You did not state the learning objectives verbally or in writing. You jumped right into the instructions.

K: "OK, you guys, have a seat. Because you just had your test, it is the day before vacation and it is snowing, we are going to play a game. I think it is best for us to dive into it (the game) rather than have me explain it ahead of time. You will work with partners today.

K: Get with a partner."

S: "Can we have three partners?"

K…

K:: "I am going to pass out a map of the U.S.

K passes out the maps.

K: Does everyone have at least one map?"

Stating the objectives at the start of the lesson would give the students a contextual framework for the upcoming learning, thereby fostering deeper understanding and longer retention of the concepts.

You quickly identified student confusion with the assignment early in the lesson. At 8:15, when the students started working independently, you noticed three groups had their hands up with questions. You stopped at one group and then looked quickly at the papers of the other groups with their hands raised. You identified the confusion and then re-explained using the LCD to demonstrate a trip one might take to maximize the number of points for a specific product. As a result, the confused students now understood their task and were able to work productively.

You did not check for understanding sufficiently before permitting students to work independently. As noted above, three groups (including six students) were confused. This only

(write-up continues)

became apparent to you after they started working independently. At this time, they self-initiated the need for greater clarity by raising their hands. Later in the lesson, when teaching the computer quiz portion, you pushed on with the quiz without checking for student understanding of how to complete the quiz (8:27): K "Now it is quiz time. Once you get to ten steps, the computer will ask you a quiz."

Some students shout out the answers (to the quiz on the teacher's computer that is projected on the screen. The students who answer are the ones sitting on the left side of the room which is where the projector is located and where you are standing. The right side of the room (all boys) does not answer the questions. (15 students are in the class: 7 boys on the right side of the room and six girls and two boys on the left side of the room near the screen).

The students are then allowed to take the quiz in their groups. At least five of the pairs are confused about how to do this portion of the assignment. The result of not checking before allowing the students to work independently was that five pairs (ten students) were unable to work independently on the task.

In the post-conference, you said that you pushed on in each instance because no one raised his/her hand to ask for help. As we discussed, using a "dipsticking" strategy or at least inviting students to ask questions at this time will help ensure that you do not push on until most of the students are ready. When you push on, you will at least know who needs help. I think your idea for assessing student readiness by having the students write their answers on the laptops and then turn the screen toward you is an excellent way to determine which students are ready to work independently and which students need re-teaching.

You did a very good job of choosing a lesson that fit the particular circumstances of the day. You connected the lesson to other areas of the curriculum and were clear in your own mind on what you wanted students to know and be able to do. Well done!

---------------------------------------　　　---------------------------------

Teacher's signature　　　　　　　　　　　Date

---------------------------------------　　　---------------------------------

Evaluator's signature　　　　　　　　　　Date

Your signature indicates only that you have read this observation. It does not signify agreement with its content.

DEVELOPING YOUR NOTE-TAKING SKILLS

The following rubric describes the three stages that observers go through as they develop their note-taking capabilities. The rubric is followed by a set of notes that represent each stage of development. It is important to note that people move through the rubric at varying rates. This means that a person might be a novice in some categories while being considered emergent in others. It also means that we seldom fall neatly into only one of the levels. Typically, our practice is flowing from one level to the next.

Novice	Emerging	Proficient
Your notes contain sporadic words and short statements that do not make sense to you when you go back and read them twenty-four hours after the observation.	Your notes are becoming more comprehensive and complete. They make some sense to you when you go back and read them twenty-four hours later. You still have some questions about the notes based on insufficient note-taking.	When you start your observation write-up (after the post-conferences), your notes make sense to you and you have adequate evidence to support your claims.
You experience very high frustration because you either write notes and miss what is happening or you watch what is happening and miss some notes.	You experience high to moderate frustration because you either write and miss some of what is happening or watch what is happening and miss some notes.	You experience a small and decreasing amount of frustration caused by your either writing and missing what is happening or watching what is happening and missing some notes.
Your notes are primarily observer narrative. The quotes are limited to single words or short phrases that don't make sense when you go back and ready them twenty-four hours later.	Your notes include most of the quotes from the teacher in a form that makes sense when you go back and read them twenty-four hours later. Observer narrative is less than 40% of the notes. Notes contain some student quotes. Your notes begin to note the arrangement of the room and the displays on the walls.	Your notes include most of the important quotes from the teacher and students. Your observer narrative is reduced to brief "stage directions" such as a description of the teacher's location in the classroom. You have noted the arrangement of the room and most of the displays on the walls.
After analyzing the notes, you correctly label some claims with terms from common language. You do not have sufficient evidence to support all of the claims you have made.	After analyzing your notes, 50% of the notes are labeled correctly with terms from educational research and practice. The rest of the notes are labeled correctly with common language. You have sufficient evidence to support most of the claims you have made. Some of your claims are still too broad and need greater specificity of the components of the claim.	After analyzing your notes, 80% or more of the notes are labeled correctly with specific terms from educational research and practice. For example, if it's momentum, the label should tell the teacher whether it is provisioning, a filler, subdividing, managing intrusions, etc. You have sufficient evidence to support all of your claims.

Novice	Emerging	Proficient
Your notes do not contain time notations.	Your notes contain time notations at least every ten minutes.	Your notes contain time notations at least every five to seven minutes and at critical times (e.g., the beginning and the end of transitions and the time it takes to get the learning started at the beginning of the class).
After your initial analysis, there are at least two non-judgmental questions to ask the teacher at the post-conference.	After your initial analysis, there are at least four non-judgmental questions to ask the teacher at the post-conference.	After your initial analysis, there are more than four non-judgmental questions to ask the teacher during the post-conference.
Immediately after the observation, more than three judgments are in the labels or notes.	Immediately after the observation, three or fewer judgments are in the labels or the notes.	Immediately after the observation, no judgments are in the labels or the notes.
Your labels and the teacher's answers to the post-conference questions are in the same color as your original notes.	Your evidence and labels primarily address classroom management, routines, teacher preparation and the teacher and student activities.	Your evidence and labels address classroom management, classroom routines, teacher preparation, the teacher and student activities, the class objectives (as stated by the teacher during the observation or one of the conferences), evidence of assessment of student learning as it relates to the classroom objectives, the teacher's beliefs related to the students' ability to meet those objectives and evidence of other important contributions to student achievement.

The following are three sets of notes taken in the same class. They represent different levels of note-taking development.

Novice to Emerging	Patricia, Sixth Grade—Novice to Emerging
Believe strongly Think creatively Posted student work on three bulletin boards Terrarium	
9:27	Students enter and go directly to their seats.
9:30 What are they writing in the notebooks at the start of the class Check to see what is on the chart paper.	Students are seated quietly while T waits quietly at the front of the room T Who is coming tomorrow ….. After today's classs you will have questions to ask Teacher reviews written agenda on the easel in the front. T take out last night's homework pelase … T What is the first thinkg you have to do tomorrow S T good for you.. T… S. T… S.. T Are you noticing a patter here. …. As students answer T writes something on the chart paper. T…… S…. T in you demons list you have just the worked…. ….. T What are the two assignment s we have for … Good T What are we doing next? S choral KWL Let's refresh our memories on what we did yesterday. S.. After we did… S T Why are we doing this? …… T we are bulding background on Why are we building background. Who is coming tomorrow? S choral ……

	T............. S.... T.... S chorally four years T good for you What are the dates for WWII S 1939 to ... T.... S.... T... S... T who was president during WWI S Franklin Rosevelt T.. S...
9:40	TWhat made the depression. What was going on in our country that caused the great depression. S the stock market crashed T exactly S... T... S... T... S... T what was going on in Germany at that tme that they elected Aldolph Hitler. S..... T Exactly T What else do you remember .... S... T that was all part of a plan that we call what..It begins with H S the holocaust T.. S.... T....
9:43	T You are going to fill out your KWL chart right now. .... S..... T.... T what does KWL stand for everybody? S Choral T you will have about five minutes to fill inytour KWL chart..... Studdents work quietly at their desks comleting the KWL charts T most of you know this.This is just to refresh you memory. Teacher circulates around the room giving assistance where needed.

		Student raises his hand and T gives assigstance. T tomorrow when ? is her you will ... T Now you have the information you need to start to develop what S the questions. Teacher has individually assisted five students. *Is there a beak in the video before the questioning*
		T who was a perpetrator in WWII? S... T Who was a bystander in WWII S... T.. S..
9:48		T What is nationalism/ S... T key word her is extreme Sasks a questions You are correct. You are just doing the k on the chart.
9:49		Claps hands to get attendtion

Emerging to Proficient	Patricia, Standard, Sixth Grade
Think creatively Posted student work on three bulletin boards Terrarium Go back and read what is on the walls	The desks are arranged in tables.
9:27	Students enter and go directly to their seats.
9:30 Whata are they writing in the notebooks at the start of the class Agenda Find Demons HW check Review WWII Background KWL … … Check to see what is on the chart paper.	Students enter and are seated quietly while T waits quietly at the front of the room Students are writing in a notebook. Teacher circulates around the room and checks student work. T Who is coming tomorrow? S Jack Lowenstein T and where is he coming from S.. T Good for you. T Let's go over the homework T prepare two thoughtful questions. Prepare the questions for who? S.. T… S… T After today's classs you will have questions to ask S.. T Question about the homework? Are you sure? Teacher reviews written agenda on the easel in the front. T take out last night's homework pelase … T What is the first thing you have to do tomorrow S .. T good for you.. T… S… T… S.. T Are you noticing a pattern here. …. As students answer T writes something on the chart paper. T…… S…. T in your demons list you have just the worked…. T on your demons list I want you to put contract w/…

	..... T What are the two assignment s we have for … S.. T Good T What are we doing next? S choral KWL T Let's refresh our memories on what we did yesterday. What did we do yesterday, Jennifer S.. T so you wrote you facts on big blue index cards. After we did… What did we do after that? S T Right, we wrote our facts on the … paper T Why are we doing this? Jack S… T Right. we are building background on T Why are we building background. Who is coming tomorrow? S choral ……Jack Lowenstein
	T…………. S…. T Let's see what we can remember from yesterday S T No, I will ask the questions and your provide the answers S chorally four years T good for you What are the dates for WWII S 1939 to1945 T Right 1939 to1945 S…. T… S… T who was president during WWI Jillian S Franklin Roosevelt T..Excellent, what year was he elected president S…
9:40	T What made the depression. What was going on in our country that caused the great depression. S the stock market crashed T exactly S… T… S… T Who was elected to office in Germany in 1933 S Adolph Hitler T Why did the German people elect Adolph Hitler S The wanted him to help them with their depression. T..

	S.. T what was going on in Germany at that tme that they elected Aldolph Hitler. S….. T Exactly, They were having a depression too T What else do you remember …. S… T What other facts can we remember from yesterday's conversation S T correct, He had a lot of people killed. T that was all part of a plan that we call what..It begins with H S the holocaust T.. S…. T….
9:43	T You are going to fill out your KWL chart right now. …. S….. T…. T what does KWL stand for everybody? S Choral T you will have about five minutes to fill inytour KWL chart….. Studdents work quietly at their desks comleting the KWL charts T most of you know this.This is just to refresh you memory. Teacher circulates around the room giving assistance where needed. Student raises his hand and T gives assigstance. T tomorrow when ? is her you will … T Now you have the information you need to start to develop what S the questions. Teacher has individually assisted five students. *Is there a beak in the video before the questioning*
Words Kill Believe Strongly Think Creatively Write passionately	T who was a perpetrator in WWII? S… T Who was a bystander in WWII S… T..
9:48	T What is nationalism/ S… T key word her is extreme Sasks a questions You are correct. You are just doing the k on the chart.
9:49	Claps hands to get attention

Proficient	Patricia, Sixth Grade
Never doubt that a small group of committed thoughtful citizens can change the world Posted student work on three bulletin boards Terrarium	The desks are arranged in tables of 4 students..
9:27	Students enter and go directly to their seats.
9:30 Whata are they writing in the notebooks at the start of the class? Agenda Find Demons HW check Review WWII Background KWL In Lamb prepare 2 thoughtful questions for ...	Students enter and are seated quietly while T waits quietly at the front of the room Students are writing in a notebook. Teacher circulates around the room and checks student work. T Who is coming tomorrow? S Jack Lowenstein T and where is he coming from S ..... T Good for you. T Let's go over the homework . to make sure everyone understands the first bullet. T prepare two thoughtful questions. Prepare the questions for who? S.. T...What is Thurday nights homework? S... T After today's classs you will have questions to ask S T Question about the homework? Are you sure? Teacher reviews written agenda on the easel in the front. T take out last night's homework please ... T What is the first thing you have to do tomorrow S T good for you.. T... S. T... S.. T Are you noticing a pattern here. .... As students answer T writes something on the chart paper. T What is the first thing we have to do S syllabicate

	T in your demons list you have just the worked....
	T what is the demon in surround
	S double r
	T on your demons list I want you to put contract w/...
	...
	T What is the demon in teacher
	S ea
	T right, the demon is the ea
	T What is the demon in tear
	S...
	T What are the two assignment s we have for ...
	S..
	T Good
	T Next terrible
	David syllabicate first
	T What is the Demon
	S double r
	T...
	S...
	T What are out two assignments with the demon lists
	S...
	T What are we doing next?
	S choral KWL
	T Let's refresh our memories on what we did yesterday. What did we do yesterday, Jennifer
	S..
	T so you wrote you facts on big blue index cards. After we did... What did we do after that?
	S
	T Right, we wrote our facts on the white paper
	T Why are we doing this? Jack
	Jack we need to build background
	T Right. we are building background on
	T Why are we building background. Who is coming tomorrow?
	S choral ......Jack Lowenstein
9:37	T he is going to discuss causes of WWI and WWII.
	S....
	T Let's see what we can remember from yesterday
	T all right three hands raised over there
	S
	T No, I will ask the questions and your provide the answers. What are the .. for WWI
	T how long did that take
	S chorally four years
	T good for you
	T What are the dates for WWII
	S 1939 to1945
	T Right 1939 to1945

	S.... T... S... T who was president during WWII Jillian S Franklin Roosevelt T..Excellent, what year was he elected president S 1932
9:40	T Excellent and what was going on in 1932 S the great deprssion T Who was elected to office in Germany in 1933 S Adolph Hitler T Why did the German people elect Adolph Hitler S The wanted him to help them with their depression. T What made the depression. What was going on in our country that caused the great depression. S the stock market crashed T exactly S... T...What year did the stock market crash. Look it is right up there S... T actually it was 1929 T.. S.. T what was going on in Germany at that tme that they elected Aldolph Hitler. S..... T Exactly, They were having a depression too T What else do you remember .... S... T What other facts can we remember from yesterday's conversation S T correct, He had a lot of people killed. T that was all part of a plan that we call what..It begins with H S the holocaust T..it was all part of the holocaust. You guys did really well. What Stacey S.... T.... S... T good for you S T..

9:43	T You are going to fill out your KWL chart right now. Title it. I will put the title on the board. I bet you can almost figure out for yourself what it is going to be. .... S..... T I want you to have as complete a K as you can. T what does KWL stand for everybody? S Choral T you will have about five minutes to fill inytour KWL chart..... Studdents work quietly at their desks comleting the KWL charts T most of you know this. This is just to refresh you memory. T today you are just filling out the K Teacher circulates around the room giving assistance where needed. Student raises his hand and T gives assigstance. T tomorrow when ? is here you will fill out the W and L T Now you have the information you need to start to develop what S the questions. Teacher has individually assisted five students. T now you have some factual information. You need to what S ask the questions T right, you need to ask the questions
9:47 Words Kill Believe Strongly Think Creatively Write passionately	T who was a perpetrator in WWII? S Italy T Italy was a perpetrator, Japan was a perpetrator T Who was a bystander in WWII S America T We were a bystander until when S Pearl harbor T We talked a bit about the definition of holocaust. What is the definition S Choral response ....
9:48	T What is nationalism/ S... T key word her is extreme S asks a questions You are correct. You are just doing the k on the chart. T do you have everything you need on your KWL S... T no, you are absolutely right you are just doing the K
9:49	Claps hands to get attention

Peer Support With Writing Observation Write-ups and End-of-Year Evaluation Reports

It will feel very cumbersome to evaluators when they first start writing observations and evaluations that

- consistently label teaching moves with the district's common language
- translate literal notes into evidence
- make impact statements that point to the impact on students and/or the school culture and use language consistent with the district's performance standards
- make value judgments that are consistent from teacher to teacher and use the district's evaluation language

The evaluators' comfort level will grow as they gain experience. The speed at which they write will also increase as they gain experience using this style.

For both beginning and seasoned evaluators, it is helpful to have them work with colleagues from whom they can get feedback about drafts of observation write-ups or final evaluation reports. Below is a peer conferencing guide that administrators can use to help each other write their evaluation documents more clearly, concisely and quickly. This is a good activity for an administrators' meeting. Much is written about the value of peer coaching for teachers, but peer coaching is equally effective for administrators. It provides them with both technical and emotional support.

Read the Write-Up You Have Been Assigned and Answer the Following Questions

1. Does the evidence (objective information) in the write-up directly support the claim, judgment and/or impact statement (subjective statements)? Do you have suggestions on how the writer can better support his/her statements with observed and/or verified information?

2. Is there a way for the writer to describe the evidence that is more concrete, observable or verifiable? Do you have suggestions for the writer for improving his/her descriptions?

3. Does the writer make it clear how the teacher's behaviors affect the students' learning or well being, negatively or positively?

4. Does the writer use the language of the district's performance standards in the write-up?

5. Does the writer make value judgments about the teaching moves observed?

6. What other comments/questions do you have about the example?

COMMON LANGUAGE AND STANDARDS

A district's supervision and evaluation is improved when the district has a common language teachers and administrators use to describe effective teaching in terms of the district's standards. Earlier in this chapter we looked at samples of evaluation write-ups that use and/or refer to a district's common language and standards for curriculum and instruction. Chapter 9 includes the performance standards used in Massachusetts and those used by districts in Texas as a common language all administrators and teachers use to describe teaching in their districts. Chapter 9 also includes the performance standards established by the state of Texas. A number of districts in Massachusetts, Vermont, New Jersey, New Hampshire, Maryland, Virginia, Maine and other states have further defined the language of their teaching performance standards by training their administrators to use the language described in books such as *Instructional Practices That Maximize Student Achievement: For Teachers, by Teachers* by Ribas, Deane and Seider (2005), *The Skillful Teacher* by Jonathon Saphier and Robert Gower (1997), *Instruction for all Students* by Paula Rutherford (1998) and *Enhancing Professional Practice: A Framework for Teaching* by Charlotte Danielson (1996).

You will note in the Massachusetts document under discussion that the first performance standard, *Principle of Effective Teaching I,* refers to the learning expectations, which are the district's curriculum standards. The last performance standard, *Principle of Effective Teaching VII,* refers to the responsibilities of teachers that reach beyond the realm of classroom teaching. This standard is helpful for generating a discussion with teachers about their role in public relations. Both standards reflect the value that a good teacher is someone who does more than teach effectively in the classroom.

The Massachusetts document is designed to provide teachers and evaluators with three levels of specificity related to the language of teaching. Moving from left to right through the columns, the teachers and evaluators are given more specific examples of the standard indicated in the left-most column.

Increasing the observability and verifiability of the language used to describe performance and curriculum standards has been particularly useful to administrators who are working with under-performing teachers. (Chapter 6 covers more about working with under-performing teachers.) The Texas document does this in a comprehensive fashion. In some districts, in addition to their staff development in the curriculum standards and the performance standards, a teacher in need of additional coaching attends a six day course that provides in-depth instruction in effective instructional strategies.

The instructors of this course use the same textbook used in the course that teaches classroom observation and analysis skills to administrators. The result is that the teacher and evaluator have a significant body of common practice information, standards and language with which to analyze and discuss the teacher's performance as measured against the performance and curriculum standards. This common basis allows more effective formative and summative evaluation relationships between the evaluators and the teachers.

Most supervision and evaluation training programs have a textbook that clearly describes behaviors leading to effective instructional performance. It is important that those districts who use an outside program (as opposed to a program developed in the district) for training administrators in clinical supervision and evaluation develop documents and/or training that connects the district's own curriculum and performance standards to the language used in the training. Larger districts who develop their own clinical training programs should make sure that there is a seamless connection in that training between curriculum standards, performance standards and the language that administrators and teachers use to describe those standards.

> It is important that those districts who use an outside program (as opposed to a program developed in the district) for training administrators in clinical supervision and evaluation develop documents and/or training that connects the district's own curriculum and performance standards to the language used in the training.

One district I work with is presently struggling with the issue of supervisors and evaluators using *three sets of terms* to describe some of the same teaching practices. One set of terms is written on their contracted evaluation forms that have existed for many years. The second set of terms was developed several years ago in response to the state Department of Education's issuing regulations that require districts to develop new performance standards meeting a minimum specified level. The standards in the evaluation documents did not meet this level, so new standards were developed without changing the evaluation forms. The third set of terms is language given to teachers and administrators in a program teaching instructional practices and promoting standards-based education. All three of these documents/programs are excellent in isolation. However, one can easily see the potential for confusion as the district works to increase inter-rater reliability between and among over sixty evaluators without a structure for connecting the three sets of language in use.

TIME-SAVING TIPS FOR SUPERVISORS AND EVALUATORS

Try These Tips!

Administrators with large evaluation loads often feel frustrated by the time it takes to provide a quality evaluation for every member of their staffs. It is important that every teacher receive evaluations that incorporate the criteria from the Evaluator Survey of Potential Areas for Training and Support for Your District's Teacher Supervisors and Evaluators, discussed earlier in this chapter. However, if the structure of an administrator's department or building leaves the administrator with a large number of evaluations, there are time-saving strategies that have a minimal negative impact or no impact on the supervision and evaluation of the staff.

Administrators also vary greatly in the time it takes them to complete the various tasks related to supervision and evaluation. Administrators are always aware that it takes a great deal of time to supervise and evaluate well, however, they are often not sure which activities take up most of that time. The amount of time spent on each activity can vary by administrator. It can be helpful to have administrators complete the survey on page 100 prior to teaching them time-saving techniques. This preparation enables each administrator to choose those techniques that will lead to the greatest benefit. It is important to remember that the techniques below are a menu, not a recipe. Administrators must pick and choose those that will save time without undermining the quality of their work. It is also important to note that the assumption is made that the evaluators have had sufficient training in the skills needed to capture, analyze and communicate orally and in writing about the complex interactions involved in teaching prior to implementing these time-saving techniques.

1. **"Imitation is the highest form of flattery,"** even if you're imitating yourself. Don't be afraid to repeat a good sentence or paragraph on several evaluations. If more than one of your teachers is experiencing success or needing a recommendation in a particular area, it is fine to use the same acknowledgment or recommendation for two or more people, as long as it fits their situations. The purpose of your evaluations is to reinforce excellent practices and cause positive changes in ineffective performances. They are not exercises in original prose.

2. The strategy above also applies to using effective text from evaluations by other evaluators. Borrowing phrases from others can be particularly helpful with areas for improvement, which are the most difficult and time-consuming to write. I have seen this work particularly well when small groups of evaluators meet and exchange evaluations (with the names concealed) of low-performing teachers. The evaluators then borrow clear,

concise but sensitive recommendations for use in their evaluations. Regarding recommendations for improvement, evaluators often spend more time deciding how to phrase them than deciding what needs to be said.

TIME STUDY SURVEY

Evaluator's name: _____

Evaluator's position: _____

Date: _____

Number of evaluations you must do this year:

Tenure _____ Non-Tenure _____ Total _____

1. How much time in the course of the year (in hours and minutes) does it take you to schedule all of your observations and pre-/post-conferences? Below, briefly describe how you do this scheduling.

_____

_____

_____

_____

_____

Tenure high	Tenure average	Tenure low	Non-tenure	
____	____	____	____	2. In what percentage of the observations do you pre-conference?
____	____	____	____	3. How many minutes does it take you to prepare for one pre-observation conference?
____	____	____	____	4. How many minutes does it take you to complete one pre-observation conference?
____	____	____	____	5. How many minutes does it take you to prepare for one observation?
____	____	____	____	6. How many minutes does it take you to complete one observation?
____	____	____	____	7. How many minutes does it take you to prepare for one post-observation conference?
____	____	____	____	8. How many minutes does it take you to complete one post-observation conference?

Tenure high	Tenure average	Tenure low	Non-tenure	
____	____	____	____	9. How many minutes does it take you to complete one observation write-up report?
____	____	____	____	10. How many minutes does it take you to write one summative evaluation document?
____	____	____	____	11. How many minutes does it take you to prepare for a meeting with one teacher about the summative evaluation document?
____	____	____	____	12. How many minutes does it take you to meet with one teacher about the summative evaluation document?

List the other activities related to evaluation that you must undertake in the course of the year and how many minutes each activity takes to complete.

Other (please describe)

_____

_____

_____

Other (please describe)

_____

_____

_____

3. In final year-end evaluation documents, don't try to write again from scratch what you observed and wrote about during the year. Cut and paste claims/judgments or evidence from your observation reports. It also saves time to refer to the report with citations such as, "In one class I observed (see observation report 3/2/97) Ed's tone was sharp and curt in reaction to the students' behavior and lack of cooperation . . ."

You can then attach the observation report or cut and paste from the report, rather than rewriting all the information related to this incident. On page 122, I included a sample final evaluation report that demonstrates both cut and paste and citing of the observation report as ways to save time.

4. A dictaphone can save time once you get used to using it. Using a dictaphone is a skill that needs to be learned both by the administrator and the secretary typing the dictation. Begin by practicing with short pieces of one or two paragraphs. This strategy will also enable your secretary to practice on small pieces. Once you have mastered the dictaphone, an observation write-up can be dictated in fifteen minutes and then revised after it is typed in draft form.

5. Laptop computers are another time-saving device that takes practice. The evaluator should only try using one if he/she is a fair-to-good typist. It is also important for an evaluator using this technique for the first time to let the teacher know ahead of time. It has been disconcerting to some teachers when the administrator who has formerly arrived in his/her room with only a pad and pen shows up with an unexpected laptop computer. However, it very soon becomes the norm with the computer causing no more anxiety than a pad and pen.

6. Voice recognition software is increasing in popularity. Evaluators take notes on paper or on a laptop computer. The notes are then transformed into chunked narrative using voice recognition software.

7. **"Give a person a fish, and he/she eats for a day. Teach a person to fish, and he/she eats for a lifetime."** This proverb applies to evaluators as well. Principals, superintendents and assistant superintendents who evaluate teacher evaluators often hesitate to delegate a sufficient number of evaluations to others. There are good reasons for this in districts where there is insufficient training and coaching of all evaluators. A poorly done evaluation can be more work for the administrator supervising the evaluator than doing the evaluation himself/herself. However, in the long run a principal, superintendent or assistant superintendent would be better off spending a year carefully coaching and closely overseeing the subordinate evaluator as he/she does the evaluations. Evaluators, like teachers, can really surprise you when they have had sufficient training, coaching, assessment and reteaching. Teach your evaluators to "fish" and it will save you time in the long run.

8. Your most extensive reports (particularly in regard to the writing of evidence) need to be those for teachers who are not performing well. These are the reports most likely to be contested by teachers and even litigated and, therefore, need to be the most thoroughly and carefully written. This is not to say that excellent teachers don't need and deserve affirmation and recommendations. However, the amount of evidence you include in the reports of high-performing teachers can be much more limited because you don't need to legally prove your claim/judgment. In all my years evaluating teachers, I have never been asked by a teacher or a teacher's union representative to provide sufficient evidence to justify a compliment! There are also many ways to acknowledge and celebrate your highest-performing teachers. Some ideas for commending their performances can be found in the sections of this book on sample lessons and peer coaching. Other ideas include sending brief handwritten notes or emails acknowledging high performance or assigning high performers to mentor new teachers.

> The amount of evidence you include in the reports of high-performing teachers can be much more limited because you don't need to legally prove your claim/judgment. In all my years evaluating teachers, I have never been asked by a teacher or a teacher's union representative to provide sufficient evidence to justify a compliment!

The following two activities are designed to help the evaluator prioritize his/her time based on a general assessment of all staff members scheduled to be evaluated. The first activity should be done just prior to the start of the school year and should include all teachers scheduled to be evaluated in that year. The second activity should be done in March or April and include all the teachers scheduled for summative evaluation in the following year. Since these designations are an estimate and not fully supported by evidence, the evaluator should keep these exercises confidential. Their purpose is only to help the evaluator prioritize his/her supervision and evaluation time. The suggested exercises make use of an overly simplified way of thinking about teaching. However, they are essential activities if you want to budget your time in a way that creates the greatest impact for students.

DIVIDING THIS YEAR'S EVALUATION LOAD INTO THIRDS

- List the *tenured* teachers (*professional status* in some states) by the three categories below, based on where you think they rank in your department or school. *Be certain to have an equal number of teachers in each category.*
- Circle the name of the teacher who is your lowest performer.
- List the ways you can recognize your top third teachers other than with lengthy evaluation write-ups.
- List the performance issues, by performance standard, of the teacher circled.

Highest-performing third:

_____

_____

_____

Middle-performing third:

_____

_____

_____

Lowest-performing third:

_____

_____

_____

Ways I can facilitate the growth of my top third teachers and acknowledge their successes, other than by lengthy observation write-ups and final evaluation documents:

_____

_____

_____

_____

The issues related to my lowest-performing tenured (professional teacher status) teacher.

_____

_____

_____

_____

DIVIDING INTO THIRDS, . . . PREPARING FOR NEXT YEAR

This activity is designed to help evaluators prioritize their time by determining which of the tenured teachers in their evaluation load in the *upcoming* year will need a disproportionate amount of time and other resources. *This information is confidential and should only be used by the evaluator.*

1. Think about the tenured (professional teacher status) teachers in your school or department whom you will evaluate next year. List them below in the appropriate category.

2. Circle the name of the teacher in the bottom list who is the lowest performer in the group.

Highest-performing third:

_____

_____

_____

_____

Middle-performing third:

_____

_____

_____

Lowest-performing third:

_____

_____

_____

The issues related to my lowest-performing tenured (professional teacher status) teacher, connected to the appropriate performance standard, and including a list of the supports I need to effectively work with this teacher.

Issues: _____

_____

_____

Performance standard: _____

_____

_____

Supports I will need to address the issues: _____

_____

_____

Where I will go for those supports: _____

_____

_____

8. Documents such as the Massachusetts performance standard document in chapter 9 enable evaluators to easily reference a small group of comprehensive resources on effective teaching. You will note that the document gives specific phrases and sentences in the second column. The third column connects each performance standard to two widely used books on the subject of classroom teaching. An evaluator can effectively write seventy-five percent or more of his/her evaluations using that document and the two reference books. For most busy evaluators, it is better to have a small group of excellent references that you use consistently, than a large library of references that become frustrating when trying to find specific information.

> For most busy evaluators, it is better to have a small group of excellent references that you use consistently, then a large library of references that become frustrating when trying to find specific information.

9. In chapter 8, we will discuss time-efficient ways for evaluators to teach sample lessons.

Evaluators can also gain the significant value of model lessons without spending a great deal of time by running one or more staff meetings as sample lessons. A good staff meeting uses many of the teaching strategies used in a good classroom lesson. The meeting can be conducted using effective classroom teaching techniques, and then leaving ten to fifteen minutes at the end for teachers to give feedback on the presentation, based on the district's performance standards. In many of the districts in which I conduct training, the teachers often complain that administrators always ask them to use interesting and engaging teaching techniques, but run dull meetings themselves. A faculty meeting designed to use effective teaching techniques would be an opportunity to run an effective meeting, discuss effective teaching techniques with the entire staff and model a school culture in which the professionals are open to experimentation and feedback on areas for improvement. Below is a sample from a handout or overhead the administrator may use at the end of the meeting to achieve this goal.

a. Read the seven teacher performance standards.

b. In your group, evaluate my running of today's meeting over the last fifty minutes in terms of my presentation related to the performance standards.

c. Agree on one area for improvement that falls within the standard assigned to your group.

d. Select one person in the group to post-conference with me about the area identified for improvement.

10. Practice may not make perfect, but it sure can make for quicker: Time yourself the next time you do a final report or an observation write-up of a teacher whose performance ranks in the top third of your school's faculty. If it takes more than ninety minutes to write these documents, try the following.

a. Get an oven timer and set it for one hour. Write as you normally would for the hour. Use cut and paste (computer or the actual scissors and paper kind) wherever possible.

b. When the oven timer dings, set it again for thirty minutes. Use that thirty minutes as a deadline for completing the report.

c. When the report is "finished", if you feel compelled to proofread and revise, set the timer again for thirty minutes. Work to finish the report before the thirty minutes is up.

d. Give it to the teacher as is. You will be very uncomfortable the first couple of times. However, after a while you will work more efficiently and learn that the world will continue to spin even if that high-performing teacher doesn't get a perfect report. There are other ways to recognize his/her hard work that are less time-consuming.

Remember: This shortcut is not for low-performing teachers.

11. Develop a question bank of conference questions for each of the district's performance standards. This can be done fairly quickly by converting the performance standards to pre-conference and post-conference questions as described on page 139 in chapter 4.

12. Peer review for your highest-performing teachers. High-performing teachers often feel (and rightfully so) that a disproportionate amount of the evaluator's time is devoted to low-performing teachers. Creating a structure that allows the evaluator to choose a pair of his/her highest-performing teachers to work together in a formal peer supervision process reduces his/her load by two evaluations for that year. It also creates a stimulating professional growth opportunity for those teachers.

Peer review/coaching should not completely replace the teacher–evaluator interaction. It is important that the evaluator complete a comprehensive summative evaluation at least every four years. Even high-performing teachers need (and most want) a comprehensive evaluation from their administrators at least every four years.[3]

In some districts, peer supervision is done formally as a contracted alternative to the administrator evaluation. In other districts where there is no formal peer supervision or coaching role within the contracted evaluation process, the evaluator prepares a "minimum contract compliance evaluation." The administrator's evaluation meets the minimal requirements of the contract or the law.

> High-performing teachers often feel (and rightfully so) that a disproportionate amount of the evaluator's time is devoted to low-performing teachers. Creating a structure that allows the evaluator to choose a pair of his/her highest-performing teachers to work together in a formal peer supervision process reduces his/her load by two evaluations for that year. It also creates a stimulating professional growth opportunity for those teachers.

The teachers involved and the evaluator are aware that the productive feedback the teachers receive for that year will come in the work they do as partners and that the evaluator will spend very little time working with them directly. (See example 1 in the peer review section that begins on page 112.) Below is a sample of an observation write-up in a district in which the evaluators had high evaluation loads. In this district, the evaluators completed

---

3 In a district in which I consult, the administration requires as few as one comprehensive evaluation every five years for a teacher with ten years of successful experience in the system. However, the district requires intensive peer coaching and supervision in at least two of the intervening years and other prescribed professional development in the other two years. The district procedures also permit the evaluator to comprehensively evaluate any teacher in any year if the evaluator wishes to do so.

the Dividing Into Thirds activity above and used minimum contract compliance evaluations with their highest-performing teachers. Teachers in the top third of the faculty received observation write-ups and final evaluations similar to the following. They were then provided with peer coaching opportunities through the staff development program as noted in the preceding discussion.

SAMPLE MINIMUM CONTRACT COMPLIANCE OBSERVATION WRITE-UP FOR A HIGH-PERFORMING TEACHER BY A PRINCIPAL WITH A LARGE EVALUATION LOAD

Wednesday, September 26, 2001   Sample School
Observer: Mr. Principal
Mr. Hamilton's Fifth Grade   9:00 to 9:35

Mr. Hamilton's review lesson on factors of whole numbers was fast-paced and clear. Mr. Hamilton checked for understanding with a series of probing questions that forced his students to use advanced thinking skills: "What is a factor?", 3 x 2 "What would be the first factor of 100?", etc. A forest of hands greeted each question, indicating that students felt familiar with the material and comfortable with sharing their thinking: "Are there others?", "What's 5's partner?" . . . As he asked questions, Mr. Hamilton used the white board to record answers, in the form of a "rainbow model." This graphic organizer/metaphor was intended to help students see the range of factors. The combination of his steady stream of questions and effective use of the board kept students focused.

He rarely used an attention move, other than one pause to wait for everyone to focus, and to remind a student to wait before sharpening his pencil: "Ben, I'm going to ask you to wait; you don't even know what we're doing yet." The management of the class seemed "invisible." You couldn't see the strings, but it was evident that in just two weeks, Mr. Hamilton had established an expectation of attention and a pattern of routines which kept students involved.

Mr. Hamilton kept momentum of the lesson going through a variety of moves. Just before he gave new instructions, he asked students to put their hands on their heads, so they would stop working, writing, etc., and pay attention to the next set of instructions. Then he continued, "I want you to work with the people at your table; I'm going to set the timer for 5 minutes." Again as he was moving toward passing out calculators, which he had on hand for each group, he anticipated that there might be some confusion with their use. "What don't I want?" Stella replied, "No fractions." "Right, whole numbers, not decimals." Mr. Hamilton gently shaped Stella's answer to remind students that while calculators will provide answers in decimals, he was looking for factors that were whole numbers. This anticipated possible confusion and kept the class on task.

The review lesson quickly moved into a practice and application session. Mr. Hamilton moved the students into groups of three, which he had drawn up ahead of time. He set them to work on a series of factoring problems to apply what they had done in their review of factors of 100. By inference, one could tell that his objective, aside from learning the concept of factoring, was for students to be able to broaden their range by working on other numbers. His lesson showed evidence of careful planning and the classroom was provisioned to keep the smooth flow going. As a result, students were able to review

(write-up continues)

and practice the factoring of multiples of 100 in a focused twenty-five minute session. Engagement was near 100% and Mr. Hamilton circulated throughout the practice time, checking in at each table to ascertain if the students had questions or were stuck. Mr. Hamilton had a lesson in which the tasks and objective were clear.

_____   _____
Signature of teacher   date

_____   _____
Signature of observer   date

Signature signifies receipt of, not concurrence with, this evaluation. Teachers are encouraged to submit comments.

13. **Effective mentoring and induction programs for teachers new to the district.** In the last five years there has been a significant increase in the hiring of teachers. In some states, districts are reporting a 100% or even 200% increase in the number of teachers hired each year compared with hiring patterns from just five years ago. As a result, evaluators are starting the year with significantly more new teachers, some of whom are less experienced than was the case five years ago. They are spending more time evaluating teachers, since many states require that teachers new to the district receive a comprehensive evaluation every year rather than every second, third or fourth year as required for tenured teachers. This is requiring an inordinate amount of the evaluators' time in working with new teachers, time which was previously available for the supervision of veteran teachers. Much of this time is spent on basic orientation, induction and, in some cases, in developing fundamental planning and classroom management skills. Providing each new teacher with an experienced and well-trained mentor, coupled with new teacher induction seminars, enables the evaluators to focus their time on the summative assessment of new teachers. This takes far less of the evaluators' time than training each new teacher to the district in Our District 101, Classroom Management 101 and Classroom Planning 101. As much as evaluators may hate to admit it, mentor teachers usually do a much better job!! For more information on establishing effective mentor and induction programs, you may wish to read the book, *Maximizing Teaching Success* (Ribas, 2003).

The next section of this chapter talks about peer review and its various forms. The evaluation of high-performing teachers, described above, is just one of many effective educational purposes for which peer review is effective.

PEER REVIEW/EVALUATION/SUPERVISION/COACHING (ALL OF THE ABOVE)?

Much has been written lately about peer involvement in the supervision and evaluation process. When people hear the terms "peer review," "peer coaching" or "assistance" they apply many meanings to the them. They often use these terms interchangeably and/or make incorrect assumptions about their definitions. Districts talking about the role of peers in changing teachers' performance need to be clear in their own minds whether they are interested in peers taking on formative or summative roles. Districts should be clear about whether they are interested in the peer interaction as a professional development function or an evaluative function.

Most districts do not yet have a formal peer program. However, those programs that do exist take forms as varied as the meanings that come to people's minds. The American Federation of Teachers and the National Education Association in their guide, *Peer Assistance & Peer Review: An AFT/NEA Handbook* (1998), defines peer review and peer assistance as very different systems.

Peer assistance aims to help new and veteran teachers improve their knowledge and skills. Such a program links new teachers or struggling teachers with consulting teachers who provide ongoing support through observing, modeling, sharing ideas and skills and recommending materials for further study.

Peer review adds one significant element to peer assistance—consulting teachers conduct formal evaluations and make recommendations regarding the continued employment of participating teachers.

An entire book can be written about the range of options for peer involvement in the process of supervision and evaluation and or that of staff development. Recent research supports the contention that peer interaction is an effective means for building teacher competency. The 1999 Milken Family Foundation Report, *A Matter of Quality*, quotes the work of The National Center for Education Information, *Profiles of Teachers in the U.S. Survey* (1996), in which educators identified the five most valuable factors in developing competency to teach as follows:

- Own teaching experience   92%
- Courses in Subject Area Taught   73%
- *Other teachers*   *72%*
- Studying on one's own   43%
- Education methods courses   37%

The concepts of peer coaching, peer assistance and/or peer review is one school boards, administrators, teachers and teachers' associations/unions support. However, the specific way such a program will operate is a question that can raise significant labor relations (*legal*) differences between school boards and teachers' associations/unions. Districts considering a peer component in their supervision and evaluation programs, therefore, must clearly define the role of the peer and the objective of the peer program.

The programs presently in use range along a continuum from peer formative assistance and feedback to peer review for the purpose of making employment decisions. In some programs, peer involvement is optional and completely formative and is identified by the district as staff development rather than as a part of the supervision and evaluation program. Example 1 below is a sample of this type of program from one of the communities in which I have worked. In this community, everyone agreed that teachers play an important role in helping other teachers improve and grow. However, the state teachers' association was adamantly opposed to teachers' involvement in the summative review of their colleagues. The state association disagreed with the national union's position paper mentioned in the preceding paragraph. The school board and teachers' association could not agree on a program within the evaluation process that would meet the objectives of both groups, therefore, we developed the program below within the professional development program as a compromise that met most of the needs of both groups. The program met the objectives of the school committee, teachers' association and many of the district's teachers to empower a group of teachers each year with the opportunity to learn and grow from one another rather than participate in a comprehensive evaluation with an administrator.

The program met the following school board objectives to

- provide an effective staff development option for high-performing teachers
- allow the evaluators to choose which teachers would participate (with final review by the superintendent), thereby recognizing the teachers' history of high performance
- reduce the administrators' evaluation time with high-performing teachers during that year to a contract minimum. This enabled administrators with large evaluation loads to focus on those teachers who needed a higher level of the evaluator's feedback and support (see the section on time-saving techniques for evaluators to see how this was done without causing the high-performing teachers to feel neglected)

The program met the following teachers' association objectives to

- ensure that teachers played no role in making summative evaluation decisions about their colleagues
- see that the program did not require large amounts of additional time from teachers
- require that the administration did not arbitrarily choose teachers for varying forms of the contract-mandated evaluation processes

This district's program falls far to the left on the continuum shown in Figure 6.

The Role of Peers in Supervision, Evaluation and Staff Development

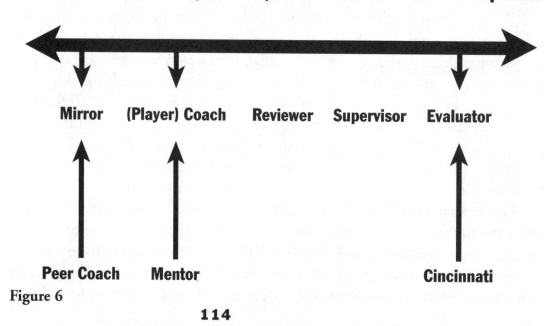

Figure 6

Those activities falling to the far left of the continuum are solely formative assistance programs. The programs to the far right require summative judgments and even employment decisions by the peer evaluator.

In another district in which I am working, the state teachers' association fully embraces the concepts identified in the national union's position paper. This district has developed a program similar to the Cincinnati model in which teachers play a significant role in making summative employment decisions about their colleagues. Teachers observe low-performing teachers and write reports, presented to a panel of fifteen people, that recommend continued employment or dismissal for these teachers. The panel reviews the recommendations and makes a final report to the superintendent. This district's program places it at the far right of the continuum below.

EXAMPLE 1

In this district, the peer review process is solely a supplemental process for teachers who have demonstrated high performance for a specified period of years. These teachers are given the option to forgo one year of extensive evaluation by their administrator to work intensively with a peer. The evaluating administrator's role is reduced to one that meets the absolute minimum required by the contract and state regulations. It is understood by the administrator and the teachers that the benefit the teachers derive from this experience will come from their self- and peer-assessment. The program provides three benefits: 1) High-performing teachers often grow more from peer- and self-assessment experiences then they do from traditional administrative evaluations; 2) The program also frees the supervisors and evaluators to focus their evaluation time on those teachers who would benefit the most from an administrative evaluation; 3) Teachers chosen for the program are the ones who would benefit most from a peer experience. The teachers chosen feel very good about being recognized for their status as excellent practitioners.

Sample School Peer-/Self-Feedback Plan for Excellence by Empowering Teachers

This year we seek to maximize the value of reflection on one's own practice and/or the extent to which we all are able to learn a great deal from our colleagues. Research indicates that reflecting on one's own teaching and honest feedback from peers are two of the most effective means of improving teachers' performance.

By September 30 of this school year, the teacher will have completed a self-assessment based on the district's performance standards. The teacher will have met with the peer colleague to develop a pre-test self-assessment plan and an observation/ meeting plan for the year. The plan should include a schedule of at least ninety minutes of observations.

By October 15 of this school year the teacher will attend the district-sponsored workshop on peer facilitation of professional growth.

By March 15 of this school year the teacher will complete a peer- and self-reflection paper or a portfolio[4] that demonstrates his/her growth during the school year, based on the district's performance standards. The teacher will have observed a colleague for a total of at least ninety minutes. The teacher will pre-conference with the colleague before each observation and post-conference after each observation.

In those classrooms without an intern or student teacher, a substitute will be provided for one day of coverage, so each peer dyad can complete observation and conferencing.

By April 1 of this school year, each teacher will have produced a reflection paper or portfolio demonstrating the learning that has emerged from this year. The report or portfolio should list areas of current growth and recommendations for future growth, based on the district's performance standards. The teacher will give the principal a two-page summary of the year's activities and the growth that has resulted from the peer- and self-reflection experience.

Principal's Role: The principal will recommend to the superintendent up to 25% of the tenured teachers scheduled for summative evaluation to participate in this program during the school year.

The teachers chosen must be deemed by the principal as excellent teachers, based on the district's performance standards as indicated in previous evaluations.

The evaluator will complete the minimum contract requirements for an evaluation of a tenured teacher. The goals will have been set out in the plan completed by the teacher by September 30. The evaluator will complete one announced formal observation that is thirty minutes in length. The observation will be followed by a one-page progress report. In addition, the evaluator will submit the Annual Report of Teacher Effectiveness by the date indicated in the contract.

The following teachers are recommended for the program above for the 200_ School Year.

_____   _____

_____   _____

_____   _____

Principal's signature: _____ Date: _____

---

[4] For information on developing portfolios, see the questions found on page 149 and the article note in the sources on which these questions are based.

EXAMPLE 2

In another school district, teacher peer review teams have a significant role in reviewing and evaluating the professional development plans of all teachers during the years in which they are not involved in an administrative evaluation. Teachers with administrative evaluation ratings at or above the district standard work with the Peer Review Committee during the three years following their administrative evaluation years. Below is a description of the Peer Review Committee's responsibilities, as they are defined in the teacher's contract for that district. The role of teachers in this supervision and evaluation process falls to the right of example 1 above on the figure 5 continuum and to the left of the Cincinnati model.

Peer Review Committees

Peer Review Committees (PRCs) play an important role in the Evaluation and Professional Growth Cycle for teachers with tenure. Peer Review Committees are to be established in each elementary school and in each high school department. All tenured teachers are expected to serve a term on a Peer Review Committee. These committees are non-evaluative in nature and are composed of three teachers who will each serve a two-year rotating term. Members of the Peer Review Committee shall be provided reasonable release time to perform these duties.

Each Peer Review Committee reviews individual and collaborative professional growth activity plans submitted by teachers to (a) make sure the plans meet the criteria established for the particular phase of the evaluation cycle and (b) provide feedback regarding the plan should the teacher request it, or if the plan does not meet the criteria.

At the end of the school year, teachers in Phases II–IV of the evaluation cycle submit a record of their professional growth activities and a one- to two-page summary statement of what they learned from the experience to the Peer Review Committee for review. The Peer Review Committee reviews all records submitted by teachers. The Peer Review Committee will not be expected to comment to the administrator on the perceived quality of any teacher's professional growth activity, but will be expected to sign and submit the Certification Form in each phase of the evaluation.

All teachers are required to serve a term on the Peer Review Committee on a rotating basis.

EXAMPLE 3

A third type of program is one in which teachers work in pairs for a year of collaborative work. An example of this type of program (Year 2 Collaborative Year) can be found in chapter 9 of this book, in the Lexington Public Schools evaluation document. The peer work is primarily formative, but it is a requirement for all teachers in the four year supervision and evaluation cycle. In this example, the peers have an equal role to one another as is the case in example 1. However, differing from example 1, all teachers are required to participate, as they are in example 2.

EXAMPLE 4

The public schools in Cincinnati, Ohio, Montgomery County, Maryland, Minneapolis, Minnesota, New York City and a number of other school districts across the country have developed comprehensive peer *assistance* and *assessment* programs. As in examples 1, 2 and 3, these programs provide teachers with peer formative assistance to improve their performances. In addition, the programs in these districts have effectively given teachers an important part of the summative assessment component for veteran teachers who were identified by their evaluators as performing below standard and probationary teachers. To quote the Cincinnati program,

> . . . through the Intervention Component, the program seeks to assist experienced teachers who exhibit serious instructional deficiencies. When assigned, consulting teachers work with those teachers to improve their instructional skills and to bring the teachers to a satisfactory level of performance. In cases where improvement of serious instructional deficiencies does not occur, peer assistance and evaluation may result in the removal of such teachers from the classroom and/or the non-renewal/termination of teaching contracts. (American Federation of Teachers and the National Education Association, 1998)

The actual description of these programs is contained in the supervision and evaluation guides for each district. However, an excellent twenty-page explanation of the NEA and AFT's recommendations for programs of this type can be found in joint publications by the two national teachers' unions/associations. I would recommend that those who are interested in learning more about these programs begin by obtaining a copy of *Peer Assistance & Peer Review: An AFT/NEA Handbook,* (American Federation of Teachers and the National Education Association [AFT/NEA], 1998). The handbook was distributed at the AFT/NEA Conference on Teacher Quality held September 25–27, 1998, in Washington, DC. The following explanation is based on the information in this guide and also on my experience in consulting to one of the districts implementing such a program.

In these peer assistance and assessment programs, the district selects and trains a group of teachers known as consulting teachers. Consulting teachers work with all probationary teachers new to the district and those probationary teachers whose contracts were renewed for a second year and are deemed by their evaluators as needing additional assistance and review. Consulting teachers are assigned to tenured teachers who are evaluated by their administrators as below standard. (AFT/NEA, 1998)

The handbook lists the following qualifications for consulting teachers:
- have taught successfully for a specified number of years
- be recognized as outstanding classroom teachers
- demonstrate deep knowledge of the disciplines they teach
- possess a repertoire of effective classroom management strategies and instructional techniques
- have strong verbal skills, both orally and in writing
- have the ability to work cooperatively and effectively with others

(AFT/NEA, 1998)

The consulting teachers are typically selected by the joint governance committee known in some districts as the Peer Assessment and Review (PAR) Panel. Consulting teachers make recommendations to the PAR panel about the teachers with whom they work. For probationary teachers, these recommendations lead the PAR panel to tenure the teacher, renew the teacher's contract without tenure or to deny renewal of the teacher's contract. For tenured teachers, the PAR recommendations lead to placement back in the professional development cycle (as opposed to continued intensive support and assessment), a second year of intensive support and assessment by the consulting teacher or dismissal.

The role of the PAR governance panel is described as follows:
- select, oversee, train and evaluate consulting teachers
- determine the process for selecting participating teachers
- review the reports and recommendations for consulting teachers
- accept or reject consulting teacher recommendations
- consider and act on appeals of participating teachers regarding the consulting process
- make recommendations concerning teacher competence (and in some districts, continued employment) to the superintendent
- ensure fair treatment for all participating teachers

(AFT/NEA, 1998)

CONCLUSIONS

Nationally, the role of teachers working with their peers to enhance professional performance is on the rise. It is important, however, that districts involved in peer programs be very clear about the purpose and structure of those programs. Teachers, teachers' unions/associations, school boards and administrators must decide whether

- the program is purely a formative professional development experience for teachers
- the program is purely a summative assessment program
- or, in cases in which it is both formative and summative, the degree and limits of the peer reviewers in making summative decisions

Final evaluation documents are also written using claims, evidence, interpretations and judgments. They differ in that they must address all of the district's performance standards rather than a chosen few. However, this requirement does not mean that the evaluator needs to rewrite all of the previous observation write-ups.

SAMPLE END-OF-YEAR REPORT THAT INCLUDES SUBJECTIVE CONCLUSIONS (CLAIMS, INTERPRETATIONS [IMPACT STATEMENTS] AND JUDGMENTS) SUPPORTED BY OBSERVABLE AND/OR VERIFIABLE DATA

Most evaluation systems require a final report at the conclusion of the summative evaluation year. For probationary teachers (nontenured), these reports are typically required every year. For tenured (professional status) teachers, districts vary in the frequency of these reports. Some districts require a final report every two years. Other districts require them every three or four years. As mentioned earlier in this chapter, one district requires a final report only every five years.

The following end-of-year report integrates subjective conclusions with the evidence used to support these conclusions.* Read this report and answer the following questions:

1. As a third party reader, did you find this style of write-up easy to read and understand? If yes, why? If not, why not?

2. Did you agree with the author's labels noted in the author's notes? If yes, why? If not, why not?

3. Francine is a very fine teacher and the evaluator frequently affirms her good work. However, please list those places in the evaluation which provide suggestions and/or questions designed to foster Francine's further growth.

4. Can you identify other claims, judgments, evidence and impact statements not identified by the author?

5. Can you determine the impact of the various teaching moves on the students' performance?

*Please note that the evaluator has used the time-saving technique of referring to supporting information in a previously written observation report rather than rewriting the information in the final evaluation. The actual excerpts from the observation reports can be found in the boxes immediately following this report.

Please also note that there are many positive claims, judgments and interpretations that are not backed up by evidence. In districts where a full time evaluator's load is limited to ten people, the evaluator is able to provide evidence for most or all of the subjective statements. However, in districts in which evaluators have over twenty evaluations (as is the case for this evaluator), valuable time documenting evidence must be focused toward the lower performers. I spoke more about this earlier in the chapter in the discussion of time-saving techniques for evaluators with large loads). — William Ribas

Sample of a Third-Year Teacher:
Annual Report of Teacher Effectiveness 2000–2001

Teacher: <u>Francine Fourth</u>   School: <u>Sample</u>   Grade/Subject: <u>4</u>

STANDARDS

I.   Currency of Curriculum
II.   Effective Planning and Assessment of Curriculum and Instruction
III. Effective Management of Classroom Environment
IV.   Effective Instruction
V.   Promotion of High Standards and Expectations for Student Achievement
VI.   Promotion of Equity and Appreciation of Diversity
VII. Fulfillment of Professional Responsibilities

Narrative

Francine is in her third year at Sample School, moving to the 4th grade this year after one year in the Learning Center. Francine agreed to teach 4th grade when there was uncertainty about the availability of the Learning Center position. Although the Learning Center position eventually became available, Francine honored her commitment to 4th grade. She did so with high spirits and a great deal of work and preparation, and she has met with significant success. Children in her class are consistently productive, engaged and thoughtful with one another. All of Francine's colleagues find her a team player. When Francine is asked to do something, her response is thoughtful and framed in terms of what is most helpful to the children. Not surprisingly, I have received numerous comments from parents such as, "Caroline adores Ms. Fourth—this is her best year in school" and "We just had our parent conference, and I was impressed with how well Francine knows Max as a person and as a student."

I.   Currency of Curriculum

Francine takes initiative around learning curriculum (**claim and judgment**). Last summer, she took a week long class at Northeastern University in order to prepare for the Math Investigations curriculum (which she was teaching for the first time this year). Francine calls on her experience teaching 4th grade at Lincoln School two years ago, and in fact met with her teaching partner from Lincoln in preparation for this assignment. Francine also works constructively with the other 4th grade teacher at Sample and has accessed the resources and expertise of the 4th grade teacher she is replacing this year. Francine also makes effective use of the Curriculum Coordinators. For example, she worked closely with the Science Coordinator in planning for the botany unit she taught at the start of this year. She met with the Language Arts Coordinator to plan both writing and spelling programs. She is likewise meeting with the Social Studies Coordinator (**evidence of the claim above**). As a result of Francine's knowledge about current curriculum expectations, students learn all the required competencies (**impact statement**).

Francine has been thoughtful about the state comprehensive assessment test as well, seeking to integrate strategies that are called for throughout the year. (See observation write-ups of 11/5/00, 11/24/00 and 12/21/00.)

(report continues)

II. Effective Planning and Assessment of Curriculum and Instruction

Francine has the ability to plan for a wide range of students within the confines of each lesson (**claim and judgment**). For example, during the human body unit, some students were expected to learn all of the parts of the cell, as well as the function of various types of cells. Other students were required to read material with a partner and draw and label a cell. If there are twenty math problems, some students are expected to do all of them; others a limited number. There are spelling programs for children learning ten words a week, children learning fifteen words and children who are working on challenge words (**evidence**).

Within each unit, each lesson meshes with the next in a seamless manner (**claim/judgment**). Because of the level of organization that Francine builds into each lesson, children are able to function quite independently (**claim/judgment/impact statement**). All of these characteristics were observed during a math lesson on November 5th.

Although the class just described utilized mixed-ability groups, Francine also utilizes performance-level groups as appropriate. The next step in Francine's development is the use of rubrics for student assessment. I recommend Francine focus next year's work with the curriculum coordinators on the development of assessment rubrics.

[The text in Box A at the end of this evaluation contains an excerpt from the November 5th observation report that supports the claims, judgments and impact statements in this part of the evaluation. See the section in this chapter titled "Time-Saving Tips for Supervisors and Evaluators" (page 98) for additional time–saving ideas.—William Ribas]

III. Effective Management of Classroom Environment

Francine is a successful manager in the classroom. So much of what happens looks like it is happening "by magic," but every moment is the result of careful planning (**claim and judgment**). The class is structured in "teams" that rotate monthly. Teams have a variety of ways to earn points for working cooperatively and productively together. Francine uses a range of mechanisms, including homework charts on which students mark off their assignments with small stickers. There are rewards such as lunch with the teacher given for a certain number of days of handing in homework on time. One of the funniest encounters I had with a child this year was with a girl from Francine's class who had left her backpack on the bus. She was unconcerned about her lunch, money and other personal possessions, but she was driven to tracking the backpack down because her homework was in it and this child was determined to maintain her perfect record (**impact statement and evidence**). Of course, all of this works because Francine's expectations are both challenging and doable at the same time (**claim and judgment**); because Francine checks with students to make sure that they understand what to do in numerous ways (**claim and judgment**); because all of the routines are predictable; because Francine speaks to her class with the utmost respect (**claim and judgment**). An observation of a science class demonstrated Francine's ability to manage a class most effectively.

Once again, this was a well organized, thoughtful class. Francine built on previous assignments— i.e., information gathering and making posters—and was moving the children to the next level of

(report continues)

application—how you would teach this information to somebody else. The posters and cards (from previous classes) were well prepared, so the kids all pretty much had the tools at hand to complete today's assignment. Each step of the research project built beautifully on the steps that preceded it. Francine is excellent at anticipating breaks to momentum and because of this, things that could become problems (i.e., who is going to be the recorder in a group, what to do about missing information, what to do about absent students) are avoided. As a result, this class was very productive; children talked in their groups in an animated, yet productive, way.

[Box B at the end of this evaluation, contains an excerpt from the December 21st evaluation report that supports this part of the evaluation.]

IV.   Effective Instruction

Francine sets clear goals, and uses these as a basis to assess instruction on a daily, weekly and monthly basis (**claim and judgment**). For example, Francine gives a weekly math assessment to review concepts taught that week. She corrects the assessment over the weekend and then on Monday divides the class into two groups; students who need to review concepts work with the special education teacher, while Francine does a supplementary lesson with the rest of the class. Francine uses the idea of pre- and post-assessments in other areas of the curriculum as well. Students are asked to draw or write on what they think about a topic (i.e., the parts of a plant or bee, what a Native American looks like) before a unit begins. As illustrated above in the description of the science class, Francine concludes units by frequently having children teach what they have learned to someone else. Francine is also skilled at using a range of instructional strategies. For example, Francine uses whole-class books, book groups, independent reading and reading aloud in her reading program. She incorporates teacher-directed lessons, hands-on activities and practice and application, as appropriate. This range of instructional approaches was evident in a math class noted in an observation on November 24th.

[Box C at the end of this evaluation, contains an excerpt from the November 24th evaluation report that supports this part of the evaluation.]

V.   Promotion of High Standards and Expectations for Students' Achievement

Francine has an academically and racially diverse group of students in her classroom (**claim**), due in part to the fact that it was not possible to accommodate a developmentally delayed child in her class at another school; Francine has thus worked effectively (**judgment**) with staff at our school to develop an interim program for the student. At the other end of the spectrum, Francine has two children in her class who are the most intellectually gifted children in 4th grade and among the highest-ability children in the school. To accommodate this range, Francine works with teachers in two learning centers, the remedial reading teacher and the E.S.L. teacher. These specialists work both on a pull-out basis and in Francine's classroom. In addition, Francine has set up a special reading group with the librarian for the highest-level children and participated in a special math pilot with the town-wide gifted and talented coordinator. Francine effectively promotes the concept of "personal best." She insists that a child put forth his or her best work, and children are required to redo work that was rushed through or incomplete. Francine works in tandem with parents around this concept, so that standards for homework and schoolwork are consistent. Francine also insists on standard writing conventions such as complete sentences, paragraphing and punctuation.

VI. Promotion of Equity and Appreciation of Diversity

Francine has respect and appreciation for each child in her class (**claim and judgment**). She honors each student for his or her strengths (**claim and judgment**). Francine takes an interest in the lives of her students outside of the classroom—be it sports, music, scouting, drama or family events (**claim and judgment**). Francine uses the curriculum as a basis for teaching about diversity (**claim and judgment**). For example, in teaching about Native Americans, Francine used this study as a sequel to previous teaching about stereotypes (**evidence**). Francine frequently uses class discussions and meetings to address issues of diversity and equity (**claim and judgment**).

VII. Fulfillment of Professional Responsibilities

Francine works effectively with everyone on our staff—the librarian, SPED staff, ESL–Bilingual staff and regular education teachers all find Francine easy to work with (**claim and judgment**). As a result of her flexibility and adaptability, two of the specialists I am evaluating this year asked me to do their observations in Francine's classrooms because it is a comfortable and positive place for other professionals as well as for children (**evidence and impact statement**).

Francine makes herself available to parents on a daily basis, yet her contacts with parents are always appropriate and professional. Like her colleagues on the faculty, parents also find Francine easy to talk to and helpful (**claim and judgment**).

Francine's enthusiasm, positive attitude, ability to forge strong and positive relationships with children, colleagues and parents, her strong work ethic and the intelligence and common sense she brings to her work, make her a valuable colleague to have on the Sample faculty.

___ This evaluation indicates performance with no areas of concern.

X This evaluation indicates performance with need for improvement in one or two areas (see recommendations).

___ This evaluation indicates performance with need for improvement in several areas (see recommendations).

___ This evaluation indicates performance which is below the standard expected of staff in the Sample Public Schools (see recommendations).

Overall Evaluation: **X**   ___
                     Satisfactory   Unsatisfactory

_____   _____
Signature of evaluator   date

_____   _____
Signature of teacher   date

Signature signifies receipt of, not concurrence with, this evaluation. Teachers are encouraged to submit comments. Please make comments on the back of this form or on an attached sheet.

Box A: Excerpt from November 5th Observation Report

This is a lesson on constructing graphs. The goal of the project is to teach children how to analyze the data they have collected from their plant unit to make a bar graph. Francine effectively frames the lesson. Francine starts the lesson with an overhead of a bar graph about the life cycle of plants. She starts by going over the parts of the graph, the title, etc. She discusses with the class how the vertical axis of the graph is constructed. She asks the children why the graph starts at 5 days and increases in increments of 5. As a result, students are prepared to receive the new concepts hat will be presented.

Francine has a nice way of guiding the discussion and of calling on a broad range of children. She also has a very good way of restating what the children say. For example, when one child says the graph would be too big if every day were labeled, Francine expanded this to talk about how the graph is used to summarize information. She presses on this issue to extend thinking—i.e., you decide what the intervals on the graph should be, based on the actual data you have. "You have to think about what numbers you have." She asks how many more days it takes one plant to develop vs. another. She has a good tolerance for wait time. When Tobias answers, she asks the class to raise hands if they agree. On another question, she asks why the answer (between 60 and 65) could be 63 or 64 but not 61. As a result, an inordinately high percentage of students participates in classroom discussions. When Francine is certain that the class has understood how to read this graph, she moves to the next part of the lesson.

For this section of the lesson, a written exercise in reading a graph, children move to their old seats so they can work with their science partners. Francine has excellent management techniques, and the children move effortlessly from one situation to the next. She reminds children to take pencils, and she tells them who will pass out graphs and how they will be distributed. When this is finished, Francine says, "You and your partner should have your question sheet and your graph." Before the children start, Francine read them a narrative about the sample graph. The questions that the children have to answer about this graph are parallel to the questions she has gone over on the overhead. The topic is different—the written exercise involves a growth chart and the overhead was about plants. The class quickly settled into the working partnerships and worked very productively. When voices were a little loud, Francine reminded them to "use one-inch voices," and this did the trick. As a result, students maintained a high level of on-task behavior.

Francine effectively checks for understanding. For the next few minutes, Francine went over the exercise with the class. She read the first question and got responses from the class. Francine again pressed the answer—she reminded the kids to pay close attention to the question being asked— i.e., the question was not to double but to find the answer as "more than twice as tall." On the second question, one student said the answer was yes—most of the kids agreed. However, Francine checked to see if anyone thought the answer was no. As a result, all students are able to complete the exercise successfully.

Francine foreshadowed the upcoming lesson. During the last part of the lesson, Francine told the class what was going to happen the next time. She told them they would be getting graph paper (she showed them a sample). She told them how they would create their own graphs. She had them get their science folders and science notebooks. Ariel distributed the graph papers. Francine referred the children to rough draft graphs they had made. She reminded them that they had these, the sample on the overhead and the graph for the practice exercise—all of these references could be used to help them. She told them that for the last few minutes of the class, they could talk with their science partners about how they would plan their graphs. As a result, students understood how today's learning connected with the learning of the next lesson.

This was an excellent class. It was carefully planned, and it met the children exactly at their learning step. One of the most impressive things about Francine's teaching is the way she presses around questioning—she routinely asks extension questions, and she checks to make sure that everyone understands. She also invites and respects minority opinions—the goal is to find out the how and why—not just to recite the right answer. The tone of the class is excellent. Francine has a very nice way of interacting with the children—she makes lots of positive remarks such as "good point, excellent." Her directions are very clear—children are able to move smoothly from one part of the lesson to the next. A lot of the class involves group work and the children stay on task and talk with each other in a respectful way. I would like to add that the classroom itself is attractive and well organized (Francine opened this room this year). Materials are well organized and easy to access. Student work is nicely displayed. Overall, Francine is an impressive teacher.

Box B: Excerpt from December 21st Observation Report

This is an observation of a science lesson. The class is going to be meeting in their "tree groups." Francine framed the day's lesson. The lesson starts with the overhead. Francine reviews by telling the class that all six research groups have presented. Francine explains that the goal of today's lesson is to have each group make a study sheet for the class. Francine explained that each student would get six study sheets which they would be able to use for a quiz; that the group that was the expert on, for example, palm trees, would make the study sheet for their group. Francine had prepared a worksheet for each group. She went over the worksheet with the class. Mickey asked about how they would get information from a student who was not here. Francine told him that they could refer to the posters of students not here. As a result, students knew how each part of the lesson fit into the big picture.

Francine gave clear directions and went through the worksheet in a question-and-answer format. The worksheet, which was very clearly laid out, asked for the names of trees included in the group, description of the trees in the group, how the tree was used and interesting facts. For each question, Francine had a student explain what was called for. Francine has a nice way of predicting and, therefore, preventing problems. For example, the worksheet called for four or five interesting facts. Francine acknowledged that kids had more than this, but that they needed to pick the most important and interesting ones. Francine reviewed the process for filling out the sheet—how to take turns and how the people who were not writing could be preparing the next question. Francine next told the kids where they were going to be working. She emphasized that if there were six groups talking, they would need to keep their voices down. The task needed to be finished before lunch (they would have about twenty-five minutes). All of this advance organizing—i.e., previewing the sheet, answering questions and predicting problems resulted in a high level of student success in completing the task. Francine pays attention to nice details—such as how to take a poster down without ripping it.

The transition to the small groups was very smooth and efficient, although it involved a lot of steps—taking down posters, getting information cards, etc. Francine made sure each group got started. The groups set to work with amazing efficiency. Due to absences, the groups ranged in size from five students to two students. Francine moved among the six groups, helping kids decide among the array of information sources available to them. She reminded kids that the information could be recorded "in note-taking form" rather than in complete sentences. Without exception, the groups stayed with the task at hand, conversations among the children in each group stayed on topic and they were all able to fill out the worksheet. The fact that these worksheets were going to be used as study sheets by their classmates gave them a clear purpose.

About five minutes before lunch, Francine stopped the groups. She said that some people were finding they needed more information to make the sheet complete. She said that they should see what information they needed to complete the sheet, who was going to get it and that they needed to bring it in tomorrow to finish the task. Francine made a final round among the groups to see what information needed to be completed. Francine had the children put everything away in a completely organized manner. She had the children organize their homework folders for the close of the day.

Box C: Excerpt from November 24th Observation Report

This is a math class—children are learning about silhouettes of solid geometric shapes. Francine activated previous learning. The first part of the lesson is a review of something they have done before. They are predicting what geometric shapes would look like on an overhead projection. They predict that a cone held upside down would be a circle—in fact, when Francine does this on the overhead, this is what they see. The children continue to give reasons why this is so. The next shape is a triangle prism—each time students say what shape they think it will be, they give a reason. When stood on end, the top is blurry—on its side, it is clear. On its side, the shape looks like a rectangle—again, Francine has children give reasons why this is so. As a result, students are better to learn today's comcepts.

Francine next has the class open their math books to page 9 of their workbook. The task is for each team to build the landscape that is pictured. Francine explains that she will be giving each group a bag of geometric solids and a sheet of paper on which to build the landscape. She answers questions about the order of the shapes, etc. Francine does a lot of advance organizing—i.e., the place where the structure is to be built, putting it all on a book so the structures won't tip, given the uneven desk surfaces. The directions are very clear, which results in the children being able to start the task in a purposeful way. As Francine walks around the class, she reminds children to look at the picture—says that there may be extra pieces in the bag. In a couple of minutes, all the groups complete this part of the task. Francine comments that in some teams there is a difference of opinion about some of the shapes. She places the diagram on the overhead and goes over it.

Francine said they were now going to talk about looking at things from different points of view. Ultimately, they would draw how things looked from different points in the room. Francine focused on the point between the two rectangles on the overhead—asked what you would see if you faced various ways. Francine said, "Pretend that you are a little person at each of these letters—what would you see from each point?" She went on to ask how the desks in the classroom would look to a little baby and to Michael Jordan. From there, they went on to do the three exercises on the worksheets with partners.

Francine told them that now they would be drawing what they saw in the classroom from their perspectives. She wanted them to draw what they saw from where they were sitting. There was a good discussion about why Charlie, for example, could see the flag and the window, whereas Alyssa would see the desk next to her. Francine said the goal was to draw your spot so clearly that if it were given to another person, they would be able to figure out who did it. There were a lot of questions about what to draw—should it be just what was in front of you, or to the left, right, etc.? Francine said they would start this today—spend five minutes on it and finish it tomorrow. The children seemed to have a fairly good idea of how to go about doing this. Francine told them not to put their names on the drawings, but to put them in their math folders, and that they would finish them tomorrow.

This lesson presented extremely challenging and often ambiguous concepts . . . Francine gave good clues as the children were drawing—i.e., think about the size of things—the size of your desk in comparison to the chalkboard . . . As always, Francine's tone with the group is very positive. Children work on the task at hand in a productive manner, even when they are confused. All of the organizational details and the preparation of the materials are well accounted for, and this keeps things flowing nicely from one activity to the next.

SOURCES

American Arbitration Association. (1995). Decision regarding the Lexington, Massachusetts, Public Schools.

American Arbitration Association. (1994). Decision regarding the Little Rock, Arkansas, School District.

American Federation of Teachers and the National Education Association. (1998). *Peer assistance & peer review: an AFT/NEA handbook*. Washington, DC.

Danielson, C. (1996). *Enhancing professional practice: A framework for teaching*. Alexandria, VA: Association for Supervision and Curriculum Development.

Curriculum frameworks. (1995). Malden, MA: Massachusetts Department of Education.

McTighe, J. & Wiggins, G. (1999). *Understanding by design*. Alexandria, VA: Association of Supervision and Curriculum Development.

Milliken Family Foundation. (1999). *A matter of quality: a strategy for assuring the high caliber of America's teachers*. Lowell Milliken.

Principles of effective teaching. (1995). Malden, MA: Massachusetts Department of Education.

Ribas, W. (2000, April). Ascending the ELPS to excellence in your district's teacher evaluation. *Phi Delta Kappan*, 585–589.

Ribas, W. (2003). *Maximizing teaching success*. Westwood, MA: Ribas Publications.

Ribas, W., Deane, J. & Seider, S. (2005). *Instructional practices that maximize student achievement: for teachers, by teachers*. Westwood, MA: Ribas Publications.

Rutherford, P. (1998). *Instruction for all students*. Alexandria, VA: Just ASK Publications.

Saphier, J. (1993). *How to make supervision and evaluation really work*. Acton, MA: Research for Better Teaching, Inc.

Saphier, J. & Gower, R. (1997). *The skillful teacher*. Acton, MA: Research for Better Teaching, Inc.

What teachers should be able to do. (1994). Washington, DC: National Board for Professional Teaching Standards.

CHAPTER 4

Sources of Observable and/or Verifiable Evidence Other Than Classroom Observations

Accurately and comprehensively evaluating a teacher requires that we use other data sources in addition to full-length classroom observations. These other data sources are referred to as **alternate data sources.** This chapter discusses a number of the more common alternate data sources that evaluators use to fully understand a teacher's performance in all the areas identified in the performance standards. In the previous chapter, we defined the two types of data, evidence and information, as follows.

Evidence is data that is sufficiently verified and is used to make a judgment. For example, in the sample observation write-up paragraphs in chapter 3, the behaviors observed by the evaluators, coupled with the data learned in the post-conferences, are sufficient to make a judgment. For those who are interested in learning more about how to determine when data is sufficient to make a judgment, chapter 6 contains a comprehensive explanation of the legal standards related to evidence.

Information is some data that leads us to make the decision that we need more data before we can make a judgment. For example, three high school math students ask to leave a teacher's class for placement in the same class with a different teacher because the teacher is "too easy" and "the class does not have the appropriate level of challenge." The supervisor's review of the teacher's first quarter grades, however, shows that two of the students had a

B+ and one had an A. A conversation with the teacher indicates that the second quarter grades for each student show that two are continuing to work at a B to B+ level and that the one with the A is continuing at that level. Two classroom walk throughs and a formal observation indicate that the content being taught is at the level of challenge prescribed in the curriculum. In this circumstance, the information initially received was not sufficient to make a judgment. The additional information collected by observation and from reviewing class grades provides sufficient data to make the judgment that the class is not "too easy" for at least two of the students. In the case of the third student, the supervisor's judgment is that providing some extension of the learning is appropriate.

Below are some of the data sources other than full-length classroom observations that are used to make a 360 degree assessment of the teacher's performance.

1. **Observing teacher-to-student interactions in non-classroom settings such as the playground, cafeteria, corridor, assemblies, before school, after school, etc.** Effective teaching requires that teachers use their skills identified in the performance standards to impact student learning and/or shape student behavior whenever the teacher comes in contact with students. These interactions typically come in two forms. The first set of interactions includes assigned duties such as recess duty, cafeteria duty, hall monitor duty, bus duty, before and after school duty, chaperoning field trips and monitoring assemblies and other large group activities during the school day. In some middle and high schools, assigned duties may include those after school hours, such as those related to sporting events, choral concerts and field trips by clubs.

   The second set of interactions is the incidental contact teachers have with students in school. This may include how the teacher interacts with students when he/she is walking through the halls during planning periods, how the teacher interacts with students other than their own when escorting their classes outside of the classroom and at other times when teachers have incidental contact with students in school.

2. **Tracking cumulative data obtained *from the parents* about teacher and student interactions in class and in other settings.** Parents frequently speak to supervisors about teachers. Many times parents give compliments. At other times, they express concerns about teachers. Both of these circumstances are data for the administrator to consider in relation to the teacher's performance. An administrator should be cautious, however, about interpreting parent comments as evidence rather than as information. Typically, the parents' statements come from secondhand information that has been originally obtained from a student. In such

cases, it is incumbent upon the administrator to gather more information prior to making a judgment. I don't mean to suggest that every time a parent complains the administrator needs to investigate the situation further. In most instances, parents' complaints should be met with the recommendation that the parents talk with the teacher about the issue. Figure 10 in chapter 6 talks more about the varied circumstances related to the handling of parent data. Chapter 6 also talks about how the administrator should address a parent concern if the parent expresses the desire to remain anonymous.

> *In most instances, parents' complaints should be met with the recommendation that the parents talk with the teacher about the issue.*

3. **Tracking cumulative data obtained *from students' reports* about teacher and student interactions in class and in other settings.** This data appears more frequently in elementary schools in the upper grades than in the primary grades. It becomes more prevalent in middle school and most prevalent in high school. Like parent data, student reports may include both positive comments and concerns. Many of the concerns may be addressed by helping students make a plan for discussing them with the teacher. At other times, however, it is appropriate for the administrator to speak directly with the teacher.

4. **Tracking cumulative data obtained from the *reports from other staff* about the teacher's interactions with students in class and in other settings.** Some of the data we receive about teachers comes from other staff members. In most cases, this data reflects the positive performance of a colleague. In some circumstances, it is related to a concern. A colleague's concern about another teacher's interactions with students may be complex for the administrator. In some circumstances, it is appropriate to suggest that the teacher express his/her concern to the colleague. The administrator must be certain, however, that the concern is addressed. Often, in these circumstances, the reporting teacher does not want his/her identity known. In those cases, the evaluator must decide whether to take the information to the identified teacher and allow the reporter to remain anonymous or to observe the teacher in question during times when the behavior might be repeated. Whichever action the evaluator takes, he/she should do so with an open mind. The intent of gathering the additional information is to determine whether or not the accusation is true. The obvious exception to this careful analysis of next steps is a report of teacher behavior that is identified as unlawful in most states. In these cases, the supervisor has a legal and moral obligation to take direct and immediate action.

5. **Observing the teacher's interactions with colleagues at meetings and in other settings.** Constructive and collegial interactions with colleagues is an important part of being a successful teacher. In the Principles of Effective Teaching document found in chapter 9, Standard VIIB, descriptors 1 and 2 (page 300) is an example of the wording of such a standard. Observing the teacher's interactions with other staff in faculty meetings, in the halls, in the teachers' room and during committee meetings are all sources of data for assessing performance in this area. Teachers are also expected to act appropriately and constructively in their interactions with support staff such as custodians, cafeteria workers and teacher assistants.

6. **Tracking the cumulative data obtained *from the reports of colleagues* about the teacher's interactions with colleagues at meetings and in other settings.** As noted above, constructive and collegial interactions with colleagues are an important part of being a successful teacher. The data about a teacher's interactions with colleagues often comes from other colleagues. Much of this data concerns reports of positive interactions among teachers. In negative circumstances, the form it typically takes is one of the reporting teacher expressing his/her displeasure with the way a colleague has treated the reporting teacher. In most cases of this type, the best strategy is to encourage the teacher to speak to the colleague. In other circumstances, the administrator should take a direct role in resolving the conflict. It is important that these situations be resolved in as open a manner as possible. Few things can be as poisonous to a school environment as teachers feeling they cannot trust their colleagues. Negative interactions are bound to happen among colleagues in any work setting. Encouraging, and at times facilitating, the teachers' discussing and resolving the conflict themselves is the best way to develop and maintain a collegial environment.

7. **Reviewing groups of corrected student work and the teacher's grade book to assess the timeliness of the teacher's responses, appropriateness of those responses and the effectiveness of recording of those responses**

8. **Reviewing the teacher-developed student assessments and how the students performed on those assessments.** Our knowledge of what makes for effective and ineffective assessment has improved considerably in recent years. Classroom observations seldom include the summative assessments of the concepts taught in the lesson. Therefore, the evaluator needs obtain the assessment instrument from the teacher to determine if the assessment does indeed measure the intended learning.

9. **Observing the teacher's interactions with parents individually (e.g., three-way conferences with the parent, teacher and evaluator).** Evaluators usually attend a parent conference only when it is related to some

mandated service or there is an unresolved issue between the teacher and the parent. As a result, the evaluator directly observes data only in the more difficult situations. By randomly selecting other conferences to attend during the teacher's summative evaluation year, the evaluator may obtain objective data on the teacher's conferencing skills.

10. **Tracking cumulative data about the teacher's interactions with parents individually as obtained from those who attended a conference that the administrator did not attend**

11. **Observing the teacher's interactions with parents in group presentations, such as during curriculum night presentations**

12. **Tracking direct data in reports received from parents and colleagues of the teacher's interactions with parents in group presentations, such as during curriculum night presentations**

13. **Reviewing the teacher's correspondence with staff, parents and students**[1]

14. **Touring the classroom with the teacher while he/she describes the reasons for the classroom set-up and displays**

15. **Tracking cumulative data obtained from high school class registration numbers (including drops and adds), which may be further substantiated by interviewing students about the reasons for their drop requests**

16. **Tracking the cumulative indirect data obtained from parents' request letters regarding elementary class placements, including requests to remove students from a classroom after the school year has started.** This evidence may be further substantiated by interviewing students and/or parents who request that their children be removed from a class after the school year begins

17. **Reviewing students' performance on criterion-referenced and norm-referenced tests over a period of several years.** It is important to note that the formal use of norm-referenced and criterion-referenced student performance data in individual teacher's evaluations is still rare and controversial. Supervisors and evaluators should be cautious about the use of these data as evidence of excellent or poor teaching performance (Holloway, 2000, p. 84). Tennessee is one of a very few states with a process for using student data from standardized tests as a measure of an individual teacher's performance. There continues to be significant research and debate about what is known as the Tennessee Value-Added Assessment System (Archer, 1999, p. 26) and other **value-added programs** that make judgments about teacher performance based on student test performance.

---

[1] For more information on effective techniques for curriculum night presentations and other parent communication skills, see the book, Maximizing Teaching Success (Ribas, 2003).

In his November 2003 *Educational Leadership* article, Harold Doran (pp. 55–59) gives one of the best explanations of the reason that test scores, other than those given careful value-added analysis, do not give us usable data about teacher performance. He explains that "test scores are subject to external variables beyond the control of the schools. A test score for an 8th grade student is invalid for evaluating 8th grade instruction because it reflects the cumulative impact of schooling over all the previous years." Doran also reminds us that the student's achievement is impacted by variables outside of the school.

Value-added testing programs use statistical analysis to estimate the impact of variables outside of the school. Doran tells us that correct implementation of these programs requires at least yearly testing. All the tests must use a consistent score metric and must measure students over an extended period of time (several years). A value-added system requires that every student in the state have a student identification number that follows the student to any school in any district to help track and account for student mobility. A district also needs to have a sufficient number of students for a sufficient sample size.

> Value-added testing programs use statistical analysis to estimate the impact of variables outside of the school.

Most districts in the country do not have the testing components needed for a value-added system. In some cases, this is by choice. Many states and districts have decided that the testing time needed for a value-added system takes away too much instructional time.[2] Others have decided that precious education funds should be spent on teaching students, rather than on the level of testing and analysis required to maintain a value-added system. Debating the pros and cons of these decisions is beyond the purview of this book. We provide this limited explanation to make the case that, in most districts, student test data is information but not evidence. For more information on the use of student achievement data, I recommend the book, *Teacher Evaluation and Student Achievement.* (Stronge, J. & Tucker, P., 2000).

18. **Reviewing students' performance as demonstrated in teacher-developed portfolios such as the Demonstrated Student Achievement Portfolios used in the Baltimore Performance Based System (Koppich, 2001, p. 29).** Oftentimes, the teacher is the best source of data. Districts are beginning to ask teachers to keep portfolios of data related to their performance on each of the district's performance standards.

---

2 This may change as a result of the No Child Left Behind legislation. Annual testing may become a requirement in all states, however, it is still unclear whether that testing will be such that it will be adequate for value-added analysis.

19. Reviewing the information provided by the teacher in answer to pre- and post-observation conference questions and/or in the course of other conversations. (See the section on conferencing later in this chapter.)

CONFERENCING TO CREATE CHANGE: WHAT YOU ASK A TEACHER AND HEAR FROM A TEACHER IS OFTEN MORE IMPORTANT THAN WHAT YOU TELL A TEACHER

In chapter 3, I spoke about the importance of writing in clear, concise and honest language. We also spoke about the importance of the above being accompanied by speaking in conferences and discussions with teachers about their performance. This is particularly true when the discussion is about areas for improvement.

The term **conferencing** refers to three distinct forms of data gathering. The first is the pre-observation conference, the second is the post-observation conference, and the third is the final evaluation conference. One of the primary complaints I hear from teachers about the classroom observation write-ups they receive is that the observations lack the contextual information that has caused the teacher to make certain instructional decisions. The pre-observation conference, post-observation conference and the final evaluation conference enable the evaluator to gather the important data that is needed to make judgments about the teaching with all the information that is available. Teaching is too complex an activity to make judgments with only the data gathered in a forty-minute observation.

> Teaching is too complex an activity to make judgments with only the data gathered in a forty-minute observation.

Pre-Observation Conference

The primary purpose of the pre-observation conference is to gather all the data the observer needs to observe the class with the greatest level of depth. There is a great deal of data that can be obtained prior to the observation that enables the observer to better understand the context within which the lesson is taught. *Pre-observation conferences are typically only available to the observer when the observation is an announced, scheduled observation.* There is some data all observers need to obtain from the teacher. Examples of data that all observers need include pre-observation data that tells the observer what the teacher expects the students will know and be able to do at the end of the observation (a.k.a. mastery objectives)? What preceded the class being observed? What will happen after the observed class? How is the teacher going to assess the students' progress toward meeting the objective of the lesson?

In other instances, there is data some observers need to obtain and others do not because they already have the data. For example, an eighth grade mathematics teacher may be observed by a middle school principal whose primary background is reading. The principal may lack the knowledge of the concepts the curriculum requires the teacher to address. In this example, the principal may ask the teacher, prior to the observation, what part of the district curriculum the class will address so the principal can familiarize herself with those concepts before observing. In another instance, the same math teacher may be observed by a K–12 mathematics curriculum administrator. In this instance, the observer may know the concepts in the curriculum, however, the observer may not know that the class contains four students who speak very limited English. That data would be helpful for the observer to obtain from the teacher prior to the observation.

Observers typically obtain pre-observation data in one of three ways. The first and most effective option is to provide the teacher with a pre-observation form that lists the information the observer needs prior to a pre-conference. Later in this chapters is an example of a pre-observation conference form used by one district. The observer reviews the data prior to the pre-conference. A pre-conference is then held to discuss that data and any other contextual data not yet obtained by the observer. The second and third options are default options and only used if there is insufficient time in the observer's schedule to choose the first option. The second option is to only use the pre-conference form. The observer gives the teacher the pre-conference form prior to the observation. The observer reviews the teacher's responses prior to the observation. The third option is to not use the form but have a pre-observation conference in which the teacher explains the contextual data to the observer.

Option one is preferable for several reasons. First, the teacher gets time to think about the data the observer wants prior to the conference. Second, the teacher knows most of what the administrator wants to talk about in the pre-observation conference and therefore is better prepared to give informative answers. Third, teachers find their anxiety leading up to the conference is decreased because they know the agenda of the pre-observation conference. It eliminates the anxiety caused when the teacher must guess what is on the evaluator's mind.

Converting Performance Standards to Conference Questions

In a standards-based environment, we are always searching for ways to obtain data that helps us determine a teacher's level of success in meeting a standard. Pre- and post-conferences are excellent sources of this data. Below are some descriptors taken from the performance standards found on pages 294 to 302 of this book. Parts of them have been converted to questions aimed at obtaining additional data about teacher performance related to the standard.

A quick and effective way to obtain good conference questions is to choose descriptors and convert part or all of the descriptors to pre- or post-conference questions.

Examples:

Principle of Effective Teaching IIA Descriptor 2:

Sets short-term and yearlong goals for curricular units which derive from unifying themes of fundamental importance to the student's present and future lives.

Pre-conference: In what way will you connect what is taught in the upcoming lesson to the students' present or future lives?

Post-conference: How can you connect what was taught in the lesson to the students' present or future lives?

Principle of Effective Teaching VI B 1:

Demonstrates sensitivity to differences in abilities, modes of contributions, and social and cultural backgrounds.

Pre-conference: What do you expect students to do when they have mastered the concepts prior to the other students and before the period has ended?

Post-conference: In what way did your lesson respond to the varying rates at which the students mastered the concepts?

PRE-CONFERENCE FORM

Please come to the pre-conference prepared to talk about the following points.

1. What do you want the students to know and be able to do by the end of the lesson? What are your goals and/or objectives?

2. What district curriculum standards or frameworks do these goals address?

3. How will you determine if the students have mastered the concepts noted in number 1 above (in your plan for assessment of student learning)?

4. Describe the sequence of events in the lesson.

5. What would you like me to focus on during the observation?

Post-Observation Conference

The purpose of the post-observation conference is two-fold. First, it is to gather additional data about the context of the observation. During an observation, observers typically have many questions that need to be answered prior to making a judgment. We know that good teaching requires the teacher to have a large repetoire of effective strategies. We also know that equally important are the decisions the teacher makes regarding which strategy to use at what time and with what students. For most teachers, observers should have more questions than statements in the post-observation conference. The second purpose of the post-observation conference is to give the teacher information about his/her teaching that will result in improved performance. This information typically comes in four categories. The first is **commendations.** One goal of giving commendations is to make the teachers feel good about those performances that were successful. A second goal which is equally or more important is to raise the teacher's consciousness about how effective strategies positively impact students. This only happens when our commendations contain specific descriptions of the behaviors rather than general statements. Within the category of commendations are two subcategories. The first is praise and the second is encouragement. **Praise** tells the person their performance meets or exceeds the standard. It says, "You have arrived." **Encouragement** tells the person that he/she is making good progress but is not yet where he/she needs to be. The following are examples of praise and encouragement.

> **Praise:** You did an excellent job of formatively assessing during the instruction to determine which students had mastered the concept and which students needed re-teaching.
>
> **Encouragement:** You are making good progress toward the standard of teaching in the target language at least 80% of the time.

The second category is **recommendations.** Recommendations also come in two forms. The first is the suggestion. **Suggestions** are those things we would like the teacher to do but he/she can choose not to do. For example, a teacher who uses an effective form of formative assessment in her class may be asked in a post-conference to describe it to the rest of the staff. In this instance, the evaluator wants the teacher to do this but does not want to compel the teacher to do so if the teacher does not want to do it. The teacher may respond "no" to this suggestion without any detriment to her evaluation. The second type of recommendation is the **direction.** These are recommendations the teacher must implement. If the teacher fails to implement the direction, it will be noted as part of the evaluation as a deficiency in the teacher's performance.

The third category is the judgment. Judgments for conferences are defined in the same way as judgments are defined in chapter 3. **Judgments** tell the teacher exactly how the evaluator rated the teacher's use (or lack there-of) of a specific strategy.

The final category is feedback. This category is often confusing because in common language we use the term to denote all of the categories above. In the language of teacher evaluation, feedback has a specific definition. **Feedback** is specific data (evidence and information) given to the teacher about his/her performance in relation to the standard. Feedback does not contain judgment by the evaluator. It is pure data from which the teacher derives his/her own judgments. For feedback to be effective, the teacher must know the standard so she can judge where her performance lies in relation to the standard. Below are some samples of feedback used by evaluators. I have written the standard in parenthesis after the feedback for the benefit of the reader of this book.

- You waited two seconds or less after 90% of the questions you asked. (Research recommends teachers wait three to five seconds after asking a question.) (Budd-Rowe, 1986, pp. 43–49)
- 20% of the students asked or answered a question. In this district, we are working toward getting more students to answer questions. (The school has set a minimum standard of 50%.)
- Group 5 was on task 60% of the time. (This is at the bottom range stated as acceptable on-task behavior.)
- You asked twelve recall questions and one comprehensive question. (In this district, the goal is to ask 50% of the questions at a higher thinking level than recall.)
- The transition from morning cycle to the centers took two minutes. (It is expected that students at this grade, at this point in the year, will complete the transition in three minutes or less.)

We should match our response to teacher performance to our objective for the response.

Figure 7

Good post-conference planning is an important step toward ensuring the post-conference achieves the observer's objectives. Below is a sample of a post-conference planning form completed by evaluators in several districts to prepare for their post-conferences.

POST-CONFERENCE PREPARATION SHEET

1. How much time do you have for the conference? What do you want to achieve by the end of this conference? (e.g., What information do you need from the teacher? Which questions do you want to ask? What points do you want to make?)

2. How will you (the observer) know if you achieved your purpose in the conference?

3. On the back, briefly outline what you will say and do in the conference.

Below is the post-conference planning sheet used for the observation write-up of Connie, found in chapter 3.

POST-CONFERENCE PREPARATION SHEET

1. How much time do you have for the conference? What do you want to achieve by the end of this conference? (e.g., What information do you need from the teacher? Which questions do you want to ask? What points do you want to make?)

   30 minutes

   - *Connie will make the connection between her relationship building techniques and the impact they have on the students.*
   - *Connie will make the connection between her effective use of clarity strategies and the impact that it has on students.*
   - *Connie will better articulate the objectives of the lesson to the students at the start of the class.*
   - *Connie will answer my questions in a way that shows me whether she knows that I think this lesson went well and that I am pleased with her performance.*
   - *Connie will answer my questions in a way that shows me that she knows the difference between activity planning and mastery planning.*

   Connie will move her practice toward mastery planning.

   I need to get more information from Connie to determine whether or not her approach to planning focuses on activities or on student mastery.

2. How will you (the observer) know if you achieved your purpose in the conference?

   After explaining each of the effective techniques Connie used, I will ask her to describe the impact of those techniques on student performance.

   I will do walk-throughs at the start of several lessons to see if the objectives are clearly stated.

   I will ask Connie to share a copy of a lesson plan in which she has focused on mastery planning. I will examine the lesson to see if it is written with an activity or a mastery focus.

   At the end of the conference, I will ask Connie how she thinks the conference went. Hopefully, she will let me know if she is feeling more criticized than praised.

3. On the back, briefly outline what you will say and do in the conference.

I will begin the conference by commenting on Connie's use of relationship building techniques and give her the examples from my notes. I will then ask Connie how she sees positive relationships with the students impacting their learning.

I will repeat this pattern with comments about Connie's use of clarity techniques. I will then build on the clarity discussion by asking Connie the following questions.

What was your objective for the lesson?

At which point do you think all the students recognized what you expected them to know and be able to do by the end of the lesson?

Hopefully, these questions will generate a discussion about mastery objectives and the need to state them at the start of the lesson.

I will then ask Connie to describe the questions she asks herself when she starts planning a lesson or a unit.

The questions Connie asks herself will give me a window into her thinking about planning. I will be able to determine whether or not she plans with an activity focus or a mastery focus.

My hunch is that she practices activity planning. If that is the case I will discuss with her the steps of mastery planning and give her a copy of a mastery lesson plan exemplar.

Final Evaluation Conference

The final evaluation conference comes after all the data for the year is collected and the evaluator is ready to write the final assessment. As with the post-conference, the evaluator uses the meeting to gather any additional data needed to write the evaluation and to verbally explain to the teacher the evaluator's judgments on all the areas for performance and the data supporting those judgments. The teacher then has an opportunity to make any final comments related to the evaluator's judgments. After the conference, the evaluator finishes writing the summative evaluation and gives it to the teacher. Some evaluators find it helpful for them and the teacher to have the final evaluation drafted prior to the final evaluation conference. This is appropriate as long as the evaluator comes to the conference knowing that the document may change as a result of new data obtained during the conference.

The next section provides a framework for effectively conducting pre-, post- and final supervision and evaluation conferences with teachers.

Pre-conferences, post-conferences and impromptu conversations with teachers are excellent opportunities to gather data to create positive change in a teacher's practice. Effective questioning and listening during conversations with a teacher give the evaluator much of the evidence he/she needs to make judgments and impact statements about the teacher's performance. Questions that force the teacher to reassess his/her practice and reconsider less effective practices can be far more effective in causing behavioral change than recommendations merely stated by the evaluator. Below are six steps evaluators can use to get teachers to think about, talk about and reassess their practices. These stages are an adaptation of the steps found on pages 54 and 55 of Thomas Gordon's book, *Leadership Effectiveness Training* (1977).

Six Stages of Listening and Questioning to Promote Behavioral Change
Stage I: Door Openers

- Choose the best location/setting for the conversation. The best setting can be determined by the situation. For example, some teachers may prefer complete privacy when you are addressing areas they need to change in their performance. In these cases, in your office behind a closed door is probably the best place. However, I have known other teachers who prefer to have conversations of this sort in their classrooms. They feel more comfortable in familiar surroundings and are more at ease discussing your assessment of their teaching.

- Door Openers indicate you want to have a two-way conversation about the teacher's practice and don't just want to give the teacher feedback. This is best achieved with questions that push the teacher to think about his/her practice in a different way. At this point, the questions should be open-ended to get the teacher talking and thinking. Some post-conference door openers can include the following:

What do you think went well in the lesson?

How did you feel during the lesson?

What did you observe about the students during the lesson?

Is there anything you would do differently?

Stage II: Passive Listening

Passive Listening is a technique you can use to create an environment where the teacher feels he/she can talk freely.

- The most important thing to do is "bite your lip and listen." Resist the urge to give the teacher the answer or advice too soon. It may be quicker (and more gratifying to you) to give the teacher your recommendations than to wait for him/ her to discover a "better way" during the discussion. However, changes in practice that are discovered by the teacher are far more likely to be implemented than those you give as advice that is not requested. Harry Truman said it best: "There is no limit to what you can achieve when you don't care who gets the credit."

- Use body language that indicates your openness to hearing what the teacher has to say. Your physical deportment can signal to the teacher that what he/she says is important to you.

Stage III: Acknowledgment Responses

Eye contact, nodding, comments such as "I hear you" and "I understand" and paraphrasing the teacher's statements all send the message that you are listening. Remember that acknowledging is not agreeing! There will be ample opportunity to discuss areas of disagreement at the appropriate time.

Stage IV: Active Listening

Active listening gives the speaker tangible evidence of the listener's understanding. For example, a listener labels a teacher's feelings about the situation (e.g., as anger, excitement, pride, frustration, confusion). The listener uses clarification questions and follow-up questions to gather additional information. For example, effective assessment is an area teachers typically struggle with because of the recent changes in practice resulting from an increased emphasis on standards. At the end of this section, you will find a set of questions that are based on one school district's performance standards on assessment. An evaluator may use these questions to learn more about how a teacher assesses students and to push the teacher to examine his/her assessment practices.

Stage V: Closing the Gap Between the Evaluator's and the Teacher's Perception of Performance

- Identify differences between your perception and the teacher's perception of the situation, and generate options that sound reasonable to both of you. Ask questions that help the teacher discover inconsistencies between his/her perception of a practice's impact on students and the real impact. You want the changes teachers make to "stick." The more teachers buy into the changes in their practices, the more likely they are to permanently implement them. Of course if a teacher's practice is detrimental to the students, you will not have the option of allowing the teacher time for self-discovery. In those situations you may need to be more direct about the inappropriateness of the behavior that you wish to change.

- Be open to the idea that you may not be completely correct in your perceptions. Listen to and consider the teacher's rationale before making a final judgment. Remember that there is a difference between a rationale and an excuse. A **rationale** is a true and convincing explanation of why the teacher's practice is better for students then your suggested change. An **excuse** is a reason why it is better for the teacher to use his/her practice, rather than to use the better practice for students.

- Do an internal check of your frustration/defensiveness meter. If your frustration and/or defensiveness is growing faster than the progress you are making in closing the gap between your perception and that of the teacher, it might be best to end the discussion and schedule a time to get together again in the near future. This will keep you from making non-productive statements and give you time to reflect and decide on whether there are other ways to word your concern that will better enable the teacher to hear and "own" those concerns.

Stage VI: Concluding the Discussion

- Generate options for next steps.
- Be aware of the consequences (alternatives to coming to agreement or ATAs) of not reaching consensus on the next steps. The extent to which you require next steps with which the teacher does not agree or continue to generate options until there is agreement often corresponds to the degree to which the teacher functions successfully or not.
- Summarize the conclusions reached in the conference.
- Set a date, time, location and tentative agenda for a follow-up discussion.

The framework as outlined in the stages of listening must always be considered within the context of the individual with whom the evaluator is meeting. Some teachers prefer that the evaluator "cut to the chase" if they believe the evaluator is working up to an area for improvement. Most, however, prefer the evaluator work through the stages and appreciate the give-and-take that this type of conference provides. Below are some sample questions that can be used with various performance standards.

Questions an Evaluator May Ask a Teacher About the Following Performance Standards on Assessment

Standard 1: The teacher effectively plans assessment of students' learning.

Standard II: The teacher monitors students' understanding of the curriculum effectively and adjusts instruction, materials or assessments when appropriate.

The following list is adapted from Colby's article (1999).
- How do you make decisions about the appropriate assessments to use?
- What types of assessments do you use in your classroom?
- How and when do you gather assessment information?
- What type of grading system do you use and how effective is it?
- What must students do to demonstrate proficiency on each curriculum standard?
- What supports do students who are not progressing receive?
- How is progress communicated to students and parents?

Questions an Evaluator Asks a Teacher About Professional Development Portfolios

Standard VII C: The teacher is a reflective and continuous learner.

The following list is based on Painter's article (2001).
- What ten to twelve artifacts can you put into your portfolio that represent your professional growth on all seven standards?
- What performance standard(s) does each artifact represent?
- Why is each artifact better than other artifacts that you could choose to represent this standard(s)?
- Can you explain the rationale for each artifact to someone who is viewing it out of the context of knowing a great deal about your classroom?
- How do the artifacts you chose represent to you and others your growth as a teacher?

Some districts are now creating a question bank of conference questions related to each of the district's performance standards.

SOURCES

Archer, J. (1999, May). Sanders 101. *Education Week,* 26.

Budd Rowe, M. (1986, January–February). Wait time! Slowing down may be a way of speeding up! *Journal of Teacher Education,* 43–49.

Colby, S. (1999, March). Grading in a standards-based system. *Educational Leadership,* 52–55.

Doran, H. (2003, December). Adding value to accountability. *Educational Leadership,* 55–59.

Gordon, T. (1979). *Leadership effectiveness training.* New York: Bantam Books.

Holloway, J. (2000, February). A value-added view of pupil performance. *Phi Delta Kappan,* 84–85.

Koppich, J. (2001). New York, New York. *Investing in teaching,* The National Alliance of Business, The Business Roundtable, National Association of Manufacturers and the U.S. Chamber of Commerce, p. 29.

Painter, B. (2001, February). Using teaching portfolios. *Educational Leadership.*

Ribas, W. (2003). *Maximizing teaching success.* Westwood, MA: Ribas Publications.

Stronge, J. & Tucker, P. (2000). *Teacher evaluation and student achievement.* Washington, DC: National Education Association of the United States.

The Public Relations (Political) Skills and Knowledge Needed to Work Effectively With Teachers' Associations/Unions and Other Constituencies

SAVVY TEACHERS' ASSOCIATIONS/UNIONS WANT TO BE YOUR PARTNER IN ENSURING EFFECTIVE SUPERVISION AND EVALUATION

In 1982 I served as vice-president of a local NEA affiliate in New Hampshire. In that position, I chaired the contract negotiations committee and the grievance committee. Over the last twenty-five years, I have moved from "labor" to "management" to a "neutral." I worked as a teacher, vice-principal, principal, director of pupil-personnel services and as an assistant superintendent for personnel. Most recently, I have been a consultant to various school districts' teacher's associations and administrators on the topic of supervision and evaluation of teachers and peer coaching, assistance and/or review. My role changed in these years, however, I saw very few changes in the basic structure and political forces that impacted school labor–management relations between 1982 and 1995.

Since 1995, the context of school labor–management relations has been changing at an accelerating pace. Public schools have been placed in a competitive environment unparalleled in other areas of public employment. Voucher programs, for-profit schools and charter schools have provided alternative education avenues to many families for whom alternatives were previously unavailable. Unlike the students who have historically attended independent schools, students who access these alternatives often take tax money that was earmarked for the local public school district with them to their new school setting. During the 1999–2000 school year, *Education Week* (Schnailberg & Walsh, 1999) ran a series of front page articles about the growth of for-profit education and for-profit schools. Since the publication of those issues, *Education Week* has included articles on the status of voucher programs and charter schools in various states and in the courts in almost every issue.

> Since 1995, the context of school labor–management relations has been changing at an accelerating pace.

We have also seen a shift in political support for voucher programs and other alternatives to public schools. During the 2000 presidential election the Democratic candidate for vice president came from a group of senators who had a record of favoring voucher programs! He significantly tempered that view once he was on the ticket. However, for most Americans, a Democratic candidate with this type of record would have been inconceivable just two years earlier.

A dozen for-profit companies now operate public schools. Beginning in the late 1990s, articles started to appear in the *Wall Street Journal* and *Business Week* describing the investment opportunities available in for-profit education. A front-page article written by Michael T. Moe, a research director for Merrill Lynch and Company, in the August 13, 1999 (Friday the 13th, mind you) *Wall Street Journal* gave the following analysis of the for-profit market.

> There are fewer than two dozen companies managing public schools now, and many operate only one or two schools. Education-management companies will grow over the next ten to fifteen years to account for 10% of U.S. elementary and secondary spending—about $36 billion dollars a year.

In these years, venture capitalists and other investors continued to invest large sums of money into those education companies, despite the fact that the companies had not yet turned a profit. An article in *Education Week* (Walsh, 2001, p. 5) indicated that venture capitalists invested 1.942 **BILLION** dollars in education companies during the year 2000 alone. The good news about the bad news is that during first half of 2001 that amount was only (if only is the right word when you are discussing this much money) 558 million dollars (Walsh, p. 5). Investors are predicting that the lobbying efforts they support to increase the number of voucher programs and charter schools will result in a significant increase in the shift of public education dollars toward for-profit education providers. From 1994 to 1999, the number of charter schools soared from 100 to 1700. In 1999, then U.S. secretary of education, Richard Riley, predicted the number of charter schools would reach 3,000 by 2002 (Symonds, 2000, p. 64). His prediction was only off by less than one year. In the fall of 2003, the web site of the organization US Charter Schools reported that there were almost 3,000 charter schools in the United States serving over 700,000 children. The proliferation of charter schools continues. The September 24, 2003 edition of *Education Week* (Keller, 2003, p. 24) reported that the Michigan legislature and the Michigan governor had reached an agreement that could add 150 charter schools in Michigan alone over the next ten years. That same issue of *Education Week* (Hendrie, 2003, p. 6) contained an article reporting that the Florida city of Pembroke Pines had established an entire school system of charter schools within Broward County, effectively seceding from the Broward County School District. With a population of 150,000 people, Pembroke Pines is larger than most of the individual city and town school districts found in the six New England States, New York, or New Jersey!

Voucher programs in various states have also opened the door for public money to leave public schools and move with the students to private schools. The 2003 United States Supreme Court ruling in Zelman vs. Simmons-Harris has given a significant boost to voucher programs. The ruling, which upheld an Ohio program of tuition aid to Cleveland students in private schools, made clear that states may choose to include religious schools in voucher programs.

United Mind Workers, a book about public school labor–management relations has been praised by the Rochester, NY, Federation of Teachers and American Federation of Teachers' leader Adam Urbanski as making "a timely and significant contribution to the future of labor management– relations." As this book states, "The assault on tenure now forming in state capitals is partly the result of the failure of school systems to create substantive evaluation systems and the failure of unions to develop peer review or other robust professional means of ensuring quality." (Kerchner, Koppich & Weeres, 1997, review on jacket)

MANY TEACHERS' ASSOCIATION/UNION LEADERS ARE LEADING THE WAY

Many school labor leaders recognize that public school boards and teachers' associations/unions need to prove to parents, taxpayers and legislators that school boards, administrators and teachers' associations/unions are working together to ensure that every child in the public schools receives a public education that is equal or better in quality then the other alternatives that are now becoming available to parents. In one district where I train, the funds for training the administrators in supervision and evaluation come from a grant written by the state affiliate of the American Federation of Teachers.

As the for-profit education, voucher and charter school movements increase their lobbying efforts in Washington, DC, and in state capitals, we see an increase in the flow of public money to public school alternatives. The proposed 2004 United States Department of Education budget increases charter school grant funds in the federal budget to $220,000,000 (Cavanagh, 2003) of taxpayer money. Savvy teachers' associations/unions, school boards and administrators see the enlightened self-interest served by developing effective systems of supervision and evaluation. They understand that an effective method of instructional quality control is one of the most powerful ways to counteract messages such as the following from a *Wall Street Journal* article:

> . . . because American public education in the 20th century has been organized much as a Soviet enterprise was . . . like one of those Soviet factories, it could just keep pumping out defective products . . . A nation made up of charter schools would entrench accountability, because every four years a district would reevaluate whether to renew the charter or hand the school to someone else . . . (*Wall Street Journal*, November 16, 1999).

The concern about charter schools, voucher programs and for-profit schools has shifted the playing field for local, state and federal leaders of teachers' associations/ unions. Prior to 1995, *A Nation at Risk* and other reports placed some public-relations (political) pressure on teachers' associations to look at their roles in ensuring high levels of performance. However, efforts of people such as Adam Urbanski, the late Albert Shanker (both from the American Federation of Teachers) and Bob Chase (past president of the National Education Association) to respond proactively to these pressures were often met with internal opposition from the membership. The opposition to the "New Unionism" was difficult for leaders to counteract because the threat to the traditional union bread and butter issues (wages, benefits, working conditions and job security) posed by these reports was more distant and abstract. These forces, coupled with the fear of lawsuits from members not given maximum protection (see the explanation in chapter 6 of a union's failure to meet the duty of fair representation) often forced all but the most visionary teachers' associations/union leaders to continue a course that protected low-performing teachers, even when management provided reasonable formative supports and adequate due process.

Today, the rapid growth of voucher programs and for-profit schools has made the threat to wages, benefits, working conditions and job security from loss of public funds more immediate for younger teachers. If these education alternatives capture ten percent of the students presently in public schools, as some predict could occur by 2010, there will be a significant decline in the number of public school teaching positions. This decline could lead to the layoff of younger staff. These teachers would be forced to take lower-paying jobs in charter, independent, religious and for-profit schools. A decline in public school jobs will also mean a decline in membership revenue for the teachers' associations/unions. This will decrease the financial ability of teachers' associations/unions to lobby and to maintain public information programs that promote public education. In my opinion, this is the *most difficult* time to be a teachers' association leader *in more than thirty years of teacher unionization.* The associations are squeezed between the financial and political pressures to reform and pressure from long-time members opposed to reforms that may negatively impact their present working conditions.

It takes a skilled and visionary local association president to balance these forces. All local presidents are elected by *today's* membership. In a time when much of the membership is within five to ten years of retirement age, it is difficult for association/union leaders to build support for programs that may increase accountability at some cost to protection. The members who will benefit from a policy geared toward maintaining the long-term viability of public education (by moving the association's support toward accountability for high performance) are likely to be in the minority of younger teachers or future teachers. Conversely, high- seniority teachers face the prospect of decreased protection without a quid pro quo benefit during their remaining years in the teaching work force. We should have tremendous respect for the many local

The Pressures on Teachers' Associations/Union Leaders as They Balance Their Role in Supervision and Evaluation Between Advocating for *More Teacher Performance Accountability* and Advocating for *Job Protections*

Prior to 1995

Duty of Fair Representation

Members' Demands

Teachers' Union Leaders

Public Reports

Accountablity ⟷ **Protection**

Figure 8

The Pressures on Teachers' Associations/Union Leaders as They Balance Their Role in Supervision and Evaluation Between Advocating for *More Teacher Performance Accountability* and Advocating for *Job Protections*

Duty of Fair Representation   **After 1995**   **Vouchers/For Profit**

⟶

Teachers' Union Leaders

Junior Members' Needs

Senior Members' Needs

⟶

⟵

Public Reports

⟵

Accountablity ⟷ **Protection**

Figure 9

presidents who maintain support for a policy that strives to achieve a balance between protecting members' rights and holding members accountable for high student performance.

SUPERVISION AND EVALUATION: QUALITY CONTROL FOR PUBLIC EDUCATION

The trust needed between management and labor to enable them to work together on quality control through supervision and evaluation takes time and work to develop. Teachers' associations/unions need to see that teachers identified as performing below standard will be given reasonable supports and a reasonable time period to improve. Evaluating administrators need to see that teachers' associations/unions will ensure reasonable supports and time to improve for their members, but they will not impede administrators from requiring all teachers to maintain a level of performance that ensures public education is competitive in quality and cost with charter, independent, religious and for-profit schools.

> The trust needed between management and labor to enable them to work together on quality control through supervision and evaluation takes time and work to develop.

In districts where this trust has been developed, I have seen teachers' associations/unions play an important role in supporting and maintaining quality programs of supervision and evaluation for tenured teachers. These are districts in which administrators and teachers' association representatives are trained to understand the E.L.P.S. factors in teacher evaluation. The administration and teachers' association have learned to work cooperatively to balance the need to be certain that due process rights are not ignored and also to require high levels of performance. Low-performing teachers receive the feedback, support and time they need to improve, resulting in adequate improvement by most. Those who do not improve, after adequate feedback and support, recognize it is time to leave and do so (often with counseling from the teachers' union/association), are asked to leave and do so or are dismissed using the appropriate legal standards for due process.

THE PUBLIC RELATIONS (POLITICAL) SOLUTION

I believe the following quote from the joint AFT/NEA manual on *Peer Assistance and Review* (1998) best sums up the public relations battle that faces teachers' associations/unions, school boards and administrators if they are to reverse the momentum in the United States toward increasing the number of voucher and charter school programs to the detriment of the public schools.

> The public, for its part, is concerned about the quality of schools and about the quality of the teachers in them. While a large majority of the public (85%) trusts teachers to make sound educational decisions (National Center for Education Information, 1996), citizens believe that a small percentage of teachers are not qualified and should not be teaching. Moreover, the public is frustrated by what it perceives as an inability to remove inadequate teachers from the classroom. The public attributes the difficulty in firing bad teachers to rules and regulations developed by teacher unions.

The 33rd Annual Phi Delta Kappan/Gallup Poll of the Public's Attitudes Toward the Public Schools

The following statistics from polls in 1993, 1998, 2001 and 2002 jointly sponsored by *Phi Delta Kappan* and Gallup, (Gallup & Rose, 2002) seem to indicate the slide in confidence in public schools began to reverse direction until the 2002 poll. We must continue to build public confidence with demonstrated high quality supervision and evaluation if we hope to receive public support for our schools.

1. Do you favor or oppose allowing students and parents to choose a private school to attend at public expense?

National Totals	2002	2001	1998	1993
Favor	46%	34%	44%	24%
Oppose	52	62	50	74
Don't know	2	4	6	2

2. A proposal has been made that would allow parents to send their school-age children to any public, private or church-related school they choose. For those parents choosing nonpublic schools, the government would **pay all or part of** the tuition. Would you favor or oppose this proposal in your state?

	National Totals				Public School Parents		
	2002	2001	1998	1994	2001	1998	1994
Favor	52%	44%	51%	45%	52%	56%	48%
Oppose	46	54	45	54	47	40	51
Don't know	2	2	4	1	1	4	1

3. In order to improve public education in America, some people think the focus should be on reforming the existing public school system. Others believe the focus should be on finding an alternative to the existing public school system. Which approach do you think is preferable—reforming the existing public school system or finding an alternative to the existing public school system?

	National Totals					No Children in School					Public School Parents				
	'02 %	'01 %	'00 %	'99 %	'97 %	'02 %	'01 %	'00 %	'99 %	'97 %	'02 %	'01 %	'00 %	'99 %	'97 %
Reforming existing system	69	72	59	71	71	69	73	59	73	70	69	73	60	68	72
Finding alternative system	27	24	34	27	23	26	23	34	24	23	27	25	34	30	24
Don't know	4	4	7	2	6	5	4	7	3	7	4	2	6	2	4

*71% of whites would reform the existing system, as compared to 60% of nonwhites.

4. Which one of these two plans would you prefer—improving and strengthening the existing public schools or providing vouchers for parents to use in selecting and paying for private and/or church-related schools?

	National Totals		No Children in School		Public School Parents	
	2002	2001	2002	2001	2002	2001
Improving and Strengthening Existing Public Schools	69%	71%	69%	71%	72%	73%
Providing Vouchers	29	27	28	26	27	25
Neither	—	—	—	—	—	—
Don't know	2	2	3	3	1	—

*38% of Republicans select providing vouchers; 24% of Democrats.

The issue of low-performing teachers not being required to improve or leave is a real one in many districts. However, it is not present in all districts. We must ask ourselves why it is that two districts in the same state, with the same statewide union leadership, the same labor laws and the same resources can exist side-by-side with one effectively dealing with low-performing teachers while the other district is virtually ineffective in dealing with this issue? To place the blame solely on the union in that state or district is unfair and inaccurate.

Chapter 6 examines the roadblocks that inhibit districts' ability to adequately address their low-performing teachers' performance issues. The chapter describes how some districts effectively address the issue. You will see that there is sufficient blame to go around. Yes, there are some state union uniserve workers and some local association presidents who still respond to the issue of addressing low-performing teachers as if the political dynamics were the same as they were in 1990. You will also see, however, that most districts have neither trained their evaluators adequately, nor created adequate support structures for evaluators so they can perform the difficult task of addressing unsatisfactory teaching. The result is that the number of districts and evaluators in those districts that can adequately address low-performing teaching is relatively low, regardless of the teachers' associations'/unions' influence.

The key to reversing the public relations and political disaster we create for ourselves by not adequately supervising and evaluating all teachers is for the following to take place.

1. Evaluators and school boards must stop pointing fingers at the associations/unions with accusations that they are protecting bad teachers and

must accept the responsibility for effectively training and supporting evaluators so they can effectively evaluate all teachers, particularly low-performing teachers. (See chapter 2 for more information about effective training.)

2. Association/union leaders must teach, coach, and assess the way their state uniserve consultants, local presidents and grievance people respond to evaluators when a teacher is being intensively supervised and evaluated for low performance. These leaders must be taught the difference between actions that ensure a member's rights and those that protect bad teachers.

EACH PARTY MUST OWN ITS PART OF THE PROBLEM! A CASE OF INSTITUTIONAL FINGER POINTING

The first time I worked with a district to improve system-wide supervision and evaluation, I met with various groups in the district to ask why supervision and evaluation didn't work in that district. The first group I spoke with was the principals. The perspective from principals was that the "union's grievance philosophy is to protect the worst-performing teachers to the fullest, regardless of how well the evaluation is completed." A number of the principals related stories ranging from one about the state uniserve person yelling at them in final evaluation meetings to another in which the uniserve representative threatened the principal physically. A high school department head, whose administrators' union was represented by the same local as the teachers' union, told of his attempt to evaluate a low-performing teacher. A local teachers' union grievance person walked into his office, closed the door and said, "We're all in this together. It's us (unionized employees) against them (the senior administration and school committee). Why are you taking their side against one of your own?"

In a subsequent conversation with the superintendent, it was confirmed that the incidents related in these stories had indeed taken place. After the physical threat, the superintendent called the local president to ask his assistance in moderating the actions of the uniserve representative. The president responded that he fully supported the uniserve person's behavior. The superintendent sent a letter to the uniserve person expressing his dismay, but felt powerless to do more. The principals felt besieged and threatened by the union and powerless to appropriately evaluate low-performing tenured teachers. Their response to parents' complaints about these tenured low performers was to tell parents that they could do very little because of the union's aggressive protection of bad teachers. This caused the concerned parents to voice their concerns to the superintendent and school committee. The superintendent, being new to the district and powerless to deal with tenured low-performing teachers because of an ineffective evaluation process, was forced to transfer low performers to other schools and/or reassign them to lower-level jobs at their teacher's salary.

When I began my work with this district, I had just finished seven years as a principal in another district. My experience had been with a local president and vice president who required any principal evaluating a low-performing teacher to be clear about expectations and provide adequate supports, frequent feedback and time to improve. If the evaluator took these steps however, the association/union ensured the teachers' rights were not violated, but also participated as a positive force for improvement in all meetings related to the evaluation. The district provided its administrators with constant training in topics such as difficult conferences and observing and documenting teachers' performance. The district also provided evaluators of low-performing teachers with legal coaching by a labor attorney well versed in teacher evaluations. Four times in those seven years I had undertaken the supervision and evaluation of teachers performing below standard. In two cases the teachers improved their performance and continued to teach for many years thereafter. In two other instances I had to find the teachers unsatisfactory and move toward further action. In the first of these two, I informed the teacher that she needed to improve in a fixed period of time or she would be dismissed. She was eventually dismissed. In the second, the teacher was started on a year-long improvement plan with intensive support and summative evaluation when I left the district. At no time did I ever feel the teachers' association/ union was threatening or in any way unreasonable in their requests.

The next group I spoke with about the district's performance on evaluation was the local president and the chairs of the grievance committee. I asked why they thought low-performing tenured teachers were not required to improve or leave. The group's response was that the evaluators weren't doing their jobs. They reported that the evaluators were not following the contracted process, nor were they meeting the due process standard and, in many cases, they were not even doing their evaluations. They further reported that there were no consistent standards among the evaluators (no inter-rater reliability). Some evaluators gave everyone glowing evaluations. Others evaluated the same performance in a very different way. After the meeting, I spent a considerable amount of time reading the evaluations that had been completed during the previous year. I found that all the claims of the association/union members were correct. Only 30% of the required evaluations had been completed in the previous year. Of those 30%, only a third had used the correct forms and procedures. Evaluators had not had any district-sponsored training in supervision and evaluation for over five years. After reading a number of evaluations, I called one principal who had been doing a good job to compliment her on her work. She stopped me midway through a sentence, saying, "I can't believe you read my evaluations! I've been a principal here for fifteen years and I don't think anyone ever read any of the evaluations before. This is wonderful."

Five years later, this district has gone from having one of the most dysfunctional supervision and evaluation systems I've worked with to having one of the most effective supervision and evaluation programs in the state. The district has gone from effectively addressing none of its low-performing tenured teachers to addressing all of its low-performing tenured teachers (2% to 3% of the teaching staff as is indicated in the literature) using the program outlined in chapter 6. Comprehensive training, coaching and assessment is provided for all evaluators. The teachers' association/union grievance people meet to discuss cases and most have responded in a far less aggressive manner as the evaluators have improved their inter-rater reliability and overall performance. It is still my hope that the quality of training for evaluators will increase and that those grievance people who are most effective in this area will train and further influence their colleagues.

> Without a commitment from superintendents and school boards to train and support evaluators so they can effectively evaluate all teachers, a district cannot have a successful system of supervision and evaluation. Without a commitment from state and local teachers' associations/unions to train uniserve people, local presidents and grievance people to ensure rights without protecting bad teachers and to avoid intimidation tactics, teachers' associations/unions are doomed to be targeted by the public as roadblocks to effective public education.

The crucial factor in the example above from a public relations (political) point of view, is that the district's evaluators and parents no longer have reason to say that supervision and evaluation of low-performing tenured teachers is impossible within the present set of state laws. Without a commitment from superintendents and school boards to train and support evaluators so they can effectively evaluate all teachers, a district cannot have a successful system of supervision and evaluation. Without a commitment from state and local teachers' associations/unions to train uniserve people, local presidents and grievance people to ensure rights without protecting bad teachers and to avoid intimidation tactics, teachers' associations/unions are doomed to be targeted by the public as roadblocks to effective public education. Unless management and labor each do their part in providing adequate training and support, public schools are destined for extinction or to be solely for those children in our society whose parents lack the knowledge, assertiveness and/or skill to access the so-called "better options" for their children.

SOURCES

American Federation of Teachers and the National Education Association. (1998). *Peer assistance & peer review: an AFT/NEA handbook.* Washington, DC.

Cavanaugh, S. (2003, December 3). Agreement reached on education spending. *Education Week,* 21.

Curriculum frameworks. (1995). Malden, MA: Massachusetts Department of Education.

Gallup, A. & Rose, L. (2002, September). The 33rd annual *Phi Delta Kappan*/Gallup Poll of the public's attitudes toward the public schools. *Phi Delta Kappan,* 41–58.

Hendrie, C. (2003, September 24). Using charter schools' powers, booming Florida city opts to build own charter schools. *Education Week,* 6.

Johnson, J. & Immerwahrl, J. (1994). *First things first: what Americans expect from public schools.* New York: The Public Agenda Foundation.

Keller, B. (2003, September 24). Michigan strikes deal on charter schools, 6.

Kerchner, Koppich & Weeres. (1997). *United mind workers.* San Francisco: Jossey & Bass.

McTighe, J. & Wiggins, G. (1999). *Understanding by design.* Alexandria, VA: Association of Supervision and Curriculum Development.

Moe, M. T. (1999, August 13). Tesseract and others march briskly ahead in school privatization. *Wall Street Journal.*

Profiles of teachers in the U.S. survey. (1996). Washington, DC: National Center for Education Information.

Ribas, W. (2000, April). Ascending the ELPS to excellence in your district's teacher evaluation. *Phi Delta Kappan,* 585–589.

Schnailberg, L. & Walsh, M. (1999, November/December). The new business of schooling. *Education Week,* Volume XIX, Nos. 13, 14, 15, and 16.

Symonds, W. (2000, February). For-profit schools. *Business Week,* 64.

Turning schools right side up. (1999, November 16).
    Wall Street Journal [Editorial].

Walsh, M. (2001, August 8) Seed money drying up for education-
    related businesses, *Education Week,* 5.

What teachers should be able to do. (1994). Washington, DC: National
    Board for Professional Teaching Standards.

CHAPTER
6

The Legal Processes and Standards as They Relate to Supervising and Evaluating Low-Performing Teachers

Successfully supervising and evaluating a low-performing tenured (aka permanent, professional status) teacher[1] is one of the most difficult, time-consuming, emotionally charged and important tasks that administrators undertake. The difficulty of the task is due in part to the natural conflict that occurs between the techniques the evaluator must employ to meet the legal requirements while balancing the social–emotional impact of the evaluation on the teacher and the department/school as a whole. The legal procedures require sensitive yet clear and frank discussion about inadequate performance and a significant amount of written documentation. These requirements in

---

1 The formative suggestions in this chapter have application to provisional teachers as well as to teachers with tenure. However, the summative standards related to the law concerning dismissal are typically only applicable to tenured teachers. In most states and Canadian provinces, provisional teachers who have not achieved tenure do not have due process protections unless they are dismissed in the middle of the year. Typically, the contract of a low-performing teacher without tenure is just not renewed for the subsequent year. Due process in these situations only becomes an issue if there is the possibility of a discrimination claim based on race, religion, age, sex or handicap.

Successfully supervising and evaluating a low-performing teacher is one of the most difficult, time-consuming, emotionally charged and important tasks that administrators undertake.

turn raise the teacher's anxiety level and, at times, that of his/her colleagues. The meetings, observations and written documents these evaluations require may make a single difficult evaluation as time-consuming as five to ten of the administrator's other evaluations.

It is important for evaluators to understand the legal basis for the evaluation procedures used by their districts. In most districts, evaluators typically become aware of the "L" in the E.L.P.S. only when one of their evaluations of a low-performing teacher is challenged. At that point it is usually too late to effectively use the legal information. An example is that of an administrator who worked collaboratively with a representative of the teachers' association on a low-performing teacher's evaluation. The administrator wrote an improvement plan and reviewed the district's performance standards with the teacher at the start of each of two years. She observed the teacher's classes frequently, providing the teacher with clear written and oral feedback, several staff development opportunities and a colleague mentor. (See the seven tests for just cause, on page 170.)

As is important, *the evaluator maintained the hope and belief that the teacher could improve* and complete her career satisfactorily.[2] Unfortunately, even with this support, the teacher still could not be successful. The administrator decided that she needed to find the teacher to be unsatisfactory and recommend dismissal. The school district's labor attorney reviewed the documents from the administrator's two years of work with this teacher and determined that the case would likely be upheld in arbitration. The assistant superintendent, who had monitored the evaluation throughout the two years, knew how much time the evaluator had devoted to the evaluation and asked the administrator how her other evaluations were progressing. The administrator became quiet. She eventually spoke up and reported that since she had been so busy with this evaluation she did not think she would be able to complete the other evaluations on time. The evaluator thought this wouldn't be a problem, since the other teachers were performing well. Fortunately, it was early enough in the school year to correct the error and have the administrator complete the other evaluations on time. Had she not done so, the administrator's evaluation of the low-performing teacher might have been open to claims that she had not applied the system's standards evenhandedly. (See the

---

2 I call this the Pollyanna Principle. At the outset of an intensive evaluation, the administrator must force him/herself to believe the teacher can improve to a satisfactory level. This is often one of the most difficult ideas to teach to an administrator. Some teachers will disappoint you and eventually need to leave the profession, however, most will surprise you by the progress they make when you have followed the procedures in this chapter.

seven tests of just cause, on page 170.) The administrator may have jeopardized the comprehensive evaluation she had prepared for the low-performing teacher.

Teachers' associations are legally bound to provide a *reasonable level* of representation to their members. An association that does not provide this level of representation leaves itself open to being sued by teachers for failure to meet its duty of fair representation. (See the explanation of the duty of fair representation legal standard, on pages 170–172.) In the example above, the teachers' association representative had

> Accepting the need to change *is one of the most significant differences* between teachers who do improve and continue in the profession and those who do not. A skilled representative is often better able to help the teacher understand and accept the need to change than the evaluator would be.

been involved as an observer and appropriate advocate and support resource for the teacher throughout the two years of the formal supervision and evaluation process. The representative knew that the administrator and the district made genuine efforts to provide support and an opportunity for the teacher to succeed and that the teacher had not sufficiently improved. Had the procedural problem mentioned above not been caught in time, however, the teachers' association may have found itself in a situation where it believed it needed to represent the teacher through arbitration in order to avoid being charged with failure to meet its duty of fair representation.

The key words related to the test of fair representation are *reasonable level* of representation. Most association representatives ensure a reasonable level to protect themselves and their members, but they will not protect a poorly-performing teacher who has received reasonable notice, support and time to improve, but still has failed to be consistently successful on the district's performance standards. At times, an association representative may unreasonably protect a teacher because he/she does not know the standard for fair representation or does not wish to offend the teacher. This is more likely to occur in districts where there has been inadequate dialogue between the association and the administration about the public relations component of the E.L.P.S. Fortunately, many association representatives are aware of the legislative and public relations implications on public education of their role in supervision and evaluation. They are committed to reasonable representation, but not to protection for low-performing teachers who have failed to improve.

Having a skilled association representative at all meetings with low-performing teachers may be helpful. Negative information about one's performance is often difficult for someone to understand and accept. The association representative may serve as a safe person with whom the teacher may discuss the information in private. Accepting the need to change *is one of the most significant differences* between teachers who do improve and continue in the profession and those who do not. A skilled representative is often better able to help the teacher understand and accept the need to change than the evaluator would be.

Involving the association representative early gives the association an opportunity to help the teacher explore all alternatives for improvement and to access emotional support such as counseling. It allows the association to put its energy and resources into assisting rather than protecting teachers. Should the evaluation not lead to improvement after a reasonable period of time and support, the association representative has access to career and retirement counseling resources for the teacher. Even in those cases in which a teacher must leave the profession, administrators and the teachers' association both want to help the teacher leave with dignity. If the representative has been involved throughout, the association has clearly met its duty of fair representation.

> Involving the association representative early gives the association an opportunity to help the teacher explore all alternatives for improvement and to access emotional support such as counseling. It allows the association to put its energy and resources into assisting rather than protecting teachers.

This section contains documents and procedures that will assist administrators in meeting the legal and educational requirements while balancing the public relations and social–emotional components of working with low-performing teachers. The work with low-performing teachers in districts using this program has resulted in some low-performing teachers leaving the profession. However, most of the teachers supervised and evaluated in accordance with the procedures outlined in this chapter have improved to a satisfactory level of teaching and consequently feel more fulfilled in their jobs.

WHAT DO DUE PROCESS AND JUST CAUSE MEAN?

A public employee's right to due process prior to discipline or dismissal is embedded in three levels of law: contract, state and constitutional.

The procedural requirement that governs the evaluation of most public employees is *just cause*. Typical contract language concerning just cause reads as follows:

> No teacher (administrator) who has acquired tenure (professional or permanent status in some states) shall be discharged or otherwise disciplined without just cause.

A typical example of state law is the following language from the Massachusetts General Laws, chapter 71, section 42:

A teacher with professional teacher status (tenure), shall not be dismissed except for inefficiency, incompetency, incapacity, conduct unbecoming a teacher, insubordination, failure on the part of the teacher to satisfy the teacher performance standards developed . . . or other *just cause*. (Finnegan, 2000, pp. *71–74*) (emphasis added)

The United States Supreme Court has determined that a person's job is a property right and is therefore protected under the Fourteenth Amendment to the United States Constitution:

No state shall make or enforce any law which shall abridge the privileges or immunities of citizens of the United States; nor shall any state deprive any person of life, liberty *or property* without *due process*. (emphasis added)

The following description is adapted from a training document that was written by Robert Fraser (1996), a partner in Stoneman, Chandler & Miller, a law firm that represents numerous school districts in labor relations and teacher evaluation matters. Dr. Fraser is a practicing attorney and has a Ph.D. in Education. He has worked as a uniserve representative for the Massachusetts Teachers Association and as an assistant superintendent of schools prior to practicing law and representing school boards in cases of labor law.

Among the earliest cases (defining just cause in teacher dismissal) was a 1984 decision in which Arbitrator Archibald Cox (of Watergate fame) stated that just cause is absent *unless* three requirements are satisfied:

1. The employee committed the offense or was guilty of the shortcoming ascribed to him;

2. The misconduct or shortcoming justified the disciplinary measure; and

3. The procedure was consistent with fundamental fairness.

(Needham Education Association and Needham School Committee, 1984)

The Cox definition, which although better than none at all, falls far short of giving school officials the guidance they need in order to determine whether or not just cause exists to discipline a teacher whose performance has been unsatisfactory. Just cause cannot include reasons that are arbitrary, unfair or generated out of some petty vendetta. (Briggs v. Board of Directors of Hinton Community School District, 1979)

Traditionally, in determining whether or not an employer had just cause to dismiss an employee, arbitrators will pose the following questions.

[The paragraphs in italics have been added by the author to connect the seven standards to the daily tasks of teacher evaluation. —William Ribas]

1. Was the employee informed of management's rules and expectations?

   Districts should make all teachers aware of the district's performance standards. Some districts give the performance standards to every teacher at the beginning of each school year. At the very least, the performance standards should be given to teachers and discussed with them at the beginning of years in which those teachers will receive a summative evaluation.

2. Were management's rules and expectations reasonable?

   In states where the performance standards are collectively bargained, the standards themselves are considered by all parties to be reasonable. It is the implementation by individual administrators that may be questioned.

3. Was the employee's alleged infraction investigated?

   Administrators must gather adequate evidence. Later in this chapter is a detailed explanation of the rules of evidence as they relate to teacher evaluation.

4. Were the procedures followed by the employer fair?

   In many states, the due process procedures are collectively bargained and therefore certified as fair by management and the union. In these states, it is often the implementation of the standards by individual administrators that may be questioned.

5. Has management applied its rules or standards evenhandedly?

   The degree to which administrators consistently implement the standards and procedures (inter-rater reliability) *is important.*

6. Was the employee given an opportunity to improve?

   The use of improvement plans that include monitoring systems and supports is discussed in depth later in this chapter.

7. Did the penalty fit the "crime"?

   The concept of progressive discipline and its connection to supervision and evaluation is discussed in chapter 7.

A negative response to any one of the foregoing questions may indicate a lack of just cause for the employer's action. (Fraser, 1993, as cited in Fraser, 1996).

THE DUTY OF FAIR REPRESENTATION

Along with the right of the union to be the exclusive representative of all employees in the bargaining unit goes the duty of the union to represent everyone fairly. The legal term for this is the duty of fair representation (a.k.a. DFR).

The collective bargaining laws in most states do not specifically refer to this duty. However, collective bargaining laws have been interpreted by judges to require the duty of fair representation. The applicable court cases have defined that duty to mean that a union

1. has a duty to fairly represent all the employees in the bargaining unit, both in collective bargaining and in the enforcement of the contract through the grievance and arbitration procedures

2. must serve the interests of all members of the unit without hostility or discrimination toward any

3. must exercise its decision-making power with good faith and honesty and must avoid arbitrary conduct; therefore, decisions, must be made in a reasonable and rational manner

Grievances: The decision of the union whether or not to process a grievance must be based on the merits of that particular grievance and on a thorough investigation of the facts of the particular situation. The decision whether or not to process a grievance may not be based on personal hostility, political opposition, illegal discrimination or any other irrational or unreasonable basis.

In many states, an individual may pursue a grievance on her/his own, without assistance from the union. However, the union must be given the opportunity to be present at any meetings between the grievant and supervisors/management representatives to ensure that any adjustments made are consistent with the terms of the contract.

Arbitration: As with grievances, the decision whether or not to take a grievance beyond the school board level (arbitration, state board or court, depending on the state or province) must be based on the merits of the grievance. The basis of the decision must be reasonable and rational. State laws vary on whether or not an individual can take a grievance beyond the school board without union approval. For example, in Massachusetts, the decision to arbitrate a grievance belongs to the union. However, in the case of dismissals, a teacher may appeal her/his dismissal to arbitration without assistance or approval from the union, as provided by the Education Reform Act of 1993, which modified Massachusetts General Law, chapter 71, section 42, which is related to the dismissal of teachers. (Dorine Levasseur, Massachusetts Teachers Association Field Consultant, 1999).

Legal Standards for Determining if the Union/Association Has Violated Its Duty of Fair Representation for a Member

The American Federation of Teachers and the National Education Association provide its state and local affiliates with information designed to inform its representatives about the duty of fair representation. The following guidelines for unions/associations appear in a jointly published document entitled *Peer Assistance & Review: An AFT/NEA Handbook* (American Federation of Teachers and National Education Association, 1998).

1. If the decision not to pursue a grievance was not arbitrary, capricious, based on discrimination or hostility toward the grievant or was rational, a court will not second-guess the wisdom of that decision (by the union/association).

2. Honest mistakes or misjudgments by the union do not constitute violations of the duty of fair representation.

3. Before finding a DFR violation, courts will look for evidence of improper motive or bad faith by the union.

WEINGARTEN RIGHT

This explanation of the Weingarten right is based on an article that first appeared a local teacher's association newsletter. It is adapted here with the permission of the local and the author, Dorine Levasseur, Massachusetts Teachers Association Field Representative.

The name comes from a 1975 United States Supreme Court case that held that it is unlawful for an employer to deny an employee's request that a union representative be present at an investigative interview which an employee reasonably believes might result in disciplinary action. The following rules tell teachers how to access those rights.

Rule 1: The teacher must make a clear request for union representation before or during an interview or meeting (*unlike the "Miranda" right that requires police officers to explain a person's rights before the meeting begins*). If the teacher believes an interview might lead to discipline somewhere down the road, or that's the way the meeting begins to unfold, the teacher may immediately tell the supervisor conducting the meeting that he/she wants to suspend the meeting until a union representative is present.

Rule 2: The supervisor must grant the request and wait until a union representative can be present, deny the request and continue the interview or give the employee the choice between having the interview without representation or ending the interview. Teachers are typically advised by their unions that in such situations the teacher should not continue without representation.

Rule 3: If the supervisor denies the request for representation and continues the interview, the teacher has the right to refuse to answer questions. However, the teacher must sit there until the supervisor terminates the interview. Teachers are typically advised by their unions/associations that if the supervisor continues the meeting, the teacher should take notes. In my experience, it may often be advantageous to the supervisor to delay the meeting for a reasonable period of time to permit representation. Most of these discussions are to obtain information and a delay of several hours or a day does not negatively impact the situation. In fact, the presence of a representative may make the conversation run more smoothly and be less confrontational. However, the administrator should not delay the meeting if there is a possibility the teacher will commit an inappropriate act if he/she is not given a clearly stated expectation by the supervisor immediately.

AN EVALUATOR'S GUIDE TO GATHERING AND VERIFYING EVIDENCE

In earlier chapters, we discussed the differences between data, information and evidence. **Data** includes everything in and out of the school environment that the evaluator comes in contact with that pertains to the teacher being supervised/evaluated. **Evidence** is data that is sufficiently verified and is used to make a judgment. **Information** is some data that leads us to make the decision that we need more data before we can make a judgment. Information can become evidence in two ways. First, the information is supported by evidence. Second, the information is of a level of accumulation that a "reasonable person" would conclude that the event inferred by the information did take place.

Gathering and documenting evidence is important in all evaluations. Stating evidence in conferences and write-ups is an effective way to recognize and acknowledge hard work and excellent performance. It is also a way to mirror for teachers their performance so they can self-evaluate. For these purposes, evidence is a formative, educational and social–emotional tool. The evaluator need not be concerned with the legal aspects of gathering and documenting evidence. The situation changes, however, when the evaluator is working with a less than satisfactory teacher.

> Gathering and documenting evidence is important in all evaluations. Stating evidence in conferences and write-ups is an effective way to recognize and acknowledge hard work and excellent performance. It is also a way to mirror for teachers their performance so they can self-evaluate.

Since in these cases there is always the possibility of a dismissal or disciplinary hearing, it is essential that the evaluator understand the legal requirements for gathering and verifying evidence. This section is written to help evaluators better understand the legal concept of *evidence* as it relates to the supervision and evaluation of low-performing teachers.

Evidence is " . . . any species of proof, or facts, legally presented at the trial or arbitration hearing of an issue" (Liacos, 1999). Administrators or supervisors involved in evaluations that may be challenged should remember that most evidence will be introduced through the evaluator's testimony, making the fact-gathering process very important. **Testimony** is "evidence given by a witness under oath either orally or in the form of affidavits or depositions" (Liacos, 1999).

Direct evidence is, " . . . evidence in the form of testimony from a witness who actually saw, heard or touched the subject of interrogation" (Garner, 1999, pp. 576–580). Direct evidence, if believed, will prove a fact without any *inference*. The most common type of *direct evidence* used in an evaluation is evaluator observation. These include observing the teacher in the classroom, outside of the classroom and reviewing artifacts such as assignments, assessments, classroom design, etc.

A second type of *direct evidence* is written or oral complaints or reports given to the evaluator by another party who witnessed the behavior. In schools, this information usually comes from another staff member, a student or a parent who has been directly impacted by or has directly observed the teacher's action. Initially, this is considered to be indirect or hearsay evidence. (See the explanation below.) However, if an evaluation goes to arbitration or another type of hearing, this evidence can be made direct if the person giving the testimony is willing to testify at the arbitration or submit an affidavit under oath.

Most frequently, this second type of evidence in an evaluation comes from parents and so, for purposes of illustration, I will use actual parent examples. In most situations when evaluators receive parents' complaints, the best course of action is to refer the parents to the teacher to discuss the issue. It often empowers the reticent parent to speak to the teacher if the evaluator also offers the person the opportunity to come back if the parent does not have a satisfactory discussion with the teacher. In cases in which the parent has already spoken to the teacher without success or the parent is afraid to speak to the teacher alone, the next course of action is usually a meeting with the teacher, the parent and the evaluator. This type of meeting serves two purposes. First, it allows the evaluator to mediate, moving the pair toward a win–win solution. Second, it enables the evaluator to thoroughly investigate the situation and determine whether or not the problem is the result of problematic teacher behavior. I have, in a select few instances, delayed this joint meeting and met with the teacher alone with permission to use the parent's name. I have done this when I felt that either party's level of emotion might preclude a productive meeting. In those cases, separate meetings allowed me to help each party work through his/her emotions, until he/she was able to resolve the issue by dealing with the facts.

> The major difficulty for evaluators with statements from other witnesses is verification of testimony by parents who refuse to have their names used.

The major difficulty for evaluators with statements from other witnesses is verification of testimony by parents who refuse to have their names used. Often a parent may call with information about an issue of which the evaluator was not aware, but the parent refuses to allow the evaluator to use his/her name. Typically, this reluctance is due to a fear that the teacher will take retribution on the student.[3] If the evaluator cannot persuade the parent to allow use of his/her name, yet judges the complaint as worthy of further investigation, the evaluator may then make observations in an attempt to establish the veracity of the complaint. (See the Indirect Data Decision Tree on page 181.) In most cases, however, a complaint from a person who wishes to remain anonymous is difficult to verify and, therefore, of little or even no use as credible evidence in an evaluation.

Circumstantial evidence is "testimony not based on actual personal knowledge or observation of the facts in controversy, but of other facts from which deductions are drawn, showing indirectly the facts sought to be proved" (Garner, 1999, pp. 576–580). An example of this type of evidence would be a consistently lower enrollment rate for a particular high school teacher as compared to that of other colleagues teaching the same class. A lower enrollment during only one year is information but not evidence of a performance issue. However, an *accumulation* of occurrences of this situation would lead a reasonable person to *infer* that there is a problem that requires further investigation and possible intervention. One school district faced with this situation took the following steps to deal effectively with the alleged problem without violating the teacher's rights.

1. The evaluator, in this case the department head, increased the level of unannounced observation in the teacher's classroom. This activity was deemed warranted to gather additional information with which to verify or negate the claims made by parents and students.

2. The principal directed the assistant principal in charge of scheduling students to fully enroll that teacher's classes for the start of the next school year.

3. The principal directed the guidance counselors (who typically removed students from the class during the summer at parents' requests) to refer disgruntled parents to the teacher and, if necessary, meet with the parents and the teacher to resolve the issues and keep the students in the class. If these interventions failed, counselors were directed to refer the parents to the department head/evaluator.

---

[3] During my nine years as a vice principal and principal, I supervised and evaluated over eighty different teachers. I had dozens of calls from parents who were initially afraid to have their names attached to a complaint about a teacher for fear that there would be retribution on their child. In every case, I encouraged the parent to speak with the teacher about the complaint. In the one instance when I suspected a teacher may punish a child for a parent's complaint, I met with the teacher early in our supervisory relationship and shared that this was a concern of the parents. I told her that I wasn't assuming it to be true, however, I wanted her to know I would consider behavior of that sort a very serious breach of professional ethics and conduct unbecoming a teacher. In nine years, I did not have one instance of a teacher taking retribution on a child. This is not to say it would never happen, but I believe the occurrence of such behavior is extremely rare.

4. The evaluator then worked with the situation in the way described earlier in the description of *direct evidence* by a witness other than the evaluator. If, after a reasonable period of time and effort, the student was not successful, the evaluator would recommend to the principal that the student be removed from the class. The evaluator kept notes of all discussions and actions taken throughout this process. When a student was removed, the evaluator documented all of these steps in a memo to the teacher.

Hearsay evidence is "evidence not proceeding from the personal knowledge of the witness, but from the mere repetition of what he has heard others say" (Garner, 1999, pp. 576–580). Hearsay evidence is often not admissible in court, but it is generally admissible in administrative hearings such as arbitrations. The arbitrators will determine the appropriate weight given to the hearsay evidence. Arbitrators place greater credibility on hearsay evidence when it is cumulative. An example of this is the parent input letters elementary principals often receive in the spring when they are making classes for the upcoming year. These letters often express the same or similar concerns about a teacher's ability to effectively teach the parents' children. In some cases, these letters are first-hand accounts from parents who previously had other children in the teacher's classes. In most cases they are hearsay accounts based on information the parents received from other parents. The accumulation of these hearsay accounts may cause a reasonable person to deduce that a problem exists, thereby making this evidence circumstantial.

CASE STUDY: USING THE VARIOUS TYPES OF EVIDENCE

One example of using various types of evidence in an evaluation was a first year principal who, upon arrival in the district, heard a number of accounts from parents and staff about a fourth grade teacher who had a reputation for intimidating students. A review of the teacher's file showed no documentation of the problem by the previous principal. In fact, the previous evaluations of the teacher had been quite positive. When the new principal asked about the teacher, however, the retiring principal shrugged his shoulders and said that the problem had been going on for years. The way the retiring principal had dealt with parents' concerns about class assignments for the upcoming year was to put only sixteen students in the class while the other fourth grade classes each had twenty-one or twenty-two students.

During the course of the next year, the new principal had two complaints from parents of students in the class about their children being afraid of this fourth grade teacher. He referred each parent to the teacher, as suggested earlier. In the case of one child, after the parents had two meetings with the teacher, the principal met with the teacher and parents to try to resolve the issue. Two other meetings of this type were required when the child refused to come to school, and the parents had to physically carry the child into the classroom. The child was eventually switched to another class. During that year, the principal had only two other complaints of children being afraid of their teachers from the parents of the other 539 students in the building. No other child needed to be removed from any class.

The principal observed the teacher six times. Three were scheduled observations and three were unannounced observations. He wrote comprehensive observation write-ups for each. The teachers' association president attended all the post-observation conference meetings between the teacher and the principal.

As was typical, in early May the principal sent a letter to parents inviting their written input to the staff about the development of class assignments for the upcoming year. There were twenty classroom teachers in grades 1 through 5. The parents of the 450 students going into grades 1 through 5 sent ninety-three input letters. (This was a K–5 school, but the input mechanism for incoming kindergarten parents was separate.) Twenty-three of the letters indicated teachers that the parents' believed could not meet the needs of their children. Twelve of those letters were about the one fourth grade teacher being investigated. The remaining eleven were scattered among the nineteen remaining teachers. No other teacher was brought up more than twice.

The upcoming school year was scheduled to be the fourth grade teacher's evaluation year. The principal met with the teacher in late May and shared the parents' concerns from the letters. The teacher said she had some minor problems with parents in previous years, however, the parents' reactions were due to inaccurate gossip rather than fact. The principal explained that he was not accepting the letters as fact at this time, though he did want the two of them to develop a plan to deal with the parents' perceptions. He also told the teacher he would be observing more often than typical in the upcoming year, so he could respond to the parents with first-hand knowledge of the teacher's performance.

The principal worked intensely with the teacher throughout the year. The principal's observations and discussions with the teacher that year indicated an inordinate use of criticism (as opposed to encouragement and positive reinforcement) by the teacher and a lack of activities that engaged her students in learning. The teacher argued that these were just philosophical differences and parents' complaints during the year, about events when the principal was not in the room, were the children's fabrications. The principal continued to work formatively with the teacher, but summatively documented the observations and parents' concerns. That year the principal and teacher had to work with two more parents who reported their children were afraid of the teacher. One child was removed from the class after a number of interventions that included several visits to a child psychiatrist to deal with the school phobia. At classroom placement time, parents' letters again showed that the teacher received more than ten times the average number of complaints. The principal wrote an unsatisfactory evaluation citing the following evidence:

1. *Direct evidence* from classroom observations and conference discussions with the teacher which indicated excessive use of criticism, a lack of smiling and positive affect and a lack of interesting and stimulating instructional activities. The direct evidence also included non-classroom observations of the teacher on the playground and at special assemblies that showed a lack of interaction and participation with the children in a way that would build the relationship between teacher and students. (See the example of a reprimand for Jane Doe in chapter 7.)

2. A large amount of *evidence* in this example was derived from the testimony of investigated complaints from the parents of students in the class that year. These complaints indicated that the teacher had frequently responded abruptly to students when the principal was not in the room. The parents' testimony of students' complaints as reported by the administrator in a hearing is often known as **double hearsay** because it was communicated from the student to the parent and then to the administrator. Some of the parents were willing to provide more direct *hearsay evidence* by testifying directly or submitting an affidavit from themselves or their children for a hearing. In this example, the age of the children led the parents and administrators to conclude that it was not in the children's best interest to testify at the hearing (*direct evidence*).

3. The following *cumulative hearsay evidence* was well documented, leading to a *reasonable person's* conclusion that there is a factual basis for the claims.

   a. Logged parents' and students' complaints and parents' letters of complaint indicating the information in 2 above (The evaluator was prepared to present this information at a hearing)

   b. Two consecutive years of an inordinate number of written and oral requests from parents not to place their children in the class

   c. The fact that of the three cases of school phobia in the building, two were in this fourth grade teacher's classroom, even though a special effort had been made during the class assignments not to place students who might be susceptible to school phobia in the class

The principal alerted the association president that he was going to find the teacher unsatisfactory. The unsatisfactory evaluation was given to the teacher and reviewed in a meeting with the association president. The teacher was informed that failure to significantly improve in the upcoming year could lead to dismissal. Two subsequent meetings were held with the association president and the teacher to develop an improvement plan.

The teacher resigned at the end of the school year. Subsequent information got back to the evaluator that indicated the teachers' association was instrumental in providing the teacher with the personal and career counseling that led the teacher toward a new career. The teacher eventually went back to school, received an MBA and went on to a career in the travel industry. (Dopazo & Ribas)

HARASSMENT?

I'm often asked by readers why the evaluator in the example above was not charged with harassment, because he began immediately to work with the teacher at a higher level than he had with other staff members. For example, six observations were conducted in the first year despite the fact that this was not a formal evaluation year for the teacher.

As described above, the administrator had heard an inordinate number of accounts from parents the summer before his first school year as principal indicating issues with the teacher. The principal correctly treated these accounts as information, not evidence. He decided he would visit the classroom early in the year so he could determine for himself if the claims were founded or not. It soon became obvious to the principal that the teacher needed to change her practice. He began working more intensely with the teacher, providing coaching and feedback. The intent of the administrator in this first year was to improve the teacher's practice, not to remove the teacher. Assisting the teacher with this change required a high level of interaction between the principal and the teacher.

In this case, the principal had the following reasons for interacting differently with this teacher than with the other tenured staff members.

1. The information of teachers' and parents' complaints led the principal to reasonably *infer* that the teacher may need assistance and/or closer monitoring.

2. The principal's direct observations supported these claims.

3. The principal's intent in increasing his interactions with the teacher was to *improve* not *remove* the teacher.

As a result, the principal was honestly and openly meeting his responsibilities as a supervisor and his responsibility to ensure the best interests of the students. Therefore, he was *not* harassing the teacher.

DECISION TREE FOR ADMINISTRATORS RESPONDING TO INDIRECT CLAIMS

The principal in the preceding example utilized a decision tree chart (figure 10 on facing page) to address parents' complaints. You will note that the principal treats all parents' complaints similarly unless he has a reason to do otherwise. Following a procedure of this type insulates the principal from charges from teachers (and parents) that he/she acts in an arbitrary or capricious manner when dealing with claims from indirect sources.

It is important to note that a procedure such as that below is a guide to administrative action. Since every incident has its own unique characteristics, it is impossible to develop a chart such as this that accounts for all the varied circumstances that may arise. Therefore, it is important that administrators effectively exercise professional judgment throughout the decision tree. The evaluating administrator must have access to a person in the senior administration (or a consultant) from whom he/she may receive coaching when confronted with a difficult judgment in responding to complaints about a teacher. The following section of this chapter describes a framework used by some districts to provide peer coaching for administrators confronted with difficult evaluation or disciplinary situations. In the chart below, those times in which the principal needed to exercise his professional judgment are shown with a dotted line around the box.

Investigation Hint: You will note that the investigation of this type of complaint may include interviews with other students to obtain information when there are no adult witnesses or only insufficient ones. When conducting such interviews of students, it is important to record the questions you asked and ask each child the same questions to the extent possible. When a union files a grievance concerning the administrator's actions in situations of this type, administrators are often accused of asking leading questions when interviewing students in an investigation. Writing down the questions and sticking to the script (to the extent possible) is one way an administrator may show he/she did not ask leading questions designed to push the students toward responses that would incriminate the staff member being investigated. Chapter 7 contains specific guidelines for conducting this type of investigation.

Indirect Data Decision Tree

Strategies for Addressing an Indirect Claim

The boxes with dotted borders indicate that the evaluator took no further action beyond that point.

Parent tells evaluator a teacher yelled at his/her child. Principal tells parent he/she should speak with the teacher and parent agrees.

Parent tells evaluator a teacher yelled at his/her child. Parent says he/she has already spoken with the teacher. Evaluator schedules 3-way meeting.

Parent tells evaluator a teacher yelled at his/her child. Parent refuses to talk to the teacher because he/she already did so.

Parent tells evaluator a teacher yelled at his/her child. Parent refuses to talk to the teacher out of fear of retribution.

In 95% or more of cases, evaluator reassures parents that retribution is not common and evaluator will take strong action if it happens. Encourages parents to meet with teacher.

Evaluator considers information about parent, teacher, student and other information and makes a judgment on the next step.

Interviews both teacher and student about claim. Observes teacher formally or informally. Encourages parents to meet with teacher and evaluator.

Evaluator decides claim is unfounded and decides no further action is needed. May or may not tell teacher about the call. (Some contracts require notification.)

Evaluator judges from investigation that claim is unfounded. No further action is needed. May make memory note to document investigation.

Evaluator is unable to judge from the investigation if claim is founded. Evaluator's previous information about teacher warrants document or memory aid.

Evaluator does not have sufficient previous accumulation of evidence and/or information.

Evaluator has sufficient previous accumulation of evidence and/or information.

Evaluator does not have sufficient previous accumulation of evidence and/or information.

No further action— evaluator makes memory note.

An expectation clarification memo is given to the teacher.

Evaluator judges from investigation that teacher's behavior is inappropriate. Makes a judgement on the next step.

Evaluator has sufficient previous accumulation of evidence and/or information.

Evaluator does not have sufficient previous accumulation of evidence and/or information.

Formally documents infraction and corrective or disciplinary action taken.

Clarify expectation orally with memory note or formally document in memo to teacher.

Figure 10

The Team Approach to Supporting and Coaching Evaluators Involved in Difficult Evaluations
or
Reducing the "Ghost Town" and "Goldilocks" Effects

Chapter 1 of this book briefly spoke about the social–emotional factors that impact the evaluators when working with a low-performing teacher. Most schools and departments are designed so the evaluator (e.g., principal, department head) is the sole evaluator of a group of teachers in the school or department. In these situations, it is a typical human reaction for the teacher's colleagues to be emotionally supportive. Even when staff members privately encourage the administrator to work more intensely with the teacher, very few ever indicate that position to the teacher or other teachers. Soon after the intensive work begins, the administrator realizes that little or none of that earlier prodding for action translates into public support of the administrator's efforts to improve the teacher's performance. The administrator steps into the "middle of the street" to confront this difficult issue and turns around to find the streets and sidewalks a "ghost town," empty of supporters. In some instances, the low-performing teacher publicly berates the administrator to other staff members. Some colleagues join the administrator bashing, but most respond with silence or active listening. These responses are taken by the teacher as concurrence with his/her complaints about the evaluator. It creates a lonely and stressful situation in which the evaluator may be prone to second-guessing whether he/she is being too direct or not direct enough with the teacher.

Neutral administrators responsible for supervision and evaluation throughout the district can help limit the ghost town effect for evaluators in three ways. First, we should maintain a reasonable level of inter-rater reliability in the district. Common practice and expectations in the district limit the evaluators' vulnerability to claims that their work is personally motivated rather than connected to system-wide expectations. Using the assessment techniques noted in chapter 2 is an important first step. The best way to achieve inter-rater reliability is with good teaching, coaching and assessment of the skills of supervision and evaluation.

Second, we should provide periodic meetings during the year when groups of administrators involved in difficult evaluations or staff discipline situations come together to discuss their work with a qualified coach. This enables administrators to learn from one another and to receive coaching from a knowledgeable expert from the senior administration or a consultant. More importantly though, the social support of this type of meeting reassures administrators that they are not alone and that the system supports them during this difficult yet very important work.

The first meeting of this type in your district should be used to analyze a sample case study together. (See the sample cases later in this section.) This activity will model for the evaluators the steps involved in productively analyzing a difficult evaluation. In subsequent meetings, the evaluators bring their own difficult cases for discussion and coaching. In preparation for the meeting, evaluators should consider the following background facts and impressions (without including the staff members' names) prior to the session. This preparation will enable evaluators to give the group and the coach the information needed to productively participate in the discussion. It should be understood by all participants that all information related to these meetings is strictly confidential and should not be discussed beyond the meeting.

Below is a questionnaire that should be given to evaluators at least a couple of days before the seminar, so they can arrive ready to talk about their cases in a way that will maximize the quality of the feedback they receive.

DIFFICULT EVALUATION/PROGRESSIVE DISCIPLINE SUPPORT AND COACHING SEMINARS

The evaluator coaching seminar we are having next week is designed to provide administrators with ideas, strategies and supports when working with difficult supervision, evaluation and/or progressive discipline situations. Often these situations involve confidential information. Because of this we ask that you not use the staff member's name when posing your questions. We also must insist that the issues discussed not be shared with anyone other than the appropriate administrator outside of the meeting.

Consider the pertinent background information requested in the questions below. What questions do you have about your case that will help you to better work with this teacher?

1. How many years has he/she been teaching? How many years in this district? (Give an estimate if you're not sure.)
2. What is the teacher's age?
3. What is the teacher's overall health (physical and mental)?
4. What is the teacher's personal support system in and out of school?
5. How does the teacher respond to recommendations for change?
6. How would parents describe the teacher?
7. How would students describe the teacher?
8. How would colleagues describe the teacher?
9. How would the teacher describe his/her performance to you?

10. How would the teacher describe his/her performance to a trusted friend?

11. How would you describe the teacher's performance? What are the issues?

12. How do the above descriptions compare to one another?

13. What supervision techniques have worked with the teacher? Why?

14. What has not worked with the teacher? Why?

15. Are there any other legal issues that might be raised (e.g., discrimination based on age, sex, race, religion or handicapping condition)?

Third, we should match these evaluators as partners or groups of three to provide each of them with constant support between the regularly scheduled meetings. Typically, there are two kinds of partner relationships. In one type of partner relationship, the second administrator has no direct contact with the teacher being evaluated. In these situations, the partner is a "critical friend" who assists the evaluator with analyzing the teacher's issues and deciding on appropriate interventions, but does not observe or meet with the teacher. The other partner relationship is the second evaluator/supervisor model. In these cases the second administrator conducts observations and participates in meetings with the teacher. I strongly advise against having the second evaluator/supervisor be a person with a full evaluation load, for this will only dilute his/her effectiveness on those evaluations. In either case, addressing the evaluation as a case study with the partner, using the information from the preceding questions, may be very helpful. It is understood by both parties that all information related to the teacher and his/her evaluation is strictly confidential.

The partners may also use one another to help with observations that are difficult to write, final evaluations and/or memos to the teacher. In chapter 3, I noted how helpful administrators find peer coaching about observation write-ups and end-of-year reports. In cases of low-performing teachers, this activity is not only helpful, it is essential! Below is a format for peer-editing evaluation documents of low-performing teachers.

Peer Conferencing to Help Your Peers With Write-Ups of Low-Performing Teachers (Evaluations, Memos, Observations, etc.)

1. Start with an area in the write-up that is done well. Be sure to be specific about what is done well and give evidence that supports why you believe that part is done well.

    - Don't say, "This is really good."
    - Do say (see C.J.E.I. examples in chapter 3), "You did a good job of supporting the claim that is underlined by indicating the time the students came in, the fact that the teacher arrived after the students and the time the teacher addressed the class."

2. Do the labeled teaching moves (claim) identify the teacher behavior in terms of one of the district performance standards?

3. Does the evidence (objective data) in the write-up directly support the claim, judgment and/or impact statements (subjective statements)? Do you have a suggestion as to how the writer may better do this?

4. Are the impact statements worded in language consistent with the performance standards?

5. Have clear judgments been made about the claims that indicate whether the teacher is satisfactory in each standard described in the document? Have the judgments been made in language that is consistent with the statements of judgments used in the district's final end-of-year evaluation document?

6. Is there sufficient evidence to support any judgments about performance standards on which the teacher has been judged unsatisfactory?

7. Is there a way for the writer to describe the evidence in a more concrete, observable or verifiable manner? Do you have a suggestion for the writer as to how he/she may better do this?

8. Do you, as the reader, understand the impact (negative or positive) on the students' learning (or well being) of the behaviors described in the write-up of the class or activity?

9. Does the document objectively state the case and avoid "digs" that may result from the evaluator's frustration with this teacher?

After the information is provided, the partners may then discuss together the Questions to Ask Yourself When You Are Supervising and/or Evaluating a Teacher (Administrator) You Suspect Is Unsatisfactory (or Barely Satisfactory), on page 193–194 and A Checklist of Tests for Unfair Evaluation found on pages 195–196 of this section. These documents will help map out a plan of action that addresses the whole E.L.P.S. As the evaluations progress, there are additional questions for the partners to discuss. These questions can be found at the end of the sample case study that follows.

CASE STUDY OF A DIFFICULT SEVENTH AND EIGHTH GRADE SCIENCE TEACHER EVALUATION (SAMPLE OF A FOUR-YEAR CYCLE)

Read the case study and follow the directions that appear at the end.

This example takes place in a district with a four-year evaluation process for tenured (professional or permanent status) teachers. The first year is a summative evaluation. Years two, three and four are formative, with significant professional development components. In those years, the principal does not complete a summative evaluation of the teacher. For an example of this type of evaluation process, see chapter 9.

Jane Doe is a seventh and eighth grade science teacher. She is forty-two years old and has taught in the system for fifteen years. Jane taught for two years in another district before coming to Sample District. She works with a staff of seventh and eighth grade teachers who, for the most part, are quite strong. However, there is one other teacher on the team, John Moe, who performs below average, but still satisfactorily. John is one of Jane's closest confidants. They typically sit together at faculty meetings and often have lunch together.

Jane is liked by other members of the staff, but by no means loved. She attends all the staff's social events and is generally cordial with colleagues. However, she can at times be moody and short with colleagues. Jane and John Moe are part of a group of six to eight teachers from the school who get together quarterly for coffee. Jane stays connected to the teachers' association by attending social events and some of the informational meetings, but she is not an active participant in the operation of the union.

Jane's first seven years were excellent. She actively took courses, eventually getting her master's degree. She served on system-wide committees, showed up at some of the seventh and eight grade sporting events and plays, and participated in the eighth grade overnight trip. During this period, she built strong relationships with parents. Parents whose children had Jane during that time still speak highly of her in the community, though they no longer have children in the school. Jane's performance warranted excellent evaluations and tenure (professional or permanent status) at the end of her third year. Years four through six were supervisory years (phases two through four) and her performance in evaluation year seven (phase one) continued to be excellent.

Years eight to ten were a plateau for Jane. One of her own two children started to have difficulties in school and at home due to some emotional issues.

Jane periodically discussed her concerns about the child with the principal, but the child's problems were a continual source of concern. As a result, Jane cut back on her committee work, professional development and attendance at events. Her teaching remained good (but not excellent) partly on the strength of the knowledge and skills she had developed in her first seven years. The principal began to notice the plateau effect in evaluation year nine (phase three of the four-year evaluation cycle). She gave the issues some thought, but decided to give an evaluation with no areas of concern because Jane's performance was still quite good in the classroom. She believed the plateau would end and Jane would again begin to grow as a teacher, if she gave Jane positive and supportive comments during Jane's phase one administrative evaluation in year ten.

Years eleven to thirteen saw a slow but steady decline. Jane stopped keeping up with changes in instructional strategies and curriculum. As her teaching declined further from her first seven years of excellence, parents' complaints increased slowly and steadily. Parents were reporting the slow return of work. Their children expressed boredom with the primarily lecture format and reported that Jane was, at times, overly critical of students. In administrative evaluation year fourteen (phase 1 of the four-year cycle), the principal realized the supportive approach of the last two years was not moving Jane forward. In fact, Jane's performance was declining due to a lack of willingness (or ability) to change at the pace needed to stay current with curriculum and instruction. She could no longer be sustained by the excellence of her first seven years.

In evaluation year fourteen (phase one) the principal made three recommendations and marked Jane as being below standard on one of the seven performance standards. The principal believed Jane should have been marked below standard on two and possibly three of the standards, but didn't do this because she was sure Jane would react very strongly to such an evaluation. There were also some fleeting hopes that Jane would still be able to turn things around. Upon receiving the evaluation, Jane made an appointment with the principal. She expressed her strong concern about receiving the below standard rating. After talking with the principal, she still disagreed but decided not to pursue the issue any further. After school closed for the year, the principal received two letters and several other comments from parents of graduating eighth graders about their disappointment with science during these last two years.

During year fifteen, when Jane was in phase two of the evaluation cycle, Jane's performance flattened out at the level of the previous year. Although the principal believed a number of improvements were needed to bring Jane up to the Sample District standard, Jane did not see the issues.

After the first principals' meeting in October, the principal takes you aside, shares this situation and asks for your advice. What will you tell her? Why?

CASE STUDY OF A DIFFICULT THIRD GRADE EVALUATION (SAMPLE OF A TWO-YEAR CYCLE)

Read the case study and follow the directions that appear at the end.

This example takes place in a district with a two-year evaluation process for tenured (professional or permanent status) teachers. The first year is a summative evaluation. The second year is a supervisory year in which no summative evaluation is completed, unless the teacher is placed in an out-of-cycle summative evaluation. For an example of this type of evaluation process, see chapter 9.

Jane Doe is a third grade classroom teacher. She is forty-two years old and has taught in the system for fifteen years. Jane taught two years in another district before coming to Sample. She works with two third grade colleagues and a grades three to six resource room teacher who are very good teachers. Next door to Jane is a fourth grade teacher, John Moe, who is below average, but still satisfactory. John is one of Jane's closest confidants.

Jane is liked by other members of the staff, but by no means loved. She attends all the staff's social events and is generally cordial with colleagues. However, she can at times be moody and short with colleagues. Jane stays connected to the teachers' association by attending social events and some of the informational meetings, but she is not an active participant in the operation of the teachers' association.

Jane's first seven years were excellent. She actively took courses, eventually getting her master's degree. She served on system-wide committees and attended some of the grade four and five after-school and evening events to support her previous students. Jane's performance warranted excellent evaluations and tenure (professional or permanent status) at the end of her third year. Years four and six were supervisory years and her performance in evaluation years five and seven continued to be excellent.

Years eight to ten were a plateau for Jane. One of her two children started to have difficulties in school and at home due to some emotional issues. Jane periodically discussed her concerns about the child with the principal, but the child's problems were a continual source of concern. As a result, Jane cut back on her committee work, professional development and attendance at events. Her teaching remained good (but not excellent) partly on the strength of the knowledge and skills she had developed in her first seven years. The principal began to notice a lack of positive change in her teaching in evaluation year nine. All of Jane's teaching seemed to be a "rerun" of previous years. She gave the issues some thought, but decided to give an evaluation with no unsatisfactory areas. Jane's performance was still satisfactory in the classroom overall, even though her currency in curriculum and in some instructional areas was below the standard. The principal believed the plateau would end, and

Jane would again begin to grow as a teacher if she were given positive and supportive comments during supervisory year ten.

Years eleven to fourteen saw a slow but steady decline. Jane stopped keeping up with changes in instructional strategies and curriculum. As her teaching declined further from her first seven years of excellence, parents' complaints increased slowly and steadily. Parents were reporting the slow return of work. Their children expressed boredom with the number of worksheets and teacher-directed activities and reported that Jane was at times negative with students. In evaluation year eleven, the principal realized the supportive approach of the last two years was not moving Jane forward. In fact, Jane's performance was declining due to a lack of willingness (or ability) to change at the pace needed to stay current with curriculum and instruction. She could no longer be sustained by the excellence of her first seven years.

In evaluation year eleven, the principal made two or three recommendations and marked Jane as below standard in one area. The principal marked Jane as "satisfactory" overall. The principal believed Jane should have been marked with two or three areas below standard, but didn't because she was sure Jane would react very strongly to such an evaluation. There were also some fleeting hopes that Jane would still be able to turn things around. Upon receiving the evaluation, Jane made an appointment with the principal. Jane expressed her strong concern about not receiving all satisfactory ratings. After talking with the principal, she still disagreed but decided not to pursue the issue any further. After school closed for the year, the principal received several comments from parents of her third graders about their disappointment with their childrens' year. The principal also received six letters from second grade parents asking that their children not be placed in Jane's class for third grade. During supervisory year twelve, Jane's performance flattened out at an overall unsatisfactory to barely satisfactory level. A number of areas for improvement persisted, however, Jane did not see most of them as issues.

After the first principals' meeting in November the principal takes you aside, shares this situation and asks for your advice. What will you tell her? Why?

CASE STUDY OF A DIFFICULT HIGH SCHOOL EVALUATION (SAMPLE OF A THREE-YEAR CYCLE)

Read the case study and follow the directions that appear at the end.

Jeff Doe is teaching French to seniors. He is forty-two years old and has taught in the district for thirteen years. Jeff taught for two years in another district before coming to this district. He works with a staff which is quite strong for the most part. However, there is one other teacher on the team, John Moe, who is below average, but still satisfactory. John is one of Jeff's closest confidants. Jeff is liked by other members of the staff, but by no means loved.

Jeff attends all the staff's social events and is generally cordial with colleagues. However, he can at times be moody and short with them. Jeff stays connected to the teachers' association by attending social events and some of the informational meetings, but he is not an active participant in the operation of the union.

Jeff's first seven years were excellent. He actively took courses, eventually getting his master's degree. He served on system-wide committees, showed up at some of the high school sporting events and plays and participated in the "Can We Talk?" diversity awareness program. Jeff's performance warranted excellent evaluations and tenure (professional or permanent status) at the end of his third year. Years four and five were alternative evaluation pathway years and his performance in evaluation year six (observation cycle) continued to be excellent.

Years eight through ten were a plateau for Jeff. One of his two children started to have difficulties in school and at home, due to some emotional issues. Jeff periodically discussed his concerns about the child with the curriculum coordinator (department head), but the child's problems were a continual source of concern. As a result, Jeff cut back on his committee work, professional development and attendance at events. His teaching remained good (but not excellent) partly on the strength of the knowledge and skills he had developed in his first seven years. The foreign language coordinator (department head) began to notice a plateau in observation cycle year nine. She gave the issues some thought, but decided not to confront the areas of concern because Jeff's performance was still quite good in the classroom. The coordinator (department head) believed the plateau would end, and Jeff would again begin to grow as a teacher if she gave Jeff positive and supportive comments in his observation cycle evaluation during year nine.

Years ten and eleven saw a slow but steady decline. Jeff stopped keeping up with changes in instructional strategies and curriculum. As his performance declined further from his first seven years of excellence, parents' complaints increased slowly but steadily. Parents were reporting the slow return of work. Their children expressed boredom with the primarily lecture format and reported that Jeff was, at times, overly critical of his students. In the observation cycle evaluation in year twelve, the Foreign Language Coordinator realized the supportive approach of the last several years was not moving Jeff forward. In fact, Jeff's performance was declining due to a lack of willingness (or ability) to change at the pace needed to stay current with curriculum and instruction. He could no longer be sustained by the excellence of his first seven years.

In evaluation year twelve, the coordinator made three recommendations and marked Jeff as barely satisfactory[4] on two of the performance standards. The coordinator believed Jeff should have been marked unsatisfactory on at

[4] The categories for summative ratings in this district were exemplary, satisfactory, barely satisfactory and unsatisfactory.

least one of those performance standards, but she didn't do it. She was sure Jeff would react very strongly, since this was the first time he was ever marked below satisfactory. There were also some fleeting hopes that Jeff would still be able to turn things around. Upon receiving the evaluation, Jeff made an appointment with the coordinator. Jeff expressed his strong concern about receiving barely satisfactory ratings. After talking with his coordinator, Jeff still disagreed, but he decided not to pursue the issue any further. After school closed for the year, the coordinator received two letters and several other comments from parents of graduating seniors about their disappointment with French class during these last two years.

At the start of year thirteen, Jeff was in the out-of-cycle stage of the evaluation cycle. Jeff's performance was no better than it had been during the previous year. Although a number of improvements were needed to bring Jeff to a satisfactory rating on all of the district's performance standards, Jeff did not see these areas of his teaching as areas for growth or unsatisfactory.

After the administrative council meeting on October 3rd, the coordinator (department head) takes you aside, shares this situation and asks for your advice. What will you tell her? Why?

CASE STUDY ACTIVITY

You have ten minutes to discuss this case with a partner. You will then have another ten minutes to discuss it as a group. If there is other information you need about this case to answer the following questions, please ask. At the end of the twenty minutes, give a report from your group on how you will advise your colleague. Some things you may want to consider in your advice are

1. Should the principal (or the curriculum coordinator in the third case) involve the central administration? If so, how? If not, why not?

2. What is the evaluator's next step?

3. How may the evaluator monitor the impact on other staff members of his work with the low-performing teacher? Will the principal's work with this teacher impact the building staff as a whole? If so, how? If not, why not?

4. What is the role of the building peer review committee or teacher support team (if one exists in your district)?

5. Does the evaluator need any more information about the low-performing teacher? If so, what?

6. What educational, legal, political or social–emotional information and support does the evaluator need? To whom should the evaluator go for this information and support?

7. Will the evaluator's work with this teacher impact the school system as a whole? If so, how? If not, why not?

8. Should the teachers' union be involved in any way? If so, how? If not, why not?

   **Your answers to the questions above are focused on helping your colleague with the evaluation from this point forward. Now, review the situation with the benefit of hindsight.

9. Is there anything this evaluator should have done differently during the prior years? If so, what?

A SECOND EVALUATOR–SUPERVISOR MODEL

When a teacher has more than one supervisor–evaluator it is important that the administrators communicate well. In cases of low-performing teachers, in which the partner is more actively involved as a second evaluator–supervisor, this partner attends meetings and observations with the teacher. For these situations, the following guidelines are essential.

1. Come to agreement on the priorities and goals of the evaluation. The administrators should review the teacher's performance related to the district's performance standards and work out any differences they may have prior to the start of the evaluation. I have seen many evaluations of low-performing teachers seriously compromised right from the beginning because of the failure of the supervising and/or evaluating administrators to provide a consistent message to the teacher. Failure to do this also makes it more difficult for the teacher's association/union to play a positive role in moving the teacher toward change.

2. Plan with your partner before each meeting, so you send the same message to the teacher. The message that a person needs to change is *emotionally* very difficult for people to hear. The more clearly and concisely the message is given and reinforced, the more likely it will be accepted by the teacher. A consistent message also helps the association representative to reinforce the suggested changes in private conversations with the teacher.

3. Use your partner's areas of strength.

4. Be ready for the period of *regression*. This process is always "two steps forward and one step back." Remind your partner of this when he/she is frustrated and ready to give up.

5. Support each other through the periods of *aggression*. There will be times when the teacher will lash out at one of you more than the other. Be willing to share the heat that results from telling the teacher about areas in which he/she needs to make a change.

6. Share the work. These evaluations require a tremendous amount of time. Try to keep the work as evenly distributed as possible.

I've developed the following questions to help evaluators align their evaluations with the seven tests of just cause described on page 170. Evaluators may use these questions alone. However, it may be extremely helpful for an evaluator to review these questions with his/her partner or supervisor for a "reality check." In districts where there are multiple evaluators you always deal with the "Goldilocks effect." Prior to a district's participating in significant training, this effect may be caused by the tendency of evaluators to function like the chairs of the three bears in the Goldilocks story. Some may have a predisposition to be *too hard,* others to be *too soft* and still others to be *just right* in their approach to a low-performing teacher.

In districts where there are multiple evaluators you always deal with the "Goldilocks effect." Prior to a district's participating in significant training, this effect may be caused by the tendency of evaluators to function like the chairs of the three bears in the Goldilocks story. Some may have a predisposition to be *too hard,* others to be *too soft* and still others to be *just right* in their approach to a low-performing teacher.

QUESTIONS TO ASK YOURSELF WHEN YOU ARE SUPERVISING AND/OR EVALUATING A TEACHER YOU SUSPECT IS UNSATISFACTORY (OR BARELY SATISFACTORY)

1. Had I reviewed the district's performance standards with the teacher with reasonable thoroughness prior to identifying problems? *Note:* Many districts now require evaluators to review the district's performance standards with their entire staff at the start of each year to ensure that all teachers are "informed of management's rules and expectations." (See the seven tests of just cause on page 170.)

2. What has changed since the last satisfactory evaluation to warrant a change in my judgement of this person's performance from satisfactory to unsatisfactory (or barely satisfactory)? Remember, this change may be in the teacher's performance or in the evaluator's and/or the district's ability to deal with the type of low performance that this teacher has previously exhibited. In cases where there has been a change in evaluator, what is the reason for the difference between my interpretation in the most recent evaluation and that of the previous evaluator?

3. On which of the district's performance standards do I believe the teacher is performing unsatisfactorily?

4. What evidence do I have that supports this belief?

5. Have I clearly and specifically communicated my concerns in language consistent with the district's performance standards? (See the questions related to editing observation and final evaluation write-ups found on pages 95 and 121.)

6. Have I factored in extenuating circumstances to a reasonable extent? For example, a teacher's health issue may require a *reasonable accommodation* to enable the teacher to perform satisfactorily on the performance standards.[5] However, it does not excuse a teacher from satisfactorily meeting the performance standards.

7. Have I given reasonable support and allowed sufficient time to enable improvement?

8. What additional knowledge do I need to be reasonably qualified to make judgments about what constitutes satisfactory teaching in this person's assignment? If I need more knowledge, where or to whom do I go for this information?

9. Is there another administrator who can give me a second opinion on the teacher's performance or act as a sounding board as I make critical decisions throughout this process?

10. To what extent does the teacher agree/disagree with my assessment of his/her performance? How do I close the gap between our differing assessments? (See the section on conferencing in chapter 4.)

11. How does the teachers' association respond when an administrator addresses the deficiencies of a low-performing teacher with tenure? How will I work with the teachers' association when addressing my concerns about this teacher?

12. Is my supervisor fully apprised of my concerns, the evidence and my plan for next steps?

[5] Edwin M. Bridges, in his book, *The Incompetent Teacher* (1992), found that in nearly half the cases of incompetent teaching that administrators described during his research, the teachers suffered from some type of emotional distress, burn-out, health problems, marital difficulties and/or financial problems.

Reasons Contributing to Teachers and Teachers' Associations Not Believing Just Cause Has Been Demonstrated in an Evaluation

The document below comes from the files of a teachers' association officer. The author is unknown. This document is a fairly comprehensive list of the claims that teachers have made over the years to refute unsatisfactory evaluations. It is an older document that comes from a time prior to the political focus on voucher programs and charter schools, when the focus of many local teachers' associations/unions was more on protection at all costs then on representation. For an in-depth explanation of this change in the manner of representation by teachers' associations, see the discussion in chapter 5 on current public relations (political) circumstances affecting how teachers' associations/unions represent their members. Despite recent political changes, the following document has value as a helpful set of questions for evaluators to ask themselves when involved in difficult evaluations.

A Checklist of Tests for Unfair Evaluation

This checklist of tests for unfair evaluation is drawn from court decisions and arbitration awards and should prove to be a classic.

The following checklist should be read by the individual in the event of a poor evaluation by the evaluator. Any one or more of the following statements that apply to your situation might be sufficient grounds to challenge the evaluation in the form of a grievance.

1. Cited facts are inaccurate.

2. The evaluation failed to consider constraints of pupil background, overcrowding, school conditions, etc.

3. The evaluator is not competent to evaluate in my field and/or lacks understanding of current acceptable pedagogical practice or board policy or law.

4. My evaluator relied on hearsay.

5. My evaluator failed to observe me for a sufficient amount of time to make a valid judgment.

6. My evaluator failed to give me adequate forewarning of this down rating, in that he did not give me sufficient time or assistance to improve, specify the incompetent performance or unprofessional conduct with such particularity as to furnish me with an adequate opportunity to make sufficient improvement or offer specific suggestions and recommendations for improvement.

checklist continues

7. This evaluation is excessive for the wrongs cited.

8. This evaluation fails to consider the extenuating and mitigating circumstances as cited on my initial conference form.

9. This evaluation is irrelevant to my fitness to teach, in that the wrongs cited do not adversely affect students or coworkers to any material extent.

10. I am being down rated for an assignment outside my field.

11. The objectives, goals, standards or rules cited are so broad as to be void for reasons of vagueness.

12. The objectives, goals, standards or rules are unreasonable, arbitrary, capricious and/or impossible of observance or attainment.

13. This evaluation is inequitable or discriminatory in that the cited standards or rules have not been consistently enforced at my school inasmuch as coworkers in the same situation have done the same thing without reprimand or down rating.

14. The wrongs cited exceed the jurisdiction of the board which jurisdiction is limited to the orderly, safe and efficient operation of the school district.

15. The citations on my evaluation form violate constitutional guarantees to my free speech, association, political advocacy or to the standards of academic freedom accepted in the profession.

16. I was given no opportunity to confront my accusers.

17. The adverse citations occurred a long time ago before the evaluation and did not recur.

18. This evaluation ignores my past record of achievement and unjustly punished me for a single recent wrong which is not likely to recur.

19. My performance has been adversely affected by extreme stress and duress due to unreasonable administrative harassment.

FORMAT FOR AN IMPROVEMENT PLAN

At a minimum, an improvement plan should be a written document that includes areas for improvement, recommendations for improving those areas, supports available to the evaluatee and the monitoring system. These plans may take many forms. Evaluators interested in other improvement plan formats are encouraged to read a book by Platt, Tripp, Ogden & Fraser (2000) called *The Skillful Leader: Confronting Mediocre Teaching*.

An improvement plan is used in years when the typical level of supervision or evaluation is insufficient to address the areas needing improvement.

It should always be used when someone has been placed in an out-of-cycle evaluation (removed from the scheduled supervisory year and placed in summative evaluation) for performance reasons. Improvement plans may also be used in a regular evaluation year or in a supervision year when it has been determined that a more intensive relationship is needed.

1. The **areas for improvement** section spells out to the teacher exactly which areas of performance are in need of improvement. Statements should relate directly to the district's performance standards (a.k.a. principles of effective teaching in some states). It is helpful to describe these areas in such a way that the teacher or administrator understands *what is not happening* and *what should be happening*. The area of concern must also be one that has been observed by or verified by the evaluator. At times, an evaluator may have circumstantial evidence pointing to a possible issue. In these cases, it should be noted as an expected area for improvement until evidence verifies or disproves what is suspected. To avoid confusion about expectations, it is important to note in the plan that the evaluation will focus on areas for improvement but will also include an assessment of all the performance standards.

2. The **recommendations for improving these areas** section explains what the employee is expected to do to overcome the concerns identified in the areas for improvement section of the plan. It is best to actively involve the evaluatee in generating these activities. This may be difficult, however, when the evaluatee does not believe there are issues. Specific, realistic and achievable activities to be pursued by the evaluatee are delineated. Some evaluators place the recommendations in a separate section. Other evaluators include the recommendations in the areas for improvement section, with connected recommendations following the description of each area identified for improvement.

3. **Supports available to the evaluatee** includes the resources (people, materials, workshops, etc.) that are available to assist the evaluatee in his/her efforts to improve. Some evaluators list the supports in a separate section. Other evaluators connect them to specific recommendations. For example, an evaluator may recommend that a teacher improve his/her knowledge of the subject matter by attending a specific course at a college or university.

4. **The monitoring system** describes how progress on the plan will be measured. It should include the pattern and approximate time lines for observations, conferences and interim and final reports. This section should also include the anticipated next steps based on whether the evaluatee is fully successful, partially successful or unsuccessful in his/her efforts to improve.

SAMPLE IMPROVEMENT PLANS

The following pages contain samples of improvement plans that have been used successfully with teachers. In the first two examples, the teacher and administrator reached agreement on the contents of the plan. Both then signed the plan without further comment. In the third example, the teacher and administrator could not reach agreement after several discussions. The administrator wrote the plan and included some of the teacher's ideas that he considered to be appropriate. The teacher was then permitted to make comments related to any areas of disagreement.

In each case, these plans were written after the end-of-year evaluation. Therefore, the evidence that lead to the judgment that improvements were needed in these areas was well established in that evaluation. In the final example, the plan for Karen Sullivan, I included the final evaluation report on which the improvement plan was based. In some cases the improvement plan is included in the final yearly evaluation.

IMPROVEMENT PLAN FOR MARK McWIRE
SAMPLE SCHOOL GRADE 5

June 10, 2004

1. Areas of Focus

Standard III. Effective Classroom Management

To ensure that the classroom environment is one in which students feel safe and comfortable

To ensure the transition of students back to class from learning center and other activities is smooth and supportive

Standard V. Promotion of High Standards

To ensure the judicious use of high quality, curriculum-related support materials (e.g., movies)

To ensure the communication of high standards in a tone and manner that is perceived by students as positive and supportive

Standard VI. Promotion of Equity and Diversity

To ensure the classroom environment, instructional techniques and management techniques are sensitive to gender differences

Standard VII. Fulfillment of Professional Responsibilities

To constructively initiate interactions with parents and solicit their contributions while being receptive to them

To work with administrators to ensure that the level of parent satisfaction is equivalent to the level that is typical for Sample School teachers

2. Recommendations for Improvement

a.   Send a summer letter to students and parents asking parents to write information about their children.

b.   Have beginning-of-the year meetings with each child's parents to learn about their child.

c.   Have a breakfast or celebration activity focused on the children and invite the parents to attend.

d.   Increase the level of constructive communication with parents.

e.   Use parents as helpers in art and/or other classroom projects.

f.   Look for opportunities early in the year to tell parents about positive things their children are doing.

g.   Think about why the majority of concerns are related to girls and if there are changes that must be made in your interactions with girls.

h.   Coordinate with Integrated Services (special education teachers, speech therapists, etc.) staff to ensure smooth transitions that are positive for the children.

3. Support Available

a.   Principal Bob Martin will meet with you on a weekly or biweekly basis to provide supervision between now and the November meeting. We will determine the frequency of meetings beyond that point at that meeting. The first meeting is scheduled for September 1 in Bob Martin's office.

b.   Bob will assist Mark in planning regular meetings with service providers.

c.   Please let Bob know if there are other supports that would be helpful.

4. Monitoring System

a.   Bob will complete at least five full length (at least 35 minutes) observations between September and April 30. At least two of these observations will be announced.

b.   Bob will make frequent walk-through visits and brief observations in and out of the classroom.

c.   Jennifer (association representative), Mark and Bob will meet in October, January and April to check the status of the evaluation to that point. We will schedule these meetings at our September 1 meeting.

d.   Bob will write an evaluation based on all of the performance standards with a focus on the areas noted above.

_____	_____
Principal's signature	date
_____	_____
Teacher's signature	date

Signature signifies receipt of, not concurrence with, this improvement plan.

IMPROVEMENT PLAN FOR SAM MAMOSA

The Sample School
Office of the Principal

MEMORANDUM

DATE: October 7, 2004
TO: Sam Mamosa
FROM: Any Principal
RE: Improvement Plan

1.   Areas for Improvement:

Standard I. Effective Planning and Assessment of Curriculum and Instruction:

A. The teacher plans instruction effectively.

- Sam needs to make sure that there is one focused learning goal for the class period and that he tailors the instruction to the wide variety of students and abilities present in his class.
- Sam must leave appropriate, complete and clear lesson plans when he will be out of school. He must not rely on phone conversations with the sub or faxed plans.

B. The teacher plans assessment of student learning effectively.

Assessment:

- Sam needs to make his expectations clear to the class and outline how the students are to meet those expectations. He must also discern, throughout the class, whether student learning is occurring. At the end of class, Sam must summarize the lesson and assess if the students have met his expectations.

C. The teacher monitors students' understanding of the curriculum and effectively adjusts instruction, materials or assessments when appropriate.

- Sam needs to make sure that all students are engaged in the activity for the day and that this is focused work, not copious idle conversation.

Standard II. Effective Management of Classroom Environment:

- Sam needs to check regularly that all students are working on the lesson for the day—not just discussing social issues.
- Sam needs to have an introduction, lesson and concluding activity for all classes.
- For behavioral problems, Sam is to deal with the students in the class, and, if he sends students to the office, he is to notify the office of the problem and indicate what he has done and what parental contact he expects to make after class.

Standard III. Effective Instruction:

Sam must plan his class with an introduction, lesson for the day and then concluding questions or a summary that refocuses his students on the purpose for the lesson. The end of the class must be more than just clean-up before the children leave the class.

Standard IV. Promotion of Equity and Appreciation of Diversity:

Sam must have consistent expectations of all students.

Standard V. Fulfillment of Professional Responsibilities:

A. The teacher constructively initiates interactions with parents and solicits and is receptive to their contributions.

Communication:

- Sam needs to continue his efforts to speak directly to parents when there is a behavioral problem in his class. Direct contact with the parents will ensure an effective resolution to the problem.

- Sam must work to develop a better relationship with the Arts Council. It is problematic to have two art programs functioning in the school. In addition, the Arts Council might be a source of funding when internal funds are limited.

B. Attendance

- Sam must continue the good attendance pattern that he established after his surgery last year.

This year's evaluation will focus on the areas noted above, but will assess all seven of the principles of effective teaching.

2. **Supports available:**

- The art curriculum coordinator is available to provide support upon request. Sam is expected to schedule appointments with the arts coordinators as he deems necessary.

- The principal and coordinator will help arrange for instructional strategies to be discussed with colleagues in other schools in the district.

- Sam is engaged in a master's program at State University; resources should also be available there.

- I am available for any discussions that will support this process.

3. **Monitoring System:**

At least four announced observations with appropriate pre-meetings and feedback will occur during the year. At least three unannounced observations will be completed during the year.

Joint observations scheduled (Coordinator and me):

11/18/2004   3/3/2005

1/13/2005   3/5/2005 visit same class

_____   _____
                Signature of evaluator   date

_____   _____
                Signature of teacher   date

Signature signifies receipt of, not concurrence with, this improvement plan.

IMPROVEMENT PLAN FOR JAMES MORGAN AUGUST 2004, SAMPLE SCHOOL

The following document sets forth a plan to support James Morgan in his efforts to address the recommendations made based on my observations and the discussions we had on April 28, 2004 and June 3, 2004. This plan will be implemented during the 2004–2005 academic year.

1.   Areas for Improvement and Related Recommendations

The primary goal is to better integrate the principles of effective teaching (district performance standards) more explicitly into daily practice. The following identifies several specific areas for improvement. The 2004–2005 evaluation will focus on these areas, but will also assess all the principles of effective teaching.

Standard I. Currency in the Curriculum
> To organize and teach the 7/8 mathematics curriculum so it follows a sequence consistent with the district's 7/8 math curriculum and the district's learning expectations for grades 7/8.

Standard II. Effective Planning, Delivery and Assessment of Curriculum and Instruction
> a.   To begin each class with an itinerary of the day's activities and make reference to it as activities change from one to another
>
> b.   To explicitly state the goals or objectives with students for units or lessons studied
>
> c.   To explicitly connect work from the previous day or previous learning to work that will take place that day
>
> d.   To spend the end of each class summarizing what has been taught and to foreshadow next steps to come

e. To develop clearer, more comprehensive handouts and other supportive materials which enhance lessons and describe projects or other major assignments

f. To consistently utilize a broad variety of active learning strategies and to incorporate an array of resources and materials in daily instruction to meet the needs of a diverse and heterogeneously grouped student body

g. To work collaboratively with the computer teacher on integrating computer technology into daily practice to enhance student understanding of mathematical concepts and their applications

Standard III. Effective Management of Classroom Environment

a. To fine tune daily classroom management routines to more smoothly transition from activity to activity and to capture students' attention more readily to focus on the learning task at hand

b. To widen the repertoire of behavior management strategies used to better contain students who are unfocused, distractible, chatty or disruptive and thereby help them to learn more successfully

Standard IV. Promotion of High Standards and Expectations for Students' Achievement

To recognize, understand and work more effectively with those students who have a history of lower math achievement or for whom math presents a particular challenge

Standard VII. Fulfillment of Professional Responsibilities

To voluntarily assume at least two additional duties which support the extra-curricular activities of the 7/8 team, such as managing the finances of a fund-raiser for the class trip

In early September, a meeting will take place with the director of personnel, principal, math coordinator, teachers' association representative and James to review and revise this improvement plan.

2. **Supports Available to the Evaluatee**

To assist James in improving the above-stated areas, the Sample Public Schools is prepared to provide him with a mentor who will work with him on a monthly basis throughout the school year. It will also pay for him to attend the Research for Better Teaching class Studying Skillful Teaching. Alternative or additional supports may be discussed at the September meeting.

3. **The Monitoring System**

James will be supervised and evaluated by the principal with contributions from the math coordinator for grades 5–8. Both announced and unannounced observations will take place. At least three announced observations will occur between September and January, 2005, all dates to be mutually agreed upon. The first will occur in late September and will be done by the principal. A second announced observation will be conducted in November by the math coordinator, who is scheduled to be at Sample School for that month. In November or December, both the principal and the math coordinator will do a joint, announced observation.

In addition, throughout the September to December period, the principal and the math coordinator each will do at least one unannounced observation. A meeting will take place at the end of November between the principal, math coordinator, mentor and James to discuss progress to date. This will be followed by a meeting in January between the director of personnel, principal, math coordinator, union representative and James to check James's progress, to determine next steps and to set a monitoring schedule for the remainder of the year. The evaluation will be written and submitted by April 30, 2000, and will include a summative assessment of the areas for improvement and the other performance standards.

Signature of evaluator	date

Signature of teacher	date

Signature signifies receipt of, not concurrence with, this improvement plan.

SAMPLE OF A TEACHER WITH MORE THAN 20 YEARS OF EXPERIENCE

Annual Report of Teacher Effectiveness

Teacher: Karen Sullivan
School: Sample
Grade/subject: Reading–Writing Specialist

STANDARDS
I.   Currency of Curriculum
II.   Effective Planning and Assessment of Curriculum and Instruction
III. Effective Management of Classroom Environment
IV.   Effective Instruction
V.   Promotion of High Standards and Expectations for Students' Achievement
VI.   Promotion of Equity and Appreciation of Diversity
VII. Fulfillment of Professional Responsibilities

Karen Sullivan has been teaching for over twenty years in the Sample Public Schools, in varying capacities. For the past six years at Sample, Karen was responsible for a tutorial and after-school homework program. This seemed to have started out strongly at the time when it was located in one of the public housing communities where many Sample children live.

Over time, however, the program moved back into the Sample building and became less effective. Attendance dropped from an average of fifteen students each day to an average of five students each day. This happened despite there being no decrease in the number of students attending Sample School from the public housing community.

In spite of repeated efforts to hold her accountable to a schedule, a procedure for keeping records and attendance, for tracking students' school performance, and for maintaining contact with parents, Karen was not able to develop and stick to a well-articulated plan. Last year, she submitted no attendance reports despite being required to submit monthly student performance and attendance reports. While Karen was kind and caring to her students, they knew there was no accountability, and the program lost its impact. As a result, other homework programs with teacher volunteers sprang up around the building. Attendance in these programs grew, and it became clear that we would need to identify another role for Karen.

It was obviously not cost-effective to pay a teacher to staff a program that would function very well in the hands of instructional aides. With the retirement of longtime reading specialist Susan Miller, Karen took on responsibility for delivering a reading program to children in grades four through six at Sample and Washington Schools. Karen accepted this in good spirit and with a commitment to do her best.

Standard I. Currency of Curriculum

In order to prepare Karen for this new job, the language arts coordinator located an excellent summer course at the University of Texas to refresh Karen's knowledge of diagnostic and pedagogical techniques for readers in the middle elementary grades. In addition, the language arts coordinator provided some days for Karen to observe and learn from a seasoned reading teacher in another building, had her attend workshops and made herself available for on-site mentoring. Nonetheless, the program has not met our expectations.

In her first year as a reading specialist at Sample, teachers reported that Karen was often late for her scheduled meetings with reading groups or misses them altogether. (See the memos of December 2, 2003, and March 4, 2004.) One described the program this way: "It's happening, but it's not dependable or productive. Kids never know whether they'll see her or not, so it undermines their commitment to keep up with their reading."

Teachers at Washington have reported to the principal that the same pattern of lateness and missed appointments has occurred there too. In addition, some of the teachers have had persistent difficulty in arranging a regular schedule with Karen. The language arts coordinator discussed the teachers' concerns and the need to be punctual in following the schedule during meetings in October, December, February and March.

It was noteworthy during a reading group observed in February (see observation write-up) that Karen did not once refer to a student by name. Since there were only four children in the group, it should have been possible to learn and use their names right away.

A lesson observed in March (see observation write-up) consisted of a preview of Lois Lowry's *The Giver*. By and large, the time was spent having students look at the book's cover and make some predictions, then take turns reading aloud and answer brief questions. While each of these techniques may have merit, in this case the group—which consisted of very bright, motivated children—was lackluster and unenthusiastic. After five minutes of rather aimless discussion, a student was asked, "And what do you think?" She responded, "Well, it's hard to know what you think when you haven't even read the first sentence of the book." Once students began reading, Karen's questions were mostly along the lines of, "How do you feel about this?" or "What do you think about this community?"—questions to which students would likely have far more substantive answers once they'd read a significant part of the text. During the post-observation conference, Karen was asked several questions about the story. It was obvious that she had not read the book prior to the class. It is essential that Karen read any book she is using with groups.

Standard II. Effective Planning and Assessment of Curriculum and Instruction and V. Promotion of High Standards and Expectations for Students' Achievement

A couple of weeks before the unit on *The Giver* got underway, the classroom teacher approached me with grave reservations about having Karen teach this beautiful and complex work. The teacher reported that she had been completely frustrated trying to work with Karen, who, as she saw it, took no initiative and showed no evidence of planning. She noted that in one case in November it was clear that Karen had not even read the book ahead of time. (See March 4, 2004 memo.)

In their January meeting (that included the classroom teacher), the language arts coordinator told Karen that she wanted her to plan a unit on *The Giver,* but she noted that when Karen showed her the unit plan, it was all work that had been done by her predecessor, Ms. Miller. Karen could not describe the unit. It was obvious that she had not read the unit before giving it to the coordinator. (See memo of January 15, 2004.)

For her part, Karen reported being treated disrespectfully by this teacher. She resented being asked to show lesson plans (she had been asked to share the plans with the teacher so the teacher could follow the students' progress) and said that the teacher had resorted to asking her to do busywork, such as copying and laminating. When I spoke to the teacher about this, she acknowledged that these allegations were true, but that she had reached a point of desperation. She felt she could not send her struggling readers to Karen and added that some teachers had begun refusing to send their students to her at all.

I have not been successful in mediating a rapprochement between Karen and this teacher. Unfortunately, the classroom teacher is not alone in finding the reading program wanting. Some teachers have been pleased to have Karen in their classrooms, finding her "helpful" and "cooperative," but they are unanimous in their conviction that a diagnostic, prescriptive program with solid planning, ongoing assessment and well-monitored progress is unavailable to their students.

Teachers at Washington have reported to the principal that they share similar frustration. While she has been helpful with individual students and specific books, there is a perception that she cannot be consistently counted on to deliver an effectively planned program. Walk-through visits by the principal and the language arts coordinator conducted at least twice per week support this information. (See memos of December 3, January 15 and March 4.)

Standard III. Effective Management of Classroom Environment

Karen maintains a calm, pleasant classroom. Students are clearly at ease with her and know they will be treated kindly.

The physical environment leaves much to be desired. No student work is on display. Books—the tools of the trade for a reading teacher—are piled untidily here and there, not displayed or stored with care. The one poster on the wall during a March visit is of autumn leaves. (See observation reports.)

To be fair, Karen shares this space with the grades 3/4 homework center. Still, there is no evident pride in maintaining a bright, inviting space in which to welcome students.

Standard IV. Effective Instruction

One of the most important functions of a reading specialist is conducting diagnostic tests. Given the centrality of reading skills to the success of students in the upper grades, the only means to effective instruction is good, ongoing assessment.

Since this was a new role for Karen, we tried to keep testing demands light in this first year. In late October, however, we received a request from the parent of a fifth grader to test his son in reading. He felt the child was not picking up on the main ideas of things he read, and he was even more deeply worried about higher-level comprehension and inferential skills. For this parent, the matter of getting this testing done and a plan in place was of particular urgency; the parent is dying of cancer and feels a deep responsibility to attend to his sons' needs and ensure that they will be met in the future.

By mid January, Karen had not yet begun testing this child, although the language arts coordinator had provided specific training in the instrument she needed to use. The principal spoke to Karen on October 5, October 25, November 10, November 30 and December 12 about the need to test this student. The father was desperate and angry. Finally, the language arts coordinator tested the child herself and met with the father to review her findings. (See memo of January 15, 2004.)

The Washington principal reports that in his conversations with Karen she has expressed that diagnostic testing is new to her and that she has found it quite challenging. The principal reports that he is appreciative of her efforts to master the testing but feels he must join with me (Sample School principal) in noting the importance and centrality of diagnostic testing in the reading specialist's role. He further states that it is imperative that she immediately focus on this task and commit all of her personal resources to mastering it.

Standard VI. Promotion of Equity and Appreciation of Diversity

There is no question that Karen cares deeply about children and wants them to succeed. Her work in former years with some of Sample's most economically disadvantaged children is evidence of her belief in the right of every child to equal opportunity through an excellent education.

Standard VII. Fulfillment of Professional Responsibilities

It seems evident that this has not been a happy year for Karen. She knows that many of her colleagues in both buildings are unhappy with her work. The fact that she is often late for school or misses scheduled meeting times with groups or individual children suggests that she has trouble sustaining enthusiasm for the job. It must be very difficult for such a warm, caring person to sense that her performance has been disappointing to people who have been friends and colleagues for many years.

I am deeply concerned that we find a way to break this cycle. The Washington principal and I therefore offer the following recommendations:

- a clearly articulated job description, with well-defined procedures for accountability has been again given to Karen
- the development of an improvement plan
- a year of intensified support with an evaluation out-of-cycle
- the identification of coursework that will have a direct impact on job effectiveness

_____ This evaluation indicates performance above district standard.

_____ This evaluation indicates performance that meets the district standard

X This evaluation indicates performance which is below the standard expected of staff in the Sample Public Schools.

Overall Evaluation: _____ Satisfactory **X** Unsatisfactory

_____   _____
Signature of evaluator   date

_____   _____
Signature of teacher   date

Signature indicates receipt of, not concurrence with, this evaluation. Teachers Are Encouraged To Submit Comments. (Please make comments on the back of this form or on an attached sheet.)

IMPROVEMENT PLAN FOR KAREN SULLIVAN

Reading–Writing Specialist
1999–2000 School Year

1.   **Areas for Improvement and Recommendations**

Standard I. Currency in the Curriculum (Performance Standard I)

In order to effectively plan for, teach and assess student learning, Karen will be familiar with and understand the language arts learning expectations for the specific grade levels of her students.

Standard II. Effective Planning and Assessment of Curriculum and Instruction Performance Standard II)

Karen will provide evidence of planning and preparation for her work with students in small groups and on a one-to-one basis. She will meet with the students' classroom teachers at least twice each month to assess students' needs, plan appropriate materials and plan a focus of instruction. Evidence of this preparation will be documented in her plan book and will indicate that she has:

- read student books before meeting with her groups
- outlined objectives for teaching the books, indicating what the students will learn during and after reading
- developed specific instructional plans for each reading class that address the objectives
- completed plans for the subsequent week before the start of school on Monday

Standard IV. Effective Instruction (Performance Standard IV)

1.   Karen will provide instruction to reteach or reinforce literacy strategies for her students. Strategies will be based on the district curriculum expectations for the grade levels of her students. The focus of instructional strategies will be on word knowledge, comprehension and response to literature and writing. Lessons will be developed to meet the specific needs of her students. For example, students who have limited word recognition skills will be provided with direct instruction in structural analysis of words followed by multiple opportunities to practice the skills taught in meaningful text. Students with difficulty in comprehending text will be given graphic organizers to identify important information and will use this information to provide an oral or written summary. Specific instructional interventions and support may include:

- modeling and demonstration of strategies
- teacher read-alouds before students read
- preteaching vocabulary
- making predictions and asking questions before reading
- opportunities for students to reread portions of text
- a variety of questions to enhance student understanding
- partially completed graphic organizers
- story frames to support summarization

2. Karen will assess student achievement and progress using specific performance samples based on instruction as well as the Qualitative Reading Inventory. Results of all assessments will be shared with the classroom teacher and, when requested, with the students' parents.

Standard VII. Standard Fulfillment of Professional Responsibilities (Performance Standard VII)

As a reading–writing specialist, Karen has specific responsibilities to students, teachers and parents. This role requires that she

1. develop a schedule during the first month of school and provide the schedule to classroom teachers, the school principal and the language arts coordinator no later than October 11. This schedule will include regular times to meet with the classroom teachers of her students;

2. assesses the literacy skills of low-performing readers and writers recommended for work with her on a pull-out basis. Assessments will be administered at the beginning of the year by October 15 and at the end of the school year by June 1;

3. arrives on time for her small group work with students both in and out of the classroom;

4. attends the monthly meetings of the reading–writing specialists with the language arts coordinator;

5. communicates effectively with parents on the progress of their children (e.g., parent conferences, telephone calls, written progress reports);

6. reviews standardized test results to identify students at risk or in need of extra help.

The focus of this improvement plan is on sections I, II, IV and VII of the performance standards for the Sample Public Schools, however, Karen's evaluation will address and assess her abilities related to all of the performance standards.

2. **Support Available**

   A. The language arts coordinator will meet individually with Karen monthly in the fall and as requested by Karen in the spring to assist her in developing and implementing her program. The meetings will focus on

   1. assessing student achievement using the QRI. Karen received one hour of training for this assessment with the other reading–writing specialists in the fall of 2003. Additional training will be provided to Karen and will include demonstrations by the language arts coordinator with several of her students;

   2. creating a schedule for work with students and teachers;

   3. developing instructional strategies to enhance students' literacy learning;

   4. using specific materials to support instructional strategies;

   5. discussing the progress of her program;

   6. creating a record-keeping system or working with another teacher to develop a record-keeping system.

3. **Monitoring System**

   A. Karen will be observed at least three times by the language arts coordinator and at least twice by the principal during the 2004–2005 school year. At least two of these observations will be announced and at least two of these observations will take place prior to January 1, 2005.

   B. Additionally, meetings involving the principal, assistant superintendent for personnel, language arts coordinator, association representative and Karen will be held in October, January and April to assess and discuss Karen's progress. The principal will schedule these meetings.

   _____   _____
   Signature of evaluator   date

   _____   _____
   Signature of the teacher   date

   Signature signifies receipt of, not concurrence with, this improvement plan.

Open Book Assessment on Improvement Plans

Define the four major areas of an improvement plan, which are listed below, and explain why each area is an integral part of an improvement plan.

1. Areas for improvement

_____

_____

_____

_____

2. Recommendations for improving these areas

_____

_____

_____

_____

3. Supports available to the evaluatee

_____

_____

_____

_____

4. Monitoring system

_____

_____

_____

_____

SOURCES

American Federation of Teachers and the National Education Association. (1998). *Peer assistance & peer review: An AFT/NEA handbook.* Washington, DC.

Bridges, E. (1992). *The incompetent teacher: Managerial responses* (2nd ed.). Washington, DC: The Falmer Press.

Briggs v. Board of Directors of Hinton Community School District, 282 N.W.2d 740, 743 (Iowa 1979).

Dopazo, J. & Ribas, W. Legal material written specifically for this book.

Finnegan, S. (2000). *MGL 2000: Selected Massachusetts general laws for school committees and personnel.* Boston, MA: Massachusetts Association of School Committees Inc.

Fraser, R. G. (1996, August 18). Untitled handout given at the workshop, *Supervising the marginal teacher*, given by the Massachusetts Association of School Personnel Administrators.

Garner, B. A. (Ed.). (1999). *Black's law dictionary* (7th ed.). St. Paul, MN: West Group.

Levasseur, D. & Ribas, W. Material written on duty of fair representation specifically for this book.

Liacos, P. (1999). *The Massachusetts handbook on evidence* (6th ed.). NY: Aspen Publishers, Inc.

Needham Education Association and Needham School Committee (Needham, Massachusetts). American Arbitration Association case no. 1139–2023–83 (July 30, 1984).

Platt, A., Tripp, C., Ogden, W. & Fraser, R. (2000). *The skillful leader: Confronting mediocre teaching.* Acton, MA: Ready About Press.

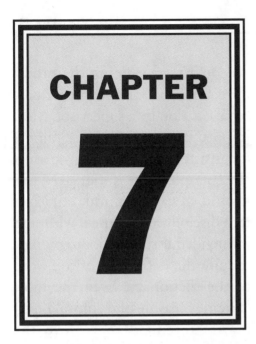

CHAPTER 7

Progressive Discipline

WHAT IS PROGRESSIVE DISCIPLINE?

The philosophy of formative supervision is one that calls for a cooperative and collegial working relationship. You will recall from chapter 2 that we defined the formative supervision and evaluation process as a positive, supportive and collaborative process designed to improve students' performance and attitudes by increasing the effectiveness and attitudes of a district's teachers.

In addition, much of a school's culture and the norms which motivate staff are predicated on the good will built up between supervisors and the 95% to 98% of the staff members who perform in the satisfactory range as they work together on a day-to-day basis in a mostly formative and collegial manner. It often presents a dilemma for school supervisors when they are faced with a situation that warrants disciplinary action toward a staff member. The definition of discipline, "punishment intended to train or correct" (Soukhanov, 1988) indicates actions which are opposite of the steps supervisors take when developing a school culture based on formative interactions and collegial relationships.

Progressive discipline is the legal and contractual concept that guides employee supervision and evaluation. Most arbitrators, courts and the just cause legal standard for due process require that a public employer follow a pattern of progressive discipline in order to sustain a disciplinary action. The word "discipline" in this term often raises discomfort because it sounds more punitive than corrective. However, progressive discipline is the universally

215

Much of a school's culture and the norms which motivate staff are predicated on the goodwill built up between supervisors and the 95% to 98% of the staff members who perform in the satisfactory range as they work together on a day-to-day basis in a mostly formative and collegial manner. It often presents a dilemma for school supervisors when they are faced with a situation that warrants disciplinary action toward a staff member.

accepted term naming the procedure for situations requiring corrective action by a supervisor. Most important, progressive discipline is a consistent and fair way to treat the people you supervise. We should always remind ourselves that discipline as we use it with staff is intended *to correct*, not to punish, despite the definition of the word in the dictionary. Even the most extreme measure of dismissal is primarily intended to remove the offender from the school house to ensure the well being of others rather than to punish the offender.

Steps in Progressive Discipline

Progressive discipline is a process that works within and parallel to a district's supervision and evaluation processes. Typically, progressive discipline has four steps: verbal warning (or reprimand), written reprimand and warning, suspension without pay (or with pay during investigation) and final warning and discharge. However, I always recommend to supervisors a preliminary step, corrective recommendation, in most situations in which the supervisor feels he/she needs to correct a behavior. A **corrective recommendation** is a private, informal conversation with a staff member about a behavior in question. The staff member should have an opportunity to explain his/her perspective on the behavior. After the discussion, the supervisor should write a brief note to his/her own file indicating date, time and substance of the conversation. Many supervisors keep track of these discussions by writing brief notes on the bottom of their appointment calendars and keeping the calendars from year to year, in case there is a need to refer to the date of earlier discussions. In most cases, they will never need to refer to these notes. However, if at some future point they need to move to a higher level of the progressive discipline process, the notes will be important in jogging the supervisor's memory and/or as evidence that the conversation actually took place.

The next step should be a **verbal warning (or reprimand).** This kind of warning details the nature of the infraction or the failure to meet an expectation and includes a statement saying that if the same infraction or concern (e.g., yelling at student, arriving at the classroom or work area after the assigned time) occurs again, more serious disciplinary action will result. This should be done at a place and time that allows for adequate opportunity for the employee to give his/her side of the incident in a private area in order to protect the employee's confidentiality. The employee has the right, known as the

Weingarten right (see the explanation of the Weingarten right in chapter 6 on pages 172–173), to ask that the discussion be postponed until the employee has representation. The subject matter of the conversation and the fact that a verbal warning has been given should always be documented in the form of a memorandum to the employee. The administrator should ask the employee to initial and return a copy. The decision of whether the copy is placed in the administrator's own file as a memory aide or placed in the personnel file is one the district-level administration should make and ensure it is carried out in a consistent manner by all supervisors. A sample of a memo sent after a verbal warning may be found later in this chapter on page 224.

The next step in the progression is a **written reprimand and warning.** The specific incident or concern is reduced to writing and presented to the employee with the clear understanding that a copy will be placed in the employee's personnel file. The written reprimand and warning should also contain a statement of what the consequences will be if there is a repetition of this or any other disciplinary incident or problem. Many districts require building-level administrators to consult with a member of the central administration prior to issuing a written reprimand and warning. This is done to ensure that there is a common administrative application of these reprimands across the district. It is suggested the written warning be given after a meeting in which the employee has an opportunity to respond to the concern. A copy of the reprimand and warning, signed or initialed by the employee, should be placed in the personnel file at the personnel office. Samples of written reprimands may be found later in this chapter on pages 225 and 229–230.

> At each stage, the supervisor should conduct *a fair and impartial investigation to establish the facts of the case.*

The next step is **suspension without pay (or suspension with pay during investigation)** and **a final written warning** stating that another incident or problem will result in discharge. This step should only be taken by the building principal after consultation with the superintendent or the superintendent's designee. If the principal cannot be reached by the administrator wishing to issue the verbal warning, the administrator should consult directly with the superintendent or the superintendent's designee. When possible, the staff member should be notified in person of the suspension and warning, then sent a written confirmation of the details of the discussion. A copy of the written confirmation, signed or initialed by the employee, should be placed in the employee's official personnel file.

The final step is **discharge.**

At each stage, the supervisor should conduct a fair and impartial investigation to establish the facts of the case (pp. 166–168 contain the Do's and Don'ts Related to Investigating an Employee Discipline Situation). The staff member's employment record should be reviewed, and the handling of other similar cases by this and other supervisors should be considered. It is only after the investigation is completed that official disciplinary action should be taken. At times, the investigation will show clear misbehavior on the part of the employee. At other times, the investigation will completely exonerate the employee. A third possibility is that the investigation will lead to conflicting evidence and no clear determination. For these types of cases, the administrator should write a memo documenting the alleged incident and the fact that a clear finding could not be reached. An example of this type of memo may be found later in this chapter on pages 230–232.

The Exceptional Situation

Not all problems with employees require each step of progressive discipline. Some incidents may be so serious in and of themselves that they justify moving immediately to one of the higher steps or even to discharge. For example, a staff member charged with an assault or other crime directly related to his/her job may be suspended and even, in some cases, discharged before the matter is resolved in the criminal justice system or in arbitration. (The structure of this explanation and some of the content is based on a handout given by Robert Fraser, 1996.)

DO'S AND DON'TS RELATED TO INVESTIGATING AN EMPLOYEE DISCIPLINE SITUATION

1. Don't Panic. Remain calm and objective. You will need to conduct your investigation from a third-party approach. Do not assume anything based on prior experiences with the subject of the complaint or the complainant. You want to avoid jumping to conclusions or making any conclusions until you have all the data in front of you and can examine it thoroughly.

2. Once you have gathered preliminary data the nature of the incident may be such that you are unsure whether or not you should continue the investigation yourself or involve others (e.g., Human Resources, labor counsel, police). If this is the case check with Human Resources (in smaller districts without a human resources administrator you should check with the superintendent's office before continuing contacting any outside agencies).

3. Read through the policies and procedures for the district regarding employee discipline prior to doing anything else. You want to make sure that you do not violate anyone's rights. Labor counsel or human

resources can guide you as to whether or not you should inform the employee(s) allegedly involved in the incident you are investigating of the right to union or legal representation before questioning (Weingarten Right). This can vary depending on the situation. For example, in administrative investigations you are not required to inform the employee of the right to representation (although you may wish to do so anyway). However, if the administrative investigation uncovers illegal activity then any evidence gathered during the questioning could be discounted if the case goes to court, (Miranda Right). **If at any point you suspect there may be illegal activity consult Human Resources immediately before proceeding.**

4. Be aware of the differences between permanent and provisional employees as they relate to investigations and disciplinary action. These are typically stipulated in the state laws and/or your district contracts. For example, in Massachusetts teachers in there first 90 calendar days of employment in the district differ from teachers without tenure who are beyond their first 90 days, who, in turn, differ from teachers with tenure.

5. Identify for interviews the witnesses who have relevant data. There may be many people involved in the incident. It's important to be discriminating in making decisions about who to interview and how many people to interview.

6. Prepare questions to ask witnesses and alleged perpetrators prior to the first interview. You may wish to ask Human Resources for advice on how to ask initial questions and follow up questions. For example, your initial questions should be general and designed to get more detailed data with which to generate more detailed questions. It is important to have a consistent list of initial questions that you put in writing. Asking consistent questions (where appropriate) helps you remain objective and helps you more accurately compare the responses received. Consistent, written questions will also insulate you from the accusation that you asked the witnesses "leading questions." This does not preclude you from asking follow up questions that enable you to get data that is unique to the witness.

7. Investigate all relevant facts pertaining to the case. If an employee has presented an "alibi" then the investigator must verify the alibi. Interview all people involved or present during the alleged incident. The

investigator may also interview non-school individuals such as an employee at the location of the incident if the incident occurred on a field trip or other off school location.

8. Take good notes. Notes should include only what is said and not interpretations and conclusion. Human Resources can guide you on whether or not you need a written and signed statement from a witness.

9. Check with Human Resources or your labor counsel at each step. Have them review any documents (e.g., results of investigation, reprimands) prior to putting them in final form. Once something is out of draft form and submitted to the "authorities", you cannot take it back, **Remember that any document you keep in draft or final form can be "discovered" by subpoena for an arbitration or court proceeding.**

10. Secure your records! Carry your folder with you and make sure that you do not leave it anywhere it can be taken or examined. Make sure that you are careful when you leave work to have all of the contents of the folder with you or in a locked location. Don't leave things around, on your computer desktop, or your desk.

11. Don't email anything specific regarding the case. Email is not secure. Also, like other documents, emails are subject to discovery by newspapers and other parties through the Freedom of Information Act.

12. Lawyers do not like surprises so tell human resources and/or labor counsel anything that could potentially have a bearing on the case. They need the complete picture to advise you about how to best address the issue(s).

> "To be a good leader, you have to be objective, fair and thorough. You have to keep the BEST interest of the students in mind at all times, even when it can create significant discomfort for you with your staff."
>
> – Margaret Maccini, principal

KNOWING HOW TO USE PROGRESSIVE DISCIPLINE IS OFTEN EASIER THAN ACTUALLY DOING IT

Educators typically have had much more practice and training in the area of student discipline than in the area of staff discipline. This leads to a higher comfort level and experience level with student discipline than with staff discipline. Staff discipline raises an entirely new set of emotions and legal issues. Delgado's work (see page 31 in chapter 2) will help the reader better understand the emotional pitfalls. A review of the legal standards (see chapter 6) will help the evaluator better understand the legal standards and processes. A good way to understand your own *emotional* reaction to staff discipline is to try the following activity.

Completing the following brainstorm activity will help you to free-associate your initial emotional responses to the concept of staff discipline. It will also give you an opportunity to begin to assess what you know and what you want to know about progressive discipline. To start, close your eyes and think of a time you or someone else had to discipline a teacher. Think of yourself as the disciplinarian. Below the directions, write emotions, questions or comments that come to your mind. Do this activity before moving on in this chapter.

List all the emotions, questions and comments that come to your mind when you think of yourself as being the administrator in a staff discipline case.

_____

_____

_____

_____

_____

_____

_____

_____

_____

DOCUMENTING YOUR PROGRESSIVE DISCIPLINE ACTIONS

The next section presents a description of the components of a memo summarizing an oral warning/reprimand and of a written reprimand. You will note that the differences in the actual documents are minor. However, the *legal* distinction is vast. When a written reprimand is given, the disciplinary action is now proceeding through the required progressive steps, and getting closer to the final resolution of discharge.

The list of components is followed by actual oral reprimands/warnings and written reprimands used in real cases. The last sample, that of Bill Murphy, is neither a reprimand nor a warning. It is documentation of the claim, investigation and the administrator's clarification of the expectation when the administrator could not find direct evidence or a sufficient accumulation of indirect evidence to determine whether or not the infraction did indeed take place.

In the sample reprimands/warnings, the names of the administrators, teachers and schools have been changed to protect confidentiality.

COMPONENTS OF A WRITTEN REPRIMAND (AND MEMO FOLLOWING AN ORAL REPRIMAND)

The components of a written reprimand and the components of a memo that follows an oral reprimand are very similar. Please note that, for those items where there are differences between the two, the wording for the oral reprimand has been written in parentheses below the language for the written reprimand.

1. The reprimand should state specific facts, such as date, place, witnesses to (or other data) and inappropriate actions of the individual(s).

2. The reprimand should identify the performance standard, policy, contract provision, law, appropriate practice or directive violated or breached.

3. The reprimand should outline all previous corrective recommendations, reprimands or warnings, if any.

4. Avoid making assumptions or using hearsay evidence from a single source. Let the direct data or accumulation of indirect data prove the case.

5. The reprimand should state that this letter constitutes a written reprimand and that it will be placed in the employee's personnel file.

    (*Oral:* The memo should state that this memo is to confirm the oral reprimand given on...)

6. It should state that if there is not sufficient improvement and/or a repeat of the inappropriate behavior the staff member will be subject to further

disciplinary action. In some circumstances, it is important to also include the outer extent of the disciplinary action (e.g., including dismissal).

(*Oral:* It should state that if there is not sufficient improvement and/or if there is a repeat of the inappropriate behavior the staff member will be subject to further disciplinary action.)

7. Give the staff member two copies of the letter and ask that one be signed and returned to you. Indicate in the signature area that the signature signifies receipt of, not concurrence with the letter.

8. Forward a copy of the signed letter to the personnel office to be included in the staff member's file. If he/she refuses to sign it, indicate the date and time you delivered the letter and the staff member's refusal on a copy of the letter and send it to the personnel office.

(*Oral:* If he/she refuses to sign, indicate the date and time you delivered the memo and the staff member's refusal on a copy of the letter and keep the copy in your file).

PEER CONFERENCING TO HELP YOUR PEERS WITH MEMOS AFTER ORAL REPRIMANDS AND/OR WRITTEN REPRIMANDS

1. Start with an area in the memo that is done well. Be sure to be specific about what is done well and give evidence to support your opinion.
   - Don't say, "This is really good."
   - Do say, "You clearly stated the date, place, time and location of the incident."

2. Has the administrator *met with the staff member* and reviewed everything that is stated in the document *in person* prior to writing and delivering the memo?

3. Does the document contain all the items in numbers 1–6 of the Components of a Written Reprimand? If not, help the writer identify what is in his/her document and what is not.

4. Is there a way the writer might revise the document to describe the items in 1–6 of the Components of a Written Reprimand in a way that is more concise, concrete, observable, verifiable or understandable? If so, give a suggestion as to how the writer might do this better.

5. Does the level of disciplinary action taken match the transgression? (Does the "penalty fit the crime"?)

6. Do you, as the reader, have any questions about the content or the intent of the written document? If so, what questions do you have?

SAMPLE HIGH SCHOOL
SCIENCE DEPARTMENT

To: Ms. Mortimer   From: Mr. Department Chair

Re: Verbal warning   Date: January 29, 2004

This memo is to confirm that on Friday, January 26, 2004, I gave you a verbal warning regarding the incident that occurred on the previous Wednesday, January 24, 2000, involving the student Margaret Herrera. The warning was for your insensitive treatment of Margaret. At a time when she was visibly upset (by the account of three adults who were present), and she was in a conversation with an adult, you interrupted and escalated the situation without adequately hearing Margaret's side or hearing from the adult.

As a background to this warning, I made reference to a meeting you and the principal had on November 13, 2003. In that meeting, he referred to two incidents this year involving confrontations between you and students outside of the classroom. His characterization to you at that time was that your manner of handling these incidents tended to "intimidate rather than educate."

Please be aware that further occurrences of this kind will lead to more serious disciplinary action.

Please sign this memo below and return to me. Your signature acknowledges receipt of the verbal warning, not agreement with it. You should feel free to meet with me again to discuss the warning; you may also include whatever comments you wish on the back of this memo.

_____   _____
Mr. Department Chair   date

_____   _____
Ms. Mortimer   date

cc: Ms. Mortimer's personnel file (optional based on district's policies or contract)

ANYWHERE PUBLIC SCHOOL
MEMORANDUM

March 12, 2004

To: Joan Doe
From: Mary Principal
Re: Written Reprimand

As I stated in our meeting on March 9, I am giving you this written reprimand for your lack of participation in the "hoe down" on March 7, 2004. Throughout this event you sat in the back of the gym while your fourth grade colleagues assisted the children with the dancing and even participated in the dancing themselves. Your lack of participation increased the burden on the other fourth grade teachers and was a negative example for the children. This event was part of our school-wide theme on the Regions of the United States, a collaborative effort with the parents (performance standards I and VII). On at least six other occasions we discussed that you have a poor reputation with the parent community (as evidenced by the negative letters from parents that I shared with you) and I have directed you to seek opportunities to enhance your reputation with parents. Your failure to assist and participate in this event, with parents attending, is inconsistent with my directive.

I will remind you that on March 1 you did not participate when the Anywhere Square Dance group visited the school. This event was also arranged and attended by the parent coordinators as part of our school- wide theme. At that time you received an oral reprimand from me for your lack of participation. Please be aware that a failure to follow my directives in the future will lead to further disciplinary action.

Please feel free to make an appointment to discuss this further or comment below. Please sign one copy of this memo and return it to me by March 19, 2004. Your signature signifies receipt of, and not concurrence with, this memo.

_____   _____
      Ms. Joan Doe   Ms. Mary Principal

cc   Ms. Joan Doe
     Ms. Mary Principal
     Ms. Doe's personnel file

STUDY GUIDE ON PROGRESSIVE DISCIPLINE

1. Why do we use the term "progressive discipline" rather than a term that sounds less threatening and more supportive?

2. The process of progressive discipline is widely understood and used by courts, arbitrators and other judiciary boards to make decisions about employee discipline. However, formal progressive discipline procedures with documentation are rarely used by most school administrators. What are the barriers that keep school administrators from using formal progressive discipline?

3. What are the four formal steps of progressive discipline used in legal circles? Is a corrective recommendation one of the formal, legal steps? If not, why is it discussed with progressive discipline and recommended for school administrators?

4. What are the components of a well-written memo summarizing an oral reprimand? What are the components of a written reprimand?

5. Explain the legal standards of *just cause, Weingarten right* and *harassment.*

6. Explain the legal standards of *insubordination* and *conduct unbecoming a teacher.*

PROGRESSIVE DISCIPLINE AND EVALUATION

Progressive discipline is primarily a supervisory process. Most instances occur without a direct connection to the teacher's summative evaluation. There are cases, however, in which there is a direct connection to the teacher's evaluation. The following examples of an oral reprimand and a written reprimand are a direct extension of the teachers' evaluation during the previous year.

In this example, the teacher was given a low evaluation and recommended for a second consecutive year of summative evaluation. During the period of time after the completion of the first year's evaluation and before the writing of the second evaluation, the teacher continued to fail to complete reports and other paperwork that were past due. The evaluator moved directly into progressive discipline as a formal written process for addressing the problem, since action could not wait until the following evaluation year was completed.

The Sample School

Office of the Principal
MEMORANDUM

DATE: September 23, 2004
TO: Ms. Sped Teacher
FROM: Ms. Principal
Re: Verbal Reprimand

This memo is to confirm that on Wednesday, September 22, 2003, I gave you a verbal reprimand regarding your failure to submit twenty-five overdue IEP reports after repeated requests.

As a background to this reprimand, I made reference to a number of meetings and conversations that we had had regarding this issue.

On April 29, 2003, during a discussion of your final evaluation report, I inquired about the status of your overdue reports and offered assistance in the form of substitute coverage to enable you to complete them. I did provide coverage on more than one occasion, but never received any reports.

On the last day of school, I asked about the status of these reports and told you I needed them by the close of school that day. I neither received the reports nor an explanation from you.

On Tuesday, June 29, I called and asked you for the reports, citing that they were long overdue. You told me you were planning to bring them in on Thursday or Friday of that same week. You never came or called.

On August 31, I again asked for the reports and told you I needed them within forty-eight hours. When I asked for the reports the following week, you told me you were working on them but hadn't completed any.

On a memo dated September 7, the special education coordinator cited that you had twenty-five overdue reports that needed to be submitted immediately. During the week of September 13, I provided daily substitute coverage so you could work on these reports. At the end of the week, you had completed five reports, leaving twenty incomplete.

On September 17, I asked if you could have ten reports completed by Tuesday, September 21 (long weekend). You said you thought that was reasonable and doable.

On Tuesday, when I came for the reports, you told me that you hadn't completed any of them, because you had things to do over the weekend. You indicated that you needed to work on the reports in school. I explained that these reports were many months overdue and that you had had the summer to complete them. I said that we needed to meet on the following day and would provide substitute coverage.

At our meeting, with the special education coordinator in attendance, you acknowledged that these reports were seriously overdue and that I had asked you on many occasions

227

(memo continues)

for them. You explained that your need for additional sleep and family responsibilities make it difficult for you to do work at home.

In addition to agreeing to a schedule for providing these reports, I explained that I would be doing an out-of-cycle evaluation because of your failure to meet Sample District Performance Standards II and VII.

The schedule we agreed to for submitting the twenty-five reports is as follows: On Monday, September 27, you will provide ten totally completed reports. The following Monday, October 4, you will provide another ten totally completed reports. The remaining five reports will be submitted no later than Tuesday, October 12. (Monday is a holiday.)

Please be aware that failure to comply with any part of this schedule will lead to more serious disciplinary action.

Please sign this memo below and return to it to me by October 5, 2004. Your signature acknowledges receipt of the verbal warning, not agreement with it. You should feel free to meet with me again to discuss the warning. You may also include whatever comments you wish on the back of this memo.

_____   _____
          Ms. Principal   date

_____   _____
        Ms. Sped Teacher   date

cc: Mrs. Sped Teacher's personnel file (optional based on district's policies or contract)

SAMPLE HIGH SCHOOL

October 22, 2004

To: Ms. Sped Teacher
From: Ms. Principal
Re: Written Reprimand

As I stated in our meeting on Tuesday, October 19, 2004, I am giving you this written reprimand for your failure to submit the overdue IEPs and reports that I have requested on at least six different occasions. On Wednesday, September 22, 2004, I gave you a verbal warning regarding your failure, after repeated requests, to submit twenty-five overdue IEPs and reports. The background to this warning, with documented occasions when requests were made for these documents, was included in a subsequent memo that you signed and returned to me on September 26, 2004.

In our discussion on September 22, 2004, you agreed to submit ten completed reports on Monday, September 27, ten completed reports on Monday, October 4, and five completed reports on Tuesday, October 12. As I explained at our meeting on October 19, 2000, you have not appropriately completed all of the IEPs and reports. There are still five reports that either were not submitted or that have been returned because they were incomplete.

Your professional responsibilities to communicate with parents and colleagues in a timely fashion and to meet mandated state and district deadlines for submitting paperwork are contained in the Principles of Effective Teaching II and VII.

Please be aware that your failure to comply with the following schedule for the submission of overdue and correctly done paperwork will result in further disciplinary action.

(memo continues)

Due: Monday, October 25, 2004		**Due: Monday, November 1, 2004**	
J. H	(review for 3/04–6/04)	M. L	(re-eval 1/04–6/04)
A. G	(IEP)	Ja L	(IEP)
G. L	(progress reports)	B. L	(testing report)
J. L	(IEP)	R. M-Scott	(progress reports)
F. R	(IEP)	A. G	(progress reports)
C. C	(IEP)	Jos. B	(IEP)
D. B	(graduation notice)	M. V	(progress reports)
		D. D	(IEP)
		M. P	(social studies goals)

We have planned a follow-up meeting for Tuesday, December 7, 2004, at 2:00 p.m. that will again include the assistant superintendent and an association representative. Please feel free to make an appointment to discuss this further or to comment in writing below. Please sign one copy of this memo and return it to me by October 26, 2004. Your signature acknowledges receipt of the written reprimand, not agreement with it.

_____   _____
            Ms. Principal   date

_____   _____
        Ms. Sped Teacher   date

cc Ms. Sped Teacher's personnel file

EXPECTATION CLARIFICATION MEMO

The following memo is known as an **expectation clarification memo.** These memos are typically used when the three following conditions exist.

1. The information comes from an indirect source.

2. The administrator's efforts to verify the veracity or inaccuracy of the claim fail to do so.

3. The administrator suspects that all or some of the claim is accurate and he/she wants to make a clear statement to the teacher about the appropriateness of the alleged behavior. You will note on page two of this example that the association representative has received a copy of the memo. This is because the association representative attended the June 17 meeting at which the incident was discussed with the teacher.

Confidential

Sample Middle School
M e m o r a n d u m

To: Bill Murphy
Date: 18 June 2004
From: Peter Principal
Re: Expectation Clarification

This memo is to review the meeting we had yesterday, during which I went over with you my notes from a meeting I had with Margie Manning on June 15. Margie asked to see me to discuss some concerns she had about her son Sean's experience in seventh grade math. This was not a meeting Margie had scheduled, so I did not have an opportunity to speak with you first. The following were the points she made.

You recently gave a test in seventh grade math. The period was ending, and Sean and Stephen Fox needed more time. (Sean's IEP specifies that he may have additional time on tests when he needs it.) Sean reported to his mother that there was no problem with his needing more time, but that when Stephen wanted more, you said no. When Stephen asked why, you said, "Because Sean has a learning disability." Margie felt that this was a hurtful and inappropriate comment to make to another child, and an invasion of Sean's privacy.

During her parent conference with you, Margie reported that you spoke entirely about yourself and your son, including his difficulties in school. She found this very inappropriate. Margie noted that she tried to redirect the conversation to focus on Sean, but that you resisted all attempts to do so. She felt that you had little information that was of any use.

When I asked Margie whether she had spoken with you about this, she said that she would feel comfortable going to any other teacher here, but that you are unapproachable. She mentioned that she had tried to work on an issue with you earlier in the year and that you had been rude and defensive. She could not recall exactly what this was about. Margie commented that the kids do not like you, because they feel you show them no respect. She said that all the other teachers take the time to work with kids.

When I asked if she could be more specific, Margie mentioned a time in the middle of the year when you called to tell her that Sean was behind in his homework, which was something she appreciated, since this is sometimes a problem for him. You then "launched into a diatribe" about having Sean tested for ADD. This made Margie feel very defensive, since she feels that she and her husband John have been very proactive in addressing Sean's needs and very open to any recommendations from the school.

231

(memo continues)

ADD has never been mentioned as a diagnosis for Sean by any of the specialists who have worked with him, in the school or in the medical field.

Margie reported that you said, "I've saved kids before who have had this." The drugs now are wonderful! She felt that this was an inappropriate discussion for a classroom teacher to initiate, and it made her very uncomfortable.

I told Margie that I thought it was very important for teachers to hear this kind of feedback and asked her permission to share it with you, since she was not comfortable approaching you herself. She said that she would not have been willing to have me do so in the middle of the year, but that since it was the end of the year she would give her permission.

When you and I spoke, you took issue with several of these points. I believe it would not be possible at this time to establish whether your account or that of the parent is more accurate. However, please be aware that events such as those described, if they occurred as described by the parent, would be inappropriate behavior for a teacher.

You are welcome to write a response to this memo. Please return a signed copy to me by Monday, June 21.

_____   _____
Signature of Peter Principal   date

_____   _____
Signature of teacher   date

Signature indicates receipt of, not concurrence with, this memo.

cc Association Representative
   Math Coordinator

SOURCES

Crew L, Everitt T. & Nunez W. (1985). *Sample written reprimands: A program of corrective discipline for school personnel.* Sacramento, CA: American Association of School Personnel.

Finnegan, S. (2000). *MGL 2000: selected Massachusetts general laws for school committees and personnel.* Boston, MA: Massachusetts Association of School Committees, Inc.

Fraser, R. G. (1996, August 18). Untitled handout passed out at the workshop, *Supervising the marginal teacher,* given by the Massachusetts Association of School Personnel Administrators.

Hirsch, J. (1999). *Labor and employment in Massachusetts: a guide to employment laws, regulations and practices* (2nd ed.). Newark, NJ: Lexis Publishing.

Procedures related to discipline of employees. (1993, September 1). Internal document from the Boston Public Schools, Boston, MA.

Soukhanov, A. H. (Ed.). (1988). *New Riverside university dictionary.* Boston: Houghton Mifflin Company.

CHAPTER 8

Creating a Culture of Openness to Change and Receiving Feedback About Areas for Improvement

Many districts in which I work have a culture that leads to most or all of the observation and evaluation write-ups including only commendations and accolades. A culture like this is called a **Tom Sawyer evaluation culture.** We call it this because it is similar to the part in Mark Twain's book when Tom Sawyer and Huckleberry Finn are presumed by the townspeople to have drowned. Tom and Huck hide in the balcony of the church during the funeral service They listen to the preacher's eulogy as he makes only superlative comments about the boys, despite their long list of indiscretions in life.

In a Tom Sawyer culture, all of the observation write-ups and final evaluation write-ups are full of the accolades. These eulogy observations and evaluations make teachers feel good. They are of little use, however, in assisting teachers in improving their performance. In districts with a Tom Sawyer evaluation culture, it is important to make changes in the culture if supervision and evaluation are to serve their designed purposes. To change the culture,

> Eulogy observations and evaluations make teachers feel good. They are of little use, however, in assisting teachers in improving their performance.

both the evaluators and the central administrators must take an active role.

Below, I have outlined the actions that districts may take to move to a culture that values the inclusion of honest, helpful feedback in evaluation documents.

1. The superintendent needs to have the objective data showing which administrators are writing accurate observations and evaluations and which are writing all "eulogies." We gather this data by randomly selecting a sample of the evaluations and supporting observation write-ups from each of the evaluators. We stratify this sample to ensure that we have at least one teacher who performs in the top third, one teacher who performs in the bottom third, and one teacher who performs in the middle third. The evaluations are read and rated on a criteria sheet similar to the one found in chapter 3. We call this a **file cabinet review.** Later in this chapter is a copy of a report that typically results from such a review.

2. The superintendent needs to convey to the evaluators the expectation that future evaluations will accurately reflect each teacher's performance.

3. Training must be provided to the evaluators to teach the concepts described in chapters 3, 4, 5, 6 and 7.

4. Coaching for evaluators on the competencies noted in chapters 3, 4, 5, 6 and 7 must also be provided.

5. Subsequent file cabinet reviews should be conducted to check the district's progress and the progress of individual evaluators toward these goals.

6. The superintendent should advise the local teachers' association and the state association's uniserve person of the plan for changing the district's supervision and evaluation culture to one that more accurately describes performance. These notifications are typically more successful when conducted in face-to-face meetings rather than solely in a memo or letter.

7. The superintendent should ask the teachers' association to advise their building representatives, grievance staff and other appropriate association members of the change in practice.

8. The superintendent must ensure that administrators' assessments of the evaluators themselves accurately reflect their performance and are based on the data from file cabinet reviews and other sources.

9. If the superintendent deems it necessary, he/she may want to advise the school board of this change.

10. Evaluators should inform the staff they supervise of the upcoming change and the reason for the change.

11. Evaluators should teach sample lessons using the format found later in this chapter. These lessons should be observed by the people they supervise.

12. Evaluators must ensure that the recommendations for change are discussed in post-conferences prior to including them in written observation reports. Teachers get very upset, and rightfully so, when they hear only

accolades or inferred recommendations in their post-conferences but then find areas for improvement and/or recommendations included in the subsequent write-ups.

13. Using documents such as the one found in chapter 2, evaluators should seek teacher feedback on their performance.

14. Evaluators should strive to make their meetings run like well planned and well taught lessons. Teachers often report their frustration with evaluators who expect their teaching to be engaging and effective but who in turn conduct boring meetings with no engagement nor any opportunity to give the administrator feedback on the meeting. Many of the components of effective instruction are applicable to running effective meetings.

15. Since evaluators are no longer using the evaluation document solely for the purpose of providing positive feedback, they must insure they have adequate structures for providing positive feedback orally and in writing.

The figure below contains a communication structure to use in developing a plan for a change in a district's evaluation culture. We have found it is most effective when central office and principals coordinate their communication to the various constituencies.

The following pages contain the sample file cabinet assessments. The first is from an urban district with approximately thirty schools. The file cabinet assessment will take place over a five-year period Approximately twenty percent of the evaluators, consulting teachers and resource teachers will have their observation and evaluation write-ups assessed each year.

The second sample is a file cabinet assessment of a small suburban district with five schools. All of the evaluators had a stratified sample of their documents assessed in a single year.

SAMPLE FILE CABINET ASSESSMENTS OF OBSERVATION AND EVALUATION WRITE-UPS

William B. Ribas, Ph.D., Consultant
9 Sherman Way   Westwood, MA 02090
Phone and Fax: 781-551-9120   E-mail: billribas2@aol.com

Dr. Alberto Hernandez
Assistant Superintendent for Human Resources
Somewhere City Public Schools
1000 Main Street
Somewhere, CA 20855

Dear Dr. Hernandez:

Attached you will find my file cabinet assessment of observation and evaluation write-ups completed at the Somewhere City Public Schools. The sample included evaluations of evaluators, consulting teachers (CT) and resource teachers (RT) from a randomly selected 20% of the district's schools. I included write-ups from five of the district's schools: three elementary, one middle and one high school. Many of the observations were missing from the high school sample, so I limited the assessment to those evaluations for which some or most of the observations were provided. Fifty-one observations from all five schools were present and assessed. Six other observations were missing and, for them, the rubric was marked as not apparent in all areas. Twenty final evaluation reports were reviewed and assessed. The purpose and desired outcomes of the file cabinet assessment are noted in sections I and II (starting on page 2) of this report.

I appreciate the opportunity to complete this file cabinet assessment in the Somewhere City Public Schools. The human resources staff were extremely gracious and helpful during both visits.

Please do not hesitate to call me at 781-551-9120 if you have any questions.

Respectfully submitted for your review and comment,

William B. Ribas, Ph.D.
President, Ribas Associates

I. Purpose

The file cabinet assessment of teacher observations and evaluations is one of the forms of data used to identify the strengths and weaknesses of the professional growth system.

Statement of Purpose

The purpose of this review of observation write-ups and final evaluation reports is both formative and summative. A reading of the rubrics and comments by the administrator, consulting teacher and resource teacher is intended to assist his/her efforts to improve. The review is also intended to be used to inform the summative evaluation judgments made by the evaluator's/observer's supervisor.

The review below is based on an assessment of the observation write-ups and the evaluation reports completed by the evaluator/observer noted above. A random number of the teachers assessed by this evaluator/supervisor were selected for review. This review is based on the rubrics for observation write-ups and final evaluation reports created by the SOMEWHERE CITY and used in the training of evaluators/observers.

To complete the review properly, the reviewer must have all the observation write-ups and final evaluation reports completed by the evaluator/observer in the year on which this assessment is based. Each observation and evaluation is read by the reviewer and assessed on the rubric form using the city-adopted anchor papers. Comments and recommendations for improvement are made for any criteria on the rubric marked as emerging or not apparent.

Please note that that the evaluator/observer did not receive narrative feedback on the areas that he/she has mastered. Evaluators/observers should assume that those areas marked as very well on the rubric meet or exceed the city's expectations.[1]

---

[1] Please note that this statement of the purpose was refined and improved in final editing. It, therefore, differs slightly from that in each of the actual evaluation reports.

II. **Desired Outcomes**

 A. Assess the level of inter-rater reliability across the city.

 B. Assess the quality of the observation and evaluation write-ups at both citywide and individual school levels.

 C. Provide data that evaluators, consulting teachers and resource teachers may use for self-assessment and professional growth.

 D. Provide data for the formative and summative evaluations of evaluators, consulting teachers and resource teachers by their respective supervisors

 E. Provide data about policy, practices and procedures that support the implementation of the professional growth system.

 F. Provide data that will enable the city to create differentiated professional development programs for evaluators, consulting teachers and resource teachers.

III. **File Cabinet Assessment of Observation and Evaluation Comments, Recommendations and Limitations**

Overall, I was impressed with the quality of the observation write-ups and evaluation reports I reviewed. They are of a higher quality then I usually find in a district that is just beginning the file cabinet assessment process for evaluating the performance of its observers. There are, however, areas for individual and citywide improvement. The following action steps are needed to prepare Somewhere City to conduct these reviews by their own staff and to improve observation and evaluation write-ups.

2003 File Cabinet Assessment—Action Steps

1. Determine which district staff will be trained to complete the file cabinet review.

2. Establish a training schedule for the district staff identified to complete the file cabinet reviews.

3. Notify administrators to keep their observation write-ups for 24 months after the close of the previous school year. This means that an observation completed during the 04–05 school year would be held through June 30, 2007. This requirement will serve two purposes. First, it will ensure that the observation reports are available for file cabinet assessments in the future. Second, since the final evaluation documents often refer to the observation write-ups as a source of evidence for corroborating claims, impact statements and judgments made in the final evaluation write-up, they will still

be available. Another administrator working with a teacher may need to refer to these observation write-ups for additional information.

4. Some schools have developed their own cover sheets that replace the electronic form developed by the city. For example, the South High School cover sheet includes the number of years the teacher has been teaching but does not include the teacher's cycle year (e.g., second year probationary, five year cycle, etc.). This omission makes it cumbersome to determine whether or not the correct number of observations have been completed for the current cycle.

Findings from the File Cabinet Assessment Related to Evaluator/ Observer Performance

5. I had a brief meeting with Dr. Hernandez on April 22. He asked me to comment specifically in this report on the extent to which the final evaluation reports address the following three questions. **Below I have given a summary of my findings in these three areas.**

   a. Do the final evaluation reports include information about teacher performance that was derived from teacher-administered surveys of parents and students that are required by the professional growth system and described in the *Professional Growth System Handbook?*

   I reviewed twenty final evaluation reports. One referred in general to the teacher seeking feedback from students. Three reports referred to positive notes or to telephone conferences that the evaluators had with parents. None of the reports indicated that the teacher had surveyed parents and students as described in the handbook or had shared the results of such a survey with his/her evaluator.

   If the city wants parent and student survey results cited, **I recommend** that this expectation be clearly articulated to those responsible for completing final evaluation reports.

   b. Does the final evaluation report reflect the evaluator's assessment of the quality of the teacher's professional development plan (PDP), as described in the *Professional Growth System Handbook,* and the extent to which it has been followed by the teacher during the professional growth years?

   This question is only pertinent to the evaluations of teachers with tenure, since probationary teachers do not have to develop PDPs. All of the seven final evaluations of tenured teachers mentioned the teacher's professional growth activities. Two of the seven specifically mentioned the teacher's professional development plan

(PDP). These were Dr. Moran's evaluation of Joseph Bellin and Dr. Moran's evaluation of Anita Cort.

c.   Does the final evaluation report contain information about student performance and growth as indicated by the data on teacher-created, city and state assessments?

Many of the observations and evaluations referred to student performance as measured by the observer's classroom observation. Several of the twenty final reports indicated that the teachers used "formal and informal" assessments but did not indicate the specific results of those assessments and how they influenced the teachers' work with individual students and the class. Samantha Rodriquez's evaluation report of Albert Lee spoke about the teacher analyzing the data and sharing the results at a weekly team meeting. The evaluation report did not describe the students' progress. A second report included comments about the students' performance on teacher-created or district-provided performance measures by describing the movement of 100% of the students from the emergent to the fluent level of reading. This was the one example that gave specific data on student performance and growth.

The criteria about student performance data speaks specifically about formal and informal measures. If the city wants evaluations to contain more specific details about student performance, **I recommend** that it provide evaluators with specific guidelines, examples and professional development activities which address the city's expectations for

- the use of formal and informal measures of student performance by teachers to impact their instruction for individual students and class groups
- how teachers' performances are described in teacher evaluation reports

6. The area in which there needs to be further professional development for most of the observers in the schools assessed is in conducting conferences and writing about areas for teacher growth and improvement. Either the teachers chosen for this initial assessment were all extraordinarily high performers in the district or there is a need for observers to give teachers more recommendations and direction for growth.

7. There is also a need for differentiated observer/evaluator professional development based on this file cabinet assessment of individual observer's/evaluator's observation and evaluation reports. As would be expected, there is a varying level of success in achieving and maintaining the

skills indicated in the rubric criteria. **I recommend** the remedial professional development for assessed observers be divided into three categories.

a. One set of observers needs only some coaching in specific areas that may be improved upon. I recommend that these people review the recommendations in this report with a supervisor or knowledgeable colleague and generate a plan for growth.

b. Another set of observers are in need of direct re-teaching related to the use of claims, judgments, evidence and impact statements. Of these four concepts, interpretations that indicate the impact on students in general and judgments about areas that need improvement need the most remediation.

c. A third group appears not to have complied with the requirements of the professional growth cycle. This could be because they do not understand the requirements or because they lack the time to complete the requirements. For at least two observations, notes were taken but no write-up was completed. In one school, there were three circumstances in which only two observations were completed of a teacher in his/her second year in the district. In each of those three cases, only one observation was sent with the evaluation for review. A number of other individual observations were missing, but this could be due to the previous district policy that allowed people to dispose of observation write-ups after eight weeks.

8. The evaluations in the pilot file cabinet review contained only one evaluation of a teacher-level position that was not a classroom teacher position. This evaluation was for a counselor. I did assess the observations and final report related to that evaluation. I don't believe it is possible, however, to make meaningful recommendations about the evaluation of counselors, instructional specialists, media specialists, occupational therapists, physical therapists, psychologists, pupil personnel workers, speech-language therapists and staff development teachers based on assessing the evaluation of one counselor.

9. **I recommend** that a time be set for this reviewer to talk with Dr. Hernandez and other any other people he designates to answer questions the city may have about this report.

10. The Richard Koerner observation of 12/18/01 had included with it a pre-observation form filled out by the teacher prior to the pre-conference. This form is used to assist administrators and teachers in their implementation of a standards-based classroom. The form is meant to be completed by the teacher prior to the pre-observation conference. If the use of such form is not standard in the city, the implementation team may

want to consider its use. These forms give evaluators considerable background information that enables them to make assessments with more depth and context.

11. Somewhere City needs to decide if the heading of the observation form should indicate whether the observation is announced or unannounced. Many evaluation systems include this designation so a third party reader can determine the level of advance notice given to the teacher prior to the observation.

The table below summarizes the recommendations made above. It includes a suggestion for the person that should take the action and when it should be taken. The suggestions above are arranged in three categories by purpose. The table below is arranged chronologically by the date each action should be taken.

Action	Recommended Person(s)	When
Evaluators/observers are notified to keep their observation write-ups on file in the schools for two school years after they were written.	Human Resources	ASAP
Review the anchor papers for use in training evaluators/observers and for incorporation in the handbook.	Human Resources and the Principal's	Summer 2004
The individual file cabinet review reports are given to the phase 1 evaluators/observers who were reviewed.	Bill Ribas	Summer 2004
Determine which members of the Somewhere City central staff will be responsible for completing future file cabinet reviews.	Human Resources	Summer 2004
Randomly select a stratified sample of 20% of the evaluators for next year's file cabinet assessment.	Human Resources	Fall 2004
Establish a training schedule for the in-district file cabinet reviewers.	Human Resources	Summer 2004
After Dr. Hernandez has read the report, a time should be set for this reviewer to talk with Dr. Hernandez and other any other people he designates to answer questions the city may have about this report.	Human Resources	Summer or Fall
Dr. Hernandez reviews the specific data he requested and takes appropriate action.	Dr. Hernandez	variable
Make a final decision on the format of the prescribed observation and evaluation forms and whether or not all evaluators/observers are expected to use the prescribed forms.	Human Resources and the Principal's Representatives	Fall 2004
If it is decided that everyone needs to use the prescribed form, all evaluators/observers should be notified of this direction.	Human Resources	Fall 2004

table continues

Action, continued	Recommended Person(s), continued	When, continued
Provide professional development for the phase 1 evaluators/observers whose file cabinet reviews indicate training is needed. Include training on conferencing about and including in observation write-ups substantive recommendations for improvement.	Department of Professional Development	Fall 2004
Remind those evaluators who did not complete the minimum observations required or who took notes in the observations but did not complete observation write-ups of the requirements in these areas. If the issue is one of time management, provide these evaluators/observers with strategies and coaching in this area.	Department of Human Resources Department of Professional Development	Fall 2004
Use the final anchor papers for the future training of evaluators/observers.	Professional Development Center	After They Are Accepted by the Implementation Committee
Decide whether or not the pre-conference form currently used is recommended or required for all observations.	Human Resources and the Principal's Representatives	Variable
Include the revised exemplar anchor papers in the Professional Growth Cycle Handbook after they have been approved by Human Resources and the Principal's Representatives.	Professional Development Center	Summer 2005

IV. Recommended Procedures for Completing Future File Cabinet Assessments

A. Choosing the Sample

The Initial Year

During the summer, the city will randomly select approximately 20% of its evaluators for the file cabinet review. In choosing this 20%, the city will assess every evaluator, consulting teacher and resource teacher at least once every five years. In addition, no evaluator who has just completed his/her final year of employment in the city or who will be in his/her final year of employment in the city should be selected. Selecting a larger or smaller percentage of evaluators will lengthen or shorten this five-year expectation accordingly. The random sample should be stratified to include a proportionate number of elementary, middle and high school evaluators. An equal number should come from each of the community clusters.

1. One teacher from the load of each selected evaluator should be randomly selected. The selected teachers should include a mix of probationary teachers and tenured teachers who were formally evaluated. All of the observations and evaluations completed in the previous year related to each

teacher should be forwarded to the file cabinet reviewers. Any observations and evaluations about that teacher written by consulting teachers or resource teachers should also be forwarded to the file cabinet reviewers.

2. The consulting teachers and resource teachers who will be reviewed are those who completed observations or evaluations of the teachers chosen in number one above.

3. If needed, additional consulting teachers and resource teachers should be selected to ensure that 20% are assessed.

Subsequent Years

1. The evaluators chosen in year one are excluded from the random sample. Steps one through three are then completed.

2. It is expected that any evaluator, consulting teacher or resource teacher whose practice was found deficient during the previous year's file cabinet assessment will pursue a plan for improvement during this year. The evaluator/observer's progress will be monitored and documented by his/her supervisor using the appropriate procedures indicated in the professional growth cycle for the respective position.

3. The process will continue in each subsequent year until the five-year cycle is complete.

Subsequent File Cabinet Cycles (five years per cycle)

1. Administrators who were hired during the first three years of the previous file cabinet assessment cycle and who were not assessed during that cycle should be selected for the initial year of the new file cabinet review cycle.

2. To complete the first year cycle, follow step one of the initial year cycle noted above until your sample reaches 20% for the evaluators.

3. Follow all the remaining steps in the Initial Year and Subsequent Years sections above.

B. Assessing the Observation and Evaluation Write-ups

1. Each observation and evaluation is read by the reviewer and assessed on the criteria form using the anchor papers. The criteria and anchor papers may be found in appendix A. The anchor papers should be used to train the reviewers to employ the criteria in a consistent manner and as a guide to the reviewers when completing the file cabinet.

2. Comments and recommendations for improvement should be made for any criteria marked as emerging or not apparent.

3. Each teacher set of documents is checked to ensure that

    a. it includes the required number of observation and evaluation documents

    b.   the documents were completed by the appropriate evaluators and observers

    c.   the documents were completed by the required dates

    d.   the documents were completed using the correct forms

C. Organizing the Data to Achieve the Desired Outcomes

1. The file cabinet assessment individual reports are designed so that each computer file contains only the observations and/or final evaluations completed by a specific evaluator/observer about a specific teacher. This will enable the city to have the flexibility to arrange the data based on the desired outcome that the city wishes to examine. The computer files are identified with the name of the observer first, followed by the name of the teacher. A slash mark (/) separates the names.

2. The individual evaluator's/observer's reports are placed in a computer folder named with the school where the teacher teaches. Teachers who teach in more than one school are typically placed in the file of the school in which they are assigned for the greatest percentage of their time. None of the teachers in the pilot review taught in more than one school.

3. The data in computer files may now be organized in the following ways to yield information about the desired outcomes.

    a.   The data, as initially organized by individual evaluator/observer and teacher, enables the city to give each evaluator/observer a report of his/her individual performance to inform the development of the evaluator's/observer's professional development plan.

    b.   The data, as initially organized by school, enables the city to give each principal a report that applies to his/her specific school. This data will be helpful to the principal in assessing the quality of observations and evaluations completed by assistant principals, CTs and RTs who work in that school.

    c.   The data, as initially organized, enables the city to give each community superintendent a report on the performance of each school in that community. This data will be helpful to the community superintendent in assessing the quality of observations and evaluations completed in each school and by the principals, assistant principals, consulting teachers and resource teachers who work in that school. It will also enable each community superintendent to ensure inter-rater reliability within his/her community cluster.

    d.   The data, as initially organized, may be used by the Department of Professional Development to create differentiated follow-up training for evaluators/observers that addresses their varied levels of success. For example, a refresher day on the writing of interpretations may be scheduled and the only people that will be required to attend are those evaluators/observers marked as emerging or needing improvement in this area.

e.   The data, as initially organized, may be used by the Department of Professional Development to increase the effectiveness of the Teacher Evaluation That Works course that is required of all evaluators, consulting teachers and resource teachers.

f.   The data, as initially organized, may be used by the Department of Human Resources to ensure inter-rater reliability among community clusters.

g.   The data, as initially organized, may be used by the Department of Human Resources to assess the city's implementation of the professional growth system.

h.   The data about all the consulting teachers assessed may be arranged into a report that contains only the consulting teachers' reports. The coordinator of the consulting teachers may use this data to help him/her in the future assessments.

i.   The data, organized by school level (e.g., elementary, middle or high), may be used by the Department of Human Resources to ensure inter-rater reliability within levels across the city.

j.   The data may be arranged by teacher-level position for use by the Department of Human Resources to ensure inter-rater reliability between positions. For example, it will tell us if the evaluations of media specialists and occupational therapists are completed with the same level of quality as those of classroom teachers.

k.   The data may be arranged by teacher-level position (e.g., counselor or speech-language therapist) for use by the head of that department in the assessment of the evaluation of its members.

4.   The purpose statement found on page 1 of this report is placed at the beginning of each evaluator's/observer's assessment report to reinforce for the evaluator/observer and his/her supervisors the purpose of this assessment.

Appendix A

Anchor Papers

1. Jerrold Stein: Example of a well-written observation write-up of a high-performing teacher

2. Latisha Soros: Example of a well-written observation write-up of a low-performing teacher

3. Joanne Pappas: Example of a well-written final evaluation of a high-performing teacher

4. Roger Negroni: Example of a well-written final evaluation of a low-performing teacher

5. Theresa Albert: Example of an observation write-up with several areas needing improvement

6. Robert Miller: Example of an evaluation report with several areas needing improvement

Note: The anchor papers were not included in the book because they are specific to this district, however, readers can find observations and a final evaluation they can use as anchor papers in chapter 3.

The following file cabinet assessment is of a small district with five schools. The district has a total of ten supervisors and evaluators. The observations of a top third, a middle third and a bottom third teacher from each of the administrator's evaluation loads were assessed. At the end of the report, I have included two of the thirty observations assessed and the assessment sheets. One is of a well written observation. The second is of an observation that needs significant improvement.

RIBAS ASSOCIATES AND PUBLICATIONS

9 Sherman Way
Westwood, MA 02090
Phone/Fax: 781-551-9120
E-mail: billribas2@aol.com
Web site: ribasassociates.com
William B. Ribas, Ph.D., President

January 16, 2004

Dr. Robert Hagel, Superintendent
Smaldistrict Public Schools
255 Mountainview Road
Smaldistrict, NY 01945

Dear Dr. Hagel:

I have completed the assessment of the observation write-ups of the Smaldistrict evaluators. Each evaluator provided me with one observation write-up of a top third teacher, a middle third teacher and a bottom third teacher. I assessed these write-ups based on the criteria sheet we used in the administrator training. Attached you will find the thirty criteria rating sheets returned to the administrators (three for each administrator). They will be discussed with administrators at the February 1, 2004 meeting.

It is our objective for Smaldistrict to have all the administrators achieving a level 3 on all of the criteria. You will note that most of the **average ratings** are lower than 3 at this time. This is because I rate the criteria based on where a district and individuals should be when they have fully reached the standard of an effective program of supervision and evaluation. This usually occurs only after all the training is completed and the administrators have had sufficient practice and coaching with the concepts taught in the training. *I do not rate based on the developmental stage of the district.*

There is cause to be pleased with the average ratings of the group, based on the district's present status of training. There is still need, however, for further growth of individuals and the group before the administrative staff is at the standard that is needed for all the criteria.

Below, I have noted each criterion with the district's average rating. This is followed by a table with the average rating for each individual administrator. I have also enclosed a copy of the actual rated criteria sheets from each of the observations assessed. The administrators each received a copy of the rated criteria sheets for their observations that included additional comments written directly on the observations.

SMALDISTRICT ADMINISTRATIVE STAFF AVERAGE RATINGS FOR THE CRITERIA FOR EFFECTIVE CLASSROOM OBSERVATIONS

NA= not applicable to this assignment
1= does not meet the standard set by the district
2= barely meets the standard set by the district
3= meets or exceeds the standard set by the district

The evaluator

A) began the observation with the grade level (or subject), number of students, time, teacher's name and any other relevant demographic data **Average Rating: 2.9**

B) ensured that all "hard-to-hear" news (e.g., areas for improvement, recommendations) is delivered in person to the teacher prior to giving it to the teacher in writing in an observation report **Average Rating: NA**

   I am unable to assess this criterion because I did not attend the post conference.

C) identified the teaching moves (made claims) using the language of the Sample District performance standards or language used by education professionals to describe effective teaching **Average Rating: 2.8**

D) limited each **claim** to a single teaching move **Average Rating: 2.2**

E) wrote value **judgments** based on the evidence about the teaching moves (claims) identified or missing from the class **Average Rating: 2.5**

F) made value **judgments** that recognized and commended examples of successful practice where appropriate **Average Rating: 2.7**

G) made value **judgments** that identified areas for improvement and offered recommendations within the text and/or in the summary of the observation write-up, after having discussed them in person with the teacher as noted in B above **Average Rating: 2.4**

H) made value **judgments** using words that leave the teacher with a clear understanding of the evaluator's meaning. In districts that require it, the evaluator used language consistent with the district performance standards. For example, if the district requires the final evaluation be marked with the judgment statements (e.g., **unsatisfactory, satisfactory or exemplary**) the evaluator should use these statements whenever appropriate in the judgments made in the observation write-ups. **Average Rating: NA**

   This is an area that cannot be addressed until the process of developing consistent definitions for the five categories of achievement has been completed.

I)   wrote **evidence** about claims, interpretations and judgments in language that is observable, verifiable and measurable in observation write-ups **Average Rating: 2.2**

J)   wrote **evidence** in the language of the Sample District performance standards or in the language of effective instructional practices when describing teacher behaviors **Average Rating: 2.7**

K)   used a variety of forms of direct and indirect **evidence** in addition to classroom observations as needed to support claims, impact statements and judgments **Average Rating: 2.3**

L)   where appropriate, connected examples of successful practice, examples of unsuccessful practice and recommendations for improvement with a description of the impact they will have on student performance, development and/or school culture (**impact statements**) in all observation write-ups **Average Rating: 1.8**

M)   wrote narratives in a way that enables a third party reading the observation write-ups to determine the varying level of success of the class observed in relation to other observations in the school and/or district **Average Rating: 2.5**

N)   applied the Sample District performance standards at levels consistent with system-wide standards (inter-rater reliability) **Average Rating: 2.5**

O)   made claims about changes in the teacher's practice that are consistent with the school and/or district goals and initiatives where appropriate **Average Rating: NA**

     I did not rate this criterion because I did not have the school or district goals.

P)   followed the contracted evaluation procedure regarding teachers' signatures or initials on written documents used in the observation cycle **Average Rating: 2.9**

Q)   followed the contracted evaluation procedure regarding number of days between each activity conducted in the observation cycle (e.g., time from observation to post-conference, time from post-conference to write-up) **Average Rating: NA**

     This could not be assessed since I did not attend all the observations and post-conferences.

R)   is clear about whom to consult for information, coaching and/or support with questions that may arise when completing an observation write-up **Average Rating: NA**

S)   goes to appropriate people for information, coaching and/or support with questions that may arise when completing an observation write-up **Average Rating: NA**

SUMMARY OF EACH EVALUATORS' PERFORMANCE

Mark Harmon   Carl Bellow
Rona Morgan   Lana Fong
Peter Vern   Dara Lanier
Bana Dabai   Joseph Raymond
Marissa Green   Sandra Martinez

Areas for Commendation and Improvement

1. All of the administrators are providing good contextual information about the class that is important for a third party reader. This is due in large part to the Smaldistrict form being so thorough in requiring the information. I recommend that the context section at the start of the observation report also include the number of students in the class.

Crit	MH	RM	PV	BD	MG	CB	LF	DL	JR	SM	Ave.
A	3.0	2.3	3.0	3.0	3.0	3.0	3.0	3.0	3.0	3.0	2.9
C	2.7	2.2	3.0	3.0	3.0	3.0	3.0	2.2	3.0	2.8	2.8
D	1.5	1.3	2.8	2.5	2.8	2.3	2.8	2.3	2.2	1.6	2.2
E	2.2	1.2	3.0	2.5	3.0	2.8	3.0	2.6	2.8	1.5	2.5
F	2.5	2.2	3.0	3.0	2.8	3.0	2.8	2.0	3.0	3.0	2.7
G	2.2	1.3	3.0	1.8	3.0	2.3	3.0	3.0	2.0	2.8	2.4
I	2.0	1.2	2.8	2.3	3.0	2.3	3.0	1.6	2.3	1.2	2.2
J	2.5	1.2	3.0	3.0	3.0	3.0	3.0	3.0	3.0	2.6	2.7
K	2.2	3.0	1.3	1.8	3.0	2.3	2.6	2.0	2.2	2.3	2.3
L	1.0	1.3	2.8	1.8	3.0	2.0	2.0	1.3	1.8	1.3	1.8
M	2.7	1.0	3.0	2.5	3.0	2.6	2.6	2.6	2.3	3.0	2.5
N	2.2	1.6	3.0	2.5	3.0	2.8	2.6	2.0	2.5	3.0	2.5
P	3.0	2.3	3.0	3.0	3.0	3.0	3.0	3.0	3.0	3.0	2.9
Ave.	2.3	1.7	2.8	2.5	3.0	2.6	2.8	2.4	2.5	2.4	

2. All the administrators are using the required form.

3. The administrators are split on their identification of claims. (See item D.) Some are doing an excellent job of making specific claims that are related to appendix L in the teacher's contract. Those who need improvement in this area are either making claims that are too broad or are trying to make multiple claims in a single paragraph. Discussion among the administrative staff related to how they can break apart appendix L[2] of the teacher's contract into specific claims will improve this situation. More specific claims will lead to write-ups that better describe to teachers the impact of their teaching on student achievement and growth.

4. Appendix L is an excellent document in that it provides a high level of specificity about the component parts of good teaching. There is a need for increased use of this specificity by some of the evaluators in the application of the language in appendix L. The workshop "Evaluating in the Standards-Based Classroom" that we have planned for February will be a very good step for addressing this area. In addition to this, I recommend that some administrative meeting time be devoted to developing specific claims for those appendix L descriptors that contain multiple claims.

5. There is a need for the district to develop and ratify through the teachers association a document similar to appendix L for counselors and other non-classroom teaching positions. Chapter nine of *Teacher Evaluation That Works!!* has excellent models of these documents from the Lexington Public Schools.

6. The workshop time scheduled to develop consistent definitions for the rating terms *excellent, exceeds expectations, meets expectations, needs improvement* and *unacceptable performance* will move the district significantly toward greater inter-rater reliability.

7. At this point in the training, the expectation for Smaldistrict is that individual administrators and the group would have an average score in the 2.4 to 2.6 range. The district scores have exceeded this range and almost all have of the individual administrators have met or exceeded this range. One administrator is well below this range and needs additional assistance to move his performance within the range of the other administrators. Peter and Marissa have a very strong grasp of note-taking and writing in the CEIJ format. I recommend that one of them work with

---

2   Appendix L refers to the section in the contract between the teachers' union and the school board that identifies the teacher performance standards.

the low-performing administrator to increase his competency on these concepts.

8. All but two of the administrators are doing an excellent job of chunking their evidence to support claims (see items I, J, and K).

9. All of the administrators wrote about the bottom third and middle third of teachers in ways that identify areas for improvement. Your administrators are to be commended for *not* falling into the common practice of writing "eulogy" observation write-ups. Some administrators were clearer when writing about areas of improvement than others. (See items G and I.) Those who struggle with this either tend to bury the area for improvement in positive text or to make more of an inference rather than a statement about the need for improvement. The workshop "Evaluating the Unsatisfactory and Barely Satisfactory Teacher" is one step toward improving this area. Another step is to have the administrators meet five or six times during the year to share their write-ups and other work with their lowest performing teachers and receive suggestions for improving this work. These meetings would give the administrators the coaching, skills instruction and support that is needed to effectively address a low-performing professional teacher status teacher. Such meetings would also increase their inter-rater reliability, thereby decreasing claims that one administrator is unreasonable in his/her expectations or that the evaluator is motivated by a personal vendetta against a teacher rather than by the teacher's performance issues.

10. Marissa and Sandra missed the guided observations.[3] A review of Marissa's work indicates that it is probably not necessary for her to have the guided observation at this time. Sandra's write-ups indicate that she should have a guided observation. I also think another guided observation would be a significant benefit to the administrator with an average score below the 2.4 to 2.6 range.

11. Impact statements (see item L) is an area in which eight of the ten evaluators still need to make significant improvement.

12. Seven of the ten administrators need to use more specific, literal evidence to support their claims (see item I). One component of this issue will be resolved as the administrators become more proficient at taking

---

3 Guided observations are observations in which the trainer observes a teacher with one or two of the administrators being assessed in this report. The purpose of a guided observation is that it enables the trainer to provide direct coaching to the administrator on a specific observation of a class they both observed. Guided observations are not needed for a file cabinet review. They are, however, often a part of administrator training designed to increase the competency of the administrators on the criteria assessed in file cabinet reports. In this report, a guided observation write-up was one of the three documents chosen for assessment.

literal notes during observations. Another component will be resolved when the administrators use greater specificity in their claims. The third component requires the administrators to move from paraphrasing what they observe to literally reporting the teacher and student behaviors and statements they observe.

As mentioned above, the Smaldistrict administrative staff has developed the competencies identified in this file cabinet assessment more quickly than is typical due to the training provided prior to the assessment. I credit them and you for this progress. Your clearly articulated expectations, as stated at the sessions, have set a clear path toward success. The effort and enthusiasm demonstrated by the administrators has moved their performance close to the objective of excellent performance on all the criteria for effective class-room observations.

Respectfully submitted,

William B. Ribas

President, Ribas Associates

EXAMPLES OF COMPLETED CRITERIA SHEETS

The file cabinet assessment report above was based on the observations completed by ten evaluators. Below, I have included the criteria sheets for two of the evaluators as an example. I have chosen the highest performing and lowest performing administrators to represent a range of performance. For each of these administrators, I have chosen the observation write-up and the criteria sheet from their middle third teacher. **In the observation write-ups, the bold print is the file cabinet assessor's comments.**

CRITERIA FOR EFFECTIVE OBSERVATION WRITE-UPS

Evaluator: *Marissa Green*—teacher performing at the middle third

NA= not applicable to this assignment
1= does not meet the standard
2= barely meets the standard
3= meets or exceeds the standard

The evaluator

A)   began the observation with the grade level (or subject), number of students, time, teacher's name and any other relevant demographic data **Rating: 3**

Please see my comments below on your observation write-up.

T)   ensured that all "hard-to-hear" news (e.g., areas for improvement, recommendations) is delivered in person to the teacher prior to giving it to the teacher in writing in an observation report **Rating: NA**

I am unable to assess this criterion because I did not attend the post-conference.

U)   identified the teaching moves (made **claims**) using the language of the Sample District performance standards or language used by education professionals to describe effective teaching **Rating: 3**

You did an excellent job of using the language in appendix L to state your claims.

V)   limited each **claim** to a single teaching move **Rating: 3**

You did an excellent job of stating your claims with specificity. As a result, you were able to chunk all the related evidence and make clearly stated impact statements.

W)   wrote value **judgments** based on the evidence about the teaching moves (claims) identified or missing from the class **Rating: 3**

X)   made value **judgments** that recognized and commended examples of successful practice where appropriate **Rating: 3**

Y)   made value **judgments** that identified areas for improvement and offered recommendations within the text and/or in the summary of the observation write-up, after having discussed them in person with the teacher as noted in B above **Rating: 3**

You did an excellent job of making clearly stated judgments. However, on one area for improvement you crossed into a bit of pointed hyperbole. Please see my notes on the observation for more information on this point.

Z)   made value **judgments** using words that leave the teacher with a clear understanding of the evaluator's meaning. In districts that require it, the evaluator used language consistent with the district performance standards. For example, if the district requires that the final evaluation be marked with a judgment statements (e.g., **unsatisfactory, satisfactory** or **exemplary**) the evaluator should use these statements whenever appropriate in the judgments made in the observation write-ups. **Rating: NA**

This is an area that cannot be addressed until the process of developing consistent definitions for the five categories of achievement has been completed.

AA)   wrote **evidence** about claims, interpretations and judgments in language that is observable, verifiable and measurable in observation write-ups **Rating: 3**

Your evidence is specific, literal and chunked with the claims. Well done!

BB)   wrote **evidence** in the language of the Sample District performance standards or in the language of effective instructional practices when describing teacher behaviors **Rating: 3**

Your evidence is directly related to the language in appendix L.

CC)   used a variety of forms of direct and indirect **evidence** in addition to classroom observations as needed to support claims, impact statements and judgments **Rating: 3**

DD)   where appropriate, connected examples of successful practice, examples of unsuccessful practice and recommendations for improvement with a description of the impact they will have on student performance, development and/or school culture (**interpretations**) in all observation write-ups **Rating: NA**

EE)   wrote narratives in a way that enables a third party reading the observation write-ups to determine the varying level of success of the class observed in relation to other observations in the school and/or district **Rating: 3**

FF)   applied the Sample District performance standards at levels consistent with system-wide standards (**inter-rater reliability**) **Rating: 3**

Your decision to point out two areas of improvement for a middle third teacher is consistent with the practice of the other Smaldistrict administrators.

GG) made **claims** about changes in the teacher's practice that are consistent with the school and/or district goals and initiatives where appropriate **Rating: NA**
I did not rate this criterion because I did not have the school or district goals.

HH) followed the contracted evaluation procedure regarding teachers' signatures or initials on written documents used in the observation cycle **Rating: 3**

II) followed the contracted evaluation procedure regarding number of days between each activity conducted in the observation cycle (e.g., time from observation to post-conference, time from post-conference to write-up) **Rating: NA**

JJ) is clear about whom to consult for information, coaching and/or support with questions that may arise when completing an observation write-up **Rating: NA**

KK) goes to appropriate people for information, coaching and/or support with questions that may arise when completing an observation write-up **Rating: NA**

SMALDISTRICT PUBLIC SCHOOLS

Report of Classroom Observation

(*Note:* The assessor's comments are in bold text.)

Teacher	Ms. ????	Supervisor	Marissa Green
Location	High School	Title	Math/Science Department Head
Date of Visit	December 9, 2003	Time	H-Block
Pre-Conference	None	Post-Conference	December 13, 2003

Observer's Comments

This was a high honors Algebra 2 class with 20 students, 12 girls and 8 boys. The room was set up in rows and columns. There were no student desks next to each other.

You have done an excellent job of providing all the information a third reader party needs to understand the context of the class.

The class began with Ms. ???? explaining the plan for the day. "We will go over homework problems you didn't understand. We will practice the even numbers from the review section of the text, and then we will go over several of these the last ten minutes of the class. You will have a quiz on this material on Monday." Quickly setting the agenda for the lesson helps focus the student and ought to make for smooth transitions from one agenda item to the next. It is good practice to present the day's agenda quickly and early in the period. **This is an excellent paragraph containing all the parts of a CJEI. Of particular note is your use of an interpretation statement that indicates the impact on students.**

Student homework was not collected nor checked in any explicit manner. **Is this piece of evidence associated with any claim? It appears to stand alone.**

The concept under study for this lesson was *log* problems (eg. $\log_b Y = X$ is the same as $Y = b^X$). The lesson reviewed previously taught material.

One of the core values of the mathematics curricula is *students will communicate their mathematical thinking as they find solutions to problems.* Ms. ???? did not honor this core value. **This is a very clearly stated claim and judgment.** A student asked to go over problem #29 ($\log(3 \times 10^{12})$). The student said "this is equivalent to $\log 3 + \log 12$." Ms. ???? asked, "...and why is this true." Instead of waiting for a student to volunteer an answer Ms. ???? stated, "Remember the *log multiplication rule*." Then Ms. ???? wrote on the board $\log 3 + \log 12 = \log 3 + 12$, and said, "why is this?" Again, instead of allowing for a student generated answer, Ms. ???? said and wrote, "Remember $7^x = 7^n$, so $\log_{10} 10^{12} = 12$." Another student asked to go over question #16. The problem was to evaluate $\log 3^6$. Ms. ???? asked, "What does it mean to have $\log 3^6$?" Ms. ???? almost immediately said and wrote "$6\log 3$." The students were not asked to state the rules or explain the rules that allowed for these transformations. The answer to these good teacher-generated questions goes to the heart of the definition of the log function. Students should be answering these questions and hence allowed to demonstrate/develop a deeper understanding of the concepts being studied. **You have sufficient literal evidence to support the claim. Once again, you have done an excellent job of including an interpretation statement that indicates the impact on the students.**

Ms. ???? stayed true to her agenda. She cut off discussion of the homework problems, and had students begin work on the even problems from the log review section of the text. There were a few remaining request to go over any of the remaining homework problems, and the new review questions from the text would offer the students another opportunity to have any remaining questions answered. The timing of the transition seemed very appropriate (i.e., *most of the material that was confusing to the majority of students was addressed, while endless time was not wasted on information that the students already knew*). **You have included all the CJEI components.**

Another core value of the department is *all students will be held to high academic expectations*. Ms. ???? expected all her students to be seriously engaged in the lesson. Following the homework review, Ms. ???? allowed 20 minutes to work on the textbook review problems. Ms. ???? moved up and down the rows helping and answering questions. She gave two students a hint: "Try dividing both sides by the common factor." She told them she would check back later. She did. Ms. ???? went over to other groups and asked, "Are you all set?" When a group said, "yes," Ms. ???? moved on. When they were troubled, she spent a few moments giving suggestions. All students were engaged doing these problems. All conversations that I was able to hear were on task. By having the students work on these problems with Ms. ???? walking up and down the rows and intervening at an individual level, all students were intellectually engaged in learning math. If Ms. ???? simply had one or two students demonstrate on the board these new problems, not nearly as many students would have been actively engaged at thinking through the solutions to these problems. **Once again, all the components are well written.**

Ms. ???? introduced a significant mathematical misconception during this lesson. While going over the review problem $17^x = 4.7$, a student said "multiply both sides by *log*." Ms. ???? also kept telling students "you multiply both sides by the *log*" to solve problems similar to the one referenced in the above sentence. A student said "I don't understand what it means when I multiply both sides by *log* ... it confuses me." Ms. ???? responded "don't you remember that it is always okay to multiply both sides of an equation by the same factor?" The student's confusion was warranted. The idea of multiplying by a *log* is a mathematically nonsensical concept. The *log* is a function. It is not a number. The correct explanation is "you apply" or "take" the *log* of both sides of an equation. A *log* is a function that is a set of rules that are applied to another function or number. This is similar to when we teach trigonometric function later in the course. You don't multiply an angle by the *sine* or *cosine*. You <u>apply</u> or <u>take</u> the *sine* or *cosine* of an angle.

This is an honors Algebra 2 class, and many of the mathematical ideas are becoming more sophisticated and sometime subtle. Nevertheless, this honors Algebra 2 class is populated by students that are likely to go on to advanced courses in mathematics. In these advanced courses, the idea of multiplying a number by a functional name would be consider mathematical heresy. **You have clearly indicated claims, evidence, interpretation and judgment of an area for improvement. Your use of words such as heresy and nonsensical sound condescending, however, and could alienate the teacher. You want to make your point with clear statements yet without hyperbole.**

It is a departmental expectation that students will be challenged at all levels and in all classes. A corollary to this expectation is that the "Advanced" level of mastery involves the student's ability to weave together several major concepts in novel problems/situations. Ms. ????'s grade distribution for the first term appears to indicate that she honors this value in her grading practices. It is noteworthy that the grade distribution for Ms. ????'s class this first term showed 20% in the advanced performance category, while last year she had 58% at this level (i.e., *The student demonstrates a thorough understanding of the material. He/she applies concepts and knowledge to problems/situations that are new and different as well as similar to those presented in class.*). There is no one correct percentage for any performance level for a given class or course. 58% of students in at the "advanced" level of performance seemed out of line with this very fast paced high-expectation honors Algebra 2 course. The 20% documented this past term appears to be more realistic. We serve our students and the educational community well when we have honest and consistent measures of excellence within our discipline and courses. **You have once again done an excellent job of including CJEI in this paragraph.**

Ms. ???? has done a commendable job with the Math Team over the last two years. The team used to consist of 80% male students. Our male:female population ratio in our honors math program is actually 45:55. Since Ms. ???? has been leading the Math team, the team male:female ratio has come into alignment with the general honors ratio. The team continues to excel, and finished 2nd in the league last year. It is important for all students to see that the fields of physical science and mathematics are open to all students regardless of gender. **Wow! This equality of gender on the math team is quite impressive. Kudos to the entire department on this success.**

Ms. ???? kept her class on task for the entire period. The class was well behaved and they were respectful to each other and to the teacher. The class was well planned and accomplished its learning objectives. I would recommend that Ms. ???? take a college calculus refresher class.

Teacher Comments are Invited	Supervisor's Signature:
Teacher's Signature does not necessarily imply agreement	
	Teacher's Signature:
	Date:

CRITERIA FOR EFFECTIVE OBSERVATION WRITE-UPS

Evaluator: <u>Rona Morgan</u>—middle third performing teacher

NA= not applicable to this assignment
1= does not meet the standard
2= barely meets the standard
3= meets or exceeds the standard

The evaluator

A) began the observation with the grade level (or subject), number of students, time, teacher's name and any other relevant demographic data **Rating: 3**

   You have included all the information that is helpful to a third party reader.

LL) ensured that all "hard-to-hear" news (e.g., areas for improvement, recommendations) is delivered in person to the teacher prior to giving it to the teacher in writing in an observation report **Rating: NA**

   I am unable to assess this criterion because I did not attend the post-conference.

MM) identified the teaching moves (made claims) using the language of the Sample District performance standards or language used by education professionals to describe effective teaching **Rating: 2**

   You made two good claims in the text of your paragraph. Please see my comments in bold below.

NN) limited each claim to a single teaching move **Rating: 1**

   Both of your claims appear in an ongoing single paragraph. You want to be stating one specific claim at the start of a paragraph and then supporting it with evidence.

OO) wrote value **judgments** based on the evidence about the teaching moves (**claims**) identified or missing from the class **Rating: 1**

   You have little or no evidence supporting the judgments you made.

PP) made value **judgments** that recognized and commended examples of successful practice where appropriate **Rating: 2**

   Both of your claims contain words that state your judgment about the claim, however, you should have at least one or two more positive claims.

QQ) made value **judgments** that identified areas for improvement and offered recommendations within the text and/or in the summary of the observation write-up, after having discussed them in person with the teacher as noted in B above **Rating: 1**

   You had no judgments or recommendations for areas for improvement.

RR) made value **judgments** using words that leave the teacher with a clear understanding of the evaluator's meaning. In districts that require it, the evaluator used language consistent with the district performance standards. For example, if the district requires the final evaluation be marked with the judgment statements (e.g., **unsatisfactory, satisfactory or exemplary**) the evaluator should use these statements whenever appropriate in the judgments made in the observation write-ups. **Rating: NA**

This is an area that cannot be addressed until the process of developing consistent definitions for the five categories of achievement has been completed.

SS) wrote **evidence** about claims, impact statements and judgments in language that is observable, verifiable and measurable in observation write-ups **Rating: 1**

You have included your notes in your observation write-up. However, you have not chunked the evidence and used it to support your claims.

TT) wrote **evidence** in the language of the Sample District performance standards or in the language of effective instructional practices when describing teacher behaviors **Rating: 1**

You have not used sufficient evidence that relates to the claims of the areas of performance identified in appendix L of the teachers contract.

UU) used a variety of forms of direct and indirect **evidence** in addition to classroom observations as needed to support claims, impact statements and judgments **Rating: 1**

You have not used evidence from alternate sources.

VV) where appropriate, connected examples of successful practice, examples of unsuccessful practice and recommendations for improvement with a description of the impact they will have on student performance, development and/or school culture (interpretations) in all observation write-ups **Rating: 1**

You did not make any impact statements that connect the teaching to its impact on students.

WW) wrote narratives in a way that enables a third party reading the observation write-ups to determine the varying level of success of the class observed in relation to other observations in the school and/or district **Rating: 1**

The narrative does not enable the reader to distinguish the teacher's level of performance as compared to other staff members.

XX) applied the Sample District performance standards at levels consistent with system-wide standards (inter-rater reliability) **Rating: 1**

The write-up does not contain recommendations and areas for improvement as is typical of the write-ups of the other Smaldistrict evaluators.

YY) made **claims** about changes in the teacher's practice that are consistent with the school and/or district goals and initiatives where appropriate **Rating: NA**
I did not rate this criterion because I did not have the school or district goals.

ZZ) followed the contracted evaluation procedure regarding teachers' signatures or initials on written documents used in the observation cycle **Rating: 3**

AAA) followed the contracted evaluation procedure regarding number of days between each activity conducted in the observation cycle (e.g., time from observation to post-conference, time from post-conference to write-up) **Rating: NA**

BBB) is clear about whom to consult for information, coaching and/or support with questions that may arise when completing an observation write-up **Rating: NA**

CCC) goes to appropriate people for information, coaching and/or support with questions that may arise when completing an observation write-up **Rating: NA**

SMALDISTRICT PUBLIC SCHOOLS

Report of Classroom Observation

(*Note:* The assessor's comments are in bold text.)

Teacher: ????	Supervisor: Rona Morgan
Location: High School	Assistant Principal
Date of Visit: 12/16/03	
Pre-Conference: 12/15/03	Post-Conference:

Observer's Comments

1:08	Class starts, students start to work without direction from teacher
	Most students are working on their autobiographical newsletter project
1:12	JS instructs students how to access digital photos they have taken
	This is a key element to their project (explained in rubric)
1:14	JS instructs students to turn off monitors, and hands out and demonstrates instructions on downloading digital photos
1:16	Teacher shows pictures on overhead screen, and class is intrigued
	JS then shows how to insert photo to their project
	JS asks class how to resize picture to fit the format
	Students reply correctly
	JS also leads class through how to crop pictures
1:20	
1:26	JS walks around the room answering questions, correcting students as they work on this new piece of the project
1:31	JS gets the digital camera out for retakes of students photos
	JS reminds students to bring in home photos to be scanned into the computer tomorrow (tomorrow's lesson)
1:37	Class continues to work on projects

The evidence in the notes above should be chunked to support your claims.

There are 15 students in today's class. This class has students working on various projects and at various levels of completion. Today's lesson involves downloading digital photos to the computer for their newsletters. Ms. ???? demonstrates a solid understanding of the technology used in this class **Good claim.** Students also demonstrate a solid understanding of desktop publishing tool/software. Ms. ???? walks around the room answering questions from students, also ensuring students are on task, and proceeding correctly. The pace of this class is very appropriate **Another good claim.** Students who are on earlier parts of the project are working to get to this point (downloading pictures) in the project. The handout given by Ms. ???? will help these students catch up. Those students who were at this point are working towards the end of the project. Some students take new digital photos and are reminded to bring in pictures for tomorrow's class. The students display confidence when using technology.

Teacher Comments are Invited	Supervisor's Signature:
Teacher's Signature does not necessarily imply agreement	
	Teacher's Signature:
	Date:

EVALUATORS TEACHING SAMPLE LESSONS AS A METHOD OF MODELING A CULTURE THAT IS OPEN TO CHANGE AND RECEIVING FEEDBACK ABOUT AREAS FOR IMPROVEMENT

Teaching sample lessons is a powerful tool for supervisors and evaluators to demonstrate a culture that is open to honest feedback about performance. However, few supervisors and evaluators ever teach sample lessons despite the fact that most agree they are very valuable. Most of the evaluators I speak with about teaching sample lessons give two reasons why they don't teach them, despite acknowledging their value. The first is the time it takes to prepare a lesson for a group of students and for a curriculum they do not teach on a regular basis. The other reason is one they tend to admit with more reluctance. It is the fear they feel about not being able to teach the lesson with the level of excellence they attained when they taught full time. They are afraid to open themselves up to the staff's ridicule. These emotions cause many evaluators to consciously or subconsciously avoid teaching model lessons.

The tips below are designed to assist evaluators with these concerns. They will help evaluators find the time and courage to maximize the use of sample lessons as a method for changing the culture.

1. Don't panic. You are supposed to make mistakes, but not on purpose. Many supervisors and evaluators believe that a sample lesson must be perfect to be of benefit to the observers. Since no lesson can be perfect, supervisors who believe they can be are reluctant to do sample lessons. A sample lesson need not be perfect or even excellent to be valuable. It should demonstrate your best teaching, given the unusual circumstances such as the limited amount of teaching you do and your lack of familiarity with the content, physical location and students, especially as compared to that of the regular teacher. Mistakes will occur during the lesson. This mistakes are as valuable supervision tools as your successes. Your mistakes are the *most valuable* tools for demonstrating an openness to feedback.

> You are teaching to create a context for discussion about teaching and learning, not to demonstrate a model of perfection. Be clear about this with the teacher when you agree/ volunteer to model a lesson.

2. As stated above, you are teaching to create a context for discussion about teaching and learning, not to demonstrate a model of perfection. Be clear about this with the teacher when you agree/volunteer to teach a sample lesson.

3. Save time! Invite several teachers for whom you think observing and the subsequent discussion would be valuable to observe the same lesson. You don't need to teach a separate lesson for each teacher to gain most of the value derived from a sample lesson. There is significant value in having several teachers give their views of the lesson in a group post-conference.

4. You are presenting a model for openness to hearing corrective feedback. In the pre-observation conference, be sure the teacher(s) knows he/she must give you specific feedback about areas for improvement. Require that the recommendations for improvement be based on the district's performance standards. By doing so you will force the teacher(s) to more thoroughly internalize the performance standards. Again, reinforce with the teacher(s) that you will do your best to make it a very good lesson. There will be areas for improvement, however, and the teachers should focus on those areas and their impact as well as on the teaching strategies that work. Hearing this feedback will be difficult the first time, however, it will get easier each time you do this. Teaching sample lessons may eventually be a lot of fun for you and the teachers!

5. Teachers may not say it to you, but most will respect and admire your "guts" in your willingness to walk in their shoes. They will respect your willingness to teach with an audience of adults and to accept feedback from them on areas for improvement. Your model lessons will increase the teachers' comfort level with being observed by supervisors and peers and increase their openness to hearing feedback about areas for improvement.

6. Ask a high-performing teacher to give you feedback on your plan before teaching. It will be helpful to you, and that teacher will feel his/her excellence is recognized and appreciated by you.

7. Keep the lesson brief. You need only teach long enough for the lesson to have a beginning, middle and end. Fifteen minute lessons take less planning and preparation and can have as much value to the observer(s) as forty-five minute lessons. There will be much to see and discuss in a fifteen minute lesson.

8. The post-conference is key to maximizing teachers' learning from the sample lesson. Here are some tips.

   a. The observing teachers will be reluctant to criticize you. If the post-conference starts off as a pep rally for your teaching, thank the observing teachers for their encouragement, but sensitively push the teachers for specific areas of weakness and suggestions for improvement.

   b. Teachers tend to give the feedback in general terms without specific evidence, because they have never received training in the effective analysis of teaching. Push them to remember specific behaviors you used that were less effective than alternative behaviors.

  c.   Get the teachers to focus on the impact of these behaviors on student performance.

  d.   When they do compliment you, push the teachers to explain how the behavior they described positively changed the performance of the students in the lesson and how it will be a benefit to students in the future.

9. Be realistic about how often you can do sample lessons. Start with just a few lessons and add more gradually. If you don't presently do any, commit to teaching two lessons in the upcoming year. Try to work yourself up to at least three or four per year. You will find that the more model lessons you do, the less time each one will take to plan. You will be better able to maximize the benefit for the teachers you observe.

Changing the district culture takes time and effort on the part of the entire administration. As noted above, there are important roles that evaluators, central administrators and the teachers' association may play in making the shift from a Tom Sawyer Culture to a culture that is open to observations and evaluations containing honest feedback about both areas of commendation and areas for improvement.

CHAPTER 9

Supervision and Evaluation Documents and Contract Language

All supervision and evaluation documents contain two major components. The first is the **performance standards**[1] section, which focuses on the educational practices. They are used during supervision and evaluation to summatively determine the teacher's level of success and to focus the teacher's formative professional growth activities in ways that maximize student success.

The second major component is the **process**[2] (often called the **evaluation procedures**). In all evaluation documents the process describes how the evaluator assists with the teacher's formative growth and how the evaluator summatively assesses the teacher's implementation of the performance standards. This assessment would include implementation of the district's curriculum if there were a performance standard addressing that topic. In recent years, evaluation documents have increasingly been integrating professional development into a three, four and even five-year cycle. In these documents, the process describes how teachers and administrators work together formatively to improve the teacher's performance through professional development activities in years when the evaluator does not complete a summative evaluation document. In many states, labor laws (*legal*) require that the school

---

[1] Examples of performance standards for Massachusetts and Texas can be found later in this chapter.

[2] Examples of evaluation processes from two districts can be found later in this chapter.

board and the teachers' association/union negotiate both the performance standards and the process section. In other states, the bargaining requirements are less demanding, however, involving the teachers through their association is often most beneficial.

This chapter contains performance standards from two different states and evaluation processes from two different districts. The first district's evaluation procedure, that of Brookline, Massachusetts, is a purely summative evaluation procedure. Example 2, that of Lexington, Massachusetts, contains both the summative evaluation component and the formative professional development component. The processes in the two sample documents differ in a variety of other ways as well. We will discuss those differences as the chapter progresses.

THE PROBLEM WITH A POORLY FUNCTIONING EVALUATION PROGRAM IS USUALLY NOT THE DOCUMENT!

When a district decides that its evaluation system is not working, it usually concludes immediately that a major cause of the problem is the document. Districts commonly reach this conclusion because there are only two possible reasons for the problems with the district's evaluation system. The first is that the document doesn't work. The second is that the people are not using the document effectively. Consciously and subconsciously, it is easier for districts to conclude that the failure is with the thing (the document) rather than to conclude it's with the people. This is particularly true when the people making these judgments are the *administrators* responsible for ensuring the effective use of the district's document!

> Consciously and subconsciously, it is easier for districts to conclude that the failure is with the thing (the document) rather than to conclude it's with the people. This is particularly true when the people making these judgments are the *administrators* responsible for ensuring the effective use of the district's document!

It's easier, personally and interpersonally, to make changes in documents than it is to change people's practices. In chapters 1, 4 and 6, we discussed the myriad of *social–emotional* and *legal* reasons why many evaluators avoid having those difficult, face-to-face conferences when they need to tell a teacher his/her performance must improve. Or, they write the negative information without ever honestly discussing it with the teacher, thus creating an even greater chasm between the administrator and the teacher.

This same reticence is true for the district-level administrators having responsibility for district-wide supervision and evaluation programs. They often have a difficult time confronting their supervisees (the evaluators) about their poor performance in evaluating the teachers. They are uncomfortable confronting teachers or the teachers' association with information about low teacher performance because of the *legal* and *public relations* (*political*) ramifications these discussions may have. Therefore, when district-level administrators are displeased with the effectiveness of their present evaluation systems, they often, due to subconscious, emotional factors, choose the costly and time-consuming direction of gathering together committees and developing and negotiating new supervision and evaluation documents, rather than thoroughly assessing the implementation of their current programs.

Bringing together a committee to develop a new document feels like the right thing to do when we have identified issues with supervision and evaluation in our districts. It allows district administrators an opportunity to work constructively and harmoniously with the evaluators, the teachers and the teachers' association on the *educational standards and processes*. It helps districts to avoid confronting the difficult *social–emotional* and *legal* issues that are the real cause for ineffective supervision and evaluation. The truth is, however, that in most cases changing the documents is unnecessary because the evaluation procedures already have most or all of the necessary components to be successful. The problems with the supervision and evaluation programs are rarely the documents themselves and are most often caused by inadequate implementation by the evaluators or by insufficient training or support for the evaluators and a lack of supervision of the evaluators by the central administrators.

Many districts have spent a year, two years and, in some cases, even longer in developing and collectively bargaining new documents. Shortly after these efforts are complete, there is a flurry of activity and excitement that leads to short term improvements in their evaluation systems. By the second or third year, however, the infatuation with the new documents fades and the supervision and evaluation programs quickly decline to their previous state. The people who passionately developed and implemented the new documents leave or move on to other projects. Over time, people find that in replacing the old documents they've eliminated the problems contained in them, but they have also eliminated many of their strengths. Before very long, the districts wonder again why their supervision and evaluation programs are not working. This is not to say that districts shouldn't assess their documents at some point, however, in ninety percent or more of the cases it should be the *last step* in seeking to improve supervision and evaluation programs.

It is for this reason that I advise districts to start their improvement efforts by addressing the implementation of the present documents. The first step in doing this is to make sure everyone is using the correct documents and using them properly. During the past eight years, I've had the opportunity to work with at least thirty districts that were unhappy with their evaluation systems. In all of these cases, I found a number of the evaluators were neither using their districts' documents nor using them correctly. People were not being negligent; they had either just fallen out of practice, or hadn't received adequate training in the effective use of the documents when beginning their administrative careers in these districts.

Evaluators first need to be trained in the proper use of the documents. They then need to be required to use the documents correctly. Requiring evaluators to use the documents without training them in their proper use would only lead to frustration for the evaluators and teachers and would feed into the general belief that the documents don't work. Evaluators must be shown the value (to the evaluators, the staff and the students) of using the prescribed documents in the correct way. Chapters 2 through 7 describe how districts might provide the teaching, coaching, assessment and reteaching to evaluators that is necessary to have an effective system of supervision and evaluation.

DEVELOPING A SUPERVISION AND EVALUATION DOCUMENT

I have just spent a considerable amount of time explaining why a district's problem may have to do with its training program rather than with the its supervision and evaluation document. After doing the organizational soul searching and/or providing the implementation training needed, some districts sometimes still conclude that they need a new set of performance standards and/or procedures for assessing and developing teaching to be consistent with them. Districts are often reaching that conclusion because of education's movement toward supervision and evaluation documents that better lend themselves to being both formative developers and summative assessors of effective teaching practice. Districts want their documents to reflect the current professional research that indicates that much of the best professional development for experienced teachers comes from teacher self-reflection and peer-facilitated reflection. This research leads districts toward documents that decrease the frequency of administrators' summative evaluations for experienced teachers and increase the frequency of formal self-reflection and peer coaching. Districts find that they currently have documents that are primarily administrator-driven and summative in nature. (See the Brookline document later in this chapter.) They wish to revise their documents to formally make teachers a part of the formative growth process. (See the Lexington document later in this chapter.)

Identifying the Stakeholders and Their Wishes and Needs

Step 1: The first step to creating a document that will withstand the test of time is to identify all the constituencies and their beliefs about what a document should contain. The following is a comprehensive but probably not all-inclusive list of constituencies.

1. School board

2. Parents

3. Taxpayers who are not parents of students

4. High-performing probationary teachers

5. Average-performing probationary teachers

6. Low-performing probationary teachers

7. High-performing elementary school tenured[3] teachers with fewer than seven to ten years of experience

8. High-performing elementary school tenured teachers with greater than seven to ten years of experience

9. Average-performing elementary school tenured teachers with fewer than seven to ten years of experience

10. Average-performing elementary school tenured teachers with greater than seven to ten years experience

11. Low-performing elementary school tenured teachers with fewer than seven to ten years of experience

12. Low-performing elementary school tenured teachers with greater than seven to ten years of experience

13. High-performing high school tenured teachers with fewer than seven to ten years of experience

14. High-performing middle school tenured teachers with greater than seven to ten years of experience

15. Average-performing middle school tenured teachers with fewer than seven to ten years of experience

16. Average-performing middle school tenured teachers with greater than seven to ten years of experience

17. Low-performing middle school tenured teachers with fewer than seven to ten years of experience

18. Low-performing middle school tenured teachers with greater than seven to ten years of experience

19. High-performing high school tenured teachers with fewer than seven to ten years of experience

20. High-performing high school tenured teachers with greater than seven to ten years of experience

---

3 I use the term "tenured" to refer to those teachers who are beyond the probationary period outlined in the laws of most states and provinces. Many states use other terms, such as "permanent status," "professional status," "continuing contract," etc.

21. Average-performing high school tenured teachers with fewer than seven to ten years of experience

22. Average-performing high school tenured teachers with greater than seven to ten years of experience

23. Low-performing high school tenured teachers with fewer than seven to ten years of experience

24. Low-performing high school tenured teachers with greater than seven to ten years of experience

25. The teachers' association as an organization. Their needs typically include organizational requirements and pressures from state and national affiliates that must be considered in addition to the specific teacher constituencies noted above.

26. Senior administrative staff

27. Elementary principals or assistants with fewer than twenty people to supervise and evaluate

28. Elementary principals or assistants with twenty to thirty people to supervise and evaluate

29. Principals and assistants with more than thirty people to supervise and evaluate

30. Middle school principals or assistants with fewer than twenty people to supervise and evaluate

31. Middle school principals or assistants with twenty to thirty people to supervise and evaluate

32. Middle school principals and assistants with greater than thirty people to supervise and evaluate

33. High school principals or assistants with fewer than twenty people to supervise and evaluate

34. High school principals or assistants with twenty to thirty people to supervise and evaluate

35. High school principals and assistants with more than thirty people to supervise and evaluate

36. Curriculum administrators with fewer than twenty people to supervise and evaluate

37. Curriculum administrators with twenty to thirty people to supervise and evaluate

38. Curriculum administrators with more than thirty people to supervise and evaluate

39. Business leaders (e.g., chamber of commerce)

40. State (or provincial in Canada) and federal education laws and regulations

Step 2: Realize that no document will ever completely meet the diverse needs and desires of this group.

Step 3: Prepare for a long and time-consuming process. The number of constituencies and the significant educational, legal, political and social-emotional factors make for a long and time-consuming process. Even with the most skilled committee leadership, the process will entail over 100 hours of the committee's meeting and working time. Districts rarely complete this process in less than one year. Some districts have taken as long as three years.

Step 4: Decide whether the committee will be advisory to the subsequent bargaining or if it will be an interest-based bargaining committee. Supervision and evaluation documents are as much legal documents as they are educational documents. The superintendent and the teachers' union/association leadership must decide on one of the three following descriptions of the committee.

1. The committee uses the steps below to develop the document. The document will then be bargained and ratified, to the extent required by law, by the bargaining teams from labor and management.

2. The committee is established with a mandate to create a document that does not require further bargaining but will require ratification by the school board and the respective unions/associations.

3. The committee is established with the mandate to create a document that will be the final document. They work simultaneously as a development committee and an interest-based bargaining committee. At the conclusion of the committee's work, there is no need to bargain and/or ratify the documents. The laws related to this type of committee vary from state to state (or province to province). Districts should get legal advice if they plan to form this type of committee.

Step 5: Create a committee that will objectively consider the needs and desires of all the constituencies. This may be one of the most difficult, yet most important, requirements in the process. One difficulty is that the committee cannot have representatives from all of these constituencies. A committee should not have greater than approximately ten to twelve members, so it isn't too large and unwieldy to complete the difficult task at hand. Having a larger committee makes it difficult to schedule meetings, and often leaves people feeling they did not have an adequate opportunity to contribute their ideas.

To create a committee that is a manageable size, the member must be able to represent more than one constituency. This may be tricky since some people who volunteer for a committee do so because they have a specific set of concerns that are unique to their position. Everyone selected for the committee must be given a definitive charge that includes all the constituencies they must represent. They must then proactively seek out information from each of these constituencies to ensure that they adequately represent each.

For example, the district may have elementary, middle and high schools, and they may vary significantly in size, but the committee only has room for two principals. In this situation, the principal representatives must know that they are representing all principals. Representatives with small evaluation loads would need to spend time talking with principals with larger evaluation loads. A high school principal chosen to represent secondary principals would need to spend time talking with middle school principals. If the principal representatives also represent the assistant principals, they would need to speak with that constituency as well.

The committee should have a balanced representation. This should include a balance of labor and management, high, middle, and elementary school, male and female, teachers and administrators. The labor–management balance may be difficult to establish because some positions straddle labor and management responsibilities. Positions such as assistant superintendents are clearly considered management. Teachers are clearly considered labor. High school department heads, on the other hand, are sometimes considered management, and sometimes considered unionized management represented by the same local association as the teachers but with different contracts. Sometimes they are represented by the same association and contract as teachers.

Make it clear to all committee members that a prerequisite for serving on the committee is that they must attend all meetings. This requirement may be achieved in one of two ways. The first way is to have all of the committee members bring their calendars to the first meeting so that subsequent meetings can be scheduled. The second is to establish the dates and times of the first five meetings and make availability to attend those meetings a prerequisite for serving on the committee. If for some reason a committee member cannot attend because of significant extenuating circumstances (e.g death in the family, illness) the member should be required to submit his/her comments, related to agenda items to be discussed, in writing prior the meeting. The member should make every effort to be available for phone consultation should the deliberations move in an unexpected direction. The member must also be made aware that decisions made by the committee during his/her absence are final and will not be revisited.

These rules may sound strict but districts have found they are very important if the committee is to make progress toward completing the document in a timely fashion.

Step 6: Establish committee chairs. Some districts elect a single chair. It is important that the chair has experience running effective meetings. It is also important that the chair operate the meetings in a way that balances the needs of the various constituent groups. Other districts elect co-chairs. A typical co-chair arrangement has one labor representative chair and one management representative chair. In co-chair arrangements, the two people must maintain good communication before, during and after each meeting. Some districts use a facilitator to assist the co-chairs. This is an outside person with experience in developing supervision and evaluation documents who remains neutral in resolving conflicts that arise among the various constituencies within the committee.

Step 7: Components of the first meeting of the committee. The first meeting is critical to the long-term success of the project. The critical nature of the first meeting makes it imperative that all committee members attend. At the first meeting, the committee should try to complete at least the following components.

1. If the committee has not already done so, it should elect the chair or the co-chairs.

2. Review the various constituencies who have a stake in the document. Reiterate the importance of each representative's responsibility to rise above their personal agenda and represent all their constituencies.

3. Clearly and specifically explain the charge to the committee. Include in the charge the fact that *it will be impossible to create a document that pleases all constituencies.* All new documents, no matter how carefully crafted, have their detractors. This is unavoidable. Repeat this part of the charge frequently through the deliberations.

4. Develop a meeting schedule. The schedule should allow adequate time for representatives to talk with their constituent groups. With groups of the committee's size, it is very difficult to find common meeting times. The best way to do this is to set the meeting times for at least the first five meetings at the initial meeting. It is much easier to schedule meetings with all the participants in the room than it is to try to find mutually agreeable times when members are dispersed.

5. Once the schedule is set, reiterate the requirement that all representatives attend all meetings.

Caution! Never wait to the last scheduled meeting to schedule future meetings. A meeting or two will inevitably be cancelled due to weather or some other unexpected set of circumstances. Be certain that the committee always has at least three more meetings scheduled before adjourning a meeting. As noted above, it is much easier to schedule meeting times when all the committee members are in the room. I worked with one district that had to cancel their last scheduled meeting. It was six months before a time was finally set for the next meeting and a great deal of momentum was lost.

Step 8: Be clear about the component parts of a supervision and evaluation document and how they interface with the various labor contracts of the employees impacted by the document. Most documents contain at least the following components.

1. An explanation of the purpose of the document

2. Performance standards. A successful document will need performance standards for all the positions that will be supervised and evaluated by the document. See the Lexington document later in this chapter for examples of standards for non-classroom teaching positions such as guidance counselors, speech and language therapists, librarians, technology teachers, etc.

3. The document needs to give examples of the various types of data that will be used to assess performance. This list should include data types that may be exclusive to certain positions and allow the omission of data types that are not relevant to certain positions. For example, psychologists cannot be easily assessed through classroom observations. Also, there jobs that require types of specific individual testing and report writing that may not be addressed in data sources set up for classroom teachers.

4. The document must, where appropriate, have processes that address all the people to be assessed. For example, many districts have processes that differ for probationary teachers and tenured teachers. Some districts have distinct processes for addressing tenured teachers who have been found to be unsatisfactory or barely satisfactory.

5. As districts have moved to less frequent summative evaluations there is a need for the document to state a process for moving an unsatisfactory or barely satisfactory tenured teachers to a more intensive summative evaluation process. See the Lexington evaluation document that follows for an example of this type of process.

6. All supervision and evaluation documents interface in some way with the teachers' contract. Some will also interface with the language in administrators' contracts. Be aware of all the contract language that

impacts supervision and evaluation. There may be a need to craft the document to fit the contract language, rewrite the contract language to match the document or a little of both.

7. The process should have clearly articulated timelines that are user-friendly for administrators and teachers.

Step 9: Set an approximate completion date for each of the document's component parts.

Step 10: Examine evaluation documents from districts which have already developed the type of documents the committee wishes to develop. In addition to reading the documents in this book, contact districts which have a document designed to meet some of the committee's goals. Each district has unique characteristics, so it is very unlikely that the committee will find a document that it will want to completely replicate. However, there will be parts in these documents that creatively address the issues with which the committee is grappling.

Step 11: Examine the district's present document to determine its strengths and weaknesses. Of particular emphasis should be the committee's analysis of the document's strengths. People typically have an intimate understanding of their document's drawbacks. If the committee doesn't take a careful look at its current document's strengths, however, then the new document may lose some of these strengths as a result of efforts to ameliorate the weaknesses that exist.

To help with step 10, I have included three documents in this chapter. The next section of is structured so the committee may critically review two of these documents as a way to isolate its preferences for a document in its district.

TALE OF TWO DOCUMENTS

The following documents are both from exemplary school districts, Brookline and Lexington, Massachusetts, with excellent systems of supervision and evaluation. In reviewing the documents, however, you will see that they are quite different, representing the districts' varying approaches to supervision and evaluation. One is not better or worse than the other; they just have different strengths and weaknesses. In both cases, the reason for effectiveness of the districts' evaluation systems is the training, coaching and supervision that evaluators receive, and not the structure of the documents.[4]

---

4   At the end of this chapter, you will find the performance standards established by the State of Texas. I included this document because it is one of the first to create a rubric type of criteria list for further quantifying the assessment of teacher performance.

The Brookline Document

The first document, Brookline's, contains both contracted components and components developed by management in collaboration with the teachers' association, to effectively implement the collectively bargained performance standards (principles of effective teaching). Contracted components are the items negotiated and agreed upon with the teachers' association through the *legal process* known as collective bargaining. Each state has its own laws that define which parts of the evaluation process and standards must be bargained between the employer and the legal representative (union or association) of the employees. Those evaluation processes and standards not indicated in the law as "mandatory subjects of bargaining" are left for management to determine by policy or other managerial instrument.

Managerial implementation processes need not always be collectively bargained because they may be outside the mandatory subjects of bargaining outlined in the laws of the state. Typically, they are designed to ensure that the collectively bargained components are carried out effectively. However, it is important to note that the line between those parts of the evaluation process and standards that are mandatory subjects of bargaining and those areas that are open to managerial implementation processes is often *gray rather than black and white*. In those cases, this line is usually further defined in the case law created by the courts and/or arbitrators.

The Brookline document section begins with the contract articles related to supervision and evaluation that have been collectively bargained. They may be found in the contract between the Brookline Educators Association and the Brookline School Committee. This document includes the procedures, which consist of the Evaluation Criteria and Format on the first five pages, the two forms on the sixth and seventh pages and the Brookline Principles of Effective Teaching (performance standards). These are the parts of the document that have been collectively bargained.

The Timeline for Teacher Evaluations, High School Evaluation Teams and the Evaluation Assignments for Integrated Services are managerial implementation documents designed to ensure that evaluators effectively implement the bargained procedures. The final document, High School Student Comment Sheet, combines the language that has been collectively bargained to govern the use of a form that exists in the School Committee Policy Manual rather than in the contract.

The Lexington Document

The second document, Lexington's, contains all the components within the collectively bargained document. The Lexington document is designed on a four-year cycle that incorporates professional development activities. For those who wish to learn more about the four-year evaluation process that incorporates staff development activities, I recommend Charlotte Danielson's and Thomas McGreal's book, *Teacher Evaluation to Enhance Professional Practice* (2000). The Lexington document is designed to be both summative and formative. In contrast, the Brookline document operates on a two-year cycle and is primarily a summative evaluation document. Formative professional development is provided outside of the evaluation system but is summatively evaluated through the performance standards.

You will note that the Lexington document contains many of the same components as the Brookline document. Time lines, observation requirements, designations of appropriate evaluators for all positions and the required forms all exist in both documents.

Analyzing the Documents

In the following section, we will analyze the documents and draw conclusions about the strengths and weaknesses of the various components of each document. I believe the best way to do this is for you to read the documents carefully before you read my comments on the strengths and weaknesses of each document. While reading, consider each document's advantages and disadvantages in addressing the E.L.P.S. components of supervision and evaluation.

People's assessments of the documents' effectiveness will vary according to their perspectives. No document can be all things to all people. There is an old truism in politics that says, "Where you sit determines where you stand." This statement is never more true than in its application to people reviewing supervision and evaluation documents. Therefore, as you read, try to assess the documents from each of the following perspectives. Although many people may agree on the educational merits of a document, where a person "sits" typically determines his/her opinion on the legal, public relations (*political*) and social–emotional merits of the documents. There are of course innumerable factors influencing where a person "stands" on any part of any document. However, I have provided the ten perspectives below to give the reader a framework for comparison. I am well aware that two high-performing teachers might feel very differently about a single provision. However, for a number of items in evaluation documents, there is at least a general consensus among the various groups.

> People's assessments of the documents' effectiveness will vary according to their perspectives. No document can be all things to all people.

1. Which part of each document would a high-performing teacher like? Why?

2. Which part of each document would a low-performing teacher (as described in the case studies in chapter 6) like? Why?

3. Which part of each document would an evaluator of a high-performing teacher like if he/she had less than ten evaluations in a given year? Why?

4. Which part of each document would an evaluator of a high-performing teacher like if he/she had more than twenty evaluations in a given year? Why?

5. Which part of each document would an evaluator of a low-performing teacher (as described in the case studies in chapter 6) like if he/she had less than ten evaluations in a given year? Why?

6. Which part of each document would an evaluator of a low-performing teacher (as described in the case studies in chapter 6) like if he/she had more than twenty evaluations in a given year? Why?

7. Which part of each document would the superintendent or assistant superintendent responsible for system-wide supervision and evaluation like? Why?

8. Which part of each document would a school district's labor attorney (assigned to sustain the dismissal of a teacher evaluated as unsatisfactory) like? Why?

9. Which part of each document would a teachers' association labor attorney (assigned to overturn the dismissal of a teacher evaluated as unsatisfactory) like? Why?

10. Which part of each document would the parents and other outside constituents like? Why?

For example:

Educational: The Brookline Annual Report of Teacher Effectiveness requires that the evaluator check a final designation from the three levels of satisfactory teaching.

Advantage: This enables the teacher to get a quantified understanding of his/her performance that is not readily apparent from the narrative.

Disadvantage: Many teachers become preoccupied with the "final grade" and have difficulty refocusing themselves on the commendations and recommendations contained in the narrative.

Advantage: Teachers who receive the top designation feel their hard work and effort is recognized and appreciated.

Disadvantage: Teachers who receive the second designation (which indicates good performance and no threat to job security) can become more focused on their anger and disappointment due to not getting the top rating rather than on the acknowledgment in this rating of what they have done well. Teachers who receive the third designation often feel very threatened and become negative toward the administrator and the supervision and evaluation process.

Advantage: Administrators working with low-performing teachers find at times that the concrete, objective nature of checking off the third level forces a teacher who has shown denial about declining performance to take a serious look at his/her teaching. The first step a low-performing teacher must take to move toward permanent improvement is "owning the problem."

Disadvantage: Administrators working with low-performing teachers find it difficult at times to refocus the teacher receiving the third level away from improvement for self-preservation (external) and toward improvement for professional fulfillment (internal). The teacher may get stuck in the belief that the problem is with the administrator or the students and fail to "own the problem." The first step a teacher must take to move toward permanent improvement is owning the problem. The angst administrators have about the time and effort it would take to overcome this ownership issue causes some administrators to avoid checking the third level even when it is appropriate.

Joint labor–management committees developing new documents inevitably have long debates on whether the final check-off should be simply a choice between "satisfactory" or "unsatisfactory" or if there should be gradations within the satisfactory level. These debates tend to be caused more by the committee members' personal beliefs (*educational* and *social–emotional*) than by whether or not they are labor or management representatives. As noted above, there are advantages and disadvantages to each structure.

BROOKLINE CONTRACT LANGUAGE ON SUPERVISION AND EVALUATION

Article 6 – Evaluation and Supervision

6.1 Evaluation and Supervision

A. Effectiveness will be based upon the Brookline Principles of Effective Teaching and Examples of Descriptors (appearing later in this chapter). The annual report for nurses will be based upon the Brookline Principles of Effective Nursing and Examples of Descriptors (later in this chapter). The procedure for evaluation shall be as set forth in Article 6.2.

B. Annual Reports and Progress Reports, as described in Article 6.2 (appearing later in this chapter), must be submitted by principals in the Elementary Schools and by secondary curriculum coordinators in the High School (in cases where there is no secondary curriculum coordinator, by the Headmaster). Annual Reports and Progress Reports may be submitted by Curriculum Coordinators, Deans, Headmaster and/or Director of Personnel.

Deans will cooperate in requested evaluations of pre-professional teachers in accordance with practices followed by housemasters in the past.

Upon the request of the Headmaster, a Dean will conduct an evaluation of a teacher with professional status following the procedures established in the contract. Absent unforeseen circumstances, the Headmaster will attempt to notify the Deans about such teachers at the beginning of the school year.

C. The Brookline School Committee and the Brookline Educators Association endorse the concept of student/teacher interaction and encourage teachers actively to seek and use student evaluation. All teachers may be required to administer the student evaluation form adopted by the BSC. The completed forms may be reviewed by a teacher with his/her Supervisor at either's request provided that a teacher shall not be required to review or share the completed form with his/her Supervisor.

A committee consisting of an equal number of representatives of the BSC and the BEA, may be convened during the terms of this contract at the request of the BSC, to study the issue of student evaluation of teachers and to make recommendations to the BSC relating to the process of student evaluation. The student evaluation process described herein shall not be changed during the term of the agreement unless otherwise mutually agreed by the BSC and the BEA.

D. The BSC encourages continual peer observation-supervision at all levels for the purpose of mutual sharing, developing and examining of teacher styles, approaches and techniques.

E. When it becomes necessary to engage teachers in the formal evaluative process (by request from Evaluators or the teacher being evaluated), then the following formula should be used:

   i. In the High School, the consensus of the teacher's department shall determine the selection of one peer evaluator, and the consensus of the teacher's house shall determine the selection of additional peer evaluators.

ii. In the Elementary Schools, the teacher involved in peer evaluation will be determined by a consensus of the building faculty; or in the case of seventh and eighth grade specialist, by a consensus of the Town-Wide Department.

iii. In both cases the number of peer evaluators and administrators shall be equal.

iv. For teachers with Professional Status, Supervisors and Evaluators always have the possibility of initiating a request for another Evaluator (administrator or peer).

F. The BSC encourages self-evaluation by teachers with pre-professional status and teachers with professional status. The mechanism for this might be either a checklist filled out by the teacher or an Annual Report of Teacher Effectiveness completed by the teacher. Self-evaluation can be requested by either the teacher or the Supervisor. It may be followed up by a conference if it is desired by either party.

G. It is strongly suggested that Supervisors provide for visitations by teachers within departments, among departments, and among buildings and other school systems. Also, Supervisors are encouraged to provide in-service workshops for teachers.

6.2 Procedure for Evaluation

A. Frequency of Evaluation – Teachers with pre-professional status will be evaluated every year and teachers with professional status will be evaluated every other year. For the remainder of Article 6.2, references to teachers with professional status refer only during their year of evaluation.

B. Orientation – In September of each year, all teachers with professional status and teachers with pre-professional status will meet with Supervisors for an orientation of the evaluation procedures. It is the intent of this meeting to allow all staff the opportunity to enter the evaluation process with full and open knowledge of what the process is.

C. Pre-Evaluation Conference – On or before October 15, Supervisors shall meet with all teachers with pre-professional status. On or before December 1, supervisors shall meet with all teachers with professional status. These pre-evaluation conferences will address goals for the year, strengths of the teacher, relationships between current and previous evaluations and support available.

D. Classroom Observations

    i. There will be one announced, formal classroom observation for each teacher with pre-professional status and for each teacher with professional status. Each formal classroom observation will be at least thirty (30) minutes in length for elementary teachers and a full period for secondary teachers.

    ii. Supervisors may informally observe teachers at any time.

E. Pre-Observation Conference – A pre-observation conference may take place prior to a formal classroom observation. Requests for these conferences may be made by either the Supervisor or the teacher.

F. Post-Observation Conference – A post-observation conference shall be held within seven (7) workdays of the classroom observation, unless the Supervisor and the teacher agree to waive the seven (7) day timeline and arrange another mutually convenient date. A classroom observation report shall be completed at or after the post-observation conference. A copy of the completed observation form, signed by the teacher and the supervisor, will be given to the teacher.

G. Staff Progress Report – Each teacher with pre-professional status shall receive a Staff Progress Report three (3) times a year, normally every two months. For teachers with professional status, Staff Progress Reports may be used if desired.

H. Annual Reports of Teacher Effectiveness – An Annual Report of Teacher Effectiveness will be made prior to February 15 each year for every teacher with pre-professional status except that the Superintendent can extend the period to a date not later than March 15 when, in his/her judgment, there is good reason for doing so. An Annual Report of Teacher Effectiveness will be made prior to May 1 of each year for every teacher with professional status.

Each teacher shall receive a copy of his/her report and have the right to discuss the report with his/her superior and submit his/her own comments within ten days. It is expected that the evaluator will have conferred periodically with the teacher concerning his/her progress before the submission of the Annual Report of Teacher Effectiveness.

I. Non-renewal of teachers with pre-professional status – A teacher with pre-professional status shall be notified, in writing, on or before April 15 if he/she is not to be employed for the following school year.

J. Out-Of-Cycle Evaluation – Any teacher with professional status may be evaluated out-of-cycle. On or before October 20, the

Supervisor will provide the teacher with substantive reasons for undertaking the out-of-cycle evaluation, and it is understood this action does not necessarily imply a negative evaluative finding. This decision to undertake an evaluation out-of-cycle, though grieveable, shall not be subject to arbitration.

When the performance of a teacher with professional status is considered satisfactory after having been evaluated out-of-cycle, that teacher's cycle will begin anew at the time of the satisfactory evaluation.

6.3 Duration of Evaluation System

For the duration of this Agreement, i.e., through August 31, 200__, present system-wide practices concerning evaluations will continue in effect.

6.4 Withholding Salary Increment

The BSC reserves the right to withhold a salary increment from any teacher who has not performed in a satisfactory manner. If a teacher is at the maximum of his/her preparation column and has not performed in a satisfactory manner, the BSC reserves the right to withhold any salary increases.

6.5 Personnel File

Each teacher shall have the right to review and make copies of the contents of his/her personnel file originating after initial employment and to have a representative of the BEA accompany him/her in such review.

6.6 Derogatory Material

Should any material which the BSC shall consider to be derogatory be placed in the teacher's personnel folder, then the teacher involved will be given the opportunity to review same prior to its placement in the personnel folder. The employee shall initial such material prior to its insertion. The employee's initials do not signify agreement with the contents but rather serve as evidence that the employee has seen the material in question. If the teacher chooses to do so, he/she may submit any statement concerning the derogatory material; and if he/she so desires, said statement shall be filed with the alleged derogatory material in the teacher's personnel folder. If such material may result in discipline or otherwise affect the teacher's status, it shall be sent to the teacher involved within twenty (20) school days. It is understood that the BSC will make an appropriate investigation before inserting derogatory material into an employee's file. In addition, with regard to nurses, any complaint to any school official regarding the performance of a nurse which the school official believes could affect the nurse's employment status, shall be called to the attention of the nurse involved within 7 working days.

THE PUBLIC SCHOOLS OF BROOKLINE, MASSACHUSETTS EVALUATION CRITERIA AND FORMAT

The teacher's central role in the schools is classroom teaching. But the teacher's other roles outside the classroom are important, too; for example, in parent and community relations and as a member of the staff. This evaluation format seeks to identify the most important areas of performance within these roles, yet remain flexible enough for educators to communicate fully and honestly about teaching performance.

The criteria listed in the attached sheets are intended to represent the image of good teaching in Brookline, to serve as an aid for teacher self evaluation, and to establish a standard towards which all members of the professional staff of the Brookline Public Schools can work cooperatively to improve instruction.

ANNUAL REPORT OF TEACHER EFFECTIVENESS

Teacher _____

School _____

Grade/subject _____

Please attach a narrative and recommendations on the following areas as outlined in detail in the Brookline Principles of Effective Teaching.

STANDARDS

I.   Currency of Curriculum

II. Effective Planning and Assessment of Curriculum and Instruction

III. Effective Management of Classroom Environment

IV. Effective Instruction

V.   Promotion of High Standards and Expectations for Student Achievement

VI. Promotion of Equity and Appreciation of Diversity

VII. Fulfillment of Professional Responsibilities

_____ This evaluation indicates performance with no areas of concern.

_____ This evaluation indicates performance with need for improvement in one or two areas (See recommendations).

_____ This evaluation indicates performance with need for improvement in several areas (See recommendations).

_____ This evaluation indicates performance which is below the standard expected of staff in the Brookline Public Schools (See recommendations).

Overall Evaluation: _____ Satisfactory _____ Unsatisfactory

_____   _____
Signature of evaluator   date

_____   _____
Signature of teacher   date

Signature signifies receipt of, not concurrence with, this evaluation. Teachers are encouraged to submit comments. (Please make comments on the back of this form or on an attached sheet.)

STAFF PROGRESS REPORT

TEACHER: _____

SCHOOL: _____

DATE: _____

Please attach the narrative of the observation if report is based on a classroom observation:

_____

_____

_____

_____

_____   _____
Signature of evaluator   date

Teacher's comments:

_____   _____
Signature of teacher   date

**Signature signifies receipt of, not concurrence with this evaluation.
Teachers are encouraged to submit comments.**

PRINCIPLES OF EFFECTIVE TEACHING
Massachusetts Department of Education

with suggested connections from

Instructional Strategies That Maximize Student Achievement: For Teachers, by Teachers by Ribas, Deane and Seider (2005)

Published by Ribas Associates

9 Sherman Way, Westwood, MA 02090

ribasassociates.com

Principles	Examples of Descriptors	Ribas, Deane and Seider (2005), published by Ribas Associates
I. CURRENCY IN THE CURRICULUM A. The teacher is up-to-date regarding curriculum content.	1. Demonstrates working knowledge of the core curriculum of the teacher's assignment	Appropriate State or Province Curriculum Standards
	2. Frames curriculum around essential questions in the discipline that provide opportunities for reasoning, logic, analsis and synthesis when planning units, lessons and assessments	Chapter 1: Mastery Objectives Chapter 2: Activators Chapter 5: Thinking Skills
	3. Keeps current in the field and applies knowledge to the instructional program	Appropriate State or Province Curriculum Standards Chapter 1, 3, 6 and 7: Content-Specific Pedagogy
	4. Contributes to the ongoing evaluation of the curriculum	Chapter 6: Assessment
II. EFFECTIVE PLANNING AND ASSESSMENT OF CURRICULUM AND INSTRUCTION A. The teacher plans instruction effectively.	1. Has a personal vision of committed, confident learners and uses that vision to guide learning goals, expectations and standards for student work	Introduction: Standards, Expectations Chapter 1: Mastery Objectives Chapter 7: Learnable Intelligence
	2. Sets short-term and yearlong goals for curricular units which derive from unifying themes of fundamental importance to students' present and future lives	Chapter 1: Mastery Objectives Chapter 2: Connecting to Students' Lives
	3. Identifies individual and group needs and plans appropriate strategies, including those that involve the use of available up-to-date technologies to meet those needs	Chapter 1: Planning Chapter 2: Activators Chapter 6: Assessing Learning

Principles		Examples of Descriptors		Ribas, Deane and Seider (2005), published by Ribas Associates
II. EFFECTIVE PLANNING AND ASSESSMENT OF CURRICULUM AND INSTRUCTION (continued)		4.	Uses materials and resources, including technologies that are appropriately matched to curricular goals and to students' learning styles	Chapter 1: Mastery Planning Chapter 4: Differentiating Instruction for Diversified Learning Styles
		5.	Frames curriculum around students' own prior knowledge and experience and identifies prerequisite skills, concepts and vocabulary that are important for students to know in order to be successful at a task	Chapter 1: Mastery Objectives Chapter 2: Connecting to Students' Prior Knowledge, Activators Chapter 5: Questioning Practices Chapter 6: Assessing Student Learning
		6.	Seeks out and collaborates with school-based specialists, resource personnel, technology specialists and administrators to better design curricula or instructional modifications to meet the special learning needs of students and to support all students to learn and apply a challenging core curriculum	Chapter 4: Diverse Learning Styles and Rates Chapter 11: Conferencing With Peers
		7.	Plans engaging ways to introduce each unit of study	Chapter 1: Mastery Planning Chapter 2: Activators
		8.	Plans frequent instructional opportunities in which students are interacting with ideas, materials, teachers and each other	Chapter 5: Questioning Practices, Developing Thinking Skills
		9.	Designs curriculum experiences in which students take increasing responsibility for their own learning	Chapter 1: Mastery Planning Chapter 5: Questioning Practices Chapter 6: Student Self-Assessment Chapter 7: Learnable Intelligence
		10.	Integrates the teaching of reading, listening, writing, speaking, viewing, and the use of appropriate learning tools (e.g., calculators, computers, etc.) within the discipline	Chapter 6: Writing Pedagogy Chapter 7: Content Area Reading Pedagogy
B. The teacher plans assessment of student learning effectively.		1.	Determines specific and challenging standards for student learning	Appropriate State or Province Curricular Standards Chapter 1: Mastery Objectives
		2.	Develops and uses authentic assessment which describes a student's learning process as well as his/her learning achievements	Chapter 6: Assessing Student Learning
		3.	Incorporates time for individual and interactive reflection including response journals, debriefings and group discussions	Chapter 1: Sample Mastery Lesson and Unit Plans Chapter 5: Questioning Practices Chapter 6: Student Self-Assessment

Principles	Examples of Descriptors	Ribas, Deane and Seider (2005), published by Ribas Associates
II. EFFECTIVE PLANNING AND ASSESSMENT OF CURRICULUM AND INSTRUCTION (continued) C. The teacher monitors students' understanding of the curriculum effectively and adjusts instruction, materials or assessments when appropriate.	1. Regularly uses a variety of formal and informal authentic assessments of students' achievement and progress for instructional revisions and decision-making	Chapter 2: Activators, Summarizers Chapter 6: Formative and Summative Assessments
	2. Implements evaluation procedures which appropriately assess the objectives taught	Chapter 1: Samples of Mastery Lesson and Unit Plans Chapter 6: Assessing Student Learning
	3. Communicates student progress to parents, students and staff members in a timely fashion using a range of information including portfolios, anecdotal records and other artifacts	Chapter 6: Assessing Student Learning Chapter 9: Parent Conferences, Student Portfolios
	4. Prepares and maintains accurate and efficient record-keeping systems of the quality and quantity of student work	Chapter 6: Assessing Student Learning
	5. Uses individual and group data appropriately; maintains confidentiality concerning individual student data and achievement	Chapter 6: National, State and District Assessments
III. EFFECTIVE MANAGEMENT OF CLASSROOM ENVIRONMENT A. The teacher creates an environment that is positive for student learning and involvement.	1. Implements instructional opportunities in which students are interacting with ideas, materials, teachers and each other	Chapter 4: Differentiating Instruction Chapter 5: Questioning Practices, Thinking Skills
	2. Implements curriculum experiences in which students take increasing responsibility for their own learning	Chapter 1: Mastery Planning Chapter 5: Questioning Practices Chapter 6: Student Self-Assessment Chapter 7: Learmab;e Intelligence
	3. Demonstrates an openness to student challenges and questions about information and ideas	Chapter 5: Questioning Practices
	4. Uses classroom time and classroom space to promote optimal learning	Chapter 3: Classroom Management Chapter 8: The Brain and Teaching
	5. Understands principles and patterns of child growth and development and uses this knowledge in working with students	Chapter 4: Differentiating Instruction Chapter 7: Theories of Intelligence Chapter 8: The Brain and Teaching
	6. Establishes classroom procedures that maintain a high level of students' time-on-task and that ensure smooth transitions from one activity to another	Chapter 3: Classroom Management
B. The teacher maintains appropriate standards of behavior, mutual respect and safety.	1. Maintains systematic approach to discipline by establishing and administering a consistent and fair set of rules supporting appropriate expectations	Chapter 3: Classroom Management

Principles	Examples of Descriptors	Ribas, Deane and Seider (2005), published by Ribas Associates
III. EFFECTIVE MANAGEMENT OF CLASSROOM ENVIRONMENT (continued) A. The teacher makes learning goals clear to students.	2. Manages routines effectively	Chapter 3: Classroom Management
	3. Maintains appropriate professional boundaries with students	Chapter 3: Classroom Management
	4. Serves as a positive role model for students	Chapter 3: Classroom Management
IV. EFFECTIVE INSTRUCTION	1. Makes connections between concepts taught and students' prior knowledge and experiences	Chapter 2: Activators, Connecting to Students' Prior Knowledge and Their Lives
	2. Regularly checks for students' understanding of content, concepts and progress on skill	Chapter 6: Formative Assessment
	3. Identifies confusions and misconceptions as indicated by student responses and regular assessment strategies: remediates, reteaches or extends teaching to meet individual and/or group need	Chapter 2: Activators Chapter 4: Differentiates Instruction Chapter 5: Questions Practices Chapter 6: Formative and Summative Assessments
	4. Communicates clearly in writing and speaking using precise language	Chapter 1: Mastery Objectives
	5. Understands and shows students the relevance of the subject to life-long learning	Chapter 2: Connecting to Students' Lives
B. The teacher uses appropriate instructional techniques.	1. Uses a variety of teaching strategies, including cooperative, peer and project-based learning, audio-visual presentations, lecture discussions and inquiry, practice and application and the teaching of others	Chapter 4: Needs of Diverse Learners Chapter 8: The Brain and Teaching
	2. Provides options for students to demonstrate competency and mastery of new material, including written work, plays, art work, oratory, visual presentations, exhibitions and portfolios	Chapter 6: Assessment
	3. Uses a variety of appropriate materials in order to reinforce and extend skills, accommodate learning styles and match instructional objectives	Chapter 1: Mastery Planning Chapter 4: Differentiates Instruction
	4. Causes students to become cognitively active in summarizing important learning and integrating them with prior knowledge	Chapter 2: Summarizers, Connecting to Prior Knowledge Chapter 5: Questioning Practices
	5. Demonstrates working knowledge of current research on optimum means for learning a particular discipline	Chapter 1: Samples of Mastery Lesson and Unit Plans Chapter 6: Student Self-Assessment Chapter 7: Learnable Intelligence Strategies in Math and Reading Chapters 1, 3, 6, and 7: Content-Speific Pedagogy

Principles	Examples of Descriptors	Ribas, Deane and Seider (2005), published by Ribas Associates
IV. EFFECTIVE INSTRUCTION (continued) C. The teacher uses appropriate questioning techniques	1. Uses a variety of questioning techniques, including those which encourage and guide critical and independent thinking and the development of ideas	.Chapter 5: Questioning Practices, Thinking Skills
	2. Presents information recognizing multiple points of view: encourages students to assess the accuracy of information presented	Chapter 1: Sample of Mastery Lesson and Unit Plans Chapter 5: Questioning Practices
D. The teacher evaluates, tries innovative approaches and refines instructional strategies, including the effective use of technologies, to increase student learning and confidence to learn.	1. Regularly tries innovative approaches to improve instructional practices	Chapters 2, 4, 5, 6, 7 and 8
	2. Conscientiously evaluates, tries innovative approaches and refines instructional strategies, including the effective use of technologies, to increase student learning and confidence about learning	Chapter 10: Self-Reflection and Classroom Research Chapter 11: Peer Reflection Partners
	3. Assesses instructional strategies in authentic ways by comparing intended and actual learning outcomes	Chapter 10: Self-Reflection and Classroom Research Chapter 11: Peer Reflection Partners
V. PROMOTION OF HIGH STANDARDS AND EXPECTATIONS FOR STUDENTS' ACHIEVEMENT A. The teacher communicates learning goals and high standards and expectations to students.	1. Regularly communicates objectives or learning outcomes to students	Chapter 1: Mastery Objectives Chapter 2: Communicating Mastery Objectives
	2. Regularly provides feedback to students on their progress on goals and objectives	Chapter 6: Formative and Summative Assessment
	3. Communicates standards, expectations and guidelines regarding quality and quantity of students' work, work procedures and interpersonal behavior to students and parents	Chapter 2: Communicating Mastery Objectives Chapter 3: Classroom Management Chapter 4: Communicating Criteria for Success Chapter 9: Parent Communication
	4. Responds to students' answers and work so as to keep students open, thinking, and willing to take risks and to persevere with challenging tasks	Chapter 5: Questioning Practices
	5. Models the skills, attitudes, values and processes central to the subject being taught	Chapter 1: Samples of Mastery Lesson and Unit Plans Chapters 1. 3. 6 and 7: Contact-Specific Pedagogy

Principles	Examples of Descriptors	Ribas, Deane and Seider (2005), published by Ribas Associates
V. PROMOTION OF HIGH STANDARDS AND EXPECTATIONS FOR STUDENTS' ACHIEVEMENT (continued) B. The teacher promotes confidence and perseverance in the student that stimulate increased personal student reppsponsibility for achieving the goals of the curriculum.	1. Uses prompt feedback and student goal setting in order to increase student motivation and ownership of learning	Chapter 2: Communicating Mastery Objectives Chapter 6: Formative and Summative Assessment, Student Self-Assessment
	2. Develops and supports students' awareness of themselves as learners and their ability to overcome self-doubt associated with learning and taking risks	Chapter 6: Student Self-Assessment Chapter 7: Learnable Intelligence
	3. Nurtures students' eagerness to do challenging work and provides incentive, interest and support for students to take responsibility to complete such tasks successfully	Chapter 4: Differentiating Instruction Chapter 6: Student Self-Assessment
	4. Acts on the belief that all students can learn and that virtually all can master a challenging core curriculum with appropriate modifications of instruction	Introduction Chapter 1: Mastery Planning Chapter 4: Differentiating Instruction Chapter 5: Questioning Practices Chapter 7: Learnable Intelligence
	5. Encourages and supports students to believe that effort is a key to high achievement and acknowledges and values student work, study and inquiry	Chapter 7: Learnable Intelligence
	6. Regularly identifies students needing extra help and secures student cooperation and participation in extra help sessions	Chapter 4: Differentiating Instruction Chapter 6: Formative and Summative Assessment
	7. Identifies students who are not meeting expectations and develops a plan that designates the teacher's and the students' responsibilities regarding learning	Introduction Chapter 4: Differentiating Instruction Chapter 6: Assessment
	8. Demonstrates attitudes of fairness, courtesy and respect that encourage students' active participation and commitment to learning	Chapter 3: Classroom Management Chapter 5: Questioning Practices
	9. Builds positive relationships with students and parents to enhance students' abilities to learn effectively	Chapter 3: Classroom Management Chapter 9: Working Effectively With Parents
	10. Recognizes and responds appropriately when an individual student is having social and/or emotional difficulties which interfere with learning and/or participating in class	Chapter 3: Classroom Management

Principles	Examples of Descriptors	Ribas, Deane and Seider (2005), published by Ribas Associates
VI. PROMOTION OF EQUITY AND APPRECIATION OF DIVERSITY A. The teacher strives to ensure equitable opportunities for student learning.	1. Provides opportunities to include all students in the full range of academic programs and activities and extracurricular activities	
	2. Addresses the needs of diverse student populations by applying and adapting constitutional and statutory laws, state regulations and Board of Education policies and guidelines	Chapter 4: Differentiates Instruction
B. The teacher demonstrates appreciation for and sensitivity to the diversity among individuals	1. Demonstrates sensitivity to differences in abilities, modes of contributions and social and cultural backgrounds	Chapter 4: Differentiates Instruction
	2. Develops and implements educational and organizational strategies that are effective in meeting the needs of a diverse student body	Chapter 4: Differentiates Instruction
	3. Functions effectively in a multilingual, multicultural and economically diverse society	Chapter 9: Working Effectively With Parents
VII. FULFILLMENT OF PROFESSIONAL RESPONSIBILITIES A. The teacher constructively initiates interactions with parents and solicits and is receptive to their contributions.	1. The teacher approaches the parent as a positive collaborator in the process of educating the student	Chapter 9: Working Effectively With Parents
	2. Keeps parents informed of students' progress and works with them to aid in the total development of the student	Chapter 9: Working Effectively With Parents
B. The teacher shares responsibility for accomplishing the goals and priorities of his/her grade, team, department, building and school district by participating on committees and in activities related to school community.	1. Works constructively with others to identify school problems and to develop and implement solutions	Chapter 11: Peer Reflection Partners
	2. Works collaboratively with other staff in planning and implementing interdisciplinary curriculum, instruction and other school programs and shares expertise and new ideas with colleagues	Chapter 11: Peer Reflection Partners

Principles	Examples of Descriptors	Ribas, Deane and Seider (2005), published by Ribas Associates
VII. FULFILLMENT OF PROFESSIONAL RESPONSIBILITIES (continued)	3. Participates in school, student, faculty and staff activities (e.g., administering "sunshine" fund, presenting at faculty meetings, beautifying school); participates in professional organizations (e.g., NCTM), teacher support groups and system-wide committees	
	4. Leads student organizations (e.g., student councils, math league, student newspapers, clubs, school plays)	
	5. Cooperates with other teachers about students' overall workload	
	6. Demonstrates a willingness to provide after-school academic support for students	
	7. Writes evaluations and recommendations for students as appropriate	
C. The teacher is a reflective and continuous learner.	1. Reflects about and acts on what students need to know and be able to do and about what the teacher can do to foster learning	Chapter 1: Mastery Objectives Chapter 10: Teacher Self-Reflection and Classroom Research Chapter 11: Peer Reflection Partners
	2. Uses available resources to analyze, expand and refine professional knowledge and skills: resources can include professional organizations, academic course work, school-based staff, administrative and community resources and other colleagues	Chapter 10: Teacher Self-Reflection and Classroom Research Chapter 11: Peer Reflection Partners
	3. Participates in activities that demonstrate a commitment to the teaching profession	
	4. Seeks out information in order to grow and improve as a professional	Chapter 10: Teacher Self-Reflection and Classroom Research Chapter 11: Peer Reflection Partners, Knowledgable About the Areas Explained in This Book

Principles	Examples of Descriptors	Ribas, Deane and Seider (2005), published by Ribas Associates
VII. FULFILLMENT OF PROFESSIONAL RESPONSIBILITIES (continued)	5. Is receptive to suggestions for growth and improvement	
D. The teacher maintains professional boundaries with parents and staff by behaving with mutual respect and discretion.		

Source: Ribas, Deane and Seider (2005)

Published by Ribas Associates

9 Sherman Way, Westwood, MA 02090

ribasassociates.com

Brookline High School Student Comment Sheet

Teacher's Name: _____

Course: _____

Date: _____

This evaluation is designed to help teachers plan courses and to improve the quality of their classes. To be used in this way, the questionnaire must be taken seriously. Please give careful consideration to your answers. Specific comments are most helpful.

Section I

Each question contains a statement. Consider the statement and decide where along the scale below the answer lies for you. Mark your response in the blank at the end of the statement. Space is provided below each question for optional comments.

Scale

1. Strongly Agree
2. Somewhat Agree
3. Neither Agree nor Disagree

4. Somewhat Disagree
5. Strongly Disagree
6. Does Not Apply to this course

1. The teacher appears to know the subject well. _____

Comment: _____

_____

_____

2. The teacher is well prepared for class. _____

Comment: _____

_____

_____

3. Class sessions are well organized. _____

Comment: _____

_____

_____

4.   The teacher gives a clear explanation of the material. _____

Comment: _____

_____

_____

5.   The teacher makes me feel free to ask questions, disagree, express ideas, etc. _____

Comment: _____

_____

_____

6.   The teacher responds effectively to questions. _____

Comment: _____

_____

_____

7.   The work outside of class is relevant to class sessions. _____

Comment: _____

_____

_____

8.   The work required outside of class is appropriate in quantity and quality. _____

Comment: _____

_____

_____

9.   The textbooks are a useful part of this course. _____

Comment: _____

_____

_____

10. The assigned reading helps me understand the subject matter of this course. _____

Comment: _____

_____

_____

11. The teacher is available for individual help. _____

Comment: _____

_____

_____

12. The teacher is interested in trying to help students. _____

Comment: _____

_____

_____

13. The teacher is fair and impartial in dealing with students. _____

Comment: _____

_____

_____

14. The grading system is reasonable. _____

Comment: _____

_____

_____

15. This course has increased my interest in the subject matter. _____

Comment: _____

_____

_____

16. This course has made a real contribution to my knowledge and under-
    standing. _____

    Comment: _____

    _____

    _____

Section II

Please check the response that most accurately reflects your answer.

1. Overall, this course is: Outstanding   Good   Fair   Poor

2. Does the teacher teach this course at the appropriate level for you?

    Yes   No, too simple   No, too difficult

3. Why are you taking this course?

    __ School Requirement __ College Requirement

    __ Interest in Subject   __ Other

4. I do all of my assignments.

    __ Most   __ Some   __ None

Section III

Please use the space below for any additional comments you may have regarding the strengths, needs, recommendations for this course. Additional paper
may be used if necessary.

HIGH SCHOOL EVALUATION TEAMS

Headmaster
Assistant Headmaster
Coordinator of School Within a School
Coordinator of Opportunity for Change
Coordinator of Integrated Services
Coordinator of Special Education 9–12
Coordinator of Differentiated Instruction
Coordinator of International Students
Coordinator for Time and Learning
Director of Athletics
Coordinator for Winthrop House

Dean of Mathematics, Science and Technology
Coordinator for Career Education
Coordinator for Health and Physical Education
Coordinator for Mathematics
Coordinator for Science
Associate Dean Grade 9
Associate Dean Grade 11

Dean of Humanities
Coordinator of English
Coordinator of Social Studies
Coordinator of World Languages
Coordinator of Visual Arts
Coordinator of Performing Arts
Associate Dean Grade 10
Associate Dean Grade 12

EVALUATION ASSIGNMENTS FOR INTEGRATED SERVICES STAFF

School Psychologists in the elementary schools based in only one school building will be evaluated by the Principal or his/her designee. Psychologists in the elementary schools who serve in more than one building will be evaluated by the Assistant Superintendent for Integrated Services. Psychologists assigned to the high school will be evaluated by the Coordinator of Integrated Services.

Guidance Counselors in the elementary schools assigned to only one building will be evaluated by the building Principal or his/her designee. Guidance counselors assigned to more than one building will be evaluated by the Assistant Superintendent for Integrated Services or his designee. Guidance counselors assigned to the high school will be evaluated by the Coordinator of Integrated Services.

Social Workers at the high school will be evaluated by the Principal or his/her designee. Social workers for Early Childhood will be evaluated by the Coordinator of Early Childhood Education. Elementary social workers will be evaluated by the building Principal.

Bilingual/E.S.L. teachers at BHS will be evaluated by the Coordinator of Bilingual/E.S.L. Elementary Bilingual/ESL teachers who are assigned to only one building will be evaluated by the building Principal or his/her designee. Elementary Bilingual/ESL teachers assigned to more than one building will be evaluated by the Coordinator of Bilingual/ESL.

Special Education Teachers in elementary schools assigned to one building will be evaluated by the building Principal or his/her designee. High school special education teachers will be evaluated by the Secondary Curriculum Coordinator for Special Education. At the high school the Program Coordinator for Winthrop House will evaluate all Winthrop House Staff. The Coordinator of Differentiated Instruction will evaluate the Learning Skills Staff and contribute to the evaluations of classroom and special education teachers. Special education teachers assigned to more than one building will be evaluated by the appropriate Curriculum Coordinator for Special Education or his/her designee.

Speech and Language Therapists in the elementary schools assigned to only one building will be evaluated by the building Principal. Speech and language therapists assigned to more than one building will be evaluated by the Coordinator of Special Education. Speech and language therapists assigned only to the Early Childhood program will be evaluated by the Coordinator of Early Childhood Education or his/her designee.

Occupational Therapists: Early Childhood O.T.s will be evaluated by the Coordinator of Early Childhood Education or designee. All other O.T.s will be evaluated by the Coordinator of Special Education.

Physical Therapists will be evaluated by the Early Childhood Education Coordinator, the school physician or the Curriculum Coordinator for Special Education.

Adaptive Physical Education teachers will be evaluated by the appropriate Coordinator of Special Education.

Visual Consultant will be evaluated by the Appropriate Curriculum Coordinator for Special Education.

Attendance Officer will be evaluated by the Assistant Superintendent for Integrated Services.

Home Instruction and **Early Childhood Teachers** will be evaluated by the Elementary Curriculum Coordinator for Special Education.

Coordinator of Outside Placements will be evaluated by the Elementary Coordinator of Special Education.

Lesley Interns will be evaluated by the Lesley College Intern Coordinator and the teacher to whom they are assigned.

School Nurses will be evaluated by the school pediatrician.

Timelines for Teacher Evaluations

The following timeline is provided for your information in connection with the implementation of the evaluation procedures as established by the Brookline School Committee. In any case when the date falls on a weekend or holiday, the Evaluator should use the prior work day as the final date. The timelines are consistent with the contract between the Brookline Educators Association and the Brookline School Committee:

September of each year – On or before this date, please discuss evaluation procedures with staff and give each staff member a copy of the Principles of Effective Teaching.

October 15 of each year – On or before this date, evaluators should meet with all preprofessional status teachers to address goals for the year, strengths of the teacher, relationships between current and previous evaluations, the Brookline Principles of Effective Teaching and the support available.

October 20 of each year – Out of Cycle Evaluation: On or before this date, any teacher with "professional teacher status" may be evaluated out-of-cycle. On or before this date, the evaluator should provide the teacher with substantive reasons for undertaking the out-of-cycle evaluation. Possible reasons are:

    a) the teacher is new to your school,

    b) previous problems,

    c) recent developments.

October 31 of each year – There are to be three staff progress reports issued annually to pre-professional status teachers. It is suggested that the first of these be issued by this date.

December 1 of each year – On or before this date, please meet with each teacher with "professional teacher status" who is to be evaluated. The purpose of this meeting is to discuss goals for the year, strengths, relationships between current and previous evaluations, the Brookline Principles of Effective Teaching and support available.

December 2 of each year – It is suggested that you issue the second staff progress reports to the pre-professional status teachers.

January 31 of each year – On or before this date, it is suggested you issue the third staff progress reports to pre-professional status teachers and the first of two progress reports to PTS teachers.

Evaluators should notify the Principal and Assistant Superintendent for Personnel of any pre-professional status teacher whose renewal is questionable and of any professional teacher status teacher who may receive a final check that is unsatisfactory or in the lowest satisfactory category.

February 14 of each year – On or before this date, you should have issued the Annual Report of Teacher Effectiveness to pre-professional status teachers. It is suggested that you issue these as early in February as possible. Please hand deliver unfavorable Annual Reports and those which contain serious reservations. Please call the Director of Personnel if you wish not to recommend a person for reappointment or if you have any doubt about there being a position for him. Kindly send the completed package, together with a cover memo listing the enclosures to this office by February 28.

March 1 of each year – Evaluators must notify the Assistant Superintendent for Personnel in writing of all pre-professional status teachers whose renewal is questionable so a non-renewal letter can be written. The teacher's name should be given even in those cases in which a decision may be made to renew the teacher prior to the April 15 date.

Evaluators must notify the Assistant Superintendent for Personnel of any professional teacher status teacher who may receive a final check that is unsatisfactory or in the lowest satisfactory category.

April 15 of each year – On or before this date all pre-professional teacher status teachers who will not be renewed for the upcoming year must be hand delivered by his/her Evaluator the letter of non-renewal.

April 30 of each year – On or before this date, Annual Reports of Teacher Effectiveness must be issued to teachers with "professional teacher status" by this date. The completed package, together with a cover memo listing the enclosures, should be sent to the personnel office by June 1, 200_. BHS Administrators should also send a copy of each package to the appropriate evaluation team leader indicated on the back. Vice/Assistant Principals should also send a copy of each package to the Principal.

LEXINGTON PUBLIC SCHOOLS

Article 10–Evaluation and Supervision

A. The philosophy of the Lexington Public Schools supervision and evaluation process emerges directly from the Lexington Public Schools core values: **Individuality and Diversity, Shared Responsibility, and Continuous Improvement.**

A diverse professional staff, by definition, comprises individuals with different backgrounds, needs, interests, and aspirations. Lexington Public Schools should afford the professional staff opportunities to explore and express their individuality and to appreciate the individuality of colleagues. Hence, the supervision and evaluation process should address the gifts, talents, and special needs of every member of the professional staff. Supervisors and evaluators should practice diverse methodologies in an effort to challenge all staff members, whatever their experience or areas of expertise. Professional excellence can only be achieved when all members of the professional staff know the high, realistic and explicitly stated expectations for them.

Members of the professional staff and administrators must work together within the supervision and evaluation process to harness the power of community, collaboration, and communication. Partnerships which maximize our professional potential, enhance our professional practices, and overcome the defensiveness which sometimes hampers our professional relationships must be developed. A collegial, supportive, non-threatening climate should be promoted by all.

Regardless of the current level of attainment, professional performance should always be improving. An environment that fosters experimentation, persistent innovation, risk taking, and continuing growth leads to a healthy school culture which in turn produces a positive place in which to teach and learn. Professional staff should be lifelong learners who develop the habit of inquiry, try new approaches to problem solving, and understand that some experiments will not work. Alternative assessments to measure the efficacy of professional performance are essential to provide professional staff with the best possible feedback so that they can continuously improve their performance. Feedback loops and constant communication among members of the school community are necessary to help guide all improvement efforts.

With these core values in mind, the purpose of a supervisory system is to provide professional staff with frequent, high quality feedback on their practice. The purpose of an evaluative system is to produce judgments about the performance level and job status of professional staff and whether or not they are performing up to district standards.

B. In accordance with state regulations, the principal or the assistant principal designee will serve as the primary evaluator for all staff assigned to a building. This evaluation will be conducted and completed in collaboration with the designated coordinator or department head as indicated on the chart below. Multi-building staff will be evaluated by the principal of the building where they have the majority of their teaching responsibilities.

CHART OF EVALUATIVE RESPONSIBILITIES

Elementary

Classroom Teachers	Principal
Teaching Specialists (Music, Art, Physical Education, Foreign Languages)	Principal/Coordinator
Elementary Subject Specialists K–5 (Mathematics, Science, Language Arts, Social Studies)	Director of Curriculum and Instruction/Coordinator

Middle School

Teachers

English, Science, Mathematics, Social Studies	Principal/Assistant Principal/ Department Head
Foreign Language, Art, Music, Physical Education, Industrial Technology, Business, Home Economics, Guidance	Principal/Assistant Principal/ Coordinator

High School

Teachers	Principal/Assistant Principal/ Department Head
Drama	Principal/Coordinator

Counselors

Elementary	Principal
Middle School	Principal
High School	Principal/High School Department Head
Librarians	Principal/Coordinator of Libraries and Instructional Materials

Cable Program Supervisor   Principal/Coordinator of Libraries
                                      and Instructional Materials

Social Workers
   High School   Principal/Guidance Department Head
   Middle School   Principal
   Elementary   Principal

Metco Staff   Principal/Coordinator

Reading
   High School   Principal/Department Head
   Middle School   Principal/Department Head
   Elementary School   Principal

Nurses   Principal/Chairperson of Nurses

Chairpersons
   Language Arts/Reading K–5   Director of Curriculum and
                                      Instruction

   Nurses   Coordinator of Health Education
   Guidance K–8   Principal

Special Needs Specialists
   Adaptive Physical Education   Principal
   Integration Specialists   Principal
   Occupational Therapists   Principal
   Psychologists   Principal
   Resource   Principal
   Self-contained Classroom Teachers Principal
   Speech and Language   Principal

Department Heads
   Mathematics and English   Principal/Director of Curriculum
                                      and Instruction

Coordinators   Superintendent/Director of
                                      Curriculum and Instruction

C. Observation Reports

1. The observation of the work performance of a staff member will be conducted openly and with full knowledge of the staff member. Frequency of observation should be a function of perceived performance. Observation of unsatisfactory performance should lead to more frequent observations and conferences.

2. Each observation will be followed by a post conference within 3 school days of the observation. A written observation report will be provided to the staff member within 15 school days after the observation. If a staff member is to be observed more than once before a written observation report is prepared, the reason must be recorded in writing on the observation report. The staff member and the evaluator will mutually agree on the dates and the number of observations.

3. Classroom observations for the purpose of collecting data for evaluation reports shall be no less than thirty (30) minutes in duration at the elementary level and one full instructional period at the middle schools and the high school. Any exception will be mutually agreed to by the staff member and the evaluator.

4. Individual observations shall not be subject to the grievance procedure except as part of a grievance concerning an evaluation. Evaluation shall be subject to the grievance and arbitration procedures, both procedurally and substantively.

5. The Superintendent, Director of Curriculum and Instruction, or the Director of Personnel and Administration may visit a staff member's classroom/workplace to assess the observation skills of an evaluator, to investigate a complaint, or for administrative purposes other than evaluation. The Superintendent, Director of Curriculum and Instruction, or the Director of Personnel and Administration may be visiting staff members' classrooms/workplaces in the course of doing a general review of teaching or they might visit staff members' classrooms/workplaces to follow up after receiving an evaluation report. They will be going into a staff member's classroom/workplace at the specific request of either the staff member or the evaluator, and they will be going into staff members' classrooms/workplaces during the professional status process.

D. Evaluation Reports

1. Normally, evaluation reports will be based on one to three observation reports.

2. Commendations and recommendations relating to Lexington's performance standards are considered to be a routine part of an evaluation report.

Adverse or negative comments or conclusions can only appear in an evaluation report if they have already appeared in an observation report or have otherwise been documented and placed in the staff member's personnel file.

3. The superintendent, director of curriculum and instruction, or the director of personnel and administration can be involved in the evaluation of a staff member.

4. One week prior to the evaluation conference, the evaluator will provide the staff member with a copy of the evaluation report. The staff member's signature on the final evaluation does not necessarily indicate agreement with the final report. Staff members shall have the right to object in writing to anything included therein; this written commentary should be attached to the evaluation report.

5. At the end of a staff member's evaluation cycle, one final evaluation report will be written. Where designated on the chart of evaluation responsibilities, the principal, assistant principal, coordinator, or department head will collaborate in writing the final evaluation report.

6. A staff member may attach a written reply to any evaluation which shall be in his/her personnel file.

E. Non-professional Status Staff Members

1. Non-professional status staff members should be observed at least twice during the school year. The interim observation is to be completed prior to December 15 and the final observation is to be completed prior to May 15. The final evaluation will be written and presented to the non-professional status staff member by May 25.

2. A non-professional status employee who is not reappointed will receive from the Administration a written statement of reasons for non-reappointment.

F. Professional Status Staff Members

1. Important dates in the evaluation process of professional status staff members are as follows:

   October 1: Observation cycle can begin. Normally, the entire evaluation process will be completed within four months of the first observation.

   May 1: The observation cycle ends.

   June 1: Final evaluations are due at the Personnel Office.

2. A comprehensive system of professional growth must give professional staff frequent, high quality feedback on their practice (supervision), and

must also produce judgments about their performance level and job status, and most importantly, whether or not they are performing up to district standards (evaluation). Therefore, a four-year cycle of evaluation and supervision has been designed to meet the needs of the professional staff and the school system:

Year 1: Comprehensive Evaluation

During this year, the staff member will be evaluated on all district performance standards and according to the principles and practices of evaluation as stated elsewhere in this article. At the end of the evaluation period (no later than May 31), the evaluator(s) will confer with the staff member and discuss the final, written evaluation. The evaluation will include a written summary of commendations and recommendations. (See model forms.)

Year 2: Collaborative Year

The purpose of the collaborative year is not only to promote professional growth but also to encourage collaboration and sharing among staff members. Staff members may also collaborate with other professionals. At some time after the comprehensive evaluation has been completed, but prior to October 1 of the collaborative year, the staff member and the evaluator(s) will confer to establish professional growth goal(s) based on the commendations and recommendations made in the comprehensive evaluation. Prior to October 15, the staff member will develop and submit a Professional Growth Plan (see model) which contains the following information:

- the proposal (see list of suggestions)
- the goals of the proposal which contribute to professional knowledge and/or skill and which are based on commendations/recommendations of the comprehensive evaluation
- the actions or procedures the staff member will follow to accomplish the goal
- a time line
- what evidence the staff member will provide to show completion of the proposal
- staff member or other participants and their roles and responsibilities
- what type of support, if any, might be needed to complete the proposal (materials, time, staff development meetings)

During the course of the collaborative professional growth activities, the evaluator(s) may make observations and hold conferences. When the activities have been completed, the staff member will confer with the primary evaluator(s) and submit a final written report (see model) by May 31. The Professional

Growth Plan and the Final Report will be placed in the staff member's personnel file.

In the unlikely event that there is an unresolvable disagreement between the staff member and the evaluator(s) over the Professional Growth Plan, each may select a colleague to participate in the resolution of the disagreement.

Should the disagreement still not be resolved, the director of curriculum and the LEA president will participate in a final resolution.

Year 3: Focused Evaluation

During this year, the staff member will be evaluated on selected district performance standards and according to the principles and practices of evaluation as stated elsewhere in this article. This focus of this evaluation will be determined in a conference between the staff member and the evaluator(s). It should grow out of the goals and outcomes of both the comprehensive evaluation (year 1) and the collaborative year (year 2). At the end of the evaluation period (no later than May 31), the evaluator(s) will confer with the staff member and discuss the final, written evaluation. The evaluation will include a written summary of commendations and recommendations. (See model forms.)

Year 4: Individual Study

This is a year in which the staff member may select a professional growth activity. The staff member will confer with the evaluator(s) and develop a Professional Growth Plan by October 15 with all of the information as listed in Year 2 with one exception: the plan may or may not include other staff member participants. The goal(s) of the plan do not have to be linked to previous evaluations, but the activity must be substantial and should contribute to one's professional knowledge or skill. At the end of the year, the staff member will submit a final report on or before May 31 and confer with his/her evaluator(s). The Professional Growth Plan and the Final Report will be placed in the staff member's personnel file.

Student Feedback

Teachers of grades 6–12 will annually solicit feedback from students in all their classes. However, those special area teachers who teach a large percentage of the student body will solicit feedback from a number of students comparable to a core subject area teacher at their school. This should occur sometime after the midpoint of the course, leaving sufficient time to allow for consultation with the peer reviewer and evaluator(s)/supervisor(s). The purpose of this feedback is to gather information that students are in a position to know which can then be used by the staff member for self-assessment and professional growth. The instrument(s) used to obtain this feedback will be created by an individual teacher or a team of teachers subject to the review of the evaluator(s)/supervisor(s) or their designees. The instruments should seek feedback in the following areas: curriculum, teaching methods, classroom management, assessment and grading, homework, classroom climate, and the teacher/student relationship.

Student completed feedback forms are the sole property of the teacher who issued them. However, the forms are to be shared with at least one of the teacher's peers in a collaborative effort to analyze the findings. The peer reviewer will hold all data and findings in confidence. The issuing teacher will discuss the findings with his/her supervisor(s)/evaluator(s) and, whenever appropriate, should use the data in goal setting activities for the coming year.

Termination of a Professional Growth Plan

If the evaluator(s) personally observes performance of a staff member participating in the Collaborative Year or the Independent Study Year that is adversely affecting the delivery of educational services, the evaluator may call for a conference with the staff member. The intent of the conference will be to address the performance issue and allow the Collaborative Year or the Independent Study Year to continue. If the issue is not resolved, the evaluator may begin a Comprehensive or Focused Evaluation Year after written notification detailing the reasons for this decision has been given to the staff member. This written notification will be placed in the Central Office personnel file.

G. Tier Two Regulations (Professional Status)

1. Normally, a staff member is placed on tier two if there are observed and documented deficiencies in more than one performance standard on the instrument; however, in unusual circumstances, which the evaluator(s) would need to define and defend, a staff member might be placed on tier two on the basis of a severe deficiency in a single category. Placement on tier two presumes that unless the reason for placement is satisfactorily remediated, recommendation for dismissal would be the result.

2. At the end of the second year on tier two, the staff member may be restored to tier one or shall be dismissed. In the second year of tier two, the staff member's increment and/or negotiated salary increase may be withheld. Any staff member restored to tier one shall be placed on the appropriate step as if he/she had never been on tier two.

3. Tier two can begin only in September of the following school year and will last no longer than two school years. No employee shall be dismissed after one year on tier two unless that employee has received a tier two warning letter on or before December 15. Placement on tier two can only be based upon an evaluation report which includes at least three observations.

The notification of possible placement on tier two can occur at any time and must be based on an evaluator's personal observations of staff member performance. The evaluator(s) must document the observations and review them with the staff member before the issuance of a notification letter. The primary evaluator shall not notify any staff member of possible placement on tier two unless there have first been at least three observations, which the evaluator(s) will have documented and reviewed with the employee.

4. Staff members who have been notified of potential placement on tier two may employ a range of activities or services in the school system including, but not limited to the following: peer consultation, peer observation, use of curriculum support personnel. The activities will not be part of the evaluation record.

5. If a professional status staff member is notified that he/she will be placed on tier two, during the period between the notification (example, May 1) and the placement, (example, September 1) there will be no additional evaluator(s), but coordinators, department heads, department chairs, assistant principals, etc., can provide support and consultation. Once a staff member is on tier two, if there is a subject-related problem, the appropriate curriculum administrator(s) must be involved as a supplementary evaluator(s). Any evaluation conclusion reached by a supplementary evaluator shall be based on observation reports.

6. Within ten school days of the tier two warning placing a staff member on tier two, the staff member and all evaluators shall meet to discuss an improvement plan which shall include: an identification of the aspects of performance which are in need of improvement; the evaluators' specific expectations; the indicators of satisfactory improvement; how the evaluators will assist the staff member, where applicable, in meeting these expectations; the time which will be allowed for improvement; and, the date by which another evaluation report will be completed.

The follow-up evaluation will be completed within two to four months, unless both the staff member and the evaluator(s) agree to a change in this time frame. The LEA president (or his/her designee) and the superintendent (or his/her designee) will have to agree to this change.

If the improvement plan does not identify one or more evaluators, or does not describe the role of any evaluator, the improvement plan shall be amended to identify any such evaluator(s) and to describe such evaluator's role in the improvement plan. This will occur within ten (10) school days from the date of the improvement plan. The staff member shall be given a copy of each amendment. The staff member and all evaluators named in the improvement plan shall meet to discuss the amendment within ten (10) school days of incorporation of the amendment to the plan. Any subsequent amendments must be agreed to by the primary evaluator, the staff member, the superintendent (or his/her designee) and the LEA president (or his/her designee).

The staff member may request a particular evaluator from the Central Office.

Before any evaluator performs any formal observation for the purpose of preparing a follow-up evaluation, pursuant to the improvement plan, he/she shall hold a pre-observation conference with the staff member. There will be a post-observation conference following the observation.

7. The primary evaluator will prepare a draft of the improvement plan and circulate copies to the staff member and all involved evaluators. Each will sign and return the tier-two improvement plan within five (5) school days to the primary evaluator. Any involved person can append suggestions or recommendations. The primary evaluator may or may not incorporate written suggestions in the final plan.

8. Copies of the final improvement plan and any subsequent amendments will be hand delivered by the primary evaluator (or his/her designee) to the superintendent and the president of the LEA each of whom will have five (5) school days in which to raise an objection to the plan and notify all of the other parties in writing of his/her concern(s).

The superintendent (or his/her designee) shall respond in writing to any written objections of the LEA president (or his/her designee). The LEA president (or his/her designee) shall respond in writing to any written objections of the superintendent (or his/her designee). Responses to objections shall be made within five (5) school days of their receipt.

The parties shall meet within seven (7) school days of the receipt of objections to resolve said objections. In the event that the parties cannot agree within five (5) school days, they shall meet with a mediator, chosen by mutual agreement, to resolve any outstanding issues. If, after an additional meeting with a mediator, they are unable to resolve any outstanding disagreements, the mediator shall resolve the disagreements. The decision of the mediator is not grieveable.

9. If a tier two improvement plan is successfully completed as evidenced by the subsequent evaluation, the staff member shall not remain on tier two.

10. Placement on tier two is grieveable. There will be an expedited grievance procedure with only one level of management review, that is the superintendent's level. The immediate step thereafter is arbitration.

PROFESSIONAL GROWTH PLAN

Name _____

School _____ Date _____

Check one: _____ Year 2 – Collaborative Year

                       _____ Year 4 – Individual Study

The PROPOSAL _____

_____

_____

_____

GOALS: State the goals of the proposal as related to the comprehensive evaluation. (**Note:** During Year 4, the goals need not be directly linked to the comprehensive evaluation.)

ACTIONS: State the actions or procedures planned to accomplish the goals.

TIME LINE: State the time line for completion.

EVIDENCE: Describe the evidence to be provided to demonstrate completion. _____

_____

_____

COLLABORATING PROFESSIONALS: Identify the collaborating teachers or other professionals involved in the proposal. Describe their roles and responsibilities. (**Note:** Collaboration is optional during Year 4 Individual Study)

ADMINISTRATIVE SUPPORT: Indicate, if any, the type of support (materials, time, staff development meetings) which might be needed from the administration to complete the proposal.

Date of conference: _____

_____   _____
Signature of evaluator   date

_____   _____
Signature of staff menber   date

FINAL REPORT ON PROFESSIONAL GROWTH PLAN

Name _____

School_____ Date _____

Check one: _____ Year 2 – Collaborative Year

                 _____ Year 4 – Individual Study

Report on your professional growth by commenting on the relevant aspects of your Professional Growth Plan. For example: Did you achieve your goals? Did the actions/procedures go according to plan? Have you provided the evidence required? How did the planned collaboration actually work? Was there sufficient time and support?

After addressing the implementation of the plan, make an assessment of the knowledge and/or skills you gained during the year. You might consider questions such as these: What did you learn and how will this knowledge impact on your professional performance? How will the year's professional growth activities affect future goal setting? What new or improved skills will make you a better professional, and how might you share them in future collaborative roles?

N.B. The staff member and the evaluator(s) should sign and date this final report which will be attached to the Professional Growth Plan and placed in the staff member's personnel file.

Date of conference _____

_____   _____
Signature of evaluator   date

_____   _____
Signature of teacher   date

SUGGESTIONS FOR A PROFESSIONAL GROWTH PLAN

Note: Most of these suggestions can be tailored to fit staff members' needs and desires, and to satisfy the requirements of either a Collaborative Year or an Individual Study Year.

- **Peer Observation:** Teachers agree to observe each other's classes several times during the year and provide and receive feedback important to their goals.

- **Study Groups:** Teachers meet with colleagues in groups to learn new strategies, experiment with these strategies and share the results of their experiments, and to problem solve. Study groups can be developed to feature content which would support a teacher's goals.

- **Field Based Research:** A teacher develops a hypothesis and a research project to test that hypothesis. A teacher might propose the hypothesis that the use of cooperative learning strategies will improve student achievement in U.S. history. The teacher can then identify a section or sections in which to use the strategy and measure student achievement. Findings could be briefly presented in a paper and discussed with other teachers.

- **Analysis of a Portfolio of Artifacts:** A teacher could develop a file of appropriate artifacts/documents in order to analyze certain relationships, such as between the instructional strategies used and student achievement. A final report could be prepared and shared with other teachers.

- **Preparing and Presenting a Staff Development Program:** A teacher with interest and expertise in a particular area of instruction could develop and present a program on the topic to other interested staff. The presentation should include what participants will know or be able to do as a result of participating in the program, why it is important to learn it, and how it relates to student learning.

- **Preparing and Presenting a Parent Education Program:** This is similar to the development of a staff development program, but specifically designed to attract parents. Topics such as how to help children with their homework or how to help children become better readers are only two of many possibilities.

- **Team Teaching with an Administrator, Principal, or Another Professional:** The "team" would create, teach, and evaluate an integrated unit of instruction. All involved share responsibility and work together to assess the unit by identifying its problems and successes.

- **Self-Analysis of Videotapes:** A teacher could videotape several lessons during the course of the year, analyze the lessons, and write up an assessment on the effectiveness of each.

- **Mentoring:** A teacher could develop and/or extend mentoring relationships throughout the school. The mentoring process should include observing the new teacher at several points during the year, providing feedback, being observed by the new teacher, and holding frequent discussions about teaching.

- **Curriculum or Instructional Strategy Development:** A group of teachers could develop and then pilot a substantively new curriculum based on state and/or local goals or requirements. A thorough process of assessing the pilot program must be prepared, implemented, and written up. Or the teachers could apply an instructional strategy such as cooperative learning to a new curriculum or to where it has not been previously used. A plan to assess the effectiveness must be prepared, implemented, and written up.

- **Course Work:** A teacher could participate in substantive in-service professional development and/or take a course.

- **Submission of Articles for Publication:** A teacher could prepare and present one or more articles on instruction and/or curriculum for publication in professional journals.

- **Other:** (Subject to administrative review and approval).

TEACHER PERFORMANCE STANDARDS

I. Currency in the Curriculum

The teacher demonstrates competency in subject area(s).

1. Has an appropriate in-depth knowledge of subject matter

2. Acts as a subject area resource person for students

3. Contributes to the ongoing evaluation of the curriculum

4. Keeps current in the field and applies knowledge to the instructional program

II. Effective Planning and Assessment of Curriculum and Instruction

A. The teacher plans instruction effectively.

1. Sets short-term and year-long goals for curricular units

2. Identifies individual and group needs and plans the use of appropriate instructional strategies

3. Uses materials and resources, including technologies, that are appropriately matched to curricular goals and to individual student needs and learning styles.

4. Seeks out and collaborates with school based specialists and administrators to better design curricula or instructional modifications to meet the special learning needs of students

5. Plans frequent instructional opportunities where students are interacting with teachers and one another while assuming increasing responsibility for their own learning

B. The teacher provides effective assessment of student learning.

1. Determines specific and challenging standards for student learning; compares intended and actual learning outcomes

2. Schedules time for individual and interactive reflection on student progress with the student

3. Regularly provides feedback to students on their progress

4. Implements innovative approaches to assessment

5. Keeps parents informed of student's progress and works with them to aid in the total development of the student

III. Effective Instruction

A. The teacher communicates effectively with students.

1. Implements clear lesson objectives and communicates these to students

2. Promotes students' independence as learners

3. Stimulates students' thinking through classroom discussion and writing activities

4. Identifies confusions and misconceptions as indicated by student responses and regular assessment strategies. Remediates, reteaches, or extends teaching to meet individual and/or group needs

5. Has enthusiasm for subject matter and makes significant efforts to communicate that enthusiasm to students and colleagues

6. Communicates clearly in writing and speaking, using precise language

7. Understands and demonstrates to students the relevance of the subject matter to life-long learning and the inter-relationship of various curricula

B. The teacher uses appropriate instructional techniques.

1. Uses a variety of teaching strategies such as cooperative learning, peer tutoring, project based learning, lecture, discussions, and technologies

2. Provides options for students to demonstrate competency and mastery of new material, such as written work, plays, artwork, oratory, visual presentations, and portfolios

3. Uses a variety of appropriate materials to reinforce and extend skills, accommodate learning styles, and match instructional objectives

4. Encourages students to summarize important learnings and to integrate them with prior knowledge

5. Demonstrates a working knowledge of current educational research

6. Refines instructional strategies to increase student learning and foster confidence in a student's ability to learn

7. Provides opportunities for creativity

8. Uses a variety of questioning techniques to stimulate student participation, including those which encourage and guide critical and independent thinking and the development of ideas

9. Presents information recognizing multiple points of view; encourages students to assess the accuracy of information presented

IV. Effective Classroom Management

A. The teacher applies classroom management techniques to establish a positive and productive learning environment.

1. Uses time and classroom space productively and efficiently in order to promote optimal learning

2. Maintains a high level of student participation and engagement with appropriate time on task

3. Establishes classroom procedures that ensure smooth transition from one activity to another

B. The teacher maintains and models appropriate standards of behavior, mutual respect, and safety.

1. Encourages student achievement and responsibility by reinforcing desired student behaviors that demonstrate attitudes of fairness and respect

2. Establishes and carries out reasonable and routine classroom rules and procedures

3. Maintains appropriate professional boundaries with students

V. Promotion of High Standards and Expectations for Student Achievement

A. The teacher promotes high standards and expectations for student achievement.

1. Communicates standards, expectations, and guidelines regarding the quality and quantity of students' work to students and parents

2. Responds to students' answers and work in a timely and appropriate way

3. Encourages students to take risks and to persevere with challenging tasks

VI. Promotion of Equity and Appreciation of Diversity
The teacher promotes equitable opportunities for student learning.

1. Provides opportunities for all students to participate in the classroom

2. Demonstrates sensitivity to differences in abilities, gender, learning style, social and cultural background

3. Develops and implements educational and organizational strategies that are effective in meeting the needs of a diverse student body

VII. Fulfillment of Professional Responsibilities
The teacher demonstrates continuing concern for professionalism.

1. Seeks out information and is receptive to suggestions for growth and improvement

2. Works collaboratively with other staff members to implement appropriate curricular and school related programs

3. Shares expertise and new ideas with colleagues

4. Works constructively with others to identify school problems and suggest possible solutions

5. Meets deadlines and fulfills routine responsibilities

6. Observes established school system policies and procedures

7. Participates in appropriate self development activities such as conferences, in-service training and professional study

8. Maintains appropriate professional behaviors in all interactions with students, parents, and colleagues

SCHOOL NURSE PERFORMANCE STANDARDS

I. Currency in School Health

1. The school nurse demonstrates competency in the area of school health. Has an appropriate in-depth knowledge of school nursing practice

2. Acts as a health resource person for students, colleagues, and parents

3. Contributes to the ongoing evaluation of the health services

4. Keeps current in the field and applies knowledge to the health care of students and staff

5. Demonstrates an interest in and concern for the prevention of disease and promotion of health

II. Effective Planning and Assessment of Student Health Status
A. The school nurse plans for health care needs effectively.

1. Sets short-term and year-long goals for health care needs of students

2. Identifies individual needs and plans for the use of appropriate nursing care

3. Uses resources, including technologies, that are appropriately matched to nursing interventions and to individual student health needs

4. Seeks out and collaborates with other school based nurses, specialists, and administrators to better design modifications to meet the special health needs of students

5. Plans for students to increase responsibility for their own health needs

B. The nurse provides effective assessment of student health status.

1. Compares intended and actual health outcomes

2. Schedules time for interaction with the student regarding health issues

3. Regularly provides feedback to students on their progress

4. Implements innovative approaches to health assessment

5. Keeps parents informed of student's health status and works with them to meet the total health needs of the student

III. Effective Instruction
A. The school nurse communicates effectively with students.

1. Implements clear health care objectives and communicates these to students

2. Promotes students' independence as learners with regard to health issues

3. Identifies confusions and misconceptions as indicated by student responses and regular assessment strategies to health care. Remediates, reteaches, or extends teaching to meet individual and/or group health needs

4. Has enthusiasm for school nursing and preventive health care and makes significant efforts to communicate that enthusiasm to students and colleagues

5. Communicates clearly in writing and speaking, using precise language

6. Understands and demonstrates to students the relevance of their health status to their life

B. The school nurse uses appropriate instructional techniques.

1. Uses a variety of strategies for individualized health teaching

2. Uses appropriate materials to reinforce health care needs to accommodate learning styles

3. Encourages students to summarize important health knowledge and to integrate it with prior knowledge

4. Demonstrates a working knowledge of current school nursing research

5. Uses a variety of questioning techniques to encourage student participation, including those which encourage self care and independent evaluation of their health issues

IV. Effective Health Room Management
A. The school nurse establishes a positive health room environment.

1. Uses time and health room space productively and efficiently

2. Maintains a high level of student participation and engagement in their own health care

B. The school nurse maintains and models appropriate standards of behavior, mutual respect, and safety.

1. Encourages student responsibility by reinforcing desired student behaviors that demonstrate attitudes of fairness and respect

2. Establishes and carries out reasonable and routine health room rules and procedures

3 Maintains appropriate professional boundaries with students

4. Handles sensitive information with discretion

V. **Promotion of Equity and Appreciation of Diversity**

The school nurse strives to ensure equitable treatment and care of all students.

1. Demonstrates sensitivity to differences in gender, social and cultural backgrounds

2. Develops and implements health programs that are effective in meeting the needs of a diverse student body

VI. **Fulfillment of Professional Responsibilities**

The school nurse demonstrates continuing concern for professionalism.

1. Seeks out information and is receptive to suggestions for growth and improvement

2. Works collaboratively with other staff members to implement appropriate nursing programs

3. Shares expertise and new ideas with colleagues

4. Works constructively with others to identify school health problems and suggest possible solutions.

5. Meets deadlines and fulfills routine responsibilities

6. Observes established school system policies and procedures

7. Participates in appropriate self development activities such as conferences, in-service training and professional study

8. Maintains appropriate professional behaviors in all interactions with students, parents, and colleagues

SPECIAL EDUCATION TEACHER PERFORMANCE STANDARDS

I. **Currency in the Curriculum**

The teacher demonstrates competency in special education practices.

1. Has an appropriate in-depth knowledge of special education practices

2. Acts as a resource person for students, colleagues and parents in special education matters

3. Keeps current in the field through professional development activities

II. **Effective Planning and Assessment of Curriculum and Instruction for Special Needs Students**

   A. The special needs teacher plans instruction effectively.

   1. Sets short term and year long goals for special education students through the education plan

   2. Identifies and plans the use of appropriate instructional strategies

   3. Uses materials and resources, including technologies that enhance learning

   B. The teacher provides effective assessment of student learning.

   1. Regularly provides feedback to students on their progress

   2. Implements varied approaches to classroom assessments

   3. Keeps parents informed of student's progress and works with them to aid in the development of the student

   4. Is familiar with relevant information from student records and consults with appropriate personnel

   5. Observes and describes student behavior as needed

   C. Participates on the school evaluation team.

   1. Selects appropriate tests and measures as part of the evaluation process

   2. Provides written documentation of testing

   3. Contributes to education plans, semi-annual reports and parent conferences as appropriate

III. **Effective Instruction**

   A. The teacher communicates effectively with students.

   1. Implements clear lesson objectives and communicates these to students

   2. Promotes students' independence as learners

   3. Stimulates students' thinking through classroom discussion and activities, when appropriate

   4. Remediates, reteaches or extends teaching to meet individual and/or group needs

   5. Communicates clearly

B. The teacher uses appropriate instructional techniques, materials and resources to assist students in achieving Individual Education Plan (IEP) objectives.

1. Provides for individual differences in student learning rates, styles, abilities and interests by such means as differentiating instruction, grouping, materials and assignments

2. Refers students to appropriate support personnel as needed

3. Uses a variety of instructional materials and strategies

4. Consults with classroom teachers about curriculum modifications

5. Provides recommendations to staff and parents to improve students' strategies in dealing with academic and/or behavioral issues

6. When appropriate, encourages creativity and independent thinking

IV. **Effective Classroom Management**

A. The teacher applies classroom management techniques to establish a positive and productive learning environment.

1. Uses time productively and efficiently

2. Reinforces desired student behaviors

3. Establishes and carries out reasonable rules and procedures

4. Uses available space effectively

B. The teacher maintains and models appropriate standards of behavior, mutual respect, and safety.

1. Encourages student attitudes of fairness and respect

2. Maintains appropriate professional boundaries with students

V. **Promotion of High Standards and Expectations for Individual Student Achievement Based on Student's Learning Profile and Educational Plan**

The teacher promotes high standards and expectations for student achievement based on the student's learning profile and educational plan.

1. Communicates standards, expectations, and guidelines regarding the quality of student's work

2. Responds to student's answers and work in a timely and appropriate way

3. Encourages student to take risks

VI. Promotion of Equity and Appreciation of Diversity
The teacher promotes equitable opportunities for student learning.

1. Provides opportunities for all students to participate in the classroom

2. Demonstrates sensitivity to differences in abilities, gender, learning style, social and cultural background

3. Develops and implements educational and organizational strategies that are effective in meeting the needs of a diverse student body

VII. Fulfillment of Professional Responsibilities
The teacher demonstrates continuing concern for professionalism.

1. Seeks out information and is receptive to suggestions

2. Works collaboratively with other staff members

3. Shares expertise and new ideas with colleagues

4. Meets deadlines and fulfills routine responsibilities

5. Observes established school system policies and procedures

6. Participates in appropriate self development activities such as conferences, in-service training and professional study

7. Maintains appropriate professional behaviors in all interactions with students, parents and colleagues

LANGUAGE ARTS/READING SPECIALIST PERFORMANCE STANDARDS

I. Currency in the Curriculum
The specialist demonstrates competency in subject area(s).

1. Has an appropriate, in-depth knowledge of literacy development and instructional strategies in all areas of the language arts

2. Acts as a subject area resource person for teachers, curriculum personnel, principals, and parents

3. Contributes to the ongoing evaluation of the curriculum

4. Keeps current in the field and applies knowledge to consultations with teachers, and to the instructional program

II.   **Effective Planning and Assessment of Curriculum and Instruction**

A. **The specialist plans instruction effectively.**

1.   Sets short-term and year-long goals for curricular units

2.   Identifies individual and group needs and plans the use of appropriate instructional strategies

3.   Uses materials and resources, including technologies, that are appropriately matched to curricular goals and to individual student needs and learning styles

4.   Seeks out and collaborates with other school based specialists and administrators to better design curricula or instructional modifications to meet the special learning needs of students

5.   Plans frequent instructional opportunities where students are interacting with teachers and one another while assuming increasing responsibility for their own learning

B. **The teacher provides effective assessment of student learning.**

1.   Determines specific and challenging standards for student learning; compares intended and actual learning outcomes

2.   Schedules time for individual and interactive reflection on student progress with the student

3.   Regularly provides feedback to students on their progress

4.   Implements innovative approaches to assessment

5.   Keeps parents informed of student's progress and works with them to aid in the total development of the student

III. **Effective Instruction**

A. **The specialist communicates effectively with students.**

1.   Implements clear lesson objectives and communicates these to students

2.   Promotes students' independence as learners through application of a modeling/guided practice/independent practice instructional model, and other appropriate instructional models

3.   Stimulates students' thinking through classroom discussion and writing activities

4.   Identifies confusions and misconceptions as indicated by student responses and regular assessment strategies. Retouches or extends teaching to meet individual and/or group needs

5. Has enthusiasm for subject matter and makes significant efforts to communicate that enthusiasm to students and colleagues

6. Communicates clearly in writing and speaking, using precise language

7. Understands and demonstrates to students the relevance of the subject matter to life-long learning and the inter-relationship of various curricula

B. The specialist uses appropriate instructional techniques.

1. Uses a variety of teaching strategies such as cooperative learning, peer tutoring, project based learning, lecture, discussions, and technologies

2. Provides options for students to demonstrate competency and mastery of new material, such as written work, plays, artwork, oratory, visual presentations, and portfolios

3. Uses a variety of appropriate materials to reinforce and extend skills, accommodate learning styles, and match instructional objectives

4. Encourages students to summarize important learnings and to integrate them with prior knowledge

5. Demonstrates a working knowledge of current educational research

6. Refines instructional strategies to increase student learning and foster confidence in a student's ability to learn

7. Provides opportunities for creativity

8. Uses a variety of questioning techniques to stimulate student participation, including those which encourage and guide critical and independent thinking and the development of ideas

9. Presents information recognizing multiple points of view; encourages students to assess the accuracy of information presented

C. The specialist consults effectively with teachers, principals, and other curriculum specialists.

1. Listens well and responds appropriately

2. Communicates positively in all interactions with teachers

3. Works effectively with teachers in a consulting capacity

4. Is available for consultation with teachers at times that are mutually convenient for both

IV. **Effective Classroom Management**

    A. **The specialist applies classroom management techniques to establish a positive and productive learning environment.**

        1. Uses time and classroom space productively and efficiently in order to promote optimal learning

        2. Maintains a high level of student participation and engagement with appropriate time on task

        3. Establishes classroom procedures that ensure smooth transition from one activity to another

    B. **The specialist maintains and models appropriate standards of behavior, mutual respect, and safety.**

        1. Encourages student achievement and responsibility by reinforcing desired student behaviors that demonstrate attitudes of fairness and respect

        2. Establishes and carries out reasonable and routine classroom rules and procedures

        3. Maintains appropriate professional boundaries with students

V. **Promotion of High Standards and Expectations for Student Achievement**

    The specialist promotes high standards and expectations for student achievement.

        1. Communicates standards, expectations, and guidelines regarding the quality and quantity of students' work to students and parents

        2. Responds to students' answers and work in a timely and appropriate way

        3. Encourages students to take risks and to persevere with challenging tasks

VI. **Promotion of Equity and Appreciation of Diversity**

    The specialist promotes equitable opportunities for student learning.

        1. Provides opportunities for all students to participate in the classroom

        2. Demonstrates sensitivity to differences in abilities, gender, learning style, social and cultural background

        3. Develops and implements educational and organizational strategies that are effective in meeting the needs of a diverse student body

VII. Fulfillment of Professional Responsibilities
The specialist demonstrates continuing concern for professionalism.

1. Seeks out information and is receptive to suggestions for growth and improvement

2. Works collaboratively with other staff members to implement appropriate curricular and school related programs

3. Shares expertise and new ideas with colleagues

4. Works constructively with others to identify school problems and suggest possible solutions

5. Meets deadlines and fulfills routine responsibilities

6. Observes established school system policies and procedures

7. Participates in appropriate self development activities such as conferences, in-service training and professional study

8. Maintains appropriate professional behaviors in all interactions with students, parents, and colleagues

PSYCHOLOGIST PERFORMANCE STANDARDS

I. Currency in the Professional Area
The psychologist demonstrates competency in professional areas.

1. Has an appropriate in-depth knowledge of psychology

2. Exhibits current awareness of sound psychological principles and practices in evaluation, consultation and counseling

3. Acts as a resource person for students, colleagues and parents in psychological matters

4. Contributes to ongoing evaluation of educational practices

II. Effective Planning and Assessment
A. The psychologist selects appropriate materials, methods, and resources to assist students in achieving learning and behavioral objectives.

1. Refers students to appropriate in-school support personnel as needed

2. Provides recommendations to staff and parents to improve students' strategies in dealing with academic and behavioral issues

3. Where appropriate, refers students and their families to outside resources

B. The psychologist establishes psychological objectives consistent with student needs.

1. Uses currently available psychological findings to make appropriate recommendations for provision of services to students

2. States objectives clearly and conveys the meaning of these objectives

3. Demonstrates concern for the affective, behavioral, and medical as well as the cognitive aspects of student learning

C. The psychologist assesses, describes, and communicates effectively student needs, strengths, weaknesses, interests, and progress.

1. Communicates clearly to students the standards and evaluative methods that will be used

2. Applies relevant information from student records

3. Consults with appropriate school personnel, parents, and other agencies and individuals outside the school in planning for students

4. Is perceptive in observing and specific in describing student behavior

5. Effectively evaluates and communicates student functioning to students, parents, staff and other appropriate liaisons

6. Provides written comprehensive documentation of testing

III. Effective Communication

A. The psychologist interacts and communicates positively and productively with students in groups and individual settings.

1. Explains importance of assessments and employs positive expectations to achieve desired outcomes

2. Provides students opportunities to meet for review of evaluations and follow-up as needed

3. Listens and responds appropriately to students

4. Maintains appropriate professional boundaries with students

B. The psychologist interacts and communicates positively and productively with parents and staff in groups and individual settings.

1. Listens and responds appropriately to staff, parents, and outside contacts

2. Communicates psychological findings clearly in writing and speaking, using precise language

IV. Effective Management

The psychologist demonstrates effective practices.

1. Employs and/or adopts appropriate psychological material and practices in evaluation, consultation, and counseling

2. Deals sensitively and effectively with the perceptions and reactions of the student, the parents, the staff, and other professionals

3. Uses time productively and efficiently

V. Promotion of High Standards and Expectations for Student Achievement

The psychologist promotes high standards and expectations for student functioning.

1. Communicates standards, expectations, and guidelines regarding the quality and quantity of student achievement and behavior

2. Encourages students to take risks and persevere with challenging tasks

VI. Promotion of Equity and Appreciation of Diversity

The psychologist promotes equitable opportunities and appreciation of diversity for all students.

1. Demonstrates sensitivity to differences in abilities, gender, learning styles, social and cultural background

2. Develops and implements educational and psychological strategies that are effective in meeting the needs of a diverse student body

3. Encourages student responsibility by reinforcing desired student behaviors that demonstrate attitudes of fairness and respect

VI. Fulfillment of Professional Responsibilities

The psychologist demonstrates continuing concern for professionalism.

1. Participates in appropriate professional development activities such as conferences, in-service training and study of journals, etc

2. Observes established school system policies and procedures

3. Meets deadlines and fulfills routine responsibilities

4. Works cooperatively with colleagues and supervisors

5. Demonstrates appropriate awareness of school program and policies in interactions with parents

6. Maintains appropriate professional behavior in all interactions with students, parents, and colleagues

SPEECH AND LANGUAGE PATHOLOGIST PERFORMANCE STANDARDS

I. **Currency in the Curriculum**

   The speech/language pathologist demonstrates competency in subject areas.

   1. Has in-depth knowledge in the field of speech/language pathology

   2. Is aware of current developments in speech/language pathology and applies this awareness in working with students and staff

   3. Acts as a subject area resource person for students, teachers, curriculum personnel, principals, and parents

II. **Effective Planning and Assessment of Curriculum and Instruction**

   A. **The speech/language pathologist plans instruction effectively.**

   1. Sets and writes goals and objectives for annual Individual Educational Plans and informs classroom teachers of them

   2. Assists teachers in planning for adjustment in instruction as needed, and in selecting appropriate instructional materials and strategies

   3. Uses materials and resources, including technologies, that are appropriately matched to student needs

   B. **The speech/language pathologist provides effective assessment of student learning.**

   1. Administers individual, diagnostic assessments of students' speech and language skills, and uses current, established testing practices and procedures, as well as innovative approaches to assessment

   2. Makes appropriate referrals for further evaluation

   3. Is specific in describing student strengths, weaknesses, and therapeutic/instructional needs in written reports

   4. Correctly interprets and effectively communicates testing data to parents and staff

5. Continuously evaluates students' progress to adjust therapeutic procedures and goals; and provides opportunities for students to reflect on progress

C. Participates on the school evaluation team.

1. Selects appropriate tests and measures as part of the evaluation process

2. Provides written documentation of testing

3. Contributes to education plans, semi-annual reports and parent conferences as appropriate

III. Effective Instruction

A. The speech/language pathologist communicates effectively with students.

1. Implements clear lesson objectives and communicates these to students

2. Encourages students' independence as learners and makes repeated efforts to support them in achieving their learning goals

3. Communicates clearly in writing and speaking, using language appropriately matched to student needs

4. Communicates positive expectations in all interactions with students, classroom teachers, and parents

5. Has enthusiasm for subject matter and makes efforts to communicate that enthusiasm to students and colleagues

B. The speech/language pathologist uses appropriate instructional techniques.

1. Employs sound therapeutic practice, as well as varied instructional strategies in small group and individual settings

2. Promotes students' independence as learners through application of instructional models

3. Stimulates students' thinking and creativity through all communication channels as appropriate to the communication disorder

4. Assists classroom teachers in providing options for students with communication disorders to demonstrate competency and mastery of new material in a variety of ways

5. Demonstrates a working knowledge of current research

6. Uses varied and effective communication strategies to stimulate student participation

7. Deals effectively with student questions, responses, and confusions

8. Remediates, reteaches or extends teaching to meet individual needs

9. Encourages students to summarize important learnings when possible, and to integrate them with prior knowledge

10. Presents information recognizing multiple points of view, and encourages students to assess the accuracy of information presented

IV. Effective Classroom Management

A. The speech/language pathologist applies classroom management techniques to establish a positive and productive learning environment.

1. Uses available instructional time productively and efficiently

2. Arranges and uses available instructional space, furnishings and display areas to facilitate and enhance learning as physical circumstances permit

3. Encourages student achievement and responsibility by reinforcing desired student behaviors to promote a high level of student participation and appropriate time on task

4. Establishes procedures that ensure smooth transitions from one activity to another

5. Is available and prepared for staffing and screenings as needed

6. Maintains accurate records of student progress

B. The speech/language pathologist maintains and models appropriate standards of behavior, mutual respect, and safety.

1. Encourages student achievement and responsibility by reinforcing desired student behaviors which demonstrate attitudes of fairness and respect

2. Establishes and carries out reasonable rules and procedures

3. Maintains appropriate professional boundaries with students

V. **Promotion of High Standards and Expectations for Student Achievement**

The speech/language pathologist promotes high standards and expectations for student achievement.

1. Communicates standards, expectations, and guidelines regarding the quality and quantity of students' work to students and parents

2. Is receptive to student concerns and responds appropriately

3. Encourages students to take risks and to persevere with challenging tasks

VI. **Displays Promotion of Equity and Appreciation of Diversity**

The speech/language pathologist promotes equitable opportunities for student learning.

1. Provides opportunities for all students to participate in the classroom

2. Demonstrates sensitivity to differences in abilities, gender, learning style, social and cultural backgrounds

3. Develops and implements educational and organizational strategies that are effective in meeting the needs of a diverse student body

VII. **Fulfillment of Professional Responsibilities**

The speech/language pathologist demonstrates continuing concern for professionalism.

1. Seeks out information and is receptive to suggestions for growth and improvement

2. Works collaboratively with other staff members to implement appropriate curricular and school related programs

3. Shares expertise and new ideas with colleagues

4. Works constructively with others to identify school problems and suggest possible solutions

5. Meets deadlines and completes routine responsibilities

6. Engages in appropriate self development activities such as conferences, in-service training, and professional study to maintain and extend subject area expertise

7. Observes established school system policies and procedures

8. Maintains appropriate professional behavior in all interactions with students, parents, and colleagues

LIBRARY MEDIA SPECIALIST PERFORMANCE STANDARDS

I.   Currency in the Curriculum

The library media specialist demonstrates competency in subject area(s).

1.   Has an appropriate in-depth knowledge of subject matters

2.   Acts as a subject area resource person for students and teachers

3.   Contributes to the ongoing evaluation of the curriculum

4.   Keeps current in the field and applies knowledge to the instructional program

II.   Effective Planning and Assessment of Curriculum and Instruction

A. The library media specialist collaborates with classroom teachers to plan effective instruction in library related units.

1.   Sets short-term and year-long goals within curricular units

2.   Identifies individual and group needs and plans the use of appropriate instructional strategies

3.   Identifies, demonstrates and uses materials and resources, including technologies, that are appropriately matched to curricular goals and to individual student needs and learning styles

4.   Seeks out and collaborates with classroom teachers, specialists and administrators to help them design curriculum, assessment strategies, and/or instructional modifications to meet the special learning needs of students

5.   Plans frequent instructional opportunities where students are interacting with teachers and one another while assuming increasing responsibility for their own learning

B. The library media specialist evaluates the library program in relation to changing needs and technology.

III.   Effective Instruction

A. The library media specialist communicates effectively with students.

1.   Implements clear lesson objectives and communicates these to students and teachers

2.   Promotes students' independence as learners

3.   Stimulates students' thinking through classroom discussion and research activities

4. Identifies students' misconceptions and reteaches or extends teaching to meet individual and/or group needs

5. Has enthusiasm for subject matter and makes significant efforts to communicate that enthusiasm to students and colleagues

6. Communicates clearly in writing and speaking, using precise language

7. Understands and demonstrates to students the relevance of the subject matter to life-long learning and inter-relationship of various curricula

B. The library media specialist uses appropriate instructional techniques.

1. Uses a variety of teaching strategies such as project based learning, discussions, and technologies

2. Helps students plan strategies for acquiring, selecting, and evaluating information and demonstrating competency and mastery of new material

3. Uses a variety of appropriate materials to reinforce and extend skills, accommodate learning styles, and match instructional objectives

4. Encourages students to summarize important learnings and to integrate them with prior knowledge

5. Demonstrates a working knowledge of current educational research and information technology

6. Refines instructional strategies to increase student learning and foster confidence in a student's ability to learn

7. Provides opportunities for creativity

8. Uses a variety of questioning techniques to stimulate student participation, including those which encourage and guide critical and independent thinking and the development of ideas

9. Presents information recognizing multiple points of view; encourages students to assess the accuracy of information presented

IV. **Effective Management**

A. **The library media specialist applies classroom management techniques to establish a positive and productive learning environment.**

1. Uses time and space productively and efficiently in order to promote optimal learning

2. Maintains a high level of student participation and engagement with appropriate time on task

3. Establishes procedures that ensure smooth transition from one activity to another

B. The library media specialist maintains and models appropriate standards of behavior, mutual respect, and safety.

1. Encourages student achievement and responsibility by reinforcing desired student behaviors that demonstrate attitudes of fairness and respect

2. Establishes and carries out reasonable and routine classroom rules and procedures

3. Maintains appropriate professional boundaries with students

V.   Promotion of High Standards and Expectations for Student Achievement

The library media specialist works with the teacher to promote high standards and expectations for student achievement.

1. Communicates standards, expectations, and guidelines regarding the quality and quantity of students' work

2. Responds to students' answers in a timely and appropriate way

3. Encourages students to take risks and to persevere with challenging tasks

VI. Promotion of Equity and Appreciation of Diversity

The library media specialist promotes equitable opportunities for student learning.

1. Provides opportunities for all students to participate in the library media center's activities

2. Demonstrates sensitivity to differences in abilities, gender, learning style, social and cultural backgrounds

3. Develops and implements educational and organizational strategies that are effective in meeting the needs of a diverse student body

VII. Fulfillment of Professional Responsibilities

The library media specialist demonstrates a concern for professionalism.

1. Seeks out information and is receptive to suggestions for growth and improvement

2. Works collaboratively with other staff members to implement appropriate curricular and school related programs

3. Shares expertise and new ideas with students, colleagues and parents

4. Works constructively with others to identify school problems and suggest possible solutions

5. Meets deadlines and fulfills routine responsibilities

6. Observes established school system policies and procedures

7. Participates in appropriate self development activities such as conferences, in-service training and professional study

8 Maintains appropriate professional behaviors in all interactions with students, parents, and colleagues

9. Articulates and models a vision of the library program that is integrated with all the school's instructional programs, provides intellectual and physical access to materials, emphasizes higher order thinking skills, manages networks of information resources and accommodates emerging information technologies

VIII. Effective Administration of the Library Media Center
The library media specialist administers the Library Media Center effectively.

1. Manages systems necessary for effective operation of the Library Media Center

2. Trains and supervises Library Media Center staff

3. Develops and administers budgets

4. Maintains information for the community about school policies, curricula and programs

5. Collaborates with Cary Memorial Library staff

COUNSELOR/SOCIAL WORKER PERFORMANCE STANDARDS

I. Currency in the Professional Area
The counselor/social worker demonstrates competency in the professional area.

1. Has appropriate in-depth knowledge of guidance and counseling practices

2. Exhibits awareness of current guidance and counseling practices

3. Employs and/or adapts sound guidance and counseling materials and practices

4. Acts as a resource person for students, parents, and staff in matters of guidance and counseling

II. Planning and Assessment of Guidance and Counseling Interventions
The counselor/social worker plans and assesses effectively.

1. Formulates objectives and appropriate strategies to assure continuity of effective guidance and counseling services

2. Identifies individual and group needs and plans the use of appropriate counseling intervention

3. Acquires pertinent information from a variety of sources:
   - Student Records
   - Consultation with appropriate school personnel
   - Consultation with students, parents, and other appropriate agencies or individuals outside of school

4. Assesses the effectiveness of intervention strategies

III. Guidance/Counseling Practices
The counselor/social worker communicates and interacts effectively.

1. Interacts positively and productively with students, parents, and teachers

2. Listens well, responds appropriately, and encourages student participation in discussion by effective counseling strategies

3. Communicates positive expectations for all students and reinforces positive behavior

IV. Effective Management
The counselor/social worker utilizes effective group techniques and activities to establish a productive learning environment.

A. The counselor/social worker applies effective group management techniques.

1. Uses time and space productively and efficiently in order to support optimal learning

2. Maintains a high level of student participation and engagement with appropriate time on task

3. Establishes procedures that ensure transition from one activity to another

B. The counselor/social worker meets individual and group case load responsibilities.

1. Attends to referrals in a timely and responsive manner

2. Refers students to appropriate support personnel as needed

3. Is available at reasonable times outside scheduled appointments

4. Employs strategies for crisis intervention

5. Actively reaches out to contact students

V. Promotion of Standards and Expectations for Personal Growth and Development

The counselor/social worker promotes high standards and expectations for personal growth and development.

1. Stimulates student's self-awareness and involvement in the learning process

2. Provides individual and group opportunities for students to develop critical and reflective skills and resourcefulness

3. Provides opportunities for parents to develop insight and understanding of students' development and appropriate parenting strategies

4. Elicits student involvement in selecting goals for personal change, selecting activities and evaluating progress consistent with age and ability levels of students

5. Helps students develop group and/or individual decision making skills

6. Assists students in learning how to assess their strengths and weaknesses

7. Encourages students to develop personal standards and methods to assess their own efforts and achievements

VI. **Promotion of Equity and Appreciation of Diversity**

The counselor/social worker promotes equitable opportunities and appreciation of diversity of all students.

1. Provides opportunities for all students to participate in guidance and counseling programs

2. Demonstrates sensitivity to differences in abilities, gender, race, and ethnicity learning style, social and cultural backgrounds

3 Develops and implements strategies that are effective in meeting the needs of a diverse student body

VII. **Fulfillment of Professional Responsibilities**

The counselor/social worker demonstrates concern for professionalism.

1. Seeks out information and is receptive to suggestions for growth and improvement

2. Works collaboratively with other staff members to implement appropriate guidance and school related programs

3. Shares expertise and new ideas with colleagues

4. Works constructively with others to identify school problems and suggest possible solutions

5. Meets deadlines and fulfills routine responsibilities

6. Observes established school system policies and procedures

7. Participates in appropriate self development activities such as conferences, in-service training, and professional study

8. Maintains appropriate level of confidentiality and professional behaviors in all interactions with students, parents, and colleagues

OCCUPATIONAL THERAPIST PERFORMANCE STANDARDS

I. **Currency in the Curriculum**

The occupational therapist demonstrates competency in professional area.

1. Has in-depth knowledge in the field of occupational therapy

2. Is aware of current developments in occupational therapy and applies this in working with students and staff

3. Acts as a resource person for all students, staff and parents

II. **Effective Planning and Assessment**

   A. **The occupational therapist plans instruction effectively.**

   1. Administers individual diagnostic assessments for varied purposes

   2. Uses current established testing practices and procedures

   3. Makes appropriate referrals for further evaluation

   4. Observes and specifically describes student strengths, weaknesses, and therapeutic/instructional needs

   5 Develops clearly stated measurable occupational therapy goals and objectives based on appropriate assessments and observations in accordance with the I.E.P.

   6. Assists teachers as needed in selecting appropriate instructional materials and strategies

   B. **The occupational therapist provides effective assessment.**

   1. Correctly interprets and effectively communicates diagnostic assessments, testing data and relevant information on student progress to parents and staff

   2. Continuously evaluates students' progress to adjust therapy procedures and goals

   3. Assists teachers in adjusting instruction as needed

   4. Provides opportunities for students to reflect on progress

III. **Effective Instruction**

   A. **The occupational therapist communicates effectively with students.**

   1. Implements clear lesson objectives and communicates these to students

   2. Promotes students' independence as learners through application of appropriate instructional models

   3. Stimulates students' thinking and creativity through discussion and, where appropriate, writing activities

   4. Uses effective questioning strategies to stimulate student participation

   5. Deals effectively with student questions, responses, and confusions and remediates, reteaches or extends teaching to meet individual and/or group needs

6. Communicates clearly in writing and in speaking using precise language. Has enthusiasm for subject matter and makes significant efforts to communicate that enthusiasm to students and colleagues

7. Interacts positively and productively with all students and teachers

B. The occupational therapist uses appropriate instructional techniques.

1. Uses a variety of appropriate material to reinforce and extend skills, accommodate learning styles and match I.E.P. objectives.

2. Sets short-term and year-long goals for mastery of goals and objectives

3. Encourages students to summarize important learnings and to integrate them with prior knowledge

4. Recognizes multiple points of view and encourages students to assess the accuracy of information presented

5. Identifies individual and group needs and plans the use of appropriate instructional strategies, materials and resources

IV. Effective Occupational Therapy Management

A. The occupational therapist applies appropriate management techniques to establish a positive and productive learning environment.

1. Uses time and space productively and efficiently in order to promote optimal learning. Maintains a high level of student participation and engagement with appropriate time on task. Establishes procedures that ensure smooth transition from one activity to another

B. The occupational therapist maintains and models appropriate standards of behavior, mutual respect, and safety.

1. Establishes and carries out reasonable rules and procedures

2. Maintains appropriate professional boundaries with students

V. Promotion of High Standards and Expectations for Student Achievement

The occupational therapist promotes high standards and expectations for student achievement.

1. Communicates standards, expectations, and guidelines regarding the quality and quantity of students' work to students, parents, and teachers

2. Accepts students' concerns and responds appropriately

3. Encourages students to take risks and to persevere with challenging tasks

VI. Promotion of Equity and Appreciation of Diversity

The occupational therapist promotes equitable opportunities for student learning.

1. Provides opportunities for all students to participate in the classroom

3. Demonstrates sensitivity to differences in abilities, gender, learning style, social and cultural background

3. Develops and implements therapeutic, educational, and organizational strategies that are effective in meeting the needs of a diverse student body

VII. Fulfillment of Professional Responsibilities

The occupational therapist demonstrates continuing concern for professionalism.

1. Actively engages in appropriate self development activities such as conferences, in-service training and professional study

2. Works cooperatively with colleagues and supervisors

3. Demonstrates an appropriate awareness of school programs and policies

4. Works constructively with others to identify school problems and suggest possible solutions

5. Meets deadlines and fulfills routine responsibilities

6. Observes established school system policies and procedures

7. Participates in appropriate self development activities such as conferences, in-service training and professional study

8. Maintains appropriate professional behaviors in all interactions with students, parents, and colleagues

ELEMENTARY CONSULTING SPECIALIST

I. Currency in the Curriculum

The elementary consulting specialist demonstrates competency in the subject area.

1. Has an appropriate in-depth knowledge of the subject area

2. Keeps current with and understands and evaluates current research literature and practice in the curriculum area to ascertain the most effective teaching/learning paradigms and practices

3. Acts as a subject area resource person for staff and colleagues

II. Effective Planning and Assessment of Curriculum and Instruction

A. The elementary consulting specialist plans instruction effectively.

1. Sets short term and long term goals for design, development, implementation and evaluation of curriculum, based upon National Standards and State Frameworks and systemic core values

2. Formulates and coordinates curriculum objectives, ensuring that there is meaningful sequence to the program goals and interrelation with other areas of curriculum wherever possible

3. Works collaboratively with principals and colleagues to develop, design and implement school organizational models, curriculum, teaching strategies and assessment techniques needed by schools to prepare students to meet the demands of the 21st century

4. Helps teachers and principals engage in systematic planning to improve curriculum and achieve coherence

B. The elementary consulting specialist provides effective assessment of curriculum, curriculum implementation, instruction and student learning.

1. Works with system administrators and teachers to determine standards for student learning and methods of assessing this learning

2. Assumes responsibility for organizing a style of curriculum design, development, implementation and assessment toward the goal of continuous improvement of curriculum and instruction

3. Promotes innovative and developmental approaches to assessment to help teachers and students reflect on learning and progress

III. Effective Instruction

The elementary consulting specialist promotes effective instruction through communication, provision of resources, and staff collaboration.

1. Works with staff to articulate a vision and standard of excellence for curriculum and pedagogy

2. Promotes a stimulating professional environment for staff which supports and encourages their own continuous learning

3. Helps teachers stay abreast of relevant research and the knowledge base related to teaching, learning, and the discipline(s)

4. Provides encouragement, models, and opportunities to help staff members develop a broad repertoire to support the engagement and achievement of all students

5. Provides colleagues with opportunities for sharing that will nurture "best practice"

6 Submit budget proposals for resources and provisions to support quality instruction

IV. Promotion of Equity and Appreciation of Diversity

The elementary consulting specialist promotes equitable opportunities for learning.

1. Works with staff to develop and implement educational and organizational strategies that are effective in meeting the needs of a diverse student body

2. Cultivates understanding of issues related to equity, diversity, and excellence so that differences are understood and accommodated, but quality of program and expectations for excellence are uniformly high

V. Fulfillment of Professional Responsibilities

The elementary consulting specialist demonstrates a continuing concern for professionalism.

1. Seeks out information and is receptive to suggestions for growth and improvement

2. Works collaboratively with other staff members to implement appropriate curricular and school related programs

3. Shares expertise and new ideas with colleagues

4. Works constructively with others to identify school/system problems and suggest possible solutions

5. Meets deadlines and fulfills routine responsibilities

6. Observes established school system policies and procedures

7. Participates in appropriate self development

8. Maintains appropriate professional behaviors in all interactions with students, parents, and colleagues

CURRICULUM LEADER PERFORMANCE STANDARDS

I. **Currency in the Curriculum**
   The curriculum leader demonstrates competency in the subject area.

   1. Has an appropriate in-depth knowledge of the subject area

   2. Acts as a subject area resource person for staff and colleagues

   3. Understands and evaluates current research, literature, and practice in curriculum and applies knowledge to the instructional program

   4. Keeps current in the field and translates that expertise into developmentally appropriate curriculum and learning environments for children

II. **Effective Planning and Assessment of Curriculum and Instruction**
   A. The curriculum leader plans instruction effectively.

   1. Addresses system core values and priorities, and solicits support and input of administrators, teachers, staff, parents and students

   2. Sets short term and long term goals for design, development, implementation and evaluation of curriculum and instruction

   3. Formulates and coordinates curriculum objectives, ensuring meaningful sequence of program goals and meaningful interrelationship with other areas of the curriculum

   4. Develops, designs and implements school organizational models, curriculum, teaching strategies and assessment techniques to prepare students for 21st century challenges

   5. Works with teachers and principals to identify individual and group needs and to plan the use of appropriate instructional strategies

6. Collaborates with specialists, administrators, and appropriate staff to design curriculum and instructional modifications to meet the special learning needs of students

B. The curriculum leader provides effective assessment of curriculum, curriculum implementation, instruction, and student learning.

1. Works with system administrators and teachers to determine specific challenging standards for student learning, to design and implement appropriate assessments, and to communicate results and recommendations to appropriate constituencies

2. Assumes responsibility for organizing a cycle of curriculum design, development, implementation and assessment toward the goal of improvement of curriculum and instruction

3. Promotes innovative and developmental approaches to assessment to help teachers and students reflect on learning and progress

4. Collaborates with system leaders to acquire and portray to the community a comprehensive overview of progress for the system

5. Helps teachers and principals engage in systematic planning to improve curriculum, instruction, and assessment

III. Effective Instruction

The curriculum leader promotes effective instruction through communication, provision of resources, and staff collaboration.

1. Works with staff to articulate a vision and standard of excellence for curriculum and pedagogy

2. Helps teachers balance interconnected responsibilities to the individual student, the group, school, and larger community

3. Promotes a stimulating professional environment for staff

4. Helps teachers stay abreast of relevant research and the knowledge base related to teaching, learning, and the disciplines

5. Ensures that staff members have opportunities to acquire and develop new materials, approaches, and pedagogical skills

6. Ensures that teachers have adequate resources and provisions for their students and their daily work

7. Provides encouragement, examples, and opportunities to help staff members develop a broad repertoire to support the engagement and achievement of all students

8. Provides opportunities for sharing and collegiality that nurture "best practice"

IV. Supervision and Evaluation

The curriculum leader supports curriculum, instruction, teacher effectiveness and student learning through quality supervision and evaluation.

1. Provides a context for supervision and evaluation by ensuring that staff understand system core values and priorities, as well as short term and long range goals of the curriculum/instruction area

2. Communicates clearly to staff about the process, timeliness and expectations related to supervision and evaluation in the Lexington Public Schools, and in their school/curriculum context

3. Creates a positive atmosphere, process and dialogue which allows the staff member to reflect on strengths and achievements, and on areas for inquiry and improvement

4. Provides opportunities for pre- and post-discussion

5. Respects staff members' reflections analysis and recommendations as major contributions in the supervision/evaluation process

6. Approaches supervision and evaluation as an opportunity to encourage self reflection and personal growth of the teacher

7. Completes observation and evaluation reports in a timely manner as specified by contract

V. Promotion of High Standards and Expectations for Student Achievement

The curriculum leader promotes high standards and expectations for student achievement.

1. Works with teachers and administrators to broadly communicate standards, expectations, and guidelines regarding the quality and quantity of students' work

2. Establishes and sustains a process to engage teachers, departments, and individual schools in meaningful conversation about assessment of students' work and development

3. Provides information that allows the public to understand standards and expectations for student achievement, and methods of assessment

4. Encourages teachers and students to take risks and to persevere with challenging tasks

VI. Promotion of Equity and Appreciation of Diversity

The curriculum leader promotes equitable opportunities for learning.

1. Promotes professional awareness and competence to ensure that all students feel welcome and affirmed in the classroom, and become full participants and active successful learners

2. Demonstrates, cultivates, and insists upon sensitivity to difference in abilities, gender, learning style, social and cultural background

3. Works with staff to develop and implement educational and organizational strategies that are effective in meeting the needs of a diverse student body

4. Cultivates understanding of issues related to equity, diversity, and excellence so that differences are understood and addressed as part of the process in maintaining quality programs

5   Cooperates with Personnel Office, system administrators and hiring committees to recruit and maintain a staff that reflects and promotes equity and appreciation of diversity

VII. Fulfillment of Professional Responsibilities

The curriculum leader demonstrates continuing concern for professionalism.

1. Seeks out information and is receptive to suggestions for growth and improvement

2. Works collaboratively with other staff members to implement appropriate curricular and school related programs

3. Shares expertise and new ideas with colleagues

4   Works constructively with others to identify school/system problems and suggest possible solutions

5. Meets deadlines and fulfills routine responsibilities

6. Observes established school system policies and procedures

7. Participates in appropriate self development

8. Maintains appropriate professional behaviors in all interactions with students, parents, and colleagues

LEXINGTON PUBLIC SCHOOLS OBSERVATION FORM

Name: _____

School: _____

Subject: _____ Grade Level: _____

Date and Time of Observation: _____

Location/setting: _____

No. of Students: _____ No. of I.E.P.'s: _____

Observation Record:

Commendations and/or Recommendations:

Dates and Duration of Conferences: _____

_____

_____   _____
Signature of evaluator   date

_____   _____
Signature of evaluatee   date

LEXINGTON PUBLIC SCHOOLS FINAL EVALUATION FORM

Name: _____

School: _____

Subject: _____ Grade Level: _____

Evaluator: _____

Total No. of Observations: _____

No. of Years in Lexington: _____ In Present Position: _____

Pre-professional Status: Year 1 _____ Year 2_____ Year 3 _____

Professional Status: Tier 1: _____ Comprehensive _____

Focused _____ Tier 2: _____

I. Currency In The Curriculum
Commendations and/or Recommendations

II. Effective Planning and Assessment of Curriculum and Instruction
Commendations and/or Recommendations:

III. Effective Instruction
Commendations and/or Recommendations:

IV. Effective Classroom Management
Commendations and/or Recommendations:

V. Promotion of High Standards and Expectations for Student Achievement
Commendations and/or Recommendations:

(form continues)

VI. Promotion of Equity and Appreciation of Diversity
Commendations and/or Recommendations:

VII. Fulfillment of Professional Responsibilities
Commendations and/or Recommendations:

Recommendation:

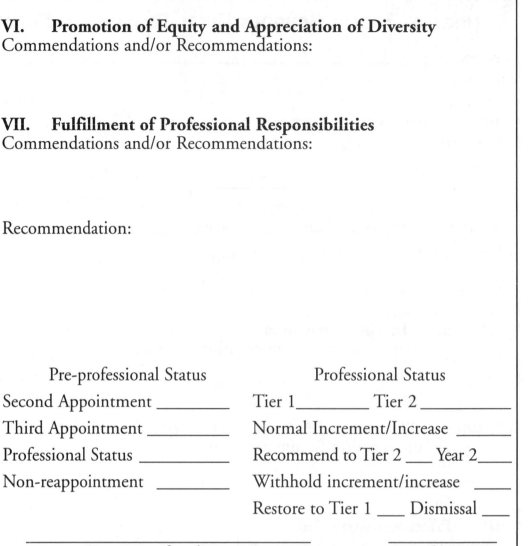

Pre-professional Status	Professional Status
Second Appointment _____	Tier 1_____ Tier 2 _____
Third Appointment _____	Normal Increment/Increase _____
Professional Status _____	Recommend to Tier 2 ___ Year 2____
Non-reappointment _____	Withhold increment/increase ____
	Restore to Tier 1 ___ Dismissal ___

_____   _____
Signature of evaluator   date

Teacher's Comments: (optional)

I have read this evaluation, a conference has been held with the evaluator, and the stated number of visits and hours are correct.

_____   _____
Signature of staff member   date

The staff member's signature does not imply agreement with the evaluation. The teacher has the right and is encouraged to comment on this evaluation.

So What Are the Correct Answers?

In actuality, the answer to all four questions posed in the section before the Brookline and Lexington documents is dependent upon the evaluator and the teacher. The Brookline document is significantly shorter and, therefore, leaves a great deal open to interpretation. This brevity gives it the ability to bend and change to fit varying needs. In some situations, this is an advantage, but in others it is a disadvantage. The second document is the inverse. It is much more specific in its requirements, providing different advantages and disadvantages than the first document. Below is an analysis of one example in each of the E.L.P.S. dimensions of how parts of each document serve as an advantage in some circumstances and as a disadvantage in others. This analysis illustrates the point that there are no perfect documents and that there rarely are unusable documents. More often the key to success lies in the training and supervision of the evaluators, not in the structure of the documents.

> . . . there are no perfect documents and . . . rarely are . . . unusable documents. More often the key to success lies in the training and supervision of the evaluators, not in the structure of the documents.

Brookline Document

Educational: The document requires only a single observation of teachers with tenure in the evaluation year. This enables evaluators with large evaluation loads to focus their observation time on those teachers that need the most attention.[5] The disadvantage to this language is that some evaluators may let their practice decline to the lowest required level, thereby not observing more often, even when it is appropriate or necessary.

Legal: The document allows administrators to recommend an out-of-cycle evaluation up to October 20 of the following year. This enables administrators to reassess a teacher's performance during the first six weeks of the next school year before making a decision about whether or not to evaluate that teacher again. The disadvantage of this language is the October 20 date. In some cases, it may be too early and, in other cases, too late. The date may be too late because in some circumstances the administrator may not have enough time to decide whether or not there has been sufficient improvement. In other cases, a date in the new school year may be too late because an administrator may be tempted to delay a decision on evaluating a teacher for a second year, even though he/she has all the information needed to make the decision at the end of the previous school year. Decisions like these are best made as soon as the necessary information is available.

---

5 This is only advised when a district has other assessment options for teachers, such as peer coaching and/or self-assessment.

Public Relations (Political): The public's primary concern about supervision and evaluation is how the process addresses low-performing teachers. The document itself offers little or no direct information about the process for improving or removing low-performing teachers. A community member who reads the document might conclude that no such procedures exist. However, all such implementation procedures are addressed in Brookline's evaluator training and in the evaluation guide designed for Brookline's administrators. This enables the district to update and improve administrators' implementation as the general performance of the administrators improves, without creating the anxiety among the teaching staff that inevitably occurs when a district seeks to change the contracted document.

Social–Emotional: The document requires a post-observation conference within seven working days of the observation. The possible seven-day delay permits an administrator to reflect on the observation, so he/she might offer helpful comments and suggestions. On the other hand, seven days might feel like a lifetime to a teacher who is anxious to hear the administrator's assessment of his/her performance.

LEXINGTON DOCUMENT

Educational: The document contains eight separate sets of principles of effective teaching (performance standards). Each set is individualized to the specific needs of the eight different categories of "teaching" positions to be evaluated. Having these separate performance standards enables administrators to better tailor their observation comments and recommendations to the specific positions. It also gives non classroom teachers a better assessment of their performance in relation to the unique characteristics of their jobs. However, it does require a significant amount of training and studying on the part of evaluators new to the district to learn eight sets of criteria. If sufficient training and discussion is not available to these evaluators to help them learn and remember the eight sets, they may be less inclined to use the principles in their write-ups and conferences.

> The internal process allows for more objective parties to review the positions of both the teacher and the evaluator, increasing the likelihood of a mutually acceptable plan.

Legal: The document has an easily implemented process to resolve differences between the evaluator and the teacher in the content of the improvement plan in the district. *The internal process allows for more objective parties to review the positions of both the teacher and the evaluator, increasing the likelihood of a mutually acceptable plan.* The document also has a provision for expedited arbitration to resolve differences in improvement plans. Resolving differences between management and the union through arbitration, prior to implementing the plan, ensures that the validity of the plan will not be an issue in the future, if the final evaluation is challenged. However, the cost of an arbitrator's time is $700 (or more) per day. A district with several plans in arbitration is forced to use scarce funds to resolve the plans rather than using them for something more productive, like mentoring or staff development opportunities for the low-performing teachers.

The next example shows the close interconnection between the E.L.P.S. dimensions. A public relations advantage in the document might also be a legal disadvantage.

Public Relations (Political): The comprehensiveness of the contracted process for addressing low-performing teachers will impress any member of the public who reads the document. However, the complexity of this procedure increases the potential for procedural errors by the evaluating administrators unless there is adequate ongoing training and coaching for administrators in the implementation of this process. As mentioned in chapter 5, if an evaluation has serious procedural flaws, a teachers' association may feel it must continue to defend a teacher whose performance has been documented as unsatisfactory to avoid being sued for failure to meet its duty of fair representation.

Social–Emotional: The post-observation conference takes place within three school days of the observation. This provides the teacher with prompt feedback and limits the period of anxiety that might exist for the teacher between the observation and the observation conference. However, teachers and administrators have busy schedules. It is not unusual for an administrator with fifteen or twenty evaluations to complete two or three observations in a single week. Finding mutually convenient times to discuss the observations within three days may be a difficult and stress-producing requirement for the administrator.

Current Trends in the Development of Evaluation Procedures and Standards

In recent years, efforts have been made to develop teacher performance standards that can be assessed in a more objective manner with a rubric type of instrument. This effort has increased in momentum as states and districts seek ways to meet the requirements about teacher qualifications found in the federal No Child Left Behind legislation. One of the first documents to do this is found in Charlotte Danielson's book, *Enhancing Professional Practice: A Framework for Teaching.*(1996, pp. 61–119). One district's work to move toward increased objectification of the teacher performance standards can be found in the Montgomery County Maryland Professional Growth System Handbook 2002–2003 (2002, pp. A-1–A-11). An example of the first statewide initiative to create rubric-type teacher performance standards was completed in the state of Texas. This is one of the few documents that moves toward the specific numeric quantification of specific teacher performance for the purpose of summatively evaluating teachers. The following is a copy of the document. It is reprinted with the permission of the State of Texas Education Agency.

SCORING CRITERIA GUIDE

Performance at the "Proficient" Level is based upon documentary evidence, as appropriate.

Documentary evidence may be collected over the entire appraisal period.

Performance at the "Proficient" Level **MAY** be inferred for a criterion if 80% of the criteria in the Domain **ARE** documented at the "Proficient" or Exceeds Expectation Level and **NO** criteria are documented at <u>Below Expectations</u> or <u>Unsatisfactory</u>.

Domain I: Active, Successful Student Participation in the Learning Process

I-1. Students are actively engaged in learning.

Things To Consider

- Students are focused on the learning objective during the academic learning time.
- Evidence of alignment of activities with the learning objective.

Quality: Engagement in the learning produces student success. Look for the level of engagement as determined by the strength, impact, variety, and alignment of the activities with the learning objective.

Quantity: Focus on the number of students actively engaged in the learning at regular intervals.

	Evaluation Criteria		
Exceeds Expectations	**Proficient**	**Below Expectations**	**Unsatisfactory**
<u>QUALITY</u> Students are consistently engaged and successful in learning that has great depth and complexity.	<u>QUALITY</u> Students are engaged and successful in learning.	<u>QUALITY</u> Students are occasionally successful in learning.	<u>QUALITY</u> Students are rarely/never successful in learning.
Student engagement is consistently self-directed/intrinsically motivated.	Student engagement is self-directed/intrinsically motivated.	Student engagement is occasionally self-directed/intrinsically motivated. **Student engagement is frequently a result of mechanical manipulation or coercion by the teacher.**	Student engagement is rarely/never self-directed/intrinsically motivated. **Student engagement is almost always/always a result of mechanical manipulation or coercion by the teacher.**
Students consistently take reasonable risks in responding, extending, questioning, and/or producing products.	Student engagement is self-directed/intrinsically motivated.	Student engagement is occasionally self-directed/intrinsically motivated. **Student engagement is frequently a result of mechanical manipulation or coercion by the teacher.**	Student engagement is rarely/never self-directed/intrinsically motivated. **Student engagement is almost always/always a result of mechanical manipulation or coercion by the teacher.**
Students are consistently engaged in connecting/applying learning to other disciplines, their own lives, and/or issues in the world beyond the classroom.	Student engagement is self-directed/intrinsically motivated.	Student engagement is occasionally self-directed/intrinsically motivated. **Student engagement is frequently a result of mechanical manipulation or coercion by the teacher.**	Student engagement is rarely/never self-directed/intrinsically motivated. **Student engagement is almost always/always a result of mechanical manipulation or coercion by the teacher.**
Multiple instructional strategies aligned with the learning objectives are used to engage learning.	Instructional strategies are aligned with the learning objectives.	Instructional strategies are frequently driven by academic content and/or activities rather than by learning objectives.	Instructional strategies are almost always/always driven by academic content and/or activities rather than by learning objectives.
<u>QUANTITY</u> ALMOST ALL OF THE TIME (90-100%) Students are active learners.	<u>QUANTITY</u> MOST OF THE TIME (80-89%) Students are active learners.	<u>QUANTITY</u> SOME OF THE TIME (50-79%) Students are active learners.	<u>QUANTITY</u> LESS THAN HALF OF THE TIME (0-49%) Students are active learners.
Students are focused on learning objectives that are at an appropriate level of difficulty.	Students are focused on learning objectives that are at an appropriate level of difficulty.	Students are focused on learning objectives that are at an appropriate level of difficulty.	Students are focused on learning objective that are at an appropriate level of difficulty.
Instructional strategies/activities reflect the unique needs/characteristics of students.	Instructional strategies/activities reflect the unique needs/characteristics of students.	Instructional strategies reflect the unique needs/characteristics of students.	Instructional strategies reflect the unique needs/characteristics of students.

SCORING CRITERIA GUIDE

Performance at the "Proficient" Level is based upon documentary evidence, as appropriate.

Documentary evidence may be collected over the entire appraisal period.

Performance at the "Proficient" Level MAY be inferred for a criterion if 80% of the criteria in the Domain ARE documented at the "Proficient" or Exceeds Expectation Level and NO criteria are documented at Below Expectations or Unsatisfactory.

Domain I: Active, Successful Student Participation in the Learning Process

I-2. Students are successful in learning.

Things To Consider

- Students demonstrate success with the stated, implied or written learning objectives.
- Assessment is aligned with the stated, implied or written learning objectives.

Quality: Assessment criteria and standards are clear and have been communicated to the student. Look at the level of success of students through strength, impact, variety and alignment of the assessment with the content and instruction.

Quantity: Focus on the number of students that are assessed. Focus on the number of students that are successful in the learning.

		Evaluation Criteria	
Exceeds Expectations	**Proficient**	**Below Expectations**	**Unsatisfactory**
QUALITY Students are consistently successful in learning. Learning objectives have great depth and complexity.	QUALITY Students are successful in learning. Learning objectives have some depth and complexity.	QUALITY Students are occasionally successful in learning. Learning objectives are frequently at low levels of complexity.	QUALITY Students are rarely/never successful in learning. Learning objectives are almost always/always at low levels of complexity.
Student engagement and success are consistently self-directed/intrinsically motivated.	Student engagement and success are self-directed/intrinsically motivated.	Students are occasionally successful in learning.	Students are rarely/never successful in learning.
Students consistently take reasonable risks in responding, extending, questioning, and/or producing products.	Students take reasonable risks in responding, extending, questioning, and/or producing products.	Students are occasionally successful in learning.	Students are rarely/never successful in learning.
Students are consistently successful in connecting/applying learning to other disciplines, their own lives, and/or issues in the world beyond the classroom. **Students are consistently assessed on learning that is aligned with the learning objectives.**	Students are successful in connecting/applying learning within the discipline. **Students are assessed on learning that is aligned with the learning objectives.**	Students are occasionally successful in learning. **Assessment strategies are frequently driven by academic content and/or activities rather than by learning objectives.**	Students are rarely/never successful in learning. **Assessment strategies are almost always/always driven by academic content and/or activities rather than by learning objectives.**
QUANTITY ALMOST ALL OF THE TIME (90-100%) Students are successful in reaching the learning objectives.	QUANTITY MOST OF THE TIME (80-89%) Students are successful in reaching the learning objectives.	QUANTITY SOME OF THE TIME (50-79%) Students are successful in reaching the learning objectives.	QUANTITY LESS THAN HALF OF THE TIME (0-49%) Students are successful in reaching the learning objectives.
Assessment strategies consistently reflect the unique needs/characteristics of students.	Assessment strategies reflect the unique needs/characteristics of students.	Assessment strategies reflect the unique needs/characteristics of students.	Assessment strategies reflect the unique needs/characteristics of students.

SCORING CRITERIA GUIDE

Performance at the "Proficient" Level is based upon documentary evidence, as appropriate.

Documentary evidence may be collected over the entire appraisal period.

Performance at the "Proficient" Level MAY be inferred for a criterion if 80% of the criteria in the Domain **ARE** documented at the "Proficient" or Exceeds Expectation Level and NO criteria are documented at Below Expectations or Unsatisfactory.

Domain I: Active, Successful Student Participation in the Learning Process

I-3. Student behaviors indicate learning is at a high cognitive level (e.g., critical thinking, creative thinking, problem solving, etc.).

Things To Consider
- Students are involved in learning activities at the application level or higher on Bloom's Taxonomy.
- Learning activities produce a logical and innovative approach, or a solution to a problem or concern.

Quality: Look at the level of thinking to determine the strength, impact, variety and alignment of the learning activity. Learning activities are at the application level or higher on Bloom's Taxonomy when appropriate to the learning objective. Students are challenged by the instruction.

Quantity: Focus on the number of students involved in learning activities at the application level or higher on Bloom's Taxonomy, when appropriate to the learning objective.

Evaluation Criteria

Exceeds Expectations	Proficient	Below Expectations	Unsatisfactory
QUALITY Students are consistently successful in learning that has depth, complexity and links to a conceptual foundation.	**QUALITY** Students are successful in the learning objectives that are at an appropriate level of difficulty.	**QUALITY** Students are occasionally successful in the learning objectives that are at an appropriate level of difficulty.	**QUALITY** Students are rarely/never successful in the learning objectives that are at an appropriate level of difficulty.
Students consistently take reasonable risks in responding, extending, questioning, and/or producing products that reflect the application level or higher on Blooms' Taxonomy.	Students take reasonable risks in responding, extending, questioning, and/or producing products that reflect the application level or higher on Blooms' Taxonomy.	Students are occasionally successful in the learning objectives that are at an appropriate level of difficulty.	Students are rarely/never successful in the learning objectives that are at an appropriate level of difficulty.
Students are consistently engaged in connecting/applying learning to other disciplines, their own lives, and/or issues in the world beyond the classroom.	Students are engaged in connecting/applying learning within the discipline.	Students are occasionally engaged in connecting/applying learning within the discipline.	Students are rarely/never engaged in connecting/applying learning within the discipline.
QUANTITY **ALMOST ALL OF THE TIME (90%-100%)** Students are focused on complex and challenging learning objectives.	**QUANTITY** **MOST OF THE TIME (80-89%)** Students are focused on challenging learning objectives.	**QUANTITY** **SOME OF THE TIME (50-79%)** Students are focused on challenging objectives.	**QUANTITY** **MOST OF THE TIME (0-49%)** Students are focused on challenging objectives.
Students are engaged in instructional activities that are driven by high level learning objectives.	Students are engaged in instructional activities that are driven by high level learning objectives.	Students are engaged in instructional activities that are driven by high level learning objectives.	Students are engaged in instructional activities that are driven by high level learning objectives.

SCORING CRITERIA GUIDE

Performance at the "Proficient" Level is based upon documentary evidence, as appropriate.
Documentary evidence may be collected over the entire appraisal period.
Performance at the "Proficient" Level MAY be inferred for a criterion if 80% of the criteria in the Domain ARE documented at the
"Proficient" or Exceeds Expectation Level and NO criteria are documented at Below Expectations or Unsatisfactory.

Domain I: Active, Successful Student Participation in the Learning Process

I-4. Students are self-directed/self-initiated as appropriate to the lesson objectives.

Things To Consider

- Students create or extend a skill, knowledge or concept connected to the learning objective.
- Students initiate or adapt activities and projects to enhance understanding.
- Students demonstrate task commitment.

Quality: Focus on appropriateness of content for self-directed/self-initiated opportunities.

Quantity: Focus on the number of students that are appropriately self-directed/self-initiated.

Evaluation Criteria

Exceeds Expectations	Proficient	Below Expectations	Unsatisfactory
QUALITY Students are consistently successful in extending the learning, appropriately questioning the teacher and/or peers and/or producing products using appropriate self-directed/self-initiated activities.	QUALITY Students are successful in appropriate self-directed/self-initiated activities.	QUALITY Students are occasionally successful in appropriate self-directed/self-initiated activities.	QUALITY Students are rarely/never successful in appropriate self-directed/self-initiated activities.
Students are consistently successful in finding their own strategies for connecting/applying learning to other disciplines, their own lives, and/or issues in the world beyond the classroom.	Students are successful in finding their own strategies for connecting/applying learning.	Students are occasionally successful in appropriate self-directed/self-initiated activities. **Most instruction is teacher directed.**	Students are rarely/never successful in appropriate self-directed/self-initiated activities. **Most instruction is teacher directed.**
The teacher uses a variety of motivational and instructional strategies to promote student responsibility/investment in appropriate self-directed/self-initiated activities.	The teacher uses motivational and instructional strategies to promote student responsibility/investment in appropriate self-directed/self-initiated activities.	The teacher occasionally uses motivational and instructional strategies to promote student responsibility/investment in appropriate self-directed/self-initiated activities.	The teacher rarely/never uses motivational and instructional strategies to promote student responsibility/investment in appropriate self-directed/self-initiated activities.
QUANTITY ALMOST ALL OF THE TIME (90%-100%) Students are engaged in appropriate self-directed/self-initiated activities.	QUANTITY ALMOST ALL OF THE TIME (80-89%) Students are engaged in appropriate self-directed/self-initiated activities.	QUANTITY SOME OF THE TIME (50-79%) Students are engaged in appropriate self-directed/self-initiated activities.	QUANTITY LESS THAN HALF OF THE TIME (0-49%) Students are engaged in appropriate self-directed/self-initiated activities.

SCORING CRITERIA GUIDE

Performance at the "Proficient" Level is based upon documentary evidence, as appropriate.

Documentary evidence may be collected over the entire appraisal period.

Performance at the "Proficient" Level MAY be inferred for a criterion if 80% of the criteria in the Domain ARE documented at the "Proficient" or Exceeds Expectation Level and NO criteria are documented at Below Expectations or Unsatisfactory.

Domain I: Active, Successful Student Participation in the Learning Process

1-5. Students connecting learning to work and life applications, both within the discipline, and with other disciplines.

Things To Consider

- Students demonstrate a connection of the learning to work and life applications.
- Students demonstrate a connection of the learning to prior/future learning within the discipline.
- Students demonstrate a connection of the learning with other disciplines.

Quality: Look for strength, impact, variety, and alignment of the connection of the learning with the learning objective.

Quantity: Focus on the number of students that can demonstrate a connection of the learning to work and life applications, both within the discipline, and with other disciplines.

	Evaluation Criteria		
Exceeds Expectations	**Proficient**	**Below Expectations**	**Unsatisfactory**
QUALITY Depth and complexity of learning are consistently characterized by successful student connection of the learning with prior/future learning within the discipline, with other disciplines, with students' interests/experiences, with issues beyond the classroom.	QUALITY Depth and complexity of learning are characterized by successful student connection of the learning with prior/future learning within the discipline.	QUALITY Students are occasionally successful in learning.	QUALITY Students are rarely/never successful in learning.
Student responsibility/investment in complex learning is consistent.	Student responsibility/investment in learning is present.	Students are occasionally successful in learning.	Students are rarely/never successful in learning.
Students consistently take reasonable risks in responding, extending, questioning, and/or producing products.	Students take reasonable risks in responding, extending, questioning, and/or producing products.	Students are occasionally successful in learning.	Students are rarely/never successful in learning.
Students are consistently engaged in producing high quality products, which connect learning with prior/future learning within the discipline, with other disciplines, with students' interests/experiences, with issues beyond the classroom.	Students are engaged in producing quality products, which connect learning with prior/future learning within the discipline.	Students are occasionally successful in learning.	Students are rarely/never successful in learning.
QUANTITY ALMOST ALL OF THE TIME (90-100%) Students are successful in connecting the learning to work and life applications, both within the discipline and with other disciplines.	QUANTITY MOST OF THE TIME (80-89%) Students are successful in connecting the learning to work and life applications, both within the discipline and with other disciplines.	QUANTITY SOME OF THE TIME (50-79%) Students are successful in connecting the learning to work and life applications, both within the discipline and with other disciplines.	QUANTITY LESS THAN HALF OF THE TIME (0-49%) Students are successful in connecting the learning to work and life applications, both within the discipline and with other disciplines.
Students are engaged in multiple activities to connect the learning to work and life applications, both within the discipline and with other disciplines.	Students are engaged in multiple activities to connect the learning to work and life applications, both within the discipline and with other disciplines.	Students are engaged in multiple activities to connect the learning to work and life applications, both within the discipline and with other disciplines.	Students are engaged in multiple activities to connect the learning to work and life applications, both within the discipline and with other disciplines.

SCORING CRITERIA GUIDE

Performance at the "Proficient" Level is based upon documentary evidence, as appropriate.
Documentary evidence may be collected over the entire appraisal period.
Performance at the "Proficient" Level MAY be inferred for a criterion if 80% of the criteria in the Domain **ARE** documented at the "Proficient" or <u>Exceeds Expectation</u> Level and **NO** criteria are documented at <u>Below Expectations</u> or <u>Unsatisfactory</u>.

Domain II: Learner-Centered Instruction

II-1. Objectives and goals include basic knowledge/skills and central themes/concepts of the discipline.

Things To Consider

- The learning objective is communicated or implied.
- The learning objective addresses a new skill or knowledge.
- The learning objective connects to a central theme/concept of the discipline.
- The learning objective addresses the TEKS, as appropriate.

Quality:　Objectives and goals reflect important learning and conceptual understanding. Look for strength, impact, variety, and alignment of the learning objective to a central theme/concept of the discipline.
Quantity:　Objectives and goals reflect needs of all students.

	Evaluation Criteria		
Exceeds Expectations	**Proficient**	**Below Expectations**	**Unsatisfactory**
QUALITY	**QUALITY**	**QUALITY**	**QUALITY**
Students are consistently successful in learning that is constructed around central themes/concepts of the discipline.	Students are successful in learning that is constructed around central themes/concepts of the discipline.	Students are occasionally successful in learning. **Instruction is occasionally constructed around central themes/concepts of the discipline.**	Students are rarely/never successful in learning. **Instruction is rarely/never constructed around central themes/concepts of the discipline.**
Students consistently find their own strategies for constructing learning and for connecting/applying learning to other disciplines, their own lives, and/or issues in the world beyond the classroom.	Students find their own strategies for constructing learning and for connecting/applying learning to other disciplines, their own lives, and/or issues in the world beyond the classroom.	Students are occasionally successful in learning. **Instruction is occasionally constructed around central themes/concepts of the discipline.**	Students are rarely/never successful in learning. **Instruction is rarely/never constructed around central themes/concepts of the discipline.**
Multiple strategies are consistently used to communicate the specific new learning objectives (skill and/or concept).	Strategies are used to communicate specific new learning objectives (skill and/or concept).	Strategies are occasionally used to communicate the specific new learning objectives (skill and/or concept).	Strategies are rarely/never are used to communicate the specific new learning objectives (skill and/or concept).
Learning is consistently constructed around concepts that are central themes/concepts in more than one discipline.	Learning is constructed around central themes/concepts of the discipline rather than miscellaneous, unconnected sets of knowledge and/or skills.	Learning is occasionally constructed around central themes/concepts of the discipline; it frequently consists of unconnected sets of knowledge/skills.	Learning is rarely/never constructed around central themes/concepts of the discipline; it almost always/always consists of unconnected sets of knowledge/skills.
QUANTITY **ALMOST ALL OF THE TIME (90-100%)**	**QUANTITY** **MOST OF THE TIME (80-89%)**	**QUANTITY** **SOME OF THE TIME (50-79%)**	**QUANTITY** **LESS THAN HALF OF THE TIME (0-49%)**
Students are consistently aware of the specific, new learning objectives (skill and/or concept).	Students are aware of the specific, new learning objectives (skill and/or concept).	Students are occasionally aware of the specific, new learning objectives (skill and/or concept).	Students are rarely/never aware of the specific, new learning objectives (skill and/or concept).
Learning objectives are appropriate to the unique needs/characteristics of all students.	Learning objectives are appropriate to the unique needs/characteristics of all students.	Learning objectives are appropriate to the unique needs/characteristics of all students.	Learning objectives are appropriate to the unique needs/characteristics of all students.
New learning is aligned with the TEKS, when appropriate.	New learning is aligned with the TEKS, when appropriate.	New learning is aligned with the TEKS, when appropriate.	New learning is aligned with the TEKS, when appropriate.
Instruction has been collaboratively planned and delivered to insure connection between/among disciplines.	Instruction has been collaboratively planned and delivered to insure connection between/among disciplines.	Instruction has been collaboratively planned and delivered to insure connection between/among disciplines.	Instruction has been collaboratively planned and delivered to insure connection between/among disciplines.

SCORING CRITERIA GUIDE

Performance at the "Proficient" Level is based upon documentary evidence, as appropriate.

Documentary evidence may be collected over the entire appraisal period.

Performance at the "Proficient" Level MAY be inferred for a criterion if 80% of the criteria in the Domain ARE documented at the "Proficient" or Exceeds Expectation Level and NO criteria are documented at Below Expectations or Unsatisfactory.

Domain II: Learner-Centered Instruction			
II-2. Instructional content is learner-centered (e.g., relates to the interests and varied characteristics of students).			

Things To Consider
- Teacher relates instruction to the interests of students.
- Teacher relates instruction to the needs of students.
- Teacher relates instruction to the varied characteristics of students.

Quality: Content is relevant to students and instructional goals. Lesson structure allows for different pathways according to student needs. Look for strength, impact, variety, and alignment of content with the varied characteristics of students.

Quantity: Look for appropriate connections to all students.

Evaluation Criteria			
Exceeds Expectations	**Proficient**	**Below Expectations**	**Unsatisfactory**
QUALITY	QUALITY	QUALITY	QUALITY
Students are consistently engaged and successful in the learning.	Students are engaged and successful in the learning.	Students are occasionally engaged and successful in the learning.	Students are rarely/never engaged and successful in the learning.
Students consistently make their own connections between the learning and their unique needs, interests, and/or characteristics.	Students are engaged and successful in the learning.	Students are occasionally engaged and successful in the learning. **Students are frequently dependent on the teacher to make connections between their learning and their unique needs.**	Students are rarely/never engaged and successful in the learning. **Students are almost always/always dependent on the teacher to make connections between their learning and their unique needs.**
The teacher consistently uses unique /creative/innovative strategies to relate the learning to the unique needs, interests, and or characteristics of the students.	Students are engaged and successful in the learning.	Students are occasionally engaged and successful in the learning.	Students are rarely/never engaged and successful in the learning.
Instruction provides students with multiple pathways/approaches for new learning that meet their unique needs, interest, and or characteristics.	Students are engaged and successful in the learning.	Students are occasionally engaged and successful in the learning.	Students are rarely/never engaged and successful in the learning.
QUANTITY	QUANTITY	QUANTITY	QUANTITY
ALMOST ALL OF THE TIME (90-100%)	MOST OF THE TIME (80-89%)	SOME OF THE TIME (50-79%)	LESS THAN HALF OF THE TIME (0-49%)
Instruction is related/connected with the unique needs, interests, and characteristics of students.	Instruction is related/connected with the unique needs, interests, and/or characteristics of students.	Instruction is related/connected with the unique needs, interests, and/or characteristics of students.	Instruction is related/connected with the unique needs, interests, and/or characteristics of students.

SCORING CRITERIA GUIDE

Performance at the "Proficient" Level is based upon documentary evidence, as appropriate.

Documentary evidence may be collected over the entire appraisal period.

Performance at the "Proficient" Level MAY be inferred for a criterion if 80% of the criteria in the Domain **ARE** documented at the "Proficient" or Exceeds Expectation Level and **NO** criteria are documented at Below Expectations or Unsatisfactory.

Domain II: Learner-Centered Instruction

II-3. Instructional strategies promote critical thinking and problem solving.

Things To Consider
- Content and activities are at the application level or higher on Bloom's Taxonomy when appropriate to the learning objective.
- Instructional strategies are research based.
- Instructional strategies reflect current knowledge and practice within the content area.

Quality: Teacher guides students to construct knowledge through experience. Instruction progresses coherently producing success in application of the learning. Look for strength, impact, variety, and alignment of the strategies with the learning objective.

Quantity: Focus on the number of students performing at the application level or higher on Bloom's Taxonomy when appropriate to the learning objective.

Evaluation Criteria			
Exceeds Expectations	**Proficient**	**Below Expectations**	**Unsatisfactory**
QUALITY Students are consistently successful in critical thinking and problem solving activities (i.e., application level or higher on Bloom's Taxonomy).	**QUALITY** Students are successful in critical thinking and problem solving activities (i.e., application level or higher on Bloom's Taxonomy).	**QUALITY** Students are occasionally successful in critical thinking and problem solving activities (i.e., application level or higher on Bloom's Taxonomy).	**QUALITY** Students are rarely/never successful in critical thinking and problem solving activities (i.e., application level or higher on Bloom's Taxonomy).
Students are consistently successfully engaged in unique, creative, and/or innovative critical thinking/problem solving activities.	Students are successfully engaged in creative, critical thinking/problem solving activities.	Students are occasionally successfully engaged in critical thinking/problem solving activities. **Students are frequently engaged in routine, rote activities.**	Students are rarely/never successfully engaged in critical thinking/problem solving activities. **Students are almost always/always engaged in routine, rote activities.**
Students' critical thinking/problem solving consistently leads to connections between new learning and prior/future learning, other disciplines, the world of the student, and/or issues in the world beyond the classroom.	Students are successfully engaged in creative, critical thinking/problem solving activities.	Students are occasionally successfully engaged in critical thinking/problem solving activities. **Students are frequently engaged in routine, rote activities.**	Students are rarely/never successfully engaged in critical thinking/problem solving activities. **Students are almost always/always engaged in routine, rote activities.**
Students consistently initiate and/or devise their own strategies for critical thinking/problem solving and or devise their own activities. **Students consistently construct their own knowledge through inquiry and experience.**	Students are successfully engaged in creative, critical thinking/problem solving activities.	Students occasionally initiate and/or devise their own strategies for critical thinking/problem solving and/or devise their own activities. **Strategies for critical thinking/problem solving are typically teacher devised and directed.**	Students rarely/never initiate and/or devise their own strategies for critical thinking/problem solving and/or devise their own activities. **Strategies for critical thinking/problem solving almost always/always teacher devised and directed.**
Students are doing the thinking and problem solving and the teacher is acting as a guide.	Students are successfully engaged in creative, critical thinking/problem solving activities.	The teacher frequently does most of the thinking and problem solving and the students are passive recipients.	The teacher almost always/always does most of the thinking and problem solving and the students are passive recipients.
QUANTITY ALMOST ALL OF THE TIME (90-100%) Students are engaged in critical thinking and problem solving activities (i.e., application level or higher on Bloom's Taxonomy).	**QUANTITY** MOST OF THE TIME (80-89%) Students are engaged in critical thinking and problem solving activities (i.e., application level or higher on Bloom's Taxonomy).	**QUANTITY** SOME OF THE TIME (50-79%) Students are engaged in critical thinking and problem solving activities (i.e., application level or higher on Bloom's Taxonomy).	**QUANTITY** LESS THAN HALF OF THE TIME (0-49%) Students are engaged in critical thinking and problem solving activities (i.e., application level or higher on Bloom's Taxonomy).
Instructional strategies are research based.	Instructional strategies are research based.	Instructional strategies are research based.	Instructional strategies are research based.
Instructional strategies reflect current knowledge and practice within the content area.	Instructional strategies reflect current knowledge and practice within the content area.	Instructional strategies reflect current knowledge and practice within the content area.	Instructional strategies reflect current knowledge and practice within the content area.

SCORING CRITERIA GUIDE

Performance at the "Proficient" Level is based upon documentary evidence, as appropriate.
Documentary evidence may be collected over the entire appraisal period.
Performance at the "Proficient" Level **MAY** be inferred for a criterion if 80% of the criteria in the Domain **ARE** documented at the "Proficient" or Exceeds Expectation Level and **NO** criteria are documented at Below Expectations or Unsatisfactory.

Domain II: Learner-Centered Instruction
II-4. Instructional strategies include motivational techniques to successfully and actively engage students in the learning process.

Things To Consider
- Strategies include elements of motivation, such as, level of concern, interest, knowledge of results, positive classroom climate and acknowledgments.
- Instructional strategies are research based.
- Instructional strategies reflect current knowledge and practice within the discipline.

Quality: Motivational techniques produce active engagement of students in the learning process. Engagement in the learning process produces learning success. Look for strength, impact, variety, and alignment of the motivational techniques and the learning success.

Quantity: Motivational techniques are used as necessary to engage students and produce learning success.

| | Evaluation Criteria | | |
Exceeds Expectations	Proficient	Below Expectations	Unsatisfactory
QUALITY	**QUALITY**	**QUALITY**	**QUALITY**
Students are consistently successfully engaged in critical thinking and problem solving, connecting new learning to their own lives, to other disciplines, and/or to issues in the world beyond the classroom.	Students are successfully engaged in learning objectives that are at an appropriate level of difficulty.	Students are occasionally successfully engaged in learning.	Students are rarely/never successfully engaged in learning.
Learning objectives are consistently at appropriate levels of complexity.	Learning objectives are at appropriate levels of complexity.	Learning objectives are occasionally at appropriate levels of complexity.	Learning objectives are rarely/never at appropriate levels of complexity.
Student engagement is consistently self-directed/intrinsically motivated.	Student engagement is self-directed/intrinsically motivated.	Students are occasionally successfully engaged in learning. **Student engagement is frequently a result of mechanical manipulation or coercion by the teacher.**	Students are rarely/never successfully engaged in learning. **Student engagement is almost always/always a result of mechanical manipulation or coercion by the teacher.**
Students consistently take reasonable risks in responding, extending, appropriately questioning the teacher and/or peers, and/or producing products that represent complex learning.	Students take risks in responding, extending, questioning, and/or producing products.	Students are occasionally successfully engaged in learning.	Students are rarely/never successfully engaged in learning.
Students are consistently engaged in connecting and/or applying learning to other disciplines, their own lives, and/or issues in the world beyond the classroom.	Students are engaged in connecting/applying learning within the discipline.	Students are occasionally engaged in connecting/applying learning within the discipline.	Students are rarely/never engaged in connecting/applying learning within the discipline.
Students are consistently eager and excited about the learning. Students are not reluctant to ask questions and/or ask for assistance when they are having difficulty.	Students are eager and excited about the learning.	Students are occasionally eager or excited about the learning.	Students are rarely/never eager or excited about the learning.
QUANTITY **ALMOST ALL OF THE TIME (90-100%)** Motivational techniques are used as necessary to engage students and produce learning success.	**QUANTITY** **MOST OF THE TIME (80-89%)** Motivational techniques are used as necessary to engage students and produce learning success.	**QUANTITY** **SOME OF THE TIME (50-79%)** Motivational techniques are used as necessary to engage students and produce learning success.	**QUANTITY** **LESS THEN HALF OF THE TIME (0-49%)** Motivational techniques are used as necessary to engage students and produce learning success.
Instructional strategies are research based.	Instructional strategies are research based.	Instructional strategies are research based.	Instructional strategies are research based.
Instructional strategies reflect current knowledge and practice within the discipline.	Instructional strategies reflect current knowledge and practice within the discipline.	Instructional strategies reflect current knowledge and practice within the discipline.	Instructional strategies reflect current knowledge and practice within the discipline.

Domain II: Learner-Centered Instruction
II-5. Instructional strategies are aligned with the objectives, activities, student characteristics, prior learning, and work and life applications, both within the discipline and with other disciplines.

SCORING CRITERIA GUIDE

Performance at the "Proficient" Level is based upon documentary evidence, as appropriate.

Documentary evidence may be collected over the entire appraisal period.

Performance at the "Proficient" Level MAY be inferred for a criterion if 80% of the criteria in the Domain **ARE** documented at the "Proficient" or Exceeds Expectation Level and **NO** criteria are documented at Below Expectations or Unsatisfactory.

Things To Consider
- Instructional strategies are aligned with the lesson objectives.
- Instructional strategies are aligned with the activities.
- Instructional strategies are aligned with student characteristics.
- Instructional strategies are aligned with prior learning.
- Instructional strategies are aligned with work and life applications.
- Instructional strategies are research based.
- Instructional strategies reflect current knowledge and practice within the content area.

Quality: Teacher connects critical attributes of the learning, personal lives, work, prior/future learning, content within the discipline, and with other disciplines. Teacher selects and organizes topics so students make connections between what is taught in school and what they experience outside the classroom.

Quantity: There is common practice of the alignment of instructional strategies to curriculum objectives.

	Evaluation Criteria		
Exceeds Expectations	**Proficient**	**Below Expectations**	**Unsatisfactory**
QUALITY The teacher uses unique, creative, and/or innovative strategies to make multiple connections between the critical attributes of the learning and students' personal lives, work, prior/future learning, content within the discipline, and/or the content in other disciplines.	**QUALITY** The teacher connects critical attributes of the learning to students' personal lives, work, and prior/future learning, content within the discipline, and content in other disciplines.	**QUALITY** The teacher occasionally connects critical attributes of the learning to students' personal lives, work, and prior/future learning, content within the discipline, and content in other disciplines.	**QUALITY** The teacher rarely/never connects learning within the discipline and rarely/never makes connections among the learning and students' personal lives, work, prior/future learning, content within the discipline, or content in other disciplines.
The teacher consistently selects topics, which are central themes and concepts of the discipline, and organizes academic content to focus it on issues in the world beyond the classroom.	The teacher selects and organizes topics so students make connections between what is taught in school and what they experience outside the classroom.	The teacher occasionally selects and organizes topics so students make connections between what is taught in school and what they experience outside the classroom.	The teacher rarely/never selects and organizes topics so students make connections between what is taught in school and what they experience outside the classroom.
The students successfully make their own and/or multiple connections between what is being learned and other disciplines, their own lives, the world of work, and/or issues in the world beyond the classroom.	The students successfully make connections between what is being taught in school and the world beyond the classroom.	The students occasionally make connections between what is being taught in school and the world beyond the classroom.	The students rarely/never make connections between what is being taught in school and the world beyond the classroom.

SCORING CRITERIA GUIDE

Performance at the "Proficient" Level is based upon documentary evidence, as appropriate.

Documentary evidence may be collected over the entire appraisal period.

Performance at the "Proficient" Level MAY be inferred for a criterion if 80% of the criteria in the Domain ARE documented at the "Proficient" or Exceeds Expectation Level and NO criteria are documented at Below Expectations or Unsatisfactory.

Domain II-5 Continued

QUANTITY ALMOST ALL OF THE TIME (90-100%)	QUANTITY MOST OF THE TIME (80-89%)	QUANTITY SOME OF THE TIME (50-79%)	QUANTITY LESS THAN HALF OF THE TIME (0-49%)
Instructional strategies are aligned with the lesson objectives.	Instructional strategies are aligned with the lesson objectives.	Instructional strategies are aligned with the lesson objectives.	Instructional strategies are aligned with the lesson objectives.
Instructional strategies are aligned with the activities.	Instructional strategies are aligned with the activities.	Instructional strategies are aligned with the activities.	Instructional strategies are aligned with the activities.
Instructional strategies are aligned with student characteristics.	Instructional strategies are aligned with student characteristics.	Instructional strategies are aligned with student characteristics.	Instructional strategies are aligned with student characteristics.
Instructional strategies are aligned with prior learning.	Instructional strategies are aligned with prior learning.	Instructional strategies are aligned with prior learning.	Instructional strategies are aligned with prior learning.
Instructional strategies are aligned with work and life applications.	Instructional strategies are aligned with work and life applications.	Instructional strategies are aligned with work and life applications.	Instructional strategies are aligned with work and life applications.
Instructional strategies reflect current knowledge and practice within the content area.	Instructional strategies reflect current knowledge and practice within the content area.	Instructional strategies reflect current knowledge and practice within the content area.	Instructional strategies reflect current knowledge and practice within the content area.

Revised June 2003

Professional Development and Appraisal System

Page 11

Scoring Criteria Guide

SCORING CRITERIA GUIDE

Performance at the "Proficient" Level is based upon documentary evidence, as appropriate.

Documentary evidence may be collected over the entire appraisal period.

Performance at the "Proficient" Level MAY be inferred for a criterion if 80% of the criteria in the Domain ARE documented at the "Proficient" or Exceeds Expectation Level and NO criteria are documented at Below Expectations or Unsatisfactory.

Domain II: Learner-Centered Instruction

II-6. The teacher varies activities appropriately and maintains appropriate pacing and sequencing of instruction.

Things To Consider
- Teacher varies activities.
- Teacher maintains pacing.
- Teacher sequences instruction.

Quality: Look for appropriateness of activities, pacing and sequence of instruction. Learning activities are relevant to students. Transitions occur without loss of instructional time. Sequence of instruction reflects recent research and/or current knowledge and practice within the content area.

Quantity: Activities are challenging for most students. Teacher demonstrates a variety of strategies, as appropriate. Focus on the number of students that are successful.

Evaluation Criteria

Exceeds Expectations	Proficient	Below Expectations	Unsatisfactory
QUALITY Students consistently complete transitions and administrative tasks quickly, with little or no direction from the teacher—procedures are in place and students know what they are.	**QUALITY** Students complete transactions and administrative tasks quickly. **Transitions and administrative tasks consume little or no instructional time.**	**QUALITY** Students occasionally complete transactions and administrative tasks quickly. **Transitions and/or administrative tasks frequently consume significant amounts of instructional time.**	**QUALITY** Students rarely/never complete transactions and administrative tasks quickly. **Transitions and/or administrative tasks almost always/always consume significant amounts of instructional time.**
The teacher consistently adjusts and/or allows students to adjust the sequence of activities and/or the pace to meet the individual needs/characteristics of students.	Student engagement and success indicate that the sequence of activities and pace of the lesson are appropriate.	Student engagement and success occasionally indicate that the sequence of activities and pace of the lesson are appropriate. **Students frequently disengage from learning and/or are unsuccessful as a result of inappropriate sequence of activities and/or inappropriate pace of the lesson (too fast or too slow).**	Student engagement and success rarely/never indicate that the sequence of activities and pace of the lesson are appropriate. **Students almost always/always disengage from learning and/or are unsuccessful as a result of inappropriate sequence of activities and/or inappropriate pace of the lesson (too fast or too slow).**
The teacher consistently uses interesting, fun, and/or relevant activities so that students are engaged in the learning process.	The teacher uses interesting, fun, and/or relevant activities so that students are engaged in the learning process.	The teacher occasionally uses interesting, fun, and/or relevant activities so that students are occasionally engaged in the learning process. **Students are frequently engaged because of teacher manipulation/coercion.**	The teacher rarely/never uses interesting, fun, and/or relevant activities so that students are never/almost never engaged in the learning process. **Students are almost always/always engaged because of teacher manipulation/coercion.**
The teacher is consistently proactive in insuring that prior learning for the new learning is in place.	The teacher is proactive in insuring that prior learning for the new learning is in place.	The teacher frequently moves from one stage of the learning to the next even when many students are not being successful.	The teacher almost always/ always moves from one stage of the learning to the next even when many students are not being successful.
The teacher consistently monitors students' understanding at every stage of the learning before moving to the next stage.	The teacher monitors students' understanding at every stage of the learning before moving to the next stage.	The teacher occasionally monitors students' understanding at every stage of the learning before moving to the next stage.	The teacher rarely/never monitors students' understanding at every stage of the learning before moving to the next stage.
QUANTITY **ALMOST ALL OF THE TIME (90-100%)** Activities are challenging for most students.	**QUANTITY** **MOST OF THE TIME (80-89%)** Activities are challenging for most students.	**QUANTITY** **SOME OF THE TIME (50-79%)** Activities are challenging for most students.	**QUANTITY** **LESS THAN HALF OF THE TIME (0-49%)** Activities are challenging for most students.
Teacher demonstrates a variety of strategies/activities, as appropriate.	Teacher demonstrates a variety of strategies/activities, as appropriate.	Teacher demonstrates a variety of strategies/activities, as appropriate.	Teacher demonstrates a variety of strategies/activities, as appropriate.
Students are successful.	Students are successful.	Students are successful.	Students are successful.

SCORING CRITERIA GUIDE

Performance at the "Proficient" Level is based upon documentary evidence, as appropriate.

Documentary evidence may be collected over the entire appraisal period.

Performance at the "Proficient" Level **MAY** be inferred for a criterion if 80% of the criteria in the Domain **ARE** documented at the "Proficient" or Exceeds Expectation Level and **NO** criteria are documented at Below Expectations or Unsatisfactory.

Domain II: Learner-Centered Instruction

II-7. The teacher emphasizes the value and importance of the activity/content.

Things To Consider
- Teacher stresses value of the activity.
- Teacher projects necessity for content into future learning objectives.
- Teacher communicates importance of content in the lives of students.

Quality: Teacher conveys genuine enthusiasm for the content. Students demonstrate commitment to the value of the activity/content. Look for strength, impact, variety, and alignment of connection to the activity/content.

Quantity: Focus on the number of students that make the connection to the learning.

Evaluation Criteria			
Exceeds Expectations	**Proficient**	**Below Expectations**	**Unsatisfactory**
QUALITY Students consistently demonstrate an understanding of the value/importance of the learning.	QUALITY Students demonstrate an understanding of the value/importance of the learning.	QUALITY Students occasionally demonstrate an understanding of the value/importance of the learning.	QUALITY Students rarely/never demonstrate an understanding of the value/importance of the learning.
Students consistently are eager and excited about the activity.	Students are eager and excited about the activity/content.	Students are occasionally eager and excited about the activity/content.	Students are rarely/never eager and excited about the activity/content.
The students consistently make their own connections between the new learning and prior learning, future learning, learning in other disciplines, their own lives, and/or the world beyond the classroom.	The students make their own connections between the new learning and prior learning, future learning, learning in other disciplines, their own lives, and/or the world beyond the classroom.	The students are occasionally able to make their own connections between the new learning and prior learning, future learning, learning in other disciplines, their own lives, and/or the world beyond the classroom.	The students are rarely/never able to make their own connections between the new learning and prior learning, future learning, learning in other disciplines, their own lives, and/or the world beyond the classroom.
The teacher consistently uses a variety of creative, unique, and/or innovative strategies to demonstrate the value/importance of the content/activity.	The teacher uses a variety of strategies to demonstrate the value/importance of the content/activity.	The teacher uses strategies to demonstrate the value/importance of the content/activity.	The teacher rarely/never uses strategies to demonstrate the value/importance of content/activity.
The teacher consistently structures the lesson in such a way that students discover for themselves the value/importance of the content/activity.	The teacher structures the lesson in such a way that students discover for themselves the value/importance of the content/activity.	The teacher occasionally structures the lesson in such a way that students discover for themselves the value/importance of the content/activity.	The teacher rarely/never structures the lesson in such a way that students discover for themselves the value/importance of the content/activity.
Students consistently apply new learning and/or produce products that demonstrate the value/importance of the content/activity.	Students apply new learning and/or produce products that demonstrate the value/importance of the content/activity.	Students occasionally apply new learning and/or produce products that demonstrate the value/importance of the content/activity.	Students rarely/never apply new learning and/or produce products that demonstrate the value/importance of the content/activity.
The teacher consistently communicates genuine excitement and enthusiasm for the content/activity.	The teacher communicates genuine excitement and enthusiasm for the content/activity.	The teacher occasionally communicates genuine excitement and enthusiasm for the content/activity.	The teacher rarely/never communicates genuine excitement and enthusiasm for the content/activity.
QUANTITY ALMOST ALL OF THE TIME (90-100%) The teacher emphasizes the value and importance of the activity/content.	QUANTITY MOST OF THE TIME (80-89%) The teacher emphasizes the value and importance of the activity/content.	QUANTITY SOME OF THE TIME (50-79%) The teacher emphasizes the value and importance of the activity/content.	QUANTITY LESS THAN HALF OF THE TIME (0-49%) The teacher emphasizes the value and importance of the activity/content.
Students make a commitment to the activity/content.	Students make a commitment to the activity/content.	Students make a commitment to the activity/content.	Students make a commitment to the activity/content.

Domain II: Learner-Centered Instruction

II-8. The teacher uses appropriate questioning and inquiry techniques to challenge students.

Scoring Criteria Guide Professional Development and Appraisal System Page 13 Revised June 2003

381

SCORING CRITERIA GUIDE

Performance at the "Proficient" Level is based upon documentary evidence, as appropriate.
Documentary evidence may be collected over the entire appraisal period.
Performance at the "Proficient" Level MAY be inferred for a criterion if 80% of the criteria in the Domain ARE documented at the "Proficient" or Exceeds Expectation Level and NO criteria are documented at Below Expectations or Unsatisfactory.

Things To Consider

- Teacher uses questioning strategies that challenge.
- Teacher uses questioning strategies that engage students.
- Teacher varies questioning strategies.

Quality: Look for evidence of student progress and/or success. Look for students initiating probes and making appropriate contributions. Look for strength, variety, impact, and alignment of questions with content.

Quantity: Focus on the number of students sampled.

Evaluation Criteria

Exceeds Expectations	Proficient	Below Expectations	Unsatisfactory
QUALITY	**QUALITY**	**QUALITY**	**QUALITY**
Students consistently participate in challenging questioning and/or inquiry techniques.	Students participate in challenging questioning and/or inquiry techniques.	Students occasionally participate in challenging questioning and/or inquiry techniques.	Students rarely/never participate in challenging questioning and/or inquiry techniques.
Instruction is consistently student-centered, inquiry-based learning and focuses on students as thinkers and problem-solvers.	Instruction is consistently student-centered, inquiry-based learning and focuses on students as thinkers and problem-solvers.	Instruction is occasionally student-centered, inquiry-based learning and focuses on students as thinkers and problem-solvers.	Instruction is rarely/never student-centered, inquiry-based learning and focuses on students as thinkers and problem-solvers.
Students consistently and successfully initiate extensions of the questions/answers and/or the inquiry process.	The teacher uses appropriate strategies for questioning and/or for guiding an inquiry process.	The teacher occasionally uses appropriate strategies for questioning and/or for guiding an inquiry process.	The teacher rarely/never uses appropriate strategies for questioning and/or for guiding an inquiry process.
Students consistently initiate contributions to the questions/answers and/or the inquiry process.	The teacher uses appropriate strategies for questioning and/or for guiding an inquiry process.	The teacher occasionally uses appropriate strategies for questioning and/or for guiding an inquiry process.	The teacher rarely/never uses appropriate strategies for questioning and/or for guiding an inquiry process.
Students consistently appropriately challenge/question the teacher and/or their peers in the inquiry process.	The teacher uses appropriate strategies for questioning and/or for guiding an inquiry process.	The teacher occasionally uses appropriate strategies for questioning and/or for guiding an inquiry process.	The teacher rarely/never uses appropriate strategies for questioning and/or for guiding an inquiry process.
Students consistently design their own guiding questions/inquiry processes.	The teacher uses appropriate strategies for questioning and/or for guiding an inquiry process.	The teacher occasionally uses appropriate strategies for questioning and/or for guiding an inquiry process.	The teacher rarely/never uses appropriate strategies for questioning and/or for guiding an inquiry process.
The teacher consistently uses a variety of creative, unique, and/or innovative strategies for questioning and/or for guiding an inquiry process.	The teacher uses appropriate strategies for questioning and/or for guiding an inquiry process. **The teacher frequently uses rote, dull repetitive strategies for questioning and/or for guiding an inquiry process.**	The teacher occasionally uses appropriate strategies for questioning and/or for guiding an inquiry process. **The teacher frequently uses rote, dull repetitive strategies for questioning and/or for guiding an inquiry process.**	The teacher rarely/never uses appropriate strategies for questioning and/or for guiding an inquiry process. **The teacher almost always/always uses rote, dull repetitive strategies for questioning and/or for guiding an inquiry process.**
Teacher and/or student questioning/inquiry strategies consistently promote successful critical thinking, problem solving, and connectivity within the discipline, with other disciplines, to the world of the student, and/or to issues in the world beyond the classroom.	Teacher and/or student questioning/inquiry strategies promote successful critical thinking, problem solving, connectivity within the discipline, and connectivity with other disciplines.	The teacher occasionally uses appropriate strategies for questioning and/or for guiding an inquiry process. **The teacher frequently uses rote, dull repetitive strategies for questioning and/or for guiding an inquiry process.**	The teacher rarely/never uses appropriate strategies for questioning and/or for guiding an inquiry process. **The teacher almost always/always uses rote, dull repetitive strategies for questioning and/or for guiding an inquiry process.**
QUANTITY **ALMOST ALL OF THE TIME (90-100%)** The teacher uses appropriate questioning and inquiry techniques to challenge students.	**QUANTITY** **MOST OF THE TIME (80-89%)** The teacher uses appropriate questioning and inquiry techniques to challenge students.	**QUANTITY** **SOME OF THE TIME (50-79%)** The teacher uses appropriate questioning and inquiry techniques to challenge students.	**QUANTITY** **LESS THAN HALF OF THE TIME (0-49%)** The teacher uses appropriate questioning and inquiry techniques to challenge students.

Revised June 2003

382

SCORING CRITERIA GUIDE

Performance at the "Proficient" Level is based upon documentary evidence, as appropriate.

Documentary evidence may be collected over the entire appraisal period.

Performance at the "Proficient" Level **MAY** be inferred for a criterion if 80% of the criteria in the Domain **ARE** documented at the "Proficient" or Exceeds Expectation Level and **NO** criteria are documented at Below Expectations or Unsatisfactory.

Domain II: Learner-Centered Instruction

II-9. The teacher makes appropriate and effective use of available technology as a part of the instructional process.

Things To Consider
- Technologies (computers, calculators, telecommunication, multimedia, videotape and film, laser disc, CD-ROM, satellite/distance learning, facsimile (fax), modem, scanners, etc.) are used as instructional tools, when available and appropriate.

Quality: Technology is suitable to the instructional goal. Technology engages the students mentally. Look for strength, impact, variety, and alignment of instructional process and technology.

Quantity: Focus on the utilization of technology as an instructional tool.

Evaluation Criteria			
Exceeds Expectations	Proficient	Below Expectations	Unsatisfactory
QUALITY The use of available technology is appropriate and aligned with the instructional goals.	QUALITY The use of available technology is appropriate and aligned with the instructional goals.	QUALITY The use of available technology is occasionally appropriate and occasionally aligned with the instructional goals.	QUALITY The use of available technology is rarely/never appropriate and rarely/never aligned with the instructional goals.
Students are highly engaged and enthusiastic as a result of the use of the technology.	Students use available technology.	Students occasionally use available technology.	Students rarely/never use available technology.
Students consistently use technology to: • promote depth and complexity of learning; • connect learning to other disciplines, their own world, and the world beyond the classroom and/or; • produce products that represent complex learning.	Students use technology to: • promote depth and complexity of learning; • connect learning to other disciplines, their own world, and the world beyond the classroom and/or; • produce products that represent complex learning.	Students occasionally use technology. **Student use of technology is frequently limited to transmission of rote information and/or for rote drill and practice.**	Students rarely/never use technology. **Student use of technology is almost always/always limited to transmission of rote information and/or for rote drill and practice.**
The teacher consistently utilizes a variety of technology resources when appropriate and available.	The teacher utilizes a variety of technology resources when appropriate and available.	The teacher occasionally utilizes a variety of technology resources when appropriate and available.	The teacher rarely/never utilizes a variety of technology resources when appropriate and available.
The teacher consistently seeks out and secures available and/or new technology.	The teacher seeks out and secures available and/or new technology.	The teacher frequently misses opportunities to secure and use available and/or new technology.	The teacher almost always/always misses opportunities to secure and use available and/or new technology.
QUANTITY ALMOST ALL OF THE TIME (90-100%) The teacher makes use of available technology as a part of the instructional process.	QUANTITY MOST OF THE TIME (80-89%) The teacher makes use of available technology as a part of the instructional process.	QUANTITY SOME OF THE TIME (50-79%) The teacher makes use of available technology as a part of the instructional process.	QUANTITY LESS THAN HALF OF THE TIME (0-49%) The teacher makes use of available technology as a part of the instructional process.

SCORING CRITERIA GUIDE

Performance at the "Proficient" Level is based upon documentary evidence, as appropriate.
Documentary evidence may be collected over the entire appraisal period.
Performance at the "Proficient" Level MAY be inferred for a criterion if 80% of the criteria in the Domain ARE documented at the "Proficient" or Exceeds Expectation Level and NO criteria are documented at Below Expectations or Unsatisfactory.

Domain III: Evaluation and Feedback on Student Progress
III-1. Academic progress of students is monitored and assessed.

Things To Consider
- Teacher monitors student work during guided practice.
- Teacher provides for formative assessment prior to independent practice.
- Teacher assesses student progress toward learning goals.

Quality:　Teacher's system for obtaining, interpreting, and acting on information on student progress is focused on student progress in learning. Look for strength, impact, variety, and alignment of the assessment with the objectives.

Quantity:　Focus on the number of students that are monitored and assessed.

Evaluation Criteria

Exceeds Expectations	Proficient	Below Expectations	Unsatisfactory
QUALITY	QUALITY	QUALITY	QUALITY
Teacher's system for obtaining, interpreting, and acting on information on student progress is consistently focused on student progress in learning.	Teacher's system for obtaining, interpreting, and acting on information on student progress is focused on student progress in learning.	Teacher's system for obtaining, interpreting, and acting on information on student progress is frequently mechanical and is only occasionally focused on student progress in learning.	Teacher's system for obtaining, interpreting, and acting on information on student progress is almost always/always mechanical and is rarely/never focused on student progress in learning.
Teacher consistently uses a variety of effective, creative, unique, and/or innovative strategies for monitoring, assessing, and/or providing feedback on student progress.	Teacher uses effective strategies for monitoring, and assessing, and/or providing feedback on student progress.	Teacher occasionally uses effective strategies for monitoring, and assessing, and/or providing feedback on student progress.	Teacher rarely/never uses effective strategies for monitoring, and assessing, and/or providing feedback on student progress.
The teacher consistently acts on assessment data before moving from one stage of instruction to the next and to plan new instruction.	The teacher consistently acts on assessment data before moving from one stage of instruction to the next and to plan new instruction.	The teacher moves from one stage of instruction to the next and plans new instruction with limited information regarding student progress.	The teacher moves from one stage of instruction to the next and plans new instruction with little/no information regarding student progress.
The teacher consistently provides positive, specific, and timely feedback, which results in student progress toward learning goals (e.g., students repeating their successes and correcting their mistakes).	The teacher provides positive, specific, and/or timely feedback, which results in student progress toward learning goals (e.g., students repeating their successes and correcting their mistakes).	The teacher's feedback to students is occasionally positive, specific, and/or timely; feedback occasionally results in student progress toward learning goals (e.g., students repeating their successes and correcting their mistakes).	The teacher's feedback to students is rarely/never positive; feedback rarely/never results in student progress toward learning goals (e.g., students repeating their successes and correcting their mistakes).
The teacher consistently uses monitoring and assessment strategies that reflect an understanding of the unique needs and characteristics of students.	The teacher uses monitoring and assessment strategies that reflect an understanding of the unique needs and characteristics of students.	The teacher occasionally uses monitoring and assessment strategies that reflect an understanding of the unique needs and characteristics of students.	The teacher rarely/never uses monitoring and assessment strategies that reflect an understanding of the unique needs and characteristics of students.
The teacher consistently conducts formal/informal formative assessments and consistently acts on that information to adjust learning to promote student learning.	The teacher consistently conducts formal/informal formative assessments and acts on that information to adjust learning to promote student learning.	The teacher occasionally conducts formal/informal formative assessments and occasionally acts on that information to adjust learning to promote student learning.	The teacher rarely/never conducts formal/informal formative assessments and rarely/never acts on that information to adjust learning to promote student learning.
QUANTITY ALMOST ALL OF THE TIME (90-100%) Academic progress of students is monitored and assessed using both formative and summative assessment.	QUANTITY MOST OF THE TIME (80-89%) Academic progress of students is monitored and assessed using both formative and summative assessment.	QUANTITY SOME OF THE TIME (50-79%) Academic progress of students is monitored and assessed using both formative and summative assessment.	QUANTITY LESS THAN HALF OF THE TIME (0-49%) Academic progress of students is monitored and assessed using both formative and summative assessment.
There is consistent alignment among objectives, instruction, and assessment.	There is consistent alignment among objectives, instruction, and assessment.	There is consistent alignment among objectives, instruction, and assessment.	There is consistent alignment among objectives, instruction, and assessment.

SCORING CRITERIA GUIDE

Performance at the "Proficient" Level is based upon documentary evidence, as appropriate.

Documentary evidence may be collected over the entire appraisal period.

Performance at the "Proficient" Level MAY be inferred for a criterion if 80% of the criteria in the Domain ARE documented at the "Proficient" or Exceeds Expectation Level and NO criteria are documented at Below Expectations or Unsatisfactory.

Domain III: Evaluation and Feedback on Student Progress

III-2. Assessment and feedback are aligned with goals and objectives and instructional strategies.

Things To Consider
- Assessment is directly linked to goals and objectives.
- Assessment is directly linked to instructional strategies.
- Feedback is directly linked to goals/objectives and instructional strategies.

Quality: Look for strength, impact, variety, and alignment of the assessment with the objectives. Feedback is specific to the assessment.

Quantity: Assessment and feedback are aligned with instructional goals, objectives, and strategies.

| | Evaluation Criteria | | |
Exceeds Expectations	Proficient	Below Expectations	Unsatisfactory
QUALITY Specific, positive feedback to all students is consistent and results in successful students repeating their success and unsuccessful students recognizing their errors and becoming successful.	**QUALITY** Positive feedback results in successful students repeating their success and unsuccessful students recognizing their errors and becoming successful.	**QUALITY** Positive feedback is occasional and/or occasionally results in successful students repeating their success and unsuccessful students recognizing their errors and becoming successful.	**QUALITY** Positive feedback is rare/absent and/or rarely/never results in successful students repeating their success and unsuccessful students recognizing their errors and becoming successful.
Teacher consistently uses a variety of effective, creative, unique, and/or innovative strategies for monitoring, assessing, and/or providing feedback on student progress.	Teacher uses strategies for monitoring, assessing, and/or providing feedback on student progress.	Teacher occasionally uses strategies for monitoring, assessing, and/or providing feedback on student progress. **Teacher's system for obtaining, interpreting, and acting on information regarding student progress is frequently mechanical and is occasionally focused on student progress in learning.**	Teacher rarely/never uses a variety of strategies for monitoring, assessing, and/or providing feedback on student progress. **Teacher's system for obtaining, interpreting, and acting on information regarding student progress is almost always/always mechanical and is rarely/never focused on student progress in learning.**
The teacher consistently acts on assessment data before moving from one stage of instruction to the next and to plan new instruction.	The teacher acts on assessment data before moving from one stage of instruction to the next and to plan new instruction.	The teacher moves from one stage of instruction to the next and plans new instruction with limited information regarding student progress in learning.	The teacher moves from one stage of instruction to the next and plans new instruction with little/no information regarding student progress in learning.
The teacher consistently provides positive, specific, and timely feedback, which results in student progress toward learning goals.	Positive feedback results in successful students repeating their success and unsuccessful students recognizing their errors and becoming successful.	Positive feedback is occasional and/or occasionally results in successful students repeating their success and unsuccessful students recognizing their errors and becoming successful.	Positive feedback is rare/absent and/or rarely/never results in successful students repeating their success and unsuccessful students recognizing their errors and becoming successful.
Monitoring and assessment strategies consistently reflect an understanding of the unique needs and characteristics of students.	Monitoring and assessment strategies reflect an understanding of the unique needs and characteristics of students.	Monitoring and assessment strategies occasionally reflect an understanding of the unique needs and characteristics of students.	Monitoring and assessment strategies rarely/never reflect an understanding of the unique needs and characteristics of students.

SCORING CRITERIA GUIDE

Performance at the "Proficient" Level is based upon documentary evidence, as appropriate.

Documentary evidence may be collected over the entire appraisal period.

Performance at the "Proficient" Level **MAY** be inferred for a criterion if 80% of the criteria in the Domain **ARE** documented at the "Proficient" or Exceeds Expectation Level and **NO** criteria are documented at Below Expectations or Unsatisfactory.

Domain III-2 Continued		
QUANTITY **ALMOST ALL OF THE TIME (90-100%)** Assessment and feedback are aligned with instructional goals, objectives, and strategies. so that goals/objectives drive the instructional activities and both formative and summative strategies are assessing the extent to which students did/did not reach the goals/objectives.	QUANTITY **MOST OF THE TIME (80-89%)** Assessment and feedback are aligned with instructional goals, objectives, and strategies so that goals/objectives drive the instructional activities and both formative and summative strategies are assessing the extent to which students did/did not reach the goals/objectives.	QUANTITY **SOME OF THE TIME (50-79%)** Assessment and feedback are aligned with instructional goals, objectives, and strategies so that goals/objectives drive the instructional activities and both formative and summative strategies are assessing the extent to which students did/did not reach the goals/objectives.	QUANTITY **LESS THAN HALF OF THE TIME (0-49%)** Assessment and feedback are aligned with instructional goals, objectives, and strategies so that goals/objectives drive the instructional activities and assessing the extent to which students did/did not reach the goals/objectives.
Students are monitored and assessed and receive feedback.	Students are monitored and assessed and receive feedback.	Students are monitored and assessed and receive feedback.	Students are monitored and assessed and receive feedback.

SCORING CRITERIA GUIDE

Performance at the "Proficient" Level is based upon documentary evidence, as appropriate.

Documentary evidence may be collected over the entire appraisal period.

Performance at the "Proficient" Level MAY be inferred for a criterion if 80% of the criteria in the Domain ARE documented at the "Proficient" or <u>Exceeds</u> Expectation Level and NO criteria are documented at <u>Below</u> Expectations or <u>Unsatisfactory</u>.

Domain III: Evaluation and Feedback on Student Progress

III-3. Assessment strategies are appropriate to the varied characteristics of students.

Things To Consider
- Assessment strategies reflect developmental level of students.
- Assessment strategies address learning needs of students.

Quality: Assessment strategies produce evidence of student success and/or the need for corrective teaching. Look for strength, impact, variety, and alignment of assessment strategies with varied characteristics of students.

Quantity: Teacher uses a variety of assessment strategies/models to check for understanding.

		Evaluation Criteria	
Exceeds Expectations	**Proficient**	**Below Expectations**	**Unsatisfactory**
QUALITY	QUALITY	QUALITY	QUALITY
Assessment strategies consistently produce evidence of student success and/or the need for corrective teaching.	Assessment strategies produce evidence of student success and/or the need for corrective teaching.	Assessment strategies occasionally produce evidence of student success and/or the need for corrective teaching.	Assessment strategies rarely/never produce evidence of student success and/or the need for corrective teaching.
Teacher consistently utilizes creative, unique, and/or innovative assessment strategies that consistently produce evidence of student success and/or the need for corrective teaching.	Assessment strategies produce evidence of student success and/or the need for corrective teaching.	Assessment strategies occasionally produce evidence of student success and/or the need for corrective teaching.	Assessment strategies rarely/never produce evidence of student success and/or the need for corrective teaching.
Teacher consistently utilizes assessment strategies, which are chosen and/or customized to fit the developmental level of students.	Teacher utilizes assessment strategies, which are appropriate to the developmental level of the students.	Teacher frequently utilizes assessment strategies, which are inappropriate for the developmental level of students.	Teacher almost always/always utilizes assessment strategies which are inappropriate to the developmental level of students.
Teacher consistently utilizes assessment strategies, which are chosen and/or customized to fit the learning styles of students.	Teacher utilizes assessment strategies, which are chosen and/or customized to fit the learning styles of students.	Teacher frequently utilizes assessment strategies, which are inappropriate to the learning styles of students.	Teacher almost always/always utilizes assessment strategies which are inappropriate to the learning styles of students.
Teacher consistently utilizes assessment strategies, which are chosen and/or customized to fit the unique, special needs of students.	Teacher utilizes assessment strategies, which are chosen and/or customized to fit the unique, special needs of students.	Teacher frequently utilizes assessment strategies, which are inappropriate to the unique, special needs of students.	Teacher almost always/always utilizes assessment strategies which are inappropriate to the unique, special needs of students.
Teacher consistently utilizes assessment strategies, which are chosen and/or customized to fit the unique language/cultural characteristics of students.	Teacher utilizes assessment strategies, which are chosen and/or customized to fit the unique language/cultural characteristics of students.	Teacher frequently utilizes assessment strategies, which are inappropriate to the unique language/cultural characteristics of students.	Teacher almost always/always utilizes assessment strategies which are inappropriate to the unique, language/cultural characteristics of students.
QUANTITY ALMOST ALL OF THE TIME (90-100%) Assessment strategies are appropriate to the varied characteristics of students.	QUANTITY MOST OF THE TIME (80-89%) Assessment strategies are appropriate to the varied characteristics of students.	QUANTITY SOME OF THE TIME (50-79%) Assessment strategies are appropriate to the varied characteristics of students.	QUANTITY LESS THAN HALF OF THE TIME (0-49%) Assessment strategies are appropriate to the varied characteristics of students.

SCORING CRITERIA GUIDE

Performance at the "Proficient" Level is based upon documentary evidence, as appropriate.
Documentary evidence may be collected over the entire appraisal period.
Performance at the "Proficient" Level **MAY** be inferred for a criterion if 80% of the criteria in the Domain **ARE** documented at the "Proficient" or Exceeds Expectation Level and **NO** criteria are documented at Below Expectations or Unsatisfactory.

Domain III: Evaluation and Feedback on Student Progress

III-4. Student learning is reinforced.

Things To Consider
- Learning is positively reinforced.
- Reinforcement communicates high expectations.
- Reinforcement techniques are research based and reflect current knowledge and practice within the content area.
- Reinforcement is appropriate to the needs of the learner.

Quality: 　Reinforcement results in student engagement and success in the learning. Look for strength, impact, variety, and alignment of reinforcement with the learning.

Quantity: 　Look for uniformity and consistency of reinforcement.

Evaluation Criteria

Exceeds Expectations	Proficient	Below Expectations	Unsatisfactory
QUALITY	**QUALITY**	**QUALITY**	**QUALITY**
Reinforcement consistently results in students understanding why they are successful and they are able to repeat their effort and success.	Reinforcement results in students understanding why they are successful and they are able to repeat their effort and success.	Reinforcement is sometimes used; it occasionally results in students understanding why they are successful and they are occasionally able to repeat their effort and success.	Reinforcement is sometimes used; it rarely/never results in students understanding why they are successful and they are rarely/never able to repeat their effort and success.
Intensity and frequency of reinforcement are consistently monitored and adjusted to fit the level of the student performance and the needs of the students.	Intensity and frequency of reinforcement are appropriate to the student performance and the needs of the students.	Intensity and frequency of reinforcement are occasionally appropriate to the student performance and the needs of the students. **Reinforcement is frequently contrived and artificial.**	Intensity and frequency of reinforcement are rarely/never appropriate to the student performance and/or the needs of the students. **Reinforcement is almost always/always contrived and artificial.**
Reinforcement of high level, complex responses and performances is consistently specific to the student and to the response/performance.	Reinforcement of student performance is specific to the student and to the response/performance.	Reinforcement of student performance is occasionally specific to the student and to the response/performance.	Reinforcement of student performance is rarely/never specific to the student and to the response/performance.
Reinforcement consistently results in an increase in the frequency, level, and/or quality of student performances.	Reinforcement results in an increase in the frequency, level, and/or quality of student performances.	Reinforcement occasionally results in an increase in the frequency, level, and/or quality of student performances.	Reinforcement rarely/never results in an increase in the frequency, level, and/or quality of student performances.
Students consistently self-assess and provide feedback for themselves and/or their peers.	Teacher appropriately reinforces learning.	Teacher occasionally appropriately reinforces learning.	Teacher rarely/never appropriately reinforces learning.
QUANTITY	**QUANTITY**	**QUANTITY**	**QUANTITY**
ALMOST ALL OF THE TIME (90-100%)	**MOST OF THE TIME (80-89%)**	**SOME OF THE TIME (50-79%)**	**LESS THAN HALF OF THE TIME (0-49%)**
Successful student learning is acknowledged/positively reinforced.	Successful student learning is acknowledged/positively reinforced.	Successful student learning is acknowledged/positively reinforced.	Successful student learning is acknowledged/positively reinforced.
Successful student learning is reinforced using a variety of verbal, nonverbal, and extrinsic strategies.	Successful student learning is reinforced using a variety of verbal, nonverbal, and extrinsic strategies.	Successful student learning is reinforced using a variety of verbal, nonverbal, and extrinsic strategies.	Successful student learning is reinforced using a variety of verbal, nonverbal, and extrinsic strategies.
Reinforcement communicates high expectations for learning and performance.	Reinforcement communicates high expectations for learning and performance.	Reinforcement communicates high expectations for learning and performance.	Reinforcement communicates high expectations for learning and performance.
Reinforcement techniques are research based and reflect current knowledge and practice within the content area.	Reinforcement techniques are research based and reflect current knowledge and practice within the content area.	Reinforcement techniques are research based and reflect current knowledge and practice within the content area.	Reinforcement techniques are research based and reflect current knowledge and practice within the content area.

SCORING CRITERIA GUIDE

Performance at the "Proficient" Level is based upon documentary evidence, as appropriate.

Documentary evidence may be collected over the entire appraisal period.

Performance at the "Proficient" Level MAY be inferred for a criterion if 80% of the criteria in the Domain ARE documented at the "Proficient" or Exceeds Expectation Level and NO criteria are documented at Below Expectations or Unsatisfactory.

Domain III: Evaluation and Feedback on Student Progress

III-6. The teacher provides opportunities for relearning and re-evaluation of material.

Things To Consider

- Teacher identifies content or skill, which needs to be re-taught or re-evaluated, as appropriate.
- Teacher utilizes a variety of re-teach and re-evaluation techniques, as appropriate.
- Techniques are research-based or reflect current knowledge and practice within the content area.

Quality: Relearning opportunities result in student success. Look for strength, impact, variety, and alignment of the re-teach technique with the learning objective.

Quantity: Focus on the impact of the re-teaching, not the number of times the teacher re-taught or re-evaluated material.

	Evaluation Criteria		
Exceeds Expectations	**Proficient**	**Below Expectations**	**Unsatisfactory**
QUALITY	QUALITY	QUALITY	QUALITY
Students are consistently successful as a result of a re-teach and/or have a higher/more complex understanding as a result of a re-evaluation of the learning.	Students are successful as a result of a re-teach and/or have better understanding as a result of a re-evaluation of the learning.	Students are occasionally successful as a result of a re-teach and/or have little additional understanding as a result of a re-evaluation of the learning.	Students are rarely/never successful as a result of a re-teach and/or have little additional understanding as a result of a re-evaluation of the learning.
Teacher consistently uses creative, unique, and/or innovative strategies that result in a high level of student success and/or a higher, more complex understanding.	Teacher uses effective strategies that result in student success in learning.	Teacher occasionally uses effective strategies that result in student success in learning.	Teacher rarely/never uses effective strategies that result in student success in learning.
Teacher consistently uses strategies that fit the unique needs/characteristics of students.	Teacher uses strategies that fit the unique needs/characteristics of students.	Teacher occasionally utilizes strategies that fit the unique needs/characteristics of students.	Teacher rarely/never utilizes strategies that fit the unique needs/characteristics of students.
The teacher consistently monitors and adjusts instruction and reflects an understanding of students by quickly adjusting instruction for additional clarification or for extension of the learning.	The teacher monitors and adjusts instruction and reflects an understanding of students by adjusting instruction for additional clarification or for extension of the learning.	The teacher occasionally monitors and adjusts instruction and/or shows a lack of understanding of students by not adjusting instruction for additional clarification or for extension of the learning.	The teacher rarely/never monitors and adjusts instruction and/or shows a lack of understanding of students by not adjusting instruction for additional clarification or for extension of the learning.
QUANTITY	QUANTITY	QUANTITY	QUANTITY
ALMOST ALL OF THE TIME (90-100%)	MOST OF THE TIME (80-89%)	SOME OF THE TIME (50-79%)	LESS THAN HALF OF THE TIME (0-49%)
The teacher provides opportunities for relearning and re-evaluation of material, when appropriate.	The teacher provides opportunities for relearning and re-evaluation of material, when appropriate.	The teacher provides opportunities for relearning and re-evaluation of material, when appropriate.	The teacher provides opportunities for relearning and re-evaluation of material, when appropriate.
Techniques for re-teaching and/or re-evaluation are researched-based and reflect current knowledge and practice within the content area.	Techniques for re-teaching and/or re-evaluation are researched-based and reflect current knowledge and practice within the correct area.	Techniques for re-teaching and/or re-evaluation are researched-based and reflect current knowledge and practice within the content area.	Techniques for re-teaching and/or re-evaluation are researched-based and reflect current knowledge and practice within the content area.
The teacher uses a variety of strategies to effectively re-teach and/or re-evaluate learning.	The teacher uses a variety of strategies to effectively re-teach and/or re-evaluate learning.	The teacher uses a variety of strategies to effectively re-teach and/or re-evaluate learning.	The teacher uses a variety of strategies to effectively re-teach and/or re-evaluate learning.

SCORING CRITERIA GUIDE

Performance at the "Proficient" Level is based upon documentary evidence, as appropriate.

Documentary evidence may be collected over the entire appraisal period.

Performance at the "Proficient" Level **MAY** be inferred for a criterion if 80% of the criteria in the Domain **ARE** documented at the "Proficient" or Exceeds Expectation Level and **NO** criteria are documented at Below Expectations or Unsatisfactory.

Domain III: Evaluation and Feedback on Student Progress

III-6. The teacher provides opportunities for relearning and re-evaluation of material.

Things To Consider
- Teacher identifies content or skill, which needs to be re-taught or re-evaluated, as appropriate.
- Teacher utilizes a variety of re-teach and re-evaluation techniques, as appropriate.
- Techniques are research-based or reflect current knowledge and practice within the content area.

Quality:　Relearning opportunities result in student success. Look for strength, impact, variety, and alignment of the re-teach technique with the learning objective.

Quantity:　Focus on the impact of the re-teaching, not the number of times the teacher re-taught or re-evaluated material.

Evaluation Criteria

Exceeds Expectations	Proficient	Below Expectations	Unsatisfactory
QUALITY	**QUALITY**	**QUALITY**	**QUALITY**
Students are consistently successful as a result of a re-teach and/or have a higher/more complex understanding as a result of a re-evaluation of the learning.	Students are successful as a result of a re-teach and/or have better understanding as a result of a re-evaluation of the learning.	Students are occasionally successful as a result of a re-teach and/or have little additional understanding as a result of a re-evaluation of the learning.	Students are rarely/never successful as a result of a re-teach and/or have little additional understanding as a result of a re-evaluation of the learning.
Teacher consistently uses creative, unique, and/or innovative strategies that result in a high level of student success and/or a higher, more complex understanding.	Teacher uses effective strategies that result in student success in learning.	Teacher occasionally uses effective strategies that result in student success in learning.	Teacher rarely/never uses effective strategies that result in student success in learning.
Teacher consistently uses strategies that fit the unique needs/characteristics of students.	Teacher uses strategies that fit the unique needs/characteristics of students.	Teacher occasionally utilizes strategies that fit the unique needs/characteristics of students.	Teacher rarely/never utilizes strategies that fit the unique needs/characteristics of students.
The teacher consistently monitors and adjusts instruction and reflects an understanding of students by quickly adjusting instruction for additional clarification or for extension of the learning.	The teacher monitors and adjusts instruction and reflects an understanding of students by adjusting instruction for additional clarification or for extension of the learning.	The teacher occasionally monitors and adjusts instruction and/or shows a lack of understanding of students by not adjusting instruction for additional clarification or for extension of the learning.	The teacher rarely/never monitors and adjusts instruction and/or shows a lack of understanding of students by not adjusting instruction for additional clarification or for extension of the learning.
QUANTITY	**QUANTITY**	**QUANTITY**	**QUANTITY**
ALMOST ALL OF THE TIME (90-100%) The teacher provides opportunities for relearning and evaluation of material, when appropriate.	**MOST OF THE TIME (80-89%)** The teacher provides opportunities for relearning and re-evaluation of material, when appropriate.	**SOME OF THE TIME (50-79%)** The teacher provides opportunities for relearning and re-evaluation of material, when appropriate.	**LESS THAN HALF OF THE TIME (0-49%)** The teacher provides opportunities for relearning and re-evaluation of material, when appropriate.
Techniques for re-teaching and/or re-evaluation are researched-based and reflect current knowledge and practice within the correct area.	Techniques for re-teaching and/or re-evaluation are researched-based and reflect current knowledge and practice within the content area.	Techniques for re-teaching and/or re-evaluation are researched-based and reflect current knowledge and practice within the content area.	Techniques for re-teaching and/or re-evaluation are researched-based and reflect current knowledge and practice within the content area.
The teacher uses a variety of strategies to effectively re-teach and/or re-evaluate learning.	The teacher uses a variety of strategies to effectively re-teach and/or re-evaluate learning.	The teacher uses a variety of strategies to effectively re-teach and/or re-evaluate learning.	The teacher uses a variety of strategies to effectively re-teach and/or re-evaluate learning.

SCORING CRITERIA GUIDE

Performance at the "Proficient" Level is based upon documentary evidence, as appropriate.

Documentary evidence may be collected over the entire appraisal period.

Performance at the "Proficient" Level **MAY** be inferred for a criterion if 80% of the criteria in the Domain **ARE** documented at the "Proficient" or Exceeds Expectation Level and **NO** criteria are documented at Below Expectations or Unsatisfactory.

Domain IV: Management of Student Discipline, Instructional Strategies, Time, and Materials
IV-1. The teacher effectively implements the discipline management procedures approved by the campus. Any lack of effective implementation is rare, inadvertent, and does not seriously compromise the needs of students or the effective operation of the classroom or campus.

Things To Consider

- Campus-adopted discipline management process is in evidence in the teacher's normal rules and routines of the classroom and school-related activities.
- Lack of implementation is "rare, inadvertent, and does not seriously compromise" the needs of students or the effective operation of the classroom or campus.
- [See NOTE (1) & (2).]

Quality: Student behavior is appropriate. The classroom is safe. Teacher response to misbehavior is highly effective and sensitive to student's individual needs. Look for strength, impact, variety, and alignment of the discipline management process with instructional goals and objectives. Look for uniformity and consistency in implementation.

Evaluation Criteria

Exceeds Expectations	Proficient	Below Expectations	Unsatisfactory
QUALITY	QUALITY	QUALITY	QUALITY
Student behavior is consistently appropriate.	Student behavior is appropriate.	Student behavior is occasionally appropriate.	Student behavior is rarely/never appropriate.
Discipline management procedures are consistently implemented. Unique, creative, and/or innovative strategies are consistently used to implement the discipline management procedures.	Discipline management procedures are implemented.	Discipline management procedures are occasionally implemented. **Any lack of effective implementation is rare, inadvertent, and does not seriously compromise the needs of students or the effective operation of the classroom or campus.**	Discipline management procedures are rarely/never implemented. **AND/OR Lack of implementation is repetitive and/or intentional and seriously compromises the needs of students or the effective operation of the classroom or campus.**
Implementation of the discipline management plan consistently reflects an understanding of the unique needs/characteristics of students.	Implementation of the discipline management plan reflects an understanding of the unique needs/characteristics of students.	Implementation of the discipline management plan occasionally reflects an understanding of the unique needs/characteristics of students. **The lack of understanding of the unique needs/characteristics of the students is repetitive and/or intentional but does not seriously compromise the needs of students.**	Implementation of the discipline management plan rarely/never reflects an understanding of the unique needs/characteristics of students. **AND/OR Lack of understanding of the unique needs/characteristics of students is repetitive and/or intentional and seriously compromises the needs of students or the effective operation of the classroom or campus.**
Implementation of the discipline management plan consistently relies on high interest/relevant classroom instruction.	Implementation of the discipline management plan relies on high interest/relevant classroom instruction.	Implementation of the discipline management plan occasionally relies on high interest/relevant classroom instruction. **Implementation frequently relies on the enforcement of rules/consequences.**	Implementation of the discipline management plan rarely/never relies on high interest/relevant classroom instruction. **Implementation almost always/always relies on the enforcement of rules/consequences.**
Students are consistently engaged in appropriate self-direction/self-management.	Students are engaged in appropriate self-direction/self-management.	Students are occasionally engaged in appropriate self-direction/self-management.	Students are rarely/never engaged in appropriate self-direction/self-management.

NOTE: (1) The "Proficient" Standard in this Domain is **HIGHER** due to needs for consistency and safety. Exceeds Expectations requires participation in the development of discipline and other management procedures.

NOTE: (2) The criteria in Domain IV relate to the **MANAGEMENT** of student discipline, instructional strategies, time, and materials which create an environment in which learning may take place. These criteria are to be evaluated in the context of student behavior as it impacts student success. The critical attributes of EACH criterion MUST be considered separately.

Scoring Criteria Guide   Professional Development and Appraisal System   Page 23   Revised June 2003

SCORING CRITERIA GUIDE

Performance at the "Proficient" Level is based upon documentary evidence, as appropriate.

Documentary evidence may be collected over the entire appraisal period.

Performance at the "Proficient" Level MAY be inferred for a criterion if 80% of the criteria in the Domain ARE documented at the "Proficient" or Exceeds Expectation Level and NO criteria are documented at Below Expectations or Unsatisfactory.

Domain IV-1 Continued

Implementation of the discipline management plan consistently results in a positive, supportive, respectful classroom environment.	Implementation of the discipline management plan results in a positive, supportive, respectful classroom environment.	Implementation of the discipline management plan occasionally results in a positive, supportive, respectful classroom environment. **Any lack of a positive, supportive, respectful classroom environment does not seriously compromise the needs of the students or the effective operation of the classroom or campus.**	Implementation of the discipline management plan rarely/never relies on a positive, supportive, respectful classroom environment. **AND/OR Lack of a positive, supportive, respectful classroom environment seriously compromises the needs of the students or the effective operation of the classroom or campus.**
The teacher participates in the development of the discipline management procedures and offers suggestions for improvement.	Discipline management procedures are implemented.	Discipline management procedures are occasionally implemented.	Discipline management procedures are rarely/never implemented.
Any lack of effective implementation is rare/inadvertent and does not seriously compromise the needs of students or the effective operation of the classroom or campus.	Any lack of effective implementation is rare/inadvertent and does not seriously compromise the needs of students or the effective operation of the classroom or campus.	There are some elements of the plan that are not implemented but the lack of effective implementation is random/inadvertent and does not seriously compromise the needs of students or the effective operation of the classroom or campus.	Lack of implementation is repetitive and/or intentional and seriously compromises the needs of students or the effective operation of the classroom or campus.

NOTE: (1) The "Proficient" Standard in this Domain is **HIGHER** due to needs for consistency and safety. Exceeds Expectations requires participation in the development of discipline and other management procedures.

NOTE: (2) The criteria in Domain IV relate to the **MANAGEMENT** of student discipline, instructional strategies, time, and materials which create an environment in which learning may take place. These criteria are to be evaluated in the context of student behavior as it impacts student success. The critical attributes of EACH criterion MUST be considered separately.

SCORING CRITERIA GUIDE

Performance at the "Proficient" Level is based upon documentary evidence, as appropriate.

Documentary evidence may be collected over the entire appraisal period.

Performance at the "Proficient" Level MAY be inferred for a criterion if 80% of the criteria in the Domain ARE documented at the "Proficient" or Exceeds Expectation Level and NO criteria are documented at Below Expectations or Unsatisfactory.

Domain IV: Management of Student Discipline, Instructional Strategies, Time, and Materials

IV-2. The teacher establishes a classroom environment that promotes and encourages self-discipline and self-directed learning.

Things To Consider

- Classroom procedures and routines result in student self-management of behavior.
- Classroom procedures and routines result in student self-directed extensions and application of learning.
- [See NOTE (2).]

Quality: Student behavior is appropriate. Students are productively engaged. Teacher establishes high expectations for the learning and behavior of all students. Look for strength, impact, variety, and alignment of classroom routines with learning objectives.

Quantity: Look for uniformity and consistency of behavior.

Evaluation Criteria

Exceeds Expectations	Proficient	Below Expectations	Unsatisfactory
QUALITY	**QUALITY**	**QUALITY**	**QUALITY**
Student behavior is consistently appropriate.	Student behavior is appropriate.	Student behavior is occasionally appropriate.	Student behavior is rarely/never appropriate.
Students are consistently engaged in appropriate self-direction/self-management learning.	Students are engaged in appropriate self-direction/self-management learning.	Students are occasionally engaged in appropriate self-direction/self-management learning. **Appropriate behavior is frequently the result of manipulation and/or enforcement of rules/consequences.**	Students are rarely/never engaged in appropriate self-direction/self-management learning. **Appropriate behavior is almost always/always the result of manipulation and/or enforcement of rules/consequences.**
Unique, creative, and/or innovative strategies are consistently used to promote and encourage self-discipline and self-directed learning and reflect an understanding of the unique needs/characteristics of students.	Strategies to promote and encourage self-discipline and self-directed learning reflect an understanding of the unique needs/characteristics of students.	Strategies to promote and encourage self-discipline and self-directed learning occasionally reflect an understanding of the unique needs/characteristics of students.	Strategies to promote and encourage self-discipline and self-directed learning rarely/never reflect an understanding of the unique needs/characteristics of students.
The teacher consistently creates a safe, positive, supportive, respectful environment so that students take appropriate risks in the learning.	The teacher creates a safe, positive, supportive, respectful environment so that students take appropriate risks in the learning.	The teacher occasionally creates a safe, positive, supportive, respectful environment so that students take appropriate risks in the learning.	The teacher rarely/never creates a safe, positive, supportive, respectful environment so that students take appropriate risks in the learning.
High-interest/relevant classroom instructions consistently provide vehicles for self-management and self-directed learning.	High-interest/relevant classroom instructions provide vehicles for self-management and self-directed learning.	High-interest/relevant classroom instructions occasionally provide vehicles for self-management and self-directed learning.	High-interest/relevant classroom instruction rarely/never provide vehicles for self-management and self-directed learning.

NOTE: (1) The "Proficient" Standard in this Domain is HIGHER due to needs for consistency and safety. Exceeds Expectations requires participation in the development of discipline and other management procedures.

NOTE: (2) The criteria in Domain IV relate to the MANAGEMENT of student discipline, instructional strategies, time, and materials which create an environment in which learning may take place. These criteria are to be evaluated in the context of student behavior as it impacts student success. The critical attributes of EACH criterion MUST be considered separately.

SCORING CRITERIA GUIDE

Performance at the "Proficient" Level is based upon documentary evidence, as appropriate.

Documentary evidence may be collected over the entire appraisal period.

Performance at the "Proficient" Level **MAY** be inferred for a criterion if 80% of the criteria in the Domain **ARE** documented at the "Proficient" or <u>Exceeds Expectation</u> Level and **NO** criteria are documented at <u>Below Expectations</u> or <u>Unsatisfactory</u>.

Domain IV-2 Continued

QUANTITY ALMOST ALL OF THE TIME (90-100%)	QUANTITY MOST OF THE TIME (80-89%)	QUANTITY SOME OF THE TIME (50-79%)	QUANTITY LESS THAN HALF OF THE TIME (0-49%)
The teacher establishes a classroom environment that promotes and encourages self-discipline and self-directed learning.	The teacher establishes a classroom environment that promotes and encourages self-discipline and self-directed learning.	The teacher establishes a classroom environment that promotes and encourages self-discipline and self-directed learning.	The teacher establishes a classroom environment that promotes and encourages self-discipline and self-directed learning.
The teacher plans and implements instruction to provide opportunities for self-directed learning.	The teacher plans and implements instruction to provide opportunities for self-directed learning.	The teacher plans and implements instruction to provide opportunities for self-directed learning.	The teacher plans and implements instruction to provide opportunities for self-directed learning.

NOTE: (1) The "Proficient" Standard in this Domain is **HIGHER** due to needs for consistency and safety. <u>Exceeds Expectations</u> requires participation in the development of discipline and other management procedures.

NOTE: (2) The criteria in Domain IV relate to the **MANAGEMENT** of student discipline, instructional strategies, time, and materials which create an environment in which learning may take place. These criteria are to be evaluated in the context of student behavior as it impacts student success. <u>The critical attributes of EACH criterion MUST be considered separately.</u>

Professional Development and Appraisal System

SCORING CRITERIA GUIDE

Performance at the "Proficient" Level is based upon documentary evidence, as appropriate.

Documentary evidence may be collected over the entire appraisal period.

Performance at the "Proficient" Level MAY be inferred for a criterion if 80% of the criteria in the Domain ARE documented at the "Proficient" or Exceeds Expectation Level and NO criteria are documented at Below Expectations or Unsatisfactory.

Domain IV: Management of Student Discipline, Instructional Strategies, Time, and Materials

IV-3. The teacher interacts with students in an equitable manner, including fair application of rules.

Things To Consider

- Teacher provides opportunities for all students to participate.
- Teacher relates to students in an equitable and consistent manner.
- Teacher is fair in the application of rules.
- [See NOTE (1) & (2).]

Quality: Teacher interactions are appropriate to developmental, cultural norms and varied characteristics of students. Teacher-student interactions demonstrate respect. Look for uniformity and consistency in interactions.

Evaluation Criteria			
Exceeds Expectations	**Proficient**	**Below Expectations**	**Unsatisfactory**
QUALITY	QUALITY	QUALITY	QUALITY
All interactions (teacher/student and student/student) are consistently courteous and respectful.	All interactions (teacher/student and student/student) are courteous and respectful.	Interactions (teacher/student and student/student) are occasionally courteous and respectful. **Interactions (teacher/student and student/student) frequently lack courtesy, but the interactions do not compromise the needs of students.**	Interactions (teacher/student and student/student) are rarely/never courteous and respectful. **Interactions (teacher/student and student/student) almost always/always lack courtesy and/or the interactions seriously compromises the needs of students.**
Rules are applied consistently and fairly to all students.	Rules are applied consistently and fairly to all students.	Rules are occasionally applied consistently and/or fairly to all students. **Inconsistency and/or unfairness in the application of rules do not compromise the needs of students.**	Rules are rarely/never-applied consistently/fairly to all students. **AND/OR Inconsistency and/or unfairness in the application of rules seriously compromise the needs of students.**
Interactions consistently reflect an awareness of the unique needs/characteristics of students.	Interactions reflect an awareness of the unique needs/characteristics of students.	Interactions occasionally reflect an awareness of the unique needs/characteristics of students. **Lack of courteousness or respect does not seriously compromise the needs of the students.**	Interactions rarely/never reflect an awareness of the unique needs/characteristics of students. **AND/OR Lack of an awareness of the unique needs/characteristics of students seriously compromises the needs of the students.**
Teacher is consistently courteous and respectful even when circumstances make it difficult to do so. Interactions are not only courteous/respectful but also serve to support, dignify, and encourage student efforts in learning.	Teacher is courteous and respectful even when circumstances make it difficult to do so.	Teacher is occasionally courteous and respectful even when circumstances make it difficult to do so. **Lack of courteousness or respect does not seriously compromise the needs of the students.**	Teacher is rarely/never courteous and respectful even when circumstances make it difficult to do so. **AND/OR Lack of courteousness or respect seriously compromises the needs of the students.**

NOTE: (1) The "Proficient" Standard in this Domain is **HIGHER** due to needs for consistency and safety. Exceeds Expectations requires participation in the development of discipline and other management procedures.

NOTE: (2) The criteria in Domain IV relate to the **MANAGEMENT** of student discipline, instructional strategies, time, and materials which create an environment in which learning may take place. These criteria are to be evaluated in the context of student behavior as it impacts student success. The critical attributes of EACH criterion MUST be considered separately.

Professional Development and Appraisal System

SCORING CRITERIA GUIDE

Performance at the "Proficient" Level is based upon documentary evidence, as appropriate.
Documentary evidence may be collected over the entire appraisal period.
Performance at the "Proficient" Level MAY be inferred for a criterion if 80% of the criteria in the Domain ARE documented at the
"Proficient" or Exceeds Expectation Level and NO criteria are documented at Below Expectations or Unsatisfactory.

Domain IV: Management of Student Discipline, Instructional Strategies, Time, and Materials

IV-4. The teacher specifies expectations for desired behavior.

Things To Consider
- Teacher explains expectations for behavior.
- Teacher restates expectations when behavior is not appropriate.
- [See NOTE (2).]

Quality: Student behavior is appropriate. Teacher states reason for desired student behavior. Student behavior is consistent with stated expectations.

Quantity: Focus on appropriate behavior, not the overt statement of expectations. Focus on the number of students behaving appropriately.

Evaluation Criteria

Exceeds Expectations	Proficient	Below Expectations	Unsatisfactory
QUALITY Students consistently understand and meet the expectations for desired behavior.	QUALITY Students understand and meet the expectations for desired behavior.	QUALITY Students occasionally understand and meet the expectations for desired behavior.	QUALITY Students rarely/never understand and meet the expectations for desired behavior.
Students are consistently engaged in appropriate self-direction/self-management and learning.	Students are engaged in appropriate self-direction/self-management and learning.	Students are occasionally engaged in appropriate self-direction/self-management and learning. **Appropriate behavior is frequently the result of teacher manipulation and enforcement of rules/consequences rather than engagement in learning.**	Students are rarely engaged in appropriate self-direction/self-management and learning. **Appropriate behavior is almost always/ always the result of teacher manipulation and enforcement of rules/consequences rather than engagement in learning.**
Unique, creative, and/or innovative strategies are consistently used to promote and encourage self-discipline and self-directed learning.	Students understand and meet the expectations for desired behavior.	Students occasionally understand and meet the expectations for desired behavior.	Students rarely/never understand and meet the expectations for desired behavior.
High-interest/relevant classroom instructions frequently and consistently provide vehicles for self-management and self-directed learning.	Students understand and meet the expectations for desired behavior.	Students occasionally understand and meet the expectations for desired behavior.	Students rarely/never understand and meet the expectations for desired behavior.
QUANTITY ALMOST ALL OF THE TIME (90-100%) The teacher specifies expectations for desired behavior.	QUANTITY MOST OF THE TIME (80-89%) The teacher specifies expectations for desired behavior.	QUANTITY SOME OF THE TIME (50-79%) The teacher specifies expectations for behavior.	QUANTITY LESS OF THE TIME (0-49%) The teacher specifies expectations for desired behavior.

NOTE: (1) The "Proficient" Standard in this Domain is HIGHER due to needs for consistency and safety. Exceeds Expectations requires participation in the development of discipline and other management procedures.

NOTE: (2) The criteria in Domain IV relate to the MANAGEMENT of student discipline, instructional strategies, time, and materials which create an environment in which learning may take place. These criteria are to be evaluated in the context of student behavior as it impacts student success. The critical attributes of EACH criterion MUST be considered separately.

SCORING CRITERIA GUIDE

Performance at the "Proficient" Level is based upon documentary evidence, as appropriate.

Documentary evidence may be collected over the entire appraisal period.

Performance at the "Proficient" Level **MAY** be inferred for a criterion if 80% of the criteria in the Domain **ARE** documented at the "Proficient" or Exceeds Expectation Level and **NO** criteria are documented at Below Expectations or Unsatisfactory.

Domain IV: Management of Student Discipline, Instructional Strategies, Time, and Materials

IV-5. The teacher intervenes and re-directs off-task, inappropriate, or disruptive behavior.

Things To Consider
- Teacher identifies students engaged in activities other than the assigned task.
- Teacher re-directs students in accordance with adopted campus discipline management policies.
- [See inference opening statement for Domain IV]
- [See Note (1) & (2).]

Quality: Student behavior is appropriate. Monitoring is subtle and preventative. Look for strength, impact, variety, impact, and alignment of intervention with the behavior. Focus on appropriate behavior not the overt redirection of behavior. Look for uniformity and consistency of interventions.

| | Evaluation Criteria | | |
Exceeds Expectations	Proficient	Below Expectations	Unsatisfactory
QUALITY The off-task, inappropriate, or disruptive behavior stops.	**QUALITY** The off-task, inappropriate, or disruptive behavior stops.	**QUALITY** The off-task, inappropriate, or disruptive behavior occasionally stops after redirection.	**QUALITY** The off-task, inappropriate, or disruptive behavior rarely/never stops after redirection.
There is little or no need to stop/redirect behavior because students are consistently engaged in quality learning and students are consistently behaving appropriately.	Students are engaged in learning and behaving appropriately.	Students are occasionally engaged in learning and behaving appropriately. The teacher frequently must redirect off-task, inappropriate or disruptive behavior because students show little interest/engagement in the learning.	Students are rarely/never engaged in learning and behaving appropriately. The teacher almost always/always must redirect off-task, inappropriate or disruptive behavior because students show little interest/engagement in the learning.
There is little or no need to stop/redirect behavior because the teacher has created a learning environment that is consistently safe, positive, supportive, and risk-free.	The teacher has created a learning environment that is safe, positive, supportive, and risk-free.	The teacher has created a learning environment that is occasionally safe, positive, supportive, and risk-free. **Where the learning environment is frequently inappropriate, the needs of the students or effective operations of the campus/district have not been seriously compromised.**	The teacher has created a learning environment that is rarely/never safe, positive, supportive, and risk-free. **AND/OR Where the learning environment is inappropriate, the needs of the students or the effective operations of the campus/district are seriously compromised.**
The teacher consistently plans instruction that is challenging and that permits students to be consistently successful.	The teacher plans instruction that is challenging and that permits students to be successful.	The teacher occasionally plans instruction that is challenging and that permits students to be successful. There is a need to frequently stop/redirect behavior.	The teacher rarely/never plans instruction that is challenging and that permits students to be successful. There is almost always/always a need to frequently stop/redirect behavior.
There is little or no need to stop/redirect behavior because the teacher patiently assists students who are frustrated and/or unsuccessful.	Students are engaged in learning and behaving appropriately.	Students are occasionally engaged in learning and behaving appropriately.	Students are rarely/never engaged in learning and behaving appropriately.

NOTE: (1) The "Proficient" Standard in this Domain is **HIGHER** due to needs for consistency and safety. Exceeds Expectations requires participation in the development of discipline and other management procedures.

NOTE: (2) The criteria in Domain IV relate to the **MANAGEMENT** of student discipline, instructional strategies, time, and materials which create an environment in which learning may take place. These criteria are to be evaluated in the context of student behavior as it impacts student success. The critical attributes of EACH criterion MUST be considered separately.

SCORING CRITERIA GUIDE

Performance at the "Proficient" Level is based upon documentary evidence, as appropriate.

Documentary evidence may be collected over the entire appraisal period.

Performance at the "Proficient" Level **MAY** be inferred for a criterion if 80% of the criteria in the Domain **ARE** documented at the "Proficient" or Exceeds Expectation Level and **NO** criteria are documented at Below Expectations or Unsatisfactory.

Domain IV-5 Continued

The teacher consistently intervenes and re-directs off-task, inappropriate, or disruptive behavior in ways that preserve the student's dignity.	The teacher intervenes and re-directs off-task, inappropriate, or disruptive behavior in ways that preserve the student's dignity.	The teacher occasionally intervenes and re-directs off-task, inappropriate, or disruptive behavior in ways that preserve the student's dignity. **The dignity and needs of students are not seriously compromised by the intervention/redirection.**	The teacher rarely/never intervenes and re-directs off-task, inappropriate, or disruptive behavior in ways that preserve the student's dignity. **AND/OR The dignity and needs of students are seriously compromised by the intervention/redirection.**
The teacher uses creative, unique, and/or innovative strategies to stop-redirect off-task and/or disruptive behavior.	Students are engaged in learning and behaving appropriately.	Students are occasionally engaged in learning and behaving appropriately.	Students are rarely/never engaged in learning and behaving appropriately.

NOTE: (1) The "Proficient" Standard in this Domain is **HIGHER** due to needs for consistency and safety. Exceeds Expectations requires participation in the development of discipline and other management procedures.

NOTE: (2) The criteria in Domain IV relate to the **MANAGEMENT** of student discipline, instructional strategies, time, and materials which create an environment in which learning may take place. These criteria are to be evaluated in the context of student behavior as it impacts student success. The critical attributes of EACH criterion MUST be considered separately.

Professional Development and Appraisal System

Scoring Criteria Guide   Page 30   Revised June 2003

SCORING CRITERIA GUIDE

Performance at the "Proficient" Level is based upon documentary evidence, as appropriate.

Documentary evidence may be collected over the entire appraisal period.

Performance at the "Proficient" Level MAY be inferred for a criterion if 80% of the criteria in the Domain **ARE** documented at the "Proficient" or Exceeds Expectation Level and **NO** criteria are documented at Below Expectations or Unsatisfactory.

Domain IV: Management of Student Discipline, Instructional Strategies, Time, and Materials

IV-6. The teacher reinforces desired behavior when appropriate.

Things To Consider

- Teacher offers accurate and specific feedback to individuals or the class.
- Teacher does not reinforce inappropriate behavior.
- [See NOTE (2).]

Quality: Reinforcement results in desired change in behavior. Look for strength, impact, variety, and alignment of teacher response with the exhibited behavior.

Quantity: Focus on the appropriateness of reinforcement, not the number of times behavior is reinforced. Look for uniformity and consistency of reinforcement.

Evaluation Criteria			
Exceeds Expectations	**Proficient**	**Below Expectations**	**Unsatisfactory**
QUALITY	QUALITY	QUALITY	QUALITY
Reinforcement results in desired behavior change or causes desired behavior to be repeated.	Reinforcement results in desired behavior change or causes desired behavior to be repeated.	Reinforcement occasionally results in desired behavior change or causes desired behavior to be repeated.	Reinforcement rarely/never results in desired behavior change or causes desired behavior to be repeated.
Inappropriate behavior is rare because of the use of positive reinforcement of appropriate behavior.	Positive reinforcement of appropriate behavior is used as a method of encouraging/promoting and establishing models of appropriate behavior.	Positive reinforcement of appropriate behavior is occasionally used as a method of encouraging/promoting and establishing models of appropriate behavior.	Positive reinforcement of appropriate behavior is rarely/never used as a method of encouraging/promoting and establishing models of appropriate behavior.
Reinforcement of behavior is consistently used to encourage/promote appropriate behavior and not simply to redirect inappropriate behavior. Reinforcement is consistently specific to the student and specific to the behavior.	Reinforcement is specific to the student and specific to the behavior.	Reinforcement is occasionally specific to the student and specific to the behavior.	Reinforcement is rarely/never specific to the student and specific to the behavior.
Use of reinforcement of behavior consistently reflects an understanding of the unique needs/characteristics of students so that reinforcement has an appropriate level of intensity appropriate to the behavior.	Use of reinforcement of behavior reflects an understanding of the unique needs/characteristics of students so that reinforcement has an appropriate level of intensity appropriate to the behavior.	Use of reinforcement of behavior occasionally reflects an understanding of the unique needs/characteristics of students so that reinforcement has an appropriate level of intensity appropriate to the behavior.	Use of reinforcement of behavior rarely/never reflects an understanding of the unique needs/characteristics of students so that reinforcement has an appropriate level of intensity appropriate to the behavior.
Use of reinforcement of behavior consistently reflects an understanding of the unique needs/characteristics of students so that reinforcement has an appropriate frequency.	Use of reinforcement of behavior reflects an understanding of the unique needs/characteristics of students so that reinforcement has an appropriate frequency.	The use of reinforcement of behavior occasionally reflects an understanding of the unique needs/characteristics of students so that reinforcement has only a limited effect on the frequency of appropriate behavior.	The use of reinforcement of behavior rarely/never reflects an understanding of the unique needs/characteristics of students so that reinforcement has little/no effect on the frequency of appropriate behavior.

NOTE: (1) The "Proficient" Standard in this Domain is **HIGHER** due to needs for consistency and safety. Exceeds Expectations requires participation in the development of discipline and other management procedures.

NOTE: (2) The criteria in Domain IV relate to the **MANAGEMENT** of student discipline, instructional strategies, time, and materials which create an environment in which learning may take place. These criteria are to be evaluated in the context of student behavior as it impacts student success. The critical attributes of EACH criterion MUST be considered separately.

Scoring Criteria Guide

Professional Development and Appraisal System

Page 31

Revised June 2003

SCORING CRITERIA GUIDE

Performance at the "Proficient" Level is based upon documentary evidence, as appropriate.

Documentary evidence may be collected over the entire appraisal period.

Performance at the "Proficient" Level **MAY** be inferred for a criterion if 80% of the criteria in the Domain **ARE** documented at the "Proficient" or Exceeds Expectation Level and **NO** criteria are documented at Below Expectations or Unsatisfactory.

Domain IV-6 Continued

QUANTITY ALMOST ALL OF THE TIME (90-100%) The teacher reinforces desired behavior when appropriate.	QUANTITY MOST OF THE TIME (80-89%) The teacher reinforces desired behavior when appropriate.	QUANTITY SOME OF THE TIME (50-79%) The teacher reinforces desired behavior when appropriate.	QUANTITY LESS THAN HALF OF THE TIME (0-49%) The teacher reinforces desired behavior when appropriate.

SCORING CRITERIA GUIDE

Performance at the "Proficient" Level is based upon documentary evidence, as appropriate.

Documentary evidence may be collected over the entire appraisal period.

Performance at the "Proficient" Level MAY be inferred for a criterion if 80% of the criteria in the Domain ARE documented at the "Proficient" or Exceeds Expectation Level and NO criteria are documented at Below Expectations or Unsatisfactory.

Domain IV: Management of Student Discipline, Instructional Strategies, Time, and Materials

IV-7. The instructional materials selected by the teacher are equitable and acknowledge the varied characteristics of all students.

Things To Consider
- Teacher selects instructional materials that reflect ethnic diversity, gender equity and the learning needs of students.
- Students have equal access to appropriate instructional materials.
- [See NOTE (2).]

Quality: Teacher is aware of resources available through the school, district, professional organizations and community. Teacher seeks out and evaluates materials needed to enhance instruction. Instructional materials contribute to student success. Look for strength, impact, variety, and alignment of instructional materials with goals and objectives.

Quantity: Focus is on the consistent use of appropriate instructional materials.

Evaluation Criteria

Exceeds Expectations	Proficient	Below Expectations	Unsatisfactory
QUALITY The teacher seeks out resources and instructional materials that are equitable and acknowledge the varied characteristics of all students.	**QUALITY** The instructional materials selected by the teacher are equitable and acknowledge the varied characteristics of all students.	**QUALITY** The instructional materials selected by the teacher are occasionally equitable and acknowledge the varied characteristics of all students.	**QUALITY** The instructional materials selected by the teacher are rarely/never equitable and acknowledge the varied characteristics of all students.
The teacher utilizes unique and creative methods for including instructional materials aligned with the learning goals/ objective that reflect ethnic diversity, gender equality and learning needs of the students.	The instructional materials selected by the teacher are equitable and acknowledge the varied characteristics of all students.	The instructional materials selected by the teacher are occasionally equitable and acknowledge the varied characteristics of all students.	The instructional materials selected by the teacher are rarely/never equitable and acknowledge the varied characteristics of all students.
The teacher utilizes unique and creative methods for including instructional materials aligned with the goals/objectives that engage students and ensure success.	The instructional materials selected by the teacher are equitable and acknowledge the varied characteristics of all students.	The instructional materials selected by the teacher are occasionally equitable and acknowledge the varied characteristics of all students.	The instructional materials selected by the teacher are rarely/never equitable and acknowledge the varied characteristics of all students.
QUANTITY **ALMOST ALL OF THE TIME (90-100%)** The teacher uses appropriate instructional materials.	**QUANTITY** **MOST OF THE TIME (80-89%)** The teacher uses appropriate instructional materials.	**QUANTITY** **SOME OF THE TIME (50-79%)** The teacher uses appropriate instructional materials.	**QUANTITY** **LESS THAN HALF OF THE TIME (0-49%)** The teacher uses appropriate instructional materials.

NOTE: (1) The "Proficient" Standard in this Domain is **HIGHER** due to needs for consistency and safety. Exceeds Expectations requires participation in the development of discipline and other management procedures.

NOTE: (2) The criteria in Domain IV relate to the **MANAGEMENT** of student discipline, instructional strategies, time, and materials which create an environment in which learning may take place. These criteria are to be evaluated in the context of student behavior as it impacts student success. The critical attributes of EACH criterion MUST be considered separately.

Professional Development and Appraisal System

SCORING CRITERIA GUIDE

Performance at the "Proficient" Level is based upon documentary evidence, as appropriate.

Documentary evidence may be collected over the entire appraisal period.

Performance at the "Proficient" Level **MAY** be inferred for a criterion if 80% of the criteria in the Domain **ARE** documented at the "Proficient" or Exceeds Expectation Level and **NO** criteria are documented at Below Expectations or Unsatisfactory.

Domain IV: Management of Student Discipline, Instructional Strategies, Time, and Materials

IV-8. The teacher effectively and efficiently manages time and materials.

Things To Consider

- Teacher has materials ready for instruction.
- Academic learning time is maximized.
- [See NOTE (2).]

Quality: Routines for handling materials occur without without loss of instructional time. Transitions are seamless. Look for strength, impact, variety, and alignment of materials with student success in the learning.

Quantity: Focus on the amount of time for teaching and learning.

Evaluation Criteria			
Exceeds Expectations	**Proficient**	**Below Expectations**	**Unsatisfactory**
QUALITY	QUALITY	QUALITY	QUALITY
The teacher organizes and uses unique and creative instructional materials aligned with the learning goals/objectives that promote student success.	The teacher has appropriate materials ready for instruction.	The teacher occasionally has appropriate materials ready for instruction. **Students frequently lose opportunities for learning.**	The teacher rarely/never has appropriate materials ready for instruction. **Students always/almost always lose opportunities for learning.**
Transitions are seamless; routines for handling materials are effective and result in student success and maximum use of instructional time.	Transitions and routines for handling materials are appropriate for the learning.	Transitions and routines for handling materials are occasionally appropriate for the learning. **Students frequently lose opportunities for learning.**	Transitions and routines for handling materials are rarely/never appropriate for the learning. **Students almost always/ always lose opportunities for learning.**
The teacher consistently establishes routines and procedures that promote student responsibility for materials and transitions in the learning.	The teacher establishes routines and procedures that promote student responsibility for materials and transitions in the learning.	The teacher occasionally establishes routines and procedures that promote student responsibility for materials and transitions in the learning.	The teacher rarely/never establishes routines and procedures that promote student responsibility for materials and transitions in the learning.
QUANTITY **ALMOST ALL OF THE TIME (90-100%)** The teacher utilizes available time as "academic learning time."	QUANTITY **MOST OF THE TIME (80-89%)** The teacher utilizes available time as "academic learning time."	QUANTITY **SOME OF THE TIME (50-79%)** The teacher utilizes available time as "academic learning time."	QUANTITY **LESS THAN HALF OF THE TIME (0-49%)** The teacher utilizes available time as "academic learning time."

NOTE: (1) The "Proficient" Standard in this Domain is **HIGHER** due to needs for consistency and safety. Exceeds Expectations requires participation in the development of discipline and other management procedures.

NOTE: (2) The criteria in Domain IV relate to the **MANAGEMENT** of student discipline, instructional strategies, time, and materials which create an environment in which learning may take place. These criteria are to be evaluated in the context of student behavior as it impacts student success. The critical attributes of EACH criterion MUST be considered separately.

SCORING CRITERIA GUIDE

Performance at the "Proficient" Level is based upon documentary evidence, as appropriate.
Documentary evidence may be collected over the entire appraisal period.
Performance at the "Proficient" Level **MAY** be inferred for a criterion if 80% of the criteria in the Domain **ARE** documented at the "Proficient" or Exceeds Expectation Level and **NO** criteria are documented at Below Expectations or Unsatisfactory.

Domain V: Professional Communication
V-1. The teacher uses appropriate and accurate written communication with students.

Things To Consider
- Teacher's written communication is without significant error in content or presentation.
- Errors are corrected.
- Errors do not interfere with the ability of students to learn.

Quality: Students are successful in the learning. Focus on the clarity of written communications. Written communications are legible. Look for strength, impact, variety, and alignment of the communication with the learning objectives.

Quantity: Focus on the extent to which written communication supports learning.

	Evaluation Criteria		
Exceeds Expectations	**Proficient**	**Below Expectations**	**Unsatisfactory**
QUALITY The teacher consistently uses appropriate and accurate written communication with students.	**QUALITY** The teacher uses appropriate and accurate written communication with students.	**QUALITY** The teacher occasionally uses appropriate and accurate written communication with students. **The teacher frequently uses inappropriate and inaccurate written communication with students.**	**QUALITY** The teacher rarely/never uses appropriate and accurate written communication with students. **The teacher almost always/always uses inappropriate and inaccurate written communication with students.**
The teacher consistently utilizes unique and creative ways to provide students with clear/accurate information, specific directives, corrective and reinforcing feedback that facilitates/encourages learning.	The teacher utilizes ways to provide students with information, directives and feedback that facilitate learning.	The teacher occasionally utilizes ways to provide students with information, directives and feedback that facilitate learning. **The teacher's written communication with students results in confusion that occasionally impedes learning.**	The teacher never/rarely utilizes ways to provide students with information, directives and feedback that facilitate learning. **The teacher's communication with students results in confusion that impedes learning.**
QUANTITY **ALMOST ALL OF THE TIME (90-100%)** The teacher uses appropriate and accurate written communication with students.	**QUANTITY** **MOST OF THE TIME (80-89%)** The teacher uses appropriate and accurate written communication with students.	**QUANTITY** **SOME OF THE TIME (50-79%)** The teacher uses appropriate and accurate written communication with students.	**QUANTITY** **LESS THAN HALF OF THE TIME (0-49%)** The teacher uses appropriate and accurate written communication with students.

NOTE: (1) The "Proficient" Standard in this Domain is **HIGHER** due to needs for consistency and safety. Exceeds Expectations requires participation in the development of discipline and other management procedures.

NOTE: (2) The criteria in Domain IV relate to the **MANAGEMENT** of student discipline, instructional strategies, time, and materials which create an environment in which learning may take place. These criteria are to be evaluated in the context of student behavior as it impacts student success. The critical attributes of EACH criterion MUST be considered separately.

SCORING CRITERIA GUIDE

Performance at the "Proficient" Level is based upon documentary evidence, as appropriate.

Documentary evidence may be collected over the entire appraisal period.

Performance at the "Proficient" Level **MAY** be inferred for a criterion if 80% of the criteria in the Domain **ARE** documented at the "Proficient" or Exceeds Expectation Level and **NO** criteria are documented at Below Expectations or Unsatisfactory.

Domain V: Professional Communication

V-2. The teacher uses appropriate and accurate verbal and non-verbal communication with students.

Things To Consider

- The teacher's verbal and non-verbal communication establishes a learning climate that enhances student's ability to learn.
- Teacher's verbal communication is without significant error in content or presentation.
- Verbal and non-verbal errors are corrected.

Quality: Students are successful in the learning. Focus on the clarity of oral communication. Oral communication is audible. Classroom environment is conducive to learning. Look for strength, impact, variety, and alignment of the communication with the learning objective.

Quantity: Focus on the extent to which oral communication supports learning.

Evaluation Criteria

Exceeds Expectations	Proficient	Below Expectations	Unsatisfactory
QUALITY The teacher's verbal and non-verbal communication consistently establishes a positive learning climate that promotes student learning and student success.	**QUALITY** The teacher's verbal and non-verbal communication establishes a learning climate that is positive and conducive to learning.	**QUALITY** The teacher's verbal and non-verbal communication occasionally establishes a learning climate that is positive and conducive to learning. **Errors are inadvertent and do not seriously compromise the needs of students or the effective and legal operation of campus/district.**	**QUALITY** The teacher's verbal and non-verbal communication rarely/never establishes a learning climate that is positive and conducive to learning. **AND/OR Errors seriously compromise the needs of students or the effective and legal operation of campus/ district.**
The teacher's verbal and non-verbal communication is consistently clear and audible.	The teacher's verbal and non-verbal communication is clear and audible.	The teacher's verbal communication is occasionally clear and audible.	The teacher's verbal communication is rarely/never audible and clear.
The teacher's verbal and non-verbal communication consistently encourages students to take responsible risks in responding, extending, questioning, and/or producing products.	The teacher's verbal and non-verbal communication encourages students to take responsible risks in responding, extending, questioning, and/or producing products.	The teacher's verbal and non-verbal communication occasionally engages students in learning.	The teacher's verbal and non-verbal communication rarely/never engages students in learning.
The teacher's verbal and non-verbal communications consistently assist in the alignment of instruction with learning objectives.	The teacher's verbal and non-verbal communications assist in the alignment of instruction with learning objectives.	The teacher's verbal and non-verbal communications occasionally assist in the alignment of instruction with learning objectives.	The teacher's verbal and non-verbal communications rarely/never assist in the alignment of instruction with learning objectives.
The teacher's verbal and non-verbal communications consistently contribute to the successful learning of students.	The teacher's verbal and non-verbal communications contribute to the successful learning of students.	The teacher's verbal and non-verbal communications occasionally contribute to the successful learning of the students.	The teacher's verbal and non-verbal communications rarely/never contribute to the successful learning of the students.
QUANTITY **ALMOST ALL OF THE TIME (90-100%)** The teacher's oral communication and non-verbal communication supports a positive learning climate that promotes student success.	**QUANTITY** **MOST OF THE TIME (80-89%)** The teacher's oral communication and non-verbal communication supports a positive learning climate that promotes student success.	**QUANTITY** **SOME OF THE TIME (50-79%)** The teacher's oral communication and non-verbal communication supports a positive learning climate that promotes student success.	**QUANTITY** **LESS THAN HALF OF THE TIME (0-49%)** The teacher's oral communication and non-verbal communication supports a positive learning climate that promotes student success.

SCORING CRITERIA GUIDE

Performance at the "Proficient" Level is based upon documentary evidence, as appropriate.

Documentary evidence may be collected over the entire appraisal period.

Performance at the "Proficient" Level **MAY** be inferred for a criterion if 80% of the criteria in the Domain **ARE** documented at the "Proficient" or Exceeds Expectation Level and **NO** criteria are documented at Below Expectations or Unsatisfactory.

Domain V: Professional Communication

V-3. The teacher encourages and supports students who are reluctant and having difficulty.

Things To Consider

- Teacher readily recognizes students who have difficulty in performance.
- Teacher modifies and positively reinforces student-learning success.

Quality: Look for strength, impact, variety, and alignment of teacher support and student success. Focus on appropriateness of the modification. Encouragement and support results in student success.

Quantity: Look for uniformity and consistency of encouragement.

Evaluation Criteria			
Exceeds Expectations	**Proficient**	**Below Expectations**	**Unsatisfactory**
QUALITY	QUALITY	QUALITY	QUALITY
The teacher consistently identifies and assesses the needs of the students who are reluctant and having difficulty. The teacher consistently encourages and supports students who are reluctant and having difficulty.	The teacher identifies and assesses the needs of the students who are reluctant and having difficulty. The teacher encourages and supports students who are reluctant and having difficulty.	The teacher occasionally identifies and assesses the needs of the students who are reluctant and having difficulty. The teacher occasionally encourages and supports students who are reluctant and having difficulty.	The teacher rarely/never identifies and assesses the needs of the students who are reluctant and having difficulty. The teacher rarely/never encourages and supports students who are reluctant and having difficulty.
The teacher consistently encourages and supports students who are reluctant and having difficulty.	The teacher encourages and supports students who are reluctant and having difficulty.	The teacher occasionally encourages and supports students who are reluctant and having difficulty.	The teacher rarely/never encourages and supports students who are reluctant and having difficulty.
The teacher consistently uses creative and unique ways to encourage and support students who are reluctant and having difficulty, which results in students taking reasonable risks, reduced frustration and willingness to continue engagement in learning.	The teacher uses strategies to encourage and support students who are reluctant and having difficulty.	The teacher occasionally uses strategies to encourage and support students who are reluctant and having difficulty. **The teacher's communication / lack of communication with students who are reluctant and having difficulty frequently results in student frustration, unwillingness to take reasonable risks and/or disengagement.**	The teacher rarely/never uses strategies to encourage and support students who are reluctant and having difficulty. **The teacher's communication / lack of communication with students who are reluctant and having difficulty almost always/ always results in student frustration, unwillingness to take reasonable risks and/or disengagement.**
QUANTITY	QUANTITY	QUANTITY	QUANTITY
ALMOST ALL OF THE TIME (90-100%)	MOST OF THE TIME (80-89%)	SOME OF THE TIME (50-79%)	LESS THAN HALF OF THE TIME (0-49%)
The teacher encourages and supports students who are reluctant or having difficulty.	The teacher encourages and supports students who are reluctant or having difficulty.	The teacher encourages and supports students who are reluctant or having difficulty.	The teacher encourages and supports students who are reluctant or having difficulty.

Revised June 2003

SCORING CRITERIA GUIDE

Performance at the "Proficient" Level is based upon documentary evidence, as appropriate.

Documentary evidence may be collected over the entire appraisal period.

Performance at the "Proficient" Level MAY be inferred for a criterion if 80% of the criteria in the Domain ARE documented at the "Proficient" or Exceeds Expectation Level and NO criteria are documented at Below Expectations or Unsatisfactory.

Domain V: Professional Communication

V-4. The teacher uses appropriate and accurate written communication with parents, staff, community members, and other professionals.

Things To Consider

- Teacher's written communication is without significant error in content or presentation.
- Written errors are corrected.
- Written errors do not interfere with the intent of the communication to parents, staff, community members, and other professionals.
- Communication reflects sensitivity to community standards.
- [NOTE: The written responses on the Teacher Self-Report are NOT to be used in the evaluation of Domain V.]

Quality: Focus on the clarity of written communication. Written communications are legible. Communication serves a purpose. Communication serves the purpose for which it was written. Look for strength, impact, variety, and alignment of the communication with the intent.

Quantity: Focus on the extent to which written communication is informative.

Evaluation Criteria

Exceeds Expectations	Proficient	Below Expectations	Unsatisfactory
QUALITY The teacher consistently uses appropriate and accurate written communication with parents, staff, community members and professionals.	QUALITY The teacher uses appropriate and accurate written communication with parents, staff, community members and professionals.	QUALITY The teacher occasionally uses appropriate and accurate written communication with parents, staff, community members and professionals. Errors in communication are inadvertent and do not seriously compromise the needs of students or the effective and legal operation of the campus/district.	QUALITY The teacher rarely/never uses appropriate and accurate written communication with parents, staff, community members and professionals. AND/OR Errors in communication seriously compromise the needs of students or the effective and legal operation of the campus/district.
The teacher's written communication with parents, staff, community members and professionals consistently results in positive responses that may include but are not limited to: increased collaboration with participants, increased involvement in the learning community.	The teacher's written communication with parents, staff, community members and professionals results in positive responses.	The teacher's written communication with parents, staff, community members and professionals occasionally results in positive responses. The teacher's written communication includes comments that are inaccurate, insensitive, or inappropriate.	The teacher's written communication with parents, staff, community members and professionals rarely/never results in positive responses. The teacher's written communication includes comments that are inaccurate, insensitive, or inappropriate.
QUANTITY ALMOST ALL OF THE TIME (90-100%) The teacher uses appropriate and accurate written communication with parents, staff, community members and other professionals.	QUANTITY MOST OF THE TIME (80-89%) The teacher uses appropriate and accurate written communication with parents, staff, community members and other professionals.	QUANTITY SOME OF THE TIME (50-79%) The teacher uses appropriate and accurate written communication with parents, staff, community members and other professionals.	QUANTITY LESS THAN HALF OF THE TIME (0-49%) The teacher uses appropriate and accurate written communication with parents, staff, community members and other professionals.

SCORING CRITERIA GUIDE

Performance at the "Proficient" Level is based upon documentary evidence, as appropriate.

Documentary evidence may be collected over the entire appraisal period.

Performance at the "Proficient" Level MAY be inferred for a criterion if 80% of the criteria in the Domain ARE documented at the "Proficient" or Exceeds Expectation Level and NO criteria are documented at Below Expectations or Unsatisfactory.

Domain V: Professional Communication

V-5. The teacher uses appropriate and accurate verbal and non-verbal communication with parents, staff, community members, and other professionals.

Things To Consider

- Teacher's verbal and non-verbal communication establishes a climate of trust and mutual respect.
- Teacher's verbal and non-verbal communication is without significant error in content or presentation.
- Verbal and non-verbal errors are corrected.

Quality: Focus on the clarity of oral communication. Oral communication is audible. Look for strength, impact, variety, and alignment of the communication with the intent.

Quantity: Focus on the extent to which communication interferes with /supports interactions between parents, staff, community members, and other professionals.

Evaluation Criteria

Exceeds Expectations	Proficient	Below Expectations	Unsatisfactory
QUALITY The teacher consistently uses appropriate and accurate verbal and non-verbal communication with parents, staff, community members and professionals.	**QUALITY** The teacher uses appropriate and accurate verbal and non-verbal communication with parents, staff, community members and professionals.	**QUALITY** The teacher occasionally uses appropriate and accurate verbal and non-verbal communication with parents, staff, community members and professionals. **AND/OR Errors in communication are inadvertent and do not seriously compromise the needs of students or the effective and legal operation of the campus/district.**	**QUALITY** The teacher rarely/never uses appropriate and accurate verbal and non-verbal communication with parents, staff, community members and professionals. **AND/OR Errors in communication seriously compromise the needs of students or the effective and legal operation of campus/district.**
The teacher's written communication with parents, staff, community members and professionals consistently results in positive responses that may include but are not limited to increased collaboration, participation, and involvement in the learning community.	The teacher's written communication with parents, staff, community members and professionals results in positive responses.	The teacher's written communication with parents, staff, community members and professionals occasionally results in positive responses. **AND/OR The teacher's use of inappropriate and/or inaccurate verbal and non-verbal communication is inadvertent and does not seriously interfere with trust and mutual respect with parents, staff, community members and professionals.**	The teacher's written communication with parents, staff, community members and professionals rarely/never results in positive responses. **AND/OR The teacher's use of inappropriate and/or inaccurate verbal and non-verbal communication seriously interferes with trust and mutual respect with parents, staff, community members and professionals.**
QUANTITY **ALMOST ALL OF THE TIME (90-100%)** The teacher uses appropriate and accurate verbal and non-verbal communication with parents, staff, community members and other professionals.	**QUANTITY** **MOST OF THE TIME (80-89%)** The teacher uses appropriate and accurate verbal and non-verbal communication with parents, staff, community members and other professionals.	**QUANTITY** **SOME OF THE TIME (50-79%)** The teacher uses appropriate and accurate verbal and non-verbal communication with parents, staff, community members and other professionals.	**QUANTITY** **LESS THAN HALF OF THE TIME (0-49%)** The teacher uses appropriate and accurate verbal and non-verbal communication with parents, staff, community members and other professionals.

SCORING CRITERIA GUIDE

Performance at the "Proficient" Level is based upon documentary evidence, as appropriate.

Documentary evidence may be collected over the entire appraisal period.

Performance at the "Proficient" Level **MAY** be inferred for a criterion if 80% of the criteria in the Domain **ARE** documented at the "Proficient" or <u>Exceeds</u> Expectation Level and **NO** criteria are documented at <u>Below Expectations</u> or <u>Unsatisfactory</u>.

Domain V: Professional Communication

V-6. The teacher's interactions are supportive, courteous, and respectful with students, parents, staff, community members, and other professionals.

Things To Consider

- Teacher models courtesy and respect through patience and active listening.
- Incorrect responses are handled with dignity.

Quality: Teacher demonstrates support, courtesy and respect for students, parents, staff, community members, and other professionals that enhance student success.

Quantity: Look for uniformity and consistency of interactions.

Evaluation Criteria

Exceeds Expectations	Proficient	Below Expectations	Unsatisfactory
QUALITY The teacher consistently models and teaches courtesy and respect by displaying patience and actively listening to students, parents, staff, community members and other professionals.	**QUALITY** The teacher models and teaches courtesy and respect by displaying patience and actively listening to students, parents, staff, community members and other professionals.	**QUALITY** The teacher occasionally models and teaches courtesy and respect by displaying patience and actively listening to students, parents, staff, community members and other professionals.	**QUALITY** The teacher rarely/never models and teaches courtesy and respect by displaying patience and actively listening to students, parents, staff, community members and other professionals.
The teacher consistently establishes a climate that allows both other students and the teacher to provide corrective information for incorrect responses.	The teacher establishes a climate that allows both other students and the teacher to provide corrective information for incorrect responses.	The teacher occasionally establishes a climate that allows both other students and the teacher to provide corrective information for incorrect responses.	The teacher rarely/never establishes a climate that allows both other students and the teacher to provide corrective information for incorrect responses.
QUANTITY <u>ALMOST ALL OF THE TIME (90-100%)</u> The teacher demonstrates support, courtesy, and respect with students, parents, staff, community members and other professionals.	**QUANTITY** <u>MOST OF THE TIME (80-89%)</u> The teacher demonstrates support, courtesy, and respect with students, parents, staff, community members and other professionals.	**QUANTITY** <u>SOME OF THE TIME (50-79%)</u> The teacher demonstrates support, courtesy, and respect with students, parents, staff, community members and other professionals.	**QUANTITY** <u>LESS THAN HALF OF THE TIME (0-49%)</u> The teacher demonstrates support, courtesy, and respect with students, parents, staff, community members and other professionals.

SCORING CRITERIA GUIDE

Performance at the "Proficient" Level is based upon documentary evidence, as appropriate.

Documentary evidence may be collected over the entire appraisal period.

Performance at the "Proficient" Level MAY be inferred for a criterion if 80% of the criteria in the Domain ARE documented at the "Proficient" or Exceeds Expectation Level and NO criteria are documented at Below Expectations or Unsatisfactory.

Domain VI: Professional Development

VI-1. The teacher successfully engages in professional development activities that positively correlate with the goals of the campus and district.

Things To Consider
- Professional development activities are directly related to the goals, the objectives and priorities of the campus or district.
- Professional development activities correlate to subject matter and past performance appraisal.
- Evidence of knowledge and skills from professional development activities are integrated in the instructional program.
- The teacher uses a variety of professional development models appropriate to the needs of students. (See Commissioner's Rules 153.1011(d)).

Quality: Look for evidence of alignment and strength through the Teacher Self-Report. How does the teacher make connections between goals and objectives, the professional development, and his/her own practice?

Quantity: Focus is on integrating practice, not the number of professional development activities. Information is primarily provided through the Teacher Self-Report.

Evaluation Criteria			
Exceeds Expectations	Proficient	Below Expectations	Unsatisfactory
QUALITY	**QUALITY**	**QUALITY**	**QUALITY**
Professional development activities consistently, thoughtfully, and positively correlate with the Teacher Self-Report and with the teacher's performance appraisal.	Professional development activities consistently correlate with the Teacher Self-Report and with the teacher's performance appraisal.	Professional development activities occasionally positively correlate with the Teacher Self-Report and/or with the teacher's performance appraisal.	Professional development activities rarely/never positively correlate with the Teacher Self-Report and/or with the teacher's performance appraisal.
Professional development activities consistently, positively and continuously correlate with the goals of the campus and the district.	Professional development activities correlate with the goals of the campus and the district.	Professional development activities occasionally positively correlate with the goals of the campus and the district.	Professional development activities rarely/never positively correlate with the goals of the campus and the district.
Professional development activities consistently result in significantly different, improved teaching and learning in the teacher's classroom.	Professional development activities result in different, improved teaching and learning in the teacher's classroom.	Professional development activities occasionally result in different, improved teaching and learning in the teacher's classroom.	Professional development activities rarely/never result in different, improved teaching and learning in the teacher's classroom.
Teacher consistently, continuously seeks out professional development opportunities, which are designed to improve teaching and learning.	Teacher seeks out professional development opportunities, which are designed to improve teaching and learning.	Teacher occasionally seeks out professional development opportunities, which are designed to improve teaching and learning.	Teacher rarely/never seeks out professional development opportunities, which are designed to improve teaching and learning.
Teacher choices for professional development consistently and continuously focus on better understanding of and improved practices for the unique needs and characteristics of students.	Teacher choices for professional development focus on better understanding of and improved practices for the unique needs and characteristics of students.	Teacher choices for professional development occasionally focus on better understanding of and improved practices for the unique needs and characteristics of students.	Teacher choices for professional development rarely/never focus on better understanding of and improved practices for the unique needs and characteristics of students.
The teacher provides formal/informal leadership in working constructively with other professionals for continuous growth and development toward meeting the needs of students and the goals of the campus/district.	The teacher works constructively with other professionals for continuous growth and development toward meeting the needs of students and the goals of the campus/district.	The teacher occasionally works constructively with other professionals for continuous growth and development toward meeting the needs of students and the goals of the campus/district.	The teacher rarely/never works constructively with other professionals for continuous growth and development toward meeting the needs of students and the goals of the campus/district.

Professional Development and Appraisal System

Revised June 2003

SCORING CRITERIA GUIDE

Performance at the "Proficient" Level is based upon documentary evidence, as appropriate.

Documentary evidence may be collected over the entire appraisal period.

Performance at the "Proficient" Level MAY be inferred for a criterion if 80% of the criteria in the Domain ARE documented at the "Proficient" or Exceeds Expectation Level and NO criteria are documented at Below Expectations or Unsatisfactory.

Domain VI-1 Continued

QUANTITY ALMOST ALL OF THE TIME (90-100%) The teacher successfully integrates professional development activities into instruction.	QUANTITY MOST OF THE TIME (80-89%) The teacher successfully integrates professional development activities into instruction.	QUANTITY SOME OF THE TIME (50-79%) The teacher successfully integrates professional development activities into instruction.	QUANTITY LESS THAN HALF OF THE TIME (0-49%) The teacher successfully integrates professional development activities into instruction.

Professional Development and Appraisal System

Revised June 2003

Scoring Criteria Guide

Page 42

SCORING CRITERIA GUIDE

Performance at the "Proficient" Level is based upon documentary evidence, as appropriate.

Documentary evidence may be collected over the entire appraisal period.

Performance at the "Proficient" Level MAY be inferred for a criterion if 80% of the criteria in the Domain ARE documented at the "Proficient" or Exceeds Expectation Level and NO criteria are documented at Below Expectations or Unsatisfactory.

Domain VI: Professional Development

VI-2. The teacher successfully correlates professional development activities with assigned subject content and the varied needs of students.

Things To Consider

- Professional development activities are directly related to the assigned grade level and/or subject content.
- Professional development activities are directly related to the needs of students.
- Evidence that knowledge and skills from professional development activities are integrated in the instructional program.

Quality: Look for evidence of strength, impact, variety and alignment through the Teacher Self-Report. The teacher makes connections between goals and objectives, the professional development, and his/her own practice.

Quantity: Focus is on integrating practice, not the number of professional development activities. Information is primarily provided through the Teacher Self-Report.

Evaluation Criteria

Exceeds Expectations	Proficient	Below Expectations	Unsatisfactory
QUALITY Professional development activities consistently result in significantly different, improved teaching and learning in the teacher's classroom.	**QUALITY** Professional development activities result in different, improved teaching and learning in the teacher's classroom.	**QUALITY** Professional development activities occasionally result in different, improved teaching and learning in the teacher's classroom.	**QUALITY** Professional development activities rarely/never result in different, improved teaching and learning in the teacher's classroom.
Professional development activities consistently, thoughtfully correlate with the Teacher Self-Report and with the teacher's performance appraisal.	Professional development activities correlate with the Teacher Self-Report and with the teacher's performance appraisal.	Professional development activities occasionally correlate with the Teacher Self-Report and/or with the teacher's performance appraisal.	Professional development activities rarely/never correlate with the Teacher Self-Report and/or with the teacher's performance appraisal.
Teacher consistently and continuously seeks out professional development opportunities, which are designed to improve teaching and learning in the content area and grade, level at which the teacher teaches.	Teacher seeks out professional development opportunities, which are designed to improve teaching and learning in the content area and grade, level at which the teacher teaches.	Teacher occasionally seeks out professional development opportunities, which are designed to improve teaching and learning in the content area and grade, level at which the teacher teaches.	Teacher rarely/never seeks out professional development opportunities, which are designed to improve teaching and learning in the content area and grade, level at which the teacher teaches.
Teacher choices for professional development consistently and continuously focus on better understanding of and improved practices for the unique needs and characteristics of students.	Teacher choices for professional development focus on better understanding of and improved practices for the unique needs and characteristics of students.	Teacher choices for professional development occasionally focus on better understanding of and improved practices for the unique needs and characteristics of students.	Teacher choices for professional development rarely/never focus on better understanding of and improved practices for the unique needs and characteristics of students.
The teacher takes a leadership role in working constructively with other professionals for continuous growth and development toward meeting the needs of students and the goals of the campus/district.	The teacher works constructively with other professionals for continuous growth and development toward meeting the needs of students and the goals of the campus/district.	The teacher occasionally works constructively with other professionals for continuous growth and development toward meeting the needs of students and the goals of the campus/district.	The teacher rarely/never works constructively with other professionals for continuous growth and development toward meeting the needs of students and the goals of the campus/district.
QUANTITY ALMOST ALL OF THE TIME (90-100%) The teacher engages in professional development activities that are related to the assigned grade level/subject area(s).	**QUANTITY** MOST OF THE TIME (80-89%). The teacher engages in professional development activities that are related to the assigned grade level/subject area(s).	**QUANTITY** SOME OF THE TIME (50-79%) The teacher engages in professional development activities that are related to the assigned grade level/subject area(s).	**QUANTITY** LESS THAN HALF OF THE TIME (0-49%) The teacher engages in professional development activities that are related to the assigned grade level/subject area(s).
The teacher engages in professional development activities that are directly related to the needs/characteristics of students.	The teacher engages in professional development activities that are directly related to the needs/characteristics of students.	The teacher engages in professional development activities that are directly related to the needs/characteristics of students.	The teacher engages in professional development activities that are directly related to the needs/characteristics of students.

SCORING CRITERIA GUIDE

Performance at the "Proficient" Level is based upon documentary evidence, as appropriate.
Documentary evidence may be collected over the entire appraisal period.
Performance at the "Proficient" Level MAY be inferred for a criterion if 80% of the criteria in the Domain ARE documented at the "Proficient" or Exceeds Expectation Level and NO criteria are documented at Below Expectations or Unsatisfactory.

Domain VI: Professional Development

VI-3. The teacher successfully engages in professional development activities that positively correlate with the prior performance appraisal.

Things To Consider
- Professional development activities directly relate to the teacher's prior performance appraisal or analysis of needs.
- Evidence that knowledge and skills from professional development activities are integrated in the instructional program.
- Continuous improvement.

Quality: Focus on how the teacher utilizes reflection and feedback for enhancing student learning. The teacher makes connections between prior performance/analysis of needs and his/her own professional development, and practice. Look for evidence of strength, impact, variety, and alignment through the Teacher Self-Report.

Quantity: Focus is on integrating practice, not the number of professional development activities. Information is primarily provided through the Teacher Self-Report.

Evaluation Criteria

Exceeds Expectations	Proficient	Below Expectations	Unsatisfactory
QUALITY Professional development activities consistently result in significantly different, improved teaching and learning in the teacher's classroom.	**QUALITY** Professional development activities result in different, improved teaching and learning in the teacher's classroom.	**QUALITY** Professional development activities occasionally result in different, improved teaching and learning in the teacher's classroom.	**QUALITY** Professional development activities rarely/never result in different, improved teaching and learning in the teacher's classroom.
Professional development activities consistently and continuously correlate with the goals of the campus and the district	Professional development activities correlate with the goals of the campus and the district.	Professional development activities occasionally correlate with the goals of the campus and the district.	Professional development activities rarely/never correlate with the goals of the campus and the district.
The teacher consistently and continuously seeks out professional development opportunities, which are designed to improve teaching and learning based on prior performance appraisal.	The teacher continuously seeks out professional development opportunities, which are designed to improve teaching and learning based on prior performance appraisal.	The teacher occasionally seeks out professional development opportunities, which are designed to improve teaching and learning based on prior performance appraisal.	The teacher rarely/never seeks out professional development opportunities, which are designed to improve teaching and learning based on prior performance appraisal.
Teacher choices for professional development continuously focus on better understanding of and improved practices for the unique needs and characteristics of students.	Teacher choices for professional development focus on better understanding of the unique needs and characteristics of students.	Teacher choices for professional development occasionally focus on better understanding of and improved practices for the unique needs and characteristics of students.	Teacher choices for professional development rarely/never focus on better understanding of and improved practices for the unique needs and characteristics of students.
QUANTITY **ALMOST ALL OF THE TIME (90-100%)** The teacher engages in professional development that is directly related to the teacher's prior performance appraisal or analysis of needs.	**QUANTITY** **MOST OF THE TIME (80-89 %)** The teacher engages in professional development that is directly related to the teacher's prior performance appraisal or analysis of needs.	**QUANTITY** **SOME OF THE TIME (50-79%)** The teacher engages in professional development that is directly related to the teacher's prior performance appraisal or analysis of needs.	**QUANTITY** **LESS THAN HALF OF THE TIME (0-49%)** The teacher engages in professional development that is directly related to the teacher's prior performance appraisal or analysis of needs.

SCORING CRITERIA GUIDE

Performance at the "Proficient" Level is based upon documentary evidence, as appropriate.

Documentary evidence may be collected over the entire appraisal period.

Performance at the "Proficient" Level MAY be inferred for a criterion if 80% of the criteria in the Domain ARE documented at the "Proficient" or Exceeds Expectation Level and NO criteria are documented at Below Expectations or Unsatisfactory.

Domain VI: Professional Development

VI-4. The teacher works collaboratively and constructively with colleagues and other professionals toward the overall improvement of student performance.

Things To Consider

- Teacher actively engages with colleagues in professional activities.
- Teacher engages in professional development activities in accordance with district/campus goals, objectives, policies, and directives.
- Collaborative activities are focused on improvement of student performance.

Quality: Look for evidence of strength, impact, variety, and alignment in implementation of knowledge and skills or collaborative activities, which impact overall student performance.

Quantity: Look for repeated evidence of formal/informal membership in collaborative partnerships or groups. Focus is on the appropriate level of participation/collaboration, not the number of groups or number of meetings.

Evaluation Criteria			
Exceeds Expectations	**Proficient**	**Below Expectations**	**Unsatisfactory**
QUALITY The teacher consistently works collaboratively and constructively with colleagues and other professionals toward the overall improvement of student performance.	**QUALITY** The teacher works collaboratively and constructively with colleagues and other professionals toward the overall improvement of student performance.	**QUALITY** The teacher occasionally works collaboratively and constructively with colleagues and other professionals toward the overall improvement of student performance.	**QUALITY** The teacher rarely/never works collaboratively and constructively with colleagues and other professionals toward the overall improvement of student performance.
Continuous collaborative professional development activities of the teacher consistently result in different, improved teaching and learning in the teacher's classroom and in the school.	Continuous collaborative professional development activities of the teacher result in different, improved teaching and learning in the teacher's classroom and in the school.	Continuous collaborative professional development activities of the teacher occasionally result in different, improved teaching and learning in the teacher's classroom and in the school.	Continuous collaborative professional development activities of the teacher rarely/never result in different, improved teaching and learning in the teacher's classroom and in the school.
The teacher consistently encourages, fosters and participates in collaborative professional development that furthers campus and district goals.	The teacher encourages, fosters and participates in collaborative professional development that furthers campus and district goals.	Professional development activities of the teacher occasionally positively correlate with the goals of the campus and the district.	Professional development activities of the teacher rarely/never positively correlate with the goals of the campus and the district.
QUANTITY **ALMOST ALL OF THE TIME (90-100%)** Teacher actively engages with colleagues in professional activities.	**QUANTITY** **MOST OF THE TIME (80-89%)** Teacher actively engages with colleagues in professional activities.	**QUANTITY** **SOME OF THE TIME (50-79%)** Teacher actively engages with colleagues in professional activities.	**QUANTITY** **LESS THAN HALF OF THE TIME (0-49%)** Teacher actively engages with colleagues in professional activities.
Teacher engages in professional development activities in accordance with district/campus goals, objectives, policies and directives.	Teacher engages in professional development activities in accordance with district/campus goals, objectives, policies and directives.	Teacher engages in professional development activities in accordance with district/campus goals, objectives, policies and directives.	Teacher engages in professional development activities in accordance with district/campus goals, objectives, policies and directives.

SCORING CRITERIA GUIDE

Performance at the "Proficient" Level is based upon documentary evidence, as appropriate.
Documentary evidence may be collected over the entire appraisal period.
Performance at the "Proficient" Level **MAY** be inferred for a criterion if 80% of the criteria in the Domain **ARE** documented at the "Proficient" or Exceeds Expectation Level and **NO** criteria are documented at Below Expectations or Unsatisfactory.

Domain VII: Compliance with Policies, Operating Procedures, and Requirements

VII-1. The teacher complies with all of the policies, operating procedures, and legal requirements (national, state, district, and campus). Any lack of compliance is rare, inadvertent, and does not seriously compromise the needs of students or the effective operations of the campus/district.

Things To Consider
- Teacher complies with all policies.
- Teacher complies with all procedures.
- Teacher complies with all legal requirements.

Quality: Look for impact and strength of non-compliance on the needs of the students. Look for impact and strength of non-compliance on the effective operation of the campus/district.

Evaluation Criteria			
Exceeds Expectations	Proficient	Below Expectations	Unsatisfactory
QUALITY The teacher consistently provides formal/informal leadership in developing; communicating; interpreting; applying policies, operating procedures, and/or legal requirements (national, state, district, and campus).	QUALITY The teacher complies with all the policies, operating procedures, and legal requirements (national, state, district, and campus).	QUALITY The teacher occasionally complies with all the policies, operating procedures, and legal requirements (national, state, district, and campus). **Any lack of compliance is rare, inadvertent, and/or does not seriously compromise the needs of students or the effective and legal operation of the campus/district.**	QUALITY The teacher rarely/never complies with all the policies, operating procedures, and legal requirements (national, state, district, and campus). **The lack of compliance is frequent and/or seriously compromises the needs of students and/or the effective and legal operation of the campus/district.**

NOTE: (1) The "Proficient" Standard in the Domain is HIGHER due to needs for consistency and safety. Exceeds Expectations requires participation in the development of discipline and other management procedures.

Revised June 2003

414

SCORING CRITERIA GUIDE

Performance at the "Proficient" Level is based upon documentary evidence, as appropriate.
Documentary evidence may be collected over the entire appraisal period.
Performance at the "Proficient" Level MAY be inferred for a criterion if 80% of the criteria in the Domain ARE documented at the "Proficient" or Exceeds Expectation Level and NO criteria are documented at Below Expectations or Unsatisfactory.

Domain VII: Compliance with Policies, Operating Procedures, and Requirements
VII-2. The teacher generally complies with all of the verbal and written directives. Any lack of compliance is rare, inadvertent, and does not seriously compromise the needs of students or the effective operations of the campus/district.

Things To Consider
- Teacher compliance with all verbal directives.
- Teacher compliance with all written directives.

Quality: Impact and strength of non-compliance on the needs of the students. Impact and strength of non-compliance on the effective operation of the campus/district.

Evaluation Criteria

Exceeds Expectations	Proficient	Below Expectations	Unsatisfactory
QUALITY The teacher consistently complies with all verbal and written directives.	QUALITY The teacher complies with all verbal and written directives.	QUALITY The teacher occasionally complies with all verbal and written directives. **Any lack of compliance with verbal and written directives is rare, inadvertent, and/or does not seriously compromise the needs of students or the effective and legal operation of the campus/district.**	QUALITY The teacher rarely/never complies with all verbal and written directives. **The lack of compliance with verbal and written directives is frequent and/or seriously compromises the needs of students and/or the effective and legal operation of the campus/district.**
The teacher consistently provides formal/informal leadership in developing; communicating; interpreting; applying verbal and written directives.	The teacher provides formal/informal leadership in developing; communicating; interpreting; applying verbal and written directives.	The teacher occasionally participates in developing; communicating; interpreting; applying verbal and written directives.	The teacher rarely/never participates in developing; communicating; interpreting; applying verbal and written directives.

NOTE: (1) The "Proficient" Standard in the Domain is HIGHER due to needs for consistency and safety.
Exceeds Expectations requires participation in the development of discipline and other management procedures.

Professional Development and Appraisal System

SCORING CRITERIA GUIDE

Performance at the "Proficient" Level is based upon documentary evidence, as appropriate.
Documentary evidence may be collected over the entire appraisal period.
Performance at the "Proficient" Level MAY be inferred for a criterion if 80% of the criteria in the Domain ARE documented at the "Proficient" or Exceeds Expectation Level and NO criteria are documented at Below Expectations or Unsatisfactory.

Domain VII: Compliance with Policies, Operating Procedures, and Requirements
VII-3. Apart from classroom responsibilities, the teacher generally contributes to making the whole school safe and orderly, and a stimulating learning environment for all children.

Things To Consider
- Teacher contributes to making the whole school safe.
- Teacher contributes to making the whole school orderly.
- Teacher contributes to creating a stimulating environment.

Quality: Teacher contributes to establishing a secure and supportive environment. Teacher is highly visible. Teacher intervenes appropriately to maintain a safe, orderly school environment.

Evaluation Criteria

Exceeds Expectations	Proficient	Below Expectations	Unsatisfactory
QUALITY	QUALITY	QUALITY	QUALITY
The teacher consistently and continuously contributes to making the school a safe and orderly environment for all students.	The teacher contributes to making the school a safe and orderly environment for all students.	The teacher occasionally contributes to making the school a safe and orderly environment for all students.	The teacher rarely/never contributes to making the school a safe and orderly environment for all students.
The teacher consistently and continuously contributes to making the school a stimulating environment for all students.	The teacher contributes to making the school a stimulating environment for all students.	The teacher occasionally contributes to making the school a stimulating environment for all students.	The teacher rarely/never contributes to making the school a stimulating environment for all students.
The teacher consistently takes appropriate, professional initiative to monitor and supervise students.	The teacher takes appropriate, professional initiative to monitor and supervise students.	The teacher occasionally takes appropriate, professional initiative to monitor and supervise students.	The teacher rarely/never takes appropriate, professional initiative to monitor and supervise students.
The teacher is consistently visible in areas of the school where students gather or are likely to gather.	The teacher is visible in areas of the school where students gather or are likely to gather.	The teacher is occasionally visible in areas of the school where students gather or are likely to gather.	The teacher is rarely/never visible in areas of the school where students gather or are likely to gather.
The teacher consistently takes appropriate initiatives to make the school a stimulating environment for students.	The teacher takes appropriate initiatives to make the school a stimulating environment for students.	Teacher occasionally takes appropriate initiatives to make the school a stimulating environment for students.	Teacher rarely/never takes appropriate initiatives to make the school a stimulating environment for students.
Teacher consistently takes actions, which make the school a positive environment for students.	Teacher takes actions, which make the school a positive environment for students.	Teacher occasionally takes actions, which make the school a positive environment for students.	Teacher rarely/never takes actions, which make the school a positive environment for students.

NOTE: (1) The "Proficient" Standard in the Domain is HIGHER due to needs for consistency and safety.
Exceeds Expectations requires participation in the development of discipline and other management procedures.

SCORING CRITERIA GUIDE

Performance at the "Proficient" Level is based upon documentary evidence, as appropriate.

Documentary evidence may be collected over the entire appraisal period.

Performance at the "Proficient" Level **MAY** be inferred for a criterion if 80% of the criteria in the Domain **ARE** documented at the "Proficient" or Exceeds Expectation Level and **NO** criteria are documented at <u>Below Expectations</u> or <u>Unsatisfactory</u>.

Domain VIII: Improvement of Academic Performance for All Students on the Campus (Based on Indicators included in the AEIS)

VIII.A-1. The teacher aligns instruction to include appropriate TEKS/TAKS objectives to support student achievement in all assigned classes.

Things To Consider
- Teacher instruction of TEKS/TAKS objectives connected to the subject matter and content.
- Instructional planning reflects the inclusion of TEKS/TAKS objectives connected to the subject matter and content.

Quality: Look for appropriate connections to the subject matter and content. Look for strength, impact, variety, and alignment of instructional delivery to TEKS/TAKS objectives.

Quantity: All classes receive instruction on appropriate TEKS/TAKS objectives.

Evaluation Criteria

Exceeds Expectations	Proficient	Below Expectations	Unsatisfactory
QUALITY There is consistent evidence of student success in using/applying the skills supportive of the TEKS/TAKS objectives in the curriculum. TEKS/TAKS objectives are consistently integrated in to regular subject matter and content.	**QUALITY** There is evidence of student success in using/applying the skills supportive of the TEKS/TAKS objectives in the curriculum. TEKS/TAKS objectives are integrated in to regular subject matter and content.	**QUALITY** There is occasional evidence of student success in using/applying the skills supportive of the TEKS/TAKS objectives in the curriculum.	**QUALITY** There is little/no evidence of student success in using/applying the skills supportive of the TEKS/TAKS objectives in the curriculum.
QUANTITY **ALMOST ALL OF THE TIME (90-100%)** The teacher aligns instruction to appropriate TEKS/TAKS objectives in all assigned classes.	**QUANTITY** **MOST OF THE TIME (80-89%)** The teacher aligns instruction to appropriate TEKS/TAKS objectives in all assigned classes.	**QUANTITY** **SOME OF THE TIME (50-79%)** The teacher aligns instruction to appropriate TEKS/TAKS objectives in all assigned classes.	**QUANTITY** **LESS THAN HALF OF THE TIME (0-49%)** The teacher aligns instruction to appropriate TEKS/TAKS objectives in all assigned classes.
TEKS/TAKS objectives are integrated in to regular subject matter and content.	TEKS/TAKS objectives are integrated in to regular subject matter and content.	TEKS/TAKS objectives are integrated in to regular subject matter and content.	TEKS/TAKS objectives are integrated in to regular subject matter and content.

SCORING CRITERIA GUIDE

Performance at the "Proficient" Level is based upon documentary evidence, as appropriate.

Documentary evidence may be collected over the entire appraisal period.

Performance at the "Proficient" Level MAY be inferred for a criterion if 80% of the criteria in the Domain ARE documented at the "Proficient" or Exceeds Expectation Level and NO criteria are documented at Below Expectations or Unsatisfactory.

Domain VIII: Improvement of Academic Performance for All Students on the Campus (Based on Indicators included in the AEIS)

VIII.A-2. The teacher analyzes TAKS performance data relevant to all students in assigned classes prior to beginning instruction.

Things To Consider

- Instructional planning reflects an analysis of TAKS performance data.
- TAKS performance data is analyzed prior to beginning instruction.

Quality: Individual student needs are addressed.

          Documentary evidence is used to support performance level.

Quantity: TAKS performance data is relevant for all assigned students.

Evaluation Criteria			
Exceeds Expectations	**Proficient**	**Below Expectations**	**Unsatisfactory**
QUALITY Instructional planning consistently reflects that TAKS performance data has been analyzed in collaboration with other professionals prior to the beginning of instruction.	**QUALITY** Instructional planning reflects that TAKS performance data has been analyzed prior to the beginning of instruction.	**QUALITY** Instructional planning occasionally reflects that TAKS performance data has been analyzed prior to the beginning of instruction.	**QUALITY** Instructional planning rarely/never reflects that TAKS performance data has been analyzed prior to the beginning of instruction.
The teacher provides formal/informal leadership in instructional planning which consistently shows evidence of addressing individual student needs as identified in the campus improvement plan.	Instructional planning shows evidence of addressing individual student needs as identified in the campus improvement plan.	Instructional planning shows occasional evidence of addressing individual student needs as identified in the campus improvement plan.	Instructional planning shows little or no evidence of addressing individual student needs as identified in the campus improvement plan.
QUANTITY **ALMOST ALL OF THE TIME (90-100%)** The teacher analyzes TAKS performance data relevant to all students in assigned classes prior to beginning instruction.	**QUANTITY** **MOST OF THE TIME (80-89%)** The teacher analyzes TAKS performance data relevant to all students in assigned classes prior to beginning instruction.	**QUANTITY** **SOME OF THE TIME (50-79%)** The teacher analyzes TAKS performance data relevant to all students in assigned classes prior to beginning instruction.	**QUANTITY** **LESS THAN HALF OF THE TIME (0-49%)** The teacher analyzes TAKS performance data relevant to all students in assigned classes prior to beginning instruction.
The teacher acts on the analyzed data by incorporating TEKS/TAKS objectives for remediation and/or reinforcement into all regular subject matter and content.	The teacher acts on the analyzed data by incorporating TEKS/TAKS objectives for remediation and/or reinforcement into all subject matter and content.	The teacher acts on the analyzed data by incorporating TEKS/TAKS objectives for remediation and/or reinforcement into all subject matter and content.	The teacher acts on the analyzed data by incorporating TEKS/TAKS objectives for remediation and/or reinforcement into all subject matter and content.

Revised June 2003

418

SCORING CRITERIA GUIDE

Performance at the "Proficient" Level is based upon documentary evidence, as appropriate.
Documentary evidence may be collected over the entire appraisal period.
Performance at the "Proficient" Level MAY be inferred for a criterion if 80% of the criteria in the Domain ARE documented at the "Proficient" or Exceeds Expectation Level and NO criteria are documented at Below Expectations or Unsatisfactory.

Domain VIII: Improvement of Academic Performance for All Students on the Campus (Based on Indicators included in the AEIS)

VIII.A-3. The teacher adjusts the sequencing of classroom instruction to appropriately incorporate TEKS/TAKS objectives.

Things To Consider
- Instructional delivery shows evidence of task analysis of TAKS performance data.
- Teacher adjusts the classroom content to include TEKS/TAKS objectives.
- Teacher adjusts the sequence of instruction in response to the timing of the TAKS test administration.

Quality: Look for the appropriateness of the sequence adjustment. Look for strength, impact, variety, and alignment of the sequence with the TAKS test administration.
Quantity: Adjustments are relevant for all students.

Evaluation Criteria

Exceeds Expectations	Proficient	Below Expectations	Unsatisfactory
QUALITY The teacher collaborates and/or provides formal/informal leadership, which encourages other colleagues to align classroom content, and sequence of instruction with skills supportive of the TEKS/TAKS objectives across content areas and grade levels.	**QUALITY** The teacher aligns classroom content and sequence of instruction with the skills supportive of the TEKS/TAKS objectives.	**QUALITY** The teacher occasionally aligns classroom content and sequence of instruction with the skills supportive of the TEKS/TAKS objectives.	**QUALITY** The teacher rarely/never aligns classroom content and sequence of instruction with the skills supportive of the TEKS/TAKS objectives.
There is consistent evidence that indicates student success has resulted due to appropriate sequence and alignment of the skills supportive of the TEKS/TAKS objectives.	There is evidence that indicates student success has resulted due to appropriate sequence and alignment of the skills supportive of the TEKS/TAKS objectives.	There is some evidence that indicates student success has resulted due to appropriate sequence and alignment of the skills supportive of the TEKS/TAKS objectives.	There is little/ no evidence that indicates student success has resulted due to appropriate sequence and alignment of the skills supportive of the TEKS/TAKS objectives.
Student needs as identified in the Campus Improvement Plan are consistently reflected in the sequence of instruction and instructional delivery.	Student needs as identified in the Campus Improvement Plan are reflected in the sequence of instruction and instructional delivery.	Student needs as identified in the Campus Improvement Plan are occasionally reflected in the sequence of instruction and instructional delivery.	Student needs as identified in the Campus Improvement Plan are rarely/never reflected in the sequence of instruction and instructional delivery.
QUANTITY **ALMOST ALL OF THE TIME (90-100%)** The teacher adjusts the sequencing of classroom instruction for all students to appropriately incorporate TEKS/TAKS objectives.	**QUANTITY** **MOST OF THE TIME (80-89%)** The teacher adjusts the sequencing of classroom instruction for all students to appropriately incorporate TEKS/TAKS objectives.	**QUANTITY** **SOME OF THE TIME (50-79%)** The teacher adjusts the sequencing of classroom instruction for all students to appropriately incorporate TEKS/TAKS objectives.	**QUANTITY** **LESS THAN HALF OF THE TIME (0-49%)** The teacher adjusts the sequencing of classroom instruction for all students to appropriately incorporate TEKS/TAKS objectives.
Skills supportive of the TEKS/TAKS objectives are integrated into all subject areas.	Skills supportive of the TEKS/TAKS objectives are integrated into all subject areas.	Skills supportive of the TEKS/TAKS objectives are integrated into all subject areas.	Skills supportive of the TEKS/TAKS objectives are integrated into all subject areas.

419

SCORING CRITERIA GUIDE

Performance at the "Proficient" Level is based upon documentary evidence, as appropriate.

Documentary evidence may be collected over the entire appraisal period.

Performance at the "Proficient" Level MAY be inferred for a criterion if 80% of the criteria in the Domain **ARE** documented at the "Proficient" or Exceeds Expectation Level and **NO** criteria are documented at Below Expectations or Unsatisfactory.

Domain VIII: Improvement of Academic Performance for All Students on the Campus (Based on Indicators included in the AEIS)

VIII.A-4. The teacher selects/adapts instructional materials and activities that are correlated with appropriate TEKS/TAKS objectives.

Things To Consider
- Teacher selects/adapts materials and techniques to support TEKS/TAKS objectives.
- Teacher selects/adapts activities and strategies to support TEKS/TAKS objectives.
- Teacher selects/adapts materials, techniques, activities, and strategies appropriate for the unique needs/characteristics of the students to support TEKS/TAKS objectives.

Quality: Look for strength, impact, variety, and alignment of strategies/techniques with appropriate TEKS/TAKS objectives.

        Look for strength, impact, variety, and alignment of material with appropriate TEKS/TAKS objectives.

        Look for strength, impact, variety, and alignment of activities with appropriate TEKS/TAKS objectives.

Quantity: All materials and activities are appropriate.

Evaluation Criteria

Exceeds Expectations	Proficient	Below Expectations	Unsatisfactory
QUALITY The teacher consistently utilizes a variety of creative, unique, and/or innovative instructional materials and techniques that are supportive of the skills that are correlated to the TEKS/TAKS objectives.	**QUALITY** The teacher utilizes instructional materials and techniques, which are supportive of the skills that are correlated with appropriate TEKS/TAKS objectives.	**QUALITY** The teacher occasionally utilizes instructional materials and techniques, which are supportive of the skills that are correlated with appropriate TEKS/TAKS objectives.	**QUALITY** The teacher rarely/never utilizes instructional materials and techniques, which are supportive of the skills that are correlated with appropriate TEKS/TAKS objectives.
The teacher consistently utilizes a variety of creative, unique, and/or innovative instructional strategies and activities, which are supportive of the skills that are correlated to the TEKS/TAKS objectives.	The teacher utilizes instructional strategies and activities, which are supportive of the skills that are correlated with appropriate TEKS/TAKS objectives.	The teacher occasionally utilizes instructional strategies and activities, which are supportive of the skills that are correlated with appropriate TEKS/TAKS objectives.	The teacher rarely/never utilizes instructional strategies and activities, which are supportive of the skills that are correlated with appropriate TEKS/TAKS objectives.
The teacher consistently utilizes a variety of creative, unique, and/or innovative instructional materials and techniques that are selected because of their relevance to the unique characteristics of the students.	The teacher utilizes instructional materials and techniques that are selected because of their relevance to the unique needs/characteristics of the students.	The teacher occasionally utilizes instructional materials and techniques that are selected because of their relevance to the unique needs/characteristics of the students.	The teacher rarely/never utilizes instructional materials and techniques that are selected because of their relevance to the unique needs/characteristics of the students.
QUANTITY **ALMOST ALL OF THE TIME (90-100%)** The teacher selects/adapts instructional materials and activities that are correlated with appropriate TEKS/TAKS objectives.	**QUANTITY** **MOST OF THE TIME (80-89%)** The teacher selects/adapts instructional materials and activities that are correlated with appropriate TEKS/TAKS objectives.	**QUANTITY** **SOME OF THE TIME (50-79%)** The teacher selects/adapts instructional materials and activities that are correlated with appropriate TEKS/TAKS objectives.	**QUANTITY** **LESS THAN HALF OF THE TIME (0-49%)** The teacher selects/adapts instructional materials and activities that are correlated with appropriate TEKS/TAKS objectives.
Students are successful in learning the skills supportive of the TEKS/TAKS objectives.	Students are successful in learning the skills supportive of the TEKS/TAKS objectives.	Students are successful in learning the skills supportive of the TEKS/TAKS objectives.	Students are successful in learning the skills supportive of the TEKS/TAKS objectives.

SCORING CRITERIA GUIDE

Performance at the "Proficient" Level is based upon documentary evidence, as appropriate.
Documentary evidence may be collected over the entire appraisal period.
Performance at the "Proficient" Level **MAY** be inferred for a criterion if 80% of the criteria in the Domain **ARE** documented at the "Proficient" or Exceeds Expectation Level and **NO** criteria are documented at Below Expectations or Unsatisfactory.

Domain VIII: Improvement of Academic Performance for All Students on the Campus (*)

VIII.A-5. The teacher provides feedback to all students regarding their learning progress on appropriate TEKS/TAKS objectives.

Things To Consider
- Teacher instruction demonstrates awareness of TEKS/TAKS objectives appropriate to the content, subject matter, grade level, and curriculum.
- Feedback is provided and provisions made for students to use the feedback in their learning.

Quality: Appropriate TEKS/TAKS objectives are addressed.
          Students are aware of their learning progress on TEKS/TAKS objectives.
Quantity: Feedback is consistently provided in a timely manner.

Evaluation Criteria

Exceeds Expectations	Proficient	Below Expectations	Unsatisfactory
QUALITY The teacher consistently provides a variety of creative, unique, and/or innovative activities and opportunities for students to use feedback to help them improve their performance on the skills supportive of the TEKS/TAKS objectives.	**QUALITY** The teacher provides activities and opportunities for students to use feedback to help them improve their performance on the skills supportive of the TEKS/TAKS objectives.	**QUALITY** The teacher occasionally provides activities and opportunities for students to use feedback to help them improve their performance on the skills supportive of the TEKS/TAKS objectives.	**QUALITY** The teacher rarely/never provides activities and opportunities for students to use feedback to help them improve their performance on the skills supportive of the TEKS/TAKS objectives.
The teacher consistently provides a variety of creative, unique, and/or innovative activities and strategies to help students understand their own strengths and weaknesses on skills supportive of TEKS/TAKS objectives.	Feedback on performance provided by the teacher helps students understand their own strengths and weaknesses on skills supportive of the TEKS/TAKS objectives.	Feedback on performance provided by the teacher occasionally helps students understand their own strengths and weaknesses on skills supportive of the TEKS/TAKS objectives.	Feedback on performance provided by the teacher rarely/never helps students understand their own strengths and weaknesses on skills supportive of the TEKS/TAKS objectives.
QUANTITY **ALMOST ALL OF THE TIME (90-100%)** The teacher provides timely feedback to all students regarding their learning progress on appropriate TEKS/TAKS objectives.	**QUANTITY** **MOST OF THE TIME (80-89%)** The teacher provides timely feedback to all students regarding their learning progress on appropriate TEKS/TAKS objectives.	**QUANTITY** **SOME OF THE TIME (50-79%)** The teacher provides timely feedback to all students regarding their learning progress on appropriate TEKS/TAKS objectives.	**QUANTITY** **LESS THAN HALF OF THE TIME (0-49%)** The teacher provides timely feedback to all students regarding their learning progress on appropriate TEKS/TAKS objectives.

* For the 2003-2004 school year, the campus performance rating will be the district performance rating as reported in the new accountability system, when determined by the State. The rating will be used **for reporting purposes only.**

Scoring Criteria Guide

Professional Development and Appraisal System

Revised June 2003

Page 53

SCORING CRITERIA GUIDE

Performance at the "Proficient" Level is based upon documentary evidence, as appropriate.

Documentary evidence may be collected over the entire appraisal period.

Performance at the "Proficient" Level MAY be inferred for a criterion if 80% of the criteria in the Domain ARE documented at the "Proficient" or Exceeds Expectation Level and NO criteria are documented at Below Expectations or Unsatisfactory.

Domain VIII: Improvement of Academic Performance for All Students on the Campus (*)

VIII.B-6. The teacher monitors attendance of all students in assigned classes and contacts parents, counselors, and other school officials for students with serious attendance problems.

Things To Consider (**)

- Teacher maintains accurate attendance records and identifies chronic attendance problems that affect student learning.
- Teacher works with appropriate staff to improve student attendance.
- Teacher works with students and parents to improve student attendance.

Quality: Teacher identifies and implements strategies/techniques that promote regular attendance.

Quantity: Teacher monitors attendance of all students.

Evaluation Criteria			
Exceeds Expectations	**Proficient**	**Below Expectations**	**Unsatisfactory**
QUALITY The teacher consistently identifies and implements creative, unique, and/or innovative strategies/techniques that promote attendance.	**QUALITY** The teacher identifies and implements strategies/techniques that promote attendance.	**QUALITY** The teacher occasionally identifies and implements strategies/techniques that promote attendance.	**QUALITY** The teacher rarely/never identifies and implements strategies/techniques that promote attendance.
The teacher consistently establishes on-going partnerships with parents/other school officials to improve attendance.	The teacher establishes on-going partnerships with parents/other school officials to improve attendance.	The teacher occasionally establishes on-going partnerships with parents/other school officials to improve attendance.	The teacher rarely/never establishes partnerships with parents/other school officials to improve attendance.
The teacher consistently establishes appropriate relationships with individual students, which result in improved attendance.	The teacher establishes appropriate relationships with individual students, which results in improved attendance.	The teacher occasionally establishes appropriate relationships with individual students, which results in improved attendance.	The teacher rarely/never establishes appropriate relationships with individual students, which results in improved attendance.
There is consistent improvement in the attendance of significant number of students.	There is improvement in the attendance of significant number of students.	There is occasional improvement in the attendance of significant number of students.	There is little or no improvement in the attendance of significant number of students.
The teacher consistently modifies the classroom-learning environment to encourage student attendance. Improvement in attendance results.	The teacher modifies the classroom-learning environment to encourage student attendance. Improvement in attendance results.	The teacher occasionally modifies the classroom environment to encourage student attendance. Some improvement in attendance results.	The teacher rarely/never modifies the classroom environment to encourage student attendance. Little/no improvement in attendance results.
The teacher consistently modifies the curriculum and instruction to encourage student attendance. Improvement in attendance results.	The teacher modifies the curriculum and instruction to encourage student attendance. Improvement in attendance results.	The teacher occasionally modifies the curriculum and instruction to encourage student attendance. Some improvement in attendance results.	The teacher rarely/never modifies the curriculum and instruction to encourage student attendance. Little/no improvement in attendance results.
QUANTITY ALMOST ALL OF THE TIME (90-100%) **The teacher monitors attendance of all students in assigned classes and contacts parents, counselors, and other school officials for students with serious attendance problems.**	**QUANTITY** MOST OF THE TIME (80-89%) The teacher monitors attendance of all students in assigned classes and contacts parents, counselors, and other school officials for students with serious attendance problems.	**QUANTITY** SOME OF THE TIME (50-79%) The teacher monitors attendance of all students in assigned classes and contacts parents, counselors, and other school officials for students with serious attendance problems.	**QUANTITY** LESS THAN HALF OF THE TIME (0-49%) The teacher monitors attendance of all students in assigned classes and contacts parents, counselors, and other school officials for students with serious attendance problems.
The teacher maintains accurate records and reports on student attendance.	The teacher maintains accurate records and reports on attendance.	The teacher maintains accurate records and reports on student attendance.	The teacher maintains accurate records and reports on student attendance.

* For the 2003-2004 school year, the campus performance rating will be the district performance rating as reported in the new accountability system, when determined by the State. The rating will be used **for reporting purposes only.**

** Although attendance is not a criteria indicator in the state accountability campus rating, the academic performance of students is largely dependent on being present in school.

SCORING CRITERIA GUIDE

Performance at the "Proficient" Level is based upon documentary evidence, as appropriate.
Documentary evidence may be collected over the entire appraisal period.
Performance at the "Proficient" Level **MAY** be inferred for a criterion if 80% of the criteria in the Domain **ARE** documented at the "Proficient" or <u>Exceeds</u> Expectation Level and **NO** criteria are documented at <u>Below</u> Expectations or <u>Unsatisfactory</u>.

Domain VIII: Improvement of Academic Performance for All Students on the Campus (*)

VIII.C-7. The teacher identifies and assesses the needs of assigned students who are in at-risk situations.

Things To Consider
- Teacher assesses instructional needs of students in at-risk situations.
- Teacher uses appropriate strategies to improve learning for students in at-risk-situations.

Quality: Teacher ensures that all students in special populations are provided opportunities to succeed. Teacher monitors the progress of students in at-risk situations. Look for impact and alignment of strategies with needs of students in at-risk situations.

Quantity: Teacher consistently meets the needs of students in at-risk situations.

Evaluation Criteria

Exceeds Expectations	Proficient	Below Expectations	Unsatisfactory
QUALITY The teacher consistently identifies and assesses the needs of students who are in at-risk situations.	**QUALITY** The teacher identifies and assesses the needs of students who are in at-risk situations.	**QUALITY** The teacher occasionally identifies and assesses the needs of students who are in at-risk situations.	**QUALITY** The teacher rarely/never identifies and assesses the needs of students who are in at-risk situations.
The teacher consistently identifies and implements creative, unique, and/or innovative strategies/techniques that result in significant changes in success/behavior for students who are are in at-risk situations.	The teacher identifies and implements strategies/techniques that result in changes in success/behavior for students who are in at-risk situations.	The teacher occasionally identifies and implements strategies/techniques that result in some changes in success/behavior for students who are in at-risk situations.	The teacher rarely/ never identifies and implements strategies/techniques; there are almost no/no changes in success/behavior for students who are in at-risk situations.
The teacher consistently establishes on-going partnerships with parents/other school officials that result in changes in success/behavior for students who are in at-risk situations.	The teacher establishes on-going partnerships with parents/other school officials that result in changes in success/behavior for students who are in at-risk situations.	The teacher occasionally establishes on-going partnerships with parents/other school officials that result in some changes in success/behavior for students who are in at-risk situations.	The teacher rarely/never establishes on-going partnerships with parents/other school officials that result in almost no/no changes in success/behavior for students who are in at-risk situations.
The teacher consistently establishes appropriate relationships with individual students that result in changes in success/behavior for students who are in at-risk situations.	The teacher establishes appropriate relationships with individual students that result in changes in success/behavior for students who are in at-risk situations.	The teacher occasionally establishes appropriate relationships with individual students that result in changes in success/behavior for students who are in at-risk situations.	The teacher rarely/never establishes appropriate relationships with individual students that result in changes in success/behavior for students who are in at-risk situations.
QUANTITY <u>ALMOST ALL OF THE TIME (90-100%)</u> The teacher identifies and assesses the needs of assigned students who are in at-risk situations.	**QUANTITY** <u>MOST OF THE TIME (80-89%)</u> The teacher identifies and assesses the needs of assigned students who are in at-risk situations.	**QUANTITY** <u>SOME OF THE TIME (50-79%)</u> The teacher identifies and assesses the needs of assigned students who are in at-risk situations.	**QUANTITY** <u>LESS THAN HALF OF THE TIME (0-49%)</u> **The teacher identifies and assesses the needs of assigned students who are in at-risk situations.**
The teacher takes action to meet the needs of assigned students who are in at-risk situations.	The teacher takes action to meet the needs of assigned students who are in at-risk situations.	The teacher takes action to meet the needs of assigned students who are in at-risk situations.	The teacher takes action to meet the needs of assigned students who are in at-risk situations.

---

* For the 2003-2004 school year, the campus performance rating will be the district performance rating as reported in the new accountability system, when determined by the State. The rating will be used **for reporting purposes only.**

SCORING CRITERIA GUIDE

Performance at the "Proficient" Level is based upon documentary evidence, as appropriate.
Documentary evidence may be collected over the entire appraisal period.
Performance at the "Proficient" Level MAY be inferred for a criterion if 80% of the criteria in the Domain ARE documented at the
"Proficient" or Exceeds Expectation Level and NO criteria are documented at Below Expectations or Unsatisfactory.

Domain VIII: Improvement of Academic Performance for All Students on the Campus (*)

VIII.C-8. The teacher meets with students who are failing or in danger of failing and develops an appropriate plan for intervention.

Things To Consider
- Teacher meets with students who are experiencing failure.
- Teacher develops short-term and long-term educational plans.

Quality: Intervention plan meets the needs of individual students. Teacher meets individually with students who are experiencing failure. Look for strength, impact, variety, and alignment of intervention plan activities with student needs.

Quantity: Focus on the results of interactions, not the number of interactions.

Evaluation Criteria			
Exceeds Expectations	**Proficient**	**Below Expectation**	**Unsatisfactory**
QUALITY The teacher consistently works cooperatively with students who are failing/in danger of failing to develop and implement a plan for intervention that results in improved student performance.	QUALITY The teacher works cooperatively with students who are failing/in danger of failing to develop and implement a plan for intervention that results in improved student performance.	QUALITY The teacher occasionally works cooperatively with students who are failing/in danger of failing to develop and implement a plan for intervention that results in improved student performance.	QUALITY The teacher rarely/never works cooperatively with students who are failing/in danger of failing to implement a plan for intervention.
Carrying out the plan consistently results in significantly improved performance for most students.	Carrying out the plan results in significantly improved performance for most students.	Carrying out the plan occasionally results in some improved performance for some students.	Carrying out the plan rarely/never results in little or no improvement in performance for most students.
The teacher consistently establishes on-going partnerships with parents/other school officials to improve student performance.	The teacher establishes on-going partnerships with parents/other school officials to improve student performance.	The teacher occasionally establishes on-going partnerships with parents/other school officials to improve student performance.	The teacher rarely/never establishes on-going partnerships with parents/other school officials to improve student performance.
The teacher consistently establishes appropriate relationships with individual students that result in improved performance.	The teacher establishes appropriate relationships with individual students that result in improved performance.	The teacher occasionally establishes appropriate relationships with individual students that result in improved performance.	The teacher rarely/never establishes appropriate relationships with individual students that result in improved performance.
QUANTITY ALMOST ALL OF THE TIME (90-100%) The teacher meets with students who are failing or in danger of failing and develops an appropriate plan for intervention.	QUANTITY MOST OF THE TIME (80-89%) The teacher meets with students who are failing or in danger of failing and develops an appropriate plan for intervention.	QUANTITY SOME OF THE TIME (50-79%) The teacher meets with students who are failing or in danger of failing and develops an appropriate plan for intervention.	QUANTITY LESS THAN HALF OF THE TIME (0-49%) The teacher meets with students who are failing or in danger of failing and develops an appropriate plan for intervention.

* For the 2003-2004 school year, the campus performance rating will be the district performance rating as reported in the new accountability system, when determined by the State. The rating will be used **for reporting purposes only.**

Scoring Criteria Guide

Professional Development and Appraisal System

Revised June 2003

Page 56

SCORING CRITERIA GUIDE

Performance at the "Proficient" Level is based upon documentary evidence, as appropriate.

Documentary evidence may be collected over the entire appraisal period.

Performance at the "Proficient" Level MAY be inferred for a criterion if 80% of the criteria in the Domain ARE documented at the "Proficient" or Exceeds Expectation Level and NO criteria are documented at Below Expectations or Unsatisfactory.

Domain VIII: Improvement of Academic Performance for All Students on the Campus (*)

VIII.C-9. The teacher modifies and adapts classroom materials and/or instruction for students in at-risk situations.

Things To Consider
- Teacher modifies/adapts materials for students in at-risk situations.
- Teacher modifies/adapts instruction for students in at-risk situations.

Quality: Materials and instruction are appropriate for students in at-risk situations. Teacher is proactive in seeking out resources. Look for strength, impact, variety, and alignment of materials/instruction with specific risk factors and learning styles of students in at-risk situations.

Quantity: Focus on the presence or absence of modifications/adaptations, when needed, for students in at-risk situations.

Evaluation Criteria

Exceeds Expectations	Proficient	Below Expectations	Unsatisfactory
QUALITY The teacher consistently modifies the classroom learning environment; resulting in changes in success/behavior for students who are in at-risk situations.	**QUALITY** The teacher modifies the classroom learning environment; resulting in changes in success/behavior for students who are in at-risk situations.	**QUALITY** The teacher occasionally modifies the classroom learning environment; resulting in some success/behavior change for students who are in at-risk situations.	**QUALITY** The teacher rarely/never modifies the classroom-learning environment, resulting in little/no success/behavior change for students who are in at-risk situations.
The teacher modifies the curriculum, instruction, and materials that consistently result in changes in success/behavior for students who are in risk situations.	The teacher modifies the curriculum, instruction, and materials that result in changes in success/behavior for students who are in at-risk situations.	The teacher occasionally modifies the curriculum, instruction, and materials. There is some success/behavior change for students who are in at-risk situations.	The teacher rarely/never modifies the curriculum, instruction, and materials. There is little/no success/behavior change for students who are in at-risk situations.
QUANTITY **ALMOST ALL OF THE TIME (90-100%)** The teacher modifies and adapts classroom materials and/or instruction for students in at-risk situations when appropriate.	**QUANTITY** **MOST OF THE TIME (80-89%)** The teacher modifies and adapts classroom materials and/or instruction for students in at-risk situations when appropriate.	**QUANTITY** **SOME OF THE TIME (50-79%)** The teacher modifies and adapts classroom materials and/or instruction for students in at-risk situations when appropriate.	**QUANTITY** **LESS THAN HALF OF THE TIME (0-49%)** The teacher modifies and adapts classroom materials and/or instruction for students in at-risk situations when appropriate.
The teacher is proactive in seeking out and using additional resources.	The teacher is proactive in seeking out and using additional resources.	The teacher is proactive in seeking out and using additional resources.	The teacher is proactive in seeking out and using additional resources.
The teacher is proactive in seeking out and acting on assistance from other professionals.	The teacher is proactive in seeking out and acting on assistance from other professionals.	The teacher is proactive in seeking out and acting on assistance from other professionals.	The teacher is proactive in seeking out and acting on assistance from other professionals.
The teacher is proactive in seeking out and acting on assistance from parents/community.	The teacher is proactive in seeking out and acting on assistance from parents/community.	The teacher is proactive in seeking out and acting on assistance from parents/community.	The teacher is proactive in seeking out and acting on assistance from parents/community.

* For the 2003-2004 school year, the campus performance rating will be the district performance rating as reported in the new accountability system, when determined by the State. The rating will be used **for reporting purposes only.**

SUMMARY

The issues noted in the preceding discussion are just a few of those related to these documents and similar ones which are inherent in every district's document. As noted in the examples, many decisions about the structure of documents lead to advantages in some circumstances and disadvantages in others. Many elements may be advantages for evaluators, but disadvantages for teachers or vice versa. Because of these dynamics, the process of developing documents is usually very time-consuming. What starts off as an effort to develop a document that better meets the needs of everyone in every situation, often ends up as an unfinished document or a document that in time proves to be only as effective as (or less effective than) the previous document. One way to avoid this problem is to initially devote your supervision and evaluation improvement efforts to training evaluators and improving the implementation of the present document. Once you have maximized the implementation of your present document, you may then assess the document from the perspective of teachers and evaluators and through the lens of the four E.L.P.S. dimensions. Having followed these recommendations, you will then be in a much better position to determine which (if any) improvements are needed to maximize the effectiveness of your supervision and evaluation program.

SOURCES

Danielson, C. (1996). *Enhancing professional practice: A teaching framework.* Alexandria, VA: Association for Supervision and Curriculum Development.

Danielson, C. & McGreal, T. (2000). Teacher evaluation to enhance professional practice. Alexandria, VA: Association for Supervision and Curriculum Development and Educational Testing Service.

McTighe, J. & Wiggins, G. (1999). *Understanding by design.* Alexandria, VA: Association for Supervision and Curriculum Development.

Montgomery County Public Schools (2002). *Professional growth system handbook: Working draft 2002–2003.* Montgomery County, MD: Montgomery County Public Schools.

Saphier, J. (1993). *How to make supervision and evaluation really work.* Acton, MA: Research for Better Teaching, Inc.

Saphier, J. & Gower, R. (1997). *The skillful teacher: Building your teaching skills.* Acton, MA: Research for Better Teaching, Inc.

Texas Education Agency (2003). *The professional development and appraisal system (PDAS) scoring criteria guide.*

CHAPTER 10

Ensuring Inter-rater Reliability and Permanent, Positive Change in Your District's Supervision and Evaluation System

The *final* and *most important standard* for assessing how well a program has been implemented in a district is the extent to which the program continues to effectively function after the key person (or people) responsible for the program's development and implementation leaves the district.

People come and go, but school districts endure forever. For this reason, it is important that programs be designed so they will continue to operate successfully as some people

> The final and most important standard for assessing how well a program has been implemented in a district is the extent to which the program continues to effectively function after the key person (or people) responsible for the program's development and implementation leaves the dsitrict.

leave and others arrive. "Operating successfully" means that a district's supervision and evaluation program maintains a high level of individual evaluator competency and a high level of inter-rater reliability. This is best achieved by designing structures that:

1. *teach* the concepts and skills needed to successfully operate the program

2. *coach* new and veteran evaluators in the implementation of those concepts and skills to create and maintain mastery

3. *assess,* at least annually, the evaluators' implementation of those concepts to ensure continued mastery and inter-rater reliability

4. *re-teach* the skills and concepts to those who need to improve and also to those who need to refresh their levels of mastery

5. *teach* new concepts and skills as they evolve in the changing educational, legal and political environment in which evaluators work

This book has provided the reader with documents and activities for the continuous assessment of supervision and evaluation. These documents include:

1. The twelve competencies districts should require of their supervision and evaluation trainer(s) (pages 21–24)

2. The five skill components (pages 18–21) that need to be taught, coached, assessed and re-taught, which, as stated in chapter 4, require an *exceptional level of skill and awareness* whenever an evaluator is evaluating a below-standard teacher or one that barely meets the standard

   a. knowledge of the district's performance standards for successful teaching
   b. ability to analyze teachers' and students' behavior (as impacted by the teacher) and determine if the performance standards are met or exceeded
   c. ability to talk with teachers honestly and openly about their performance on the standards
   d. ability to document in writing teachers' levels of performance on the standards
   e. ability to assess teachers' performance using numerous sources of information in addition to classroom observations

3. The Evaluator's Survey of Potential Areas for Training and Support for Your District's Teacher Supervisors and Evaluators (pages 39–42).

4. The Teacher's Assessment of His/Her Evaluator's Performance as a Supervisor and Evaluator (pages 35–36)

5. The Criteria for Effective Observations . . . (both the self-assessment [pages 43–45] and the one for those assessing evaluators [pages 46–47])

6. File Cabinet Assessment of evaluation documents. (See chapter 8.) File cabinet assessments are designed to ensure that evaluators are meeting

the criteria required for writing observation write-ups, evaluation reports and other evaluation documents.

The use of these activities also maintains the common level of practice throughout a district that ensures inter-rater reliability. Later in this chapter, I have included some sample lessons that also improve and maintain the level of inter-rater reliability.

PLEASE DON'T MAKE ME TRAIN THE ADMINISTRATORS![1]

In chapter 2, I spoke about the importance of good training, listing twelve characteristics of a good trainer and training program for supervision and evaluation. During my career, I have taught elementary students, middle school students, high school students, graduate students, in-service teachers and in-service administrators. I found the last group to be the most difficult to keep interested and involved. This is especially true when I'm teaching about supervision and evaluation. The reasons for this are probably many, however, here are two of the more obvious ones.

First, administrators hate to leave their buildings or districts, because they are never sure what they will find when they return. When teachers go to workshops, it is true that substitute teachers cannot really replace the regular teacher. However, a good substitute can keep the classroom running at a reasonable level and can at least correct some papers or teach some of the curriculum. There will be some clean up for the teacher, but the contracted day is completed by the substitute and need not be made up by the teacher. There are no substitutes for administrators. All of the work they are not doing while attending a workshop is piling up back at the office. No one else will write those evaluations, handle the discipline problems, plan the faculty meetings, return the parents' calls or be certain that the custodians are cleaning the bathrooms. This may make administrators unwilling and even angry workshop participants at worst and distracted attendees at best.

Second, supervision and evaluation is a time-consuming, difficult and emotionally charged responsibility. Inevitably, the content of the workshop will include training in activities which evaluators don't do well and would prefer to avoid. I find this dynamic most apparent when teaching about supervising and evaluating low-performing teachers. For the reasons discussed in chapter 6, many evaluators avoid this task. They have learned to work around the low-performing teacher, rather than address the issues. Teaching administrators the skills to address these issues and challenging them to do so often causes a great deal of angst and defensiveness in the workshops.

---

[1] In some of the most progressive districts, teachers are becoming evaluators of low-performing teachers. (See the section on peer evaluation in chapter 3 on pages 112–120.) At this point, however, the vast majority of evaluators nationally are administrators and so my comments reflect that reality.

For these reasons, supervision and evaluation workshops for administrators must employ the very best teaching techniques. The trainer must keep administrators actively involved and constantly feeling that the content is useful and supportive of their work.

Keep Them Interested

Below I have provided some sample lessons for teaching the standards and processes described in this book in a way that will keep administrators interested. I have specifically chosen lessons that will increase administrators' collaboration when dealing with difficult issues, thereby increasing inter-rater reliability. The activities chosen are in no way an all-inclusive group. I typically spend ten to fifteen full days[2] in a district over a two- to three-year period when implementing the E.L.P.S. program. In that time, I use a minimum of forty to sixty activities.

> Supervision and evaluation workshops for administrators must employ the very best teaching techniques. The trainer must keep administrators actively involved and constantly feeling that the content is useful and supportive of their work.

The order in which the activities are presented in this chapter is just one possible sequence. Districts should arrange and/or rearrange the order, rewrite the activities and/or write their own activities based on the specific needs of the participants and their districts. The sample activities may be easily revised to match the configuration of your local performance standards, curriculum standards and evaluation procedures.

Creating Training Groups

Good training requires a mix of teaching configurations. Whole class, large group, small group, pairs and independent work should all be part of the teaching repertoire. Before beginning group or pair work, the trainer should decide whether he/she wants to construct the groups, randomly make them or have the participants pick the groups themselves. There are times when any one of these choices is preferable to the others. However, more times than not, careful structuring of the groups will enhance the training experience. For example, in districts where there has not been much previous training, it is often advantageous early in the training program to have evaluators with similar jobs and expectations grouped together. This enables the administrators to begin the process of understanding their colleagues' practice and work toward common expectations (increasing inter-rater reliability). At other times, however, the trainer may determine that one group of administrators has skills from which

---

[2] I spend this amount of time in districts with approximately 6,000 students, with more days in larger districts and fewer in smaller districts.

the others may learn. In this case, it may make sense to arrange the groups by mixed skill level, rather than by job similarity. Group structure may have a significant impact on a session's level of success.

Consider the example of one large high school with 1800 students, 230 teachers, 21 evaluators and 6 non-evaluating administrators. The evaluators were divided for the first year of training into three groups based on the school's administrative structure. The school had a headmaster who supervised and evaluated one group of administrators, an assistant headmaster for the humanities and an assistant headmaster for math, science and technology, each of whom supervised and evaluated their own group of department heads, who in turn evaluated the teachers. The high school supervision and evaluation workshops during the first year of E.L.P.S. training were done with six groups made by dividing each of the three groups in half. During the course of the year, the three recombined groups met with their leaders each quarter for coaching support. The district's trainer would attend these meetings as needed to answer questions and provide assistance.

During the second year, the groups continued to have their quarterly meetings. However, for workshop sessions, the trainer varied the groups throughout the year. When re-teaching, the trainer would often mix the groups to increase the inter-rater reliability among them. When new information was presented, the trainer had the evaluators work in their original support/coaching groups. (See chapter 2 for a discussion about the need for group and partner support for evaluators.)

Changing the Groups When Confronted With a Negative Dynamic

Even the most carefully crafted groups may result in a poor mix of members due to factors that were unknown or not anticipated. In these situations, transition times are a good point to change the membership in the groups. A shift in activity that coincides with a break is often a good transition period. It enables a change without signaling that the change is due to some participants' "misbehavior."

I was once hired by a superintendent to train the administrators in a district. The district had about seventy administrators. Each training day was given twice with approximately thirty-five administrators in each session. The first day of training was for the elementary administrators and the second day was for the high school administrators and sixth to twelfth grade administrators. The elementary day went without a hitch. The superintendent introduced the workshop and two of the assistant superintendents stayed for the day. The principals, assistant principals and elementary curriculum people were all eager and positive participants. As a result, I kept principals and assistants together and rotated the district-wide curriculum people to promote inter-rater reliability in the buildings and K–8 throughout the district.

The high school was a different story. People wandered in late and no central administrators came that day. Fifteen minutes into the workshop, the high school principal, who was the ranking administrator in the room, announced that he did not want to be there and did not want his administrators there because there were more important things they should be doing back at the building. "His" administrators were only there because the superintendent required their attendance.

I had originally put together groups of people with the same responsibilities (job-alike). During the first two hours, it became obvious to me which people were following the principal's lead by functioning minimally, looking for opportunities to be oppositional or using the group work times to conduct other business. At the break, I restructured the groups, as I explained, "to provide people with different jobs the opportunity to work together." In addition, I tried to place no more than one discontented participant in each group. I made this change to ensure the groups stayed on the assigned task rather than conducting other business during the group work times or just complaining about being in the workshop rather than back at the building.

Assigning Tasks to Group Members

Once the groups are made, another strategy for groups is assigning tasks to the various members. Typically, at a minimum, groups need a **leader**, **scribe** and **reporter**. The leader's job is to see that the group completes the task in the time allotted. The leader also makes sure that the ideas of all the group members are heard and that no one member monopolizes the discussions. The scribe keeps notes of the key points in the discussion. The reporter presents these points to the larger group. These assignments may be given in a variety of ways.

1. Let the group choose the roles.
2. The trainer assigns the roles.
3. The trainer assigns the leader and then the leader assigns the other roles.
4. Assign the roles through a random selection such as by using the following criteria.

    leader: person who has lived in the place farthest from the district
    reporter: person who has lived in the state for the longest amount of time
    scribe: person who has lived in the state for the least amount of time

Assigning jobs using criteria number 4 may have the positive side effect of helping the group members to better know one another on a personal level.

5. This is a variation of the criteria used in number 4 to assign roles. Assign them initially by using the preceding criteria. Then rotate the jobs for each activity, as indicated below:

	Activity 1	Activity 2	Activity 3
lives farthest from	leader	scribe	reporter
longest in state	reporter	leader	scribe
least in state	scribe	reporter	leader

Getting Started

It is usually good practice to begin your first session with some type of ice-breaker or community builder. This helps participants become acquainted (or better acquainted) and prepares people for the content area discussions to come. It is easier to be open and honest with someone you know and trust than with a "stranger." The following are examples of the many conversation starters that may serve this purpose.

WHY AM I HERE? (THINK, PAIR, SHARE)

- How long have you been a supervisor and/or evaluator of teachers?
- Why did you become a supervisor/evaluator of teachers?[3]
- What is the most significant similarity between teaching students and supervising/evaluating teachers?
- What is the most significant difference between teaching students and supervising/evaluating teachers?
- What do you want to learn about supervision and evaluation?
- What age students and/or which curriculum areas have you taught?

The participants share the information above with the group.

Each group makes a list and reports to the entire training group the two most important things they want to learn about supervision and evaluation. This exercise serves two purposes. First, it gives the trainer a sense of the group's priorities and needs. Second, it illustrates to the group the varied priorities that exist among the participants. This enhances each participant's willingness to be supportive of the trainer's work in teaching concepts that not all participants might personally consider to be a priority.

---

3 This is a great question for stimulating a more personal discussion and connection among the group members. However, it may be too personal for use at the early stages of the group's work and, therefore, may be better left for later in the workshop series. The decision is dependent upon the trainer's interpretation of the group's level of readiness for looking at some of their own social–emotional motivations.

The trainer should limit each ice-breaker to two questions in addition to the question asking participants "What do you want to learn?" so as not to take too much time from the day's curriculum.

SAMPLE INTRODUCTORY ACTIVITY

The following sample introductory activity is designed to assess the group's previous learning about the educational, legal, public relations and social–emotional standards and processes of supervision and evaluation.

1. It allows the group's collective knowledge on the subject to be brought forward for all to see and learn.

2. It is a pre-assessment that gives the trainer information on the accuracy of the group's present knowledge.

3. It enables the administrators to learn from one another and examine their own beliefs. Information and techniques the participants are helped to discover for themselves or learn from one another, often have *greater credibility* and, therefore, are *retained longer* than those described directly by the trainer.

A side effect of using techniques of this type when training administrators is that they may use some of them when they run their own staff meetings. One of the biggest complaints I get from teachers and teachers' associations about principals and department heads (a.k.a. secondary curriculum coordinators) is that meetings are often presented with the talking head approach to administrator presentation. This is boring to staff because it does not take into account the varied level of knowledge teachers already have on the topic of discussion or the teachers' different learning styles. Throughout supervision and evaluation training, the trainer should remind the administrators of the importance of using varied teaching techniques in their own meetings. Varying their meeting style would demonstrate to teachers the administrators' willingness to walk the walk and not just talk the talk.

Throughout supervision and evaluation training, the trainer should remind the administrators of the importance of using varied teaching techniques in their own meetings. Varying their meeting style would demonstrate to teachers the administrators' willingness to walk the walk and not just talk the talk.

Procedures

1. Divide the participants into groups of three, four or five. Setting the room up cafeteria style will help facilitate group work. However, if the room is set up as a theater, participants may turn their chairs into circles. In

large groups, people may be asked to partner rather than work in groups and the four assignments may be given out based on the area of the room where people are sitting.

2. Refer to the overhead (sample below) and have each group follow the steps to answer questions 1 through 4. Each group should be assigned one question. The extension for those groups that finish early is to discuss the other questions. Additional extension activities can be found later in this chapter.

Handouts

Adult learners, like children and adolescents, need directions presented in more than one modality to maximize their retention and understanding. Some administrators follow directions best when presented orally, some when presented visually and some when the activity is demonstrated. Make an overhead or wall chart of the steps of each activity. Use the overhead while giving the directions orally. The various graphs and lists in this book can easily be copied and made into overheads on a copy machine or typed into presentation software such as PowerPoint®. It is suggested that you give the participants a handout packet containing a copy of all the overheads you use. (Trainers using this book as a text will not need to duplicate in a handout packet those charts and lists that are found in the book.) Most presentation software has a function that allows you to put the text of several overheads on a single sheet of paper. Doing this will allow the participants to take notes directly on the handout while you are speaking, saving them time, keeping their notes organized and limiting the amount of content they might miss while hurrying to write notes.

These ideas and the following ones are just a few of the considerations when developing and providing training for groups of in-service evaluators. For those who are interested in learning more about giving interesting and helpful training presentations, I strongly recommend you read the book by Robert Garmston, entitled *The Presenter's Fieldbook: A Practical Guide* (1997).

INTER-RATER RELIABILITY ACTIVITY 1: CLIMBING THE E.L.P.S.

Objective: The following activity is designed to assess the group's previous learning about the educational, legal, public relations and social–emotional standards and processes of supervision and evaluation. It allows the group's collective knowledge on the subject to be brought forward and connects to the group's previous learning in clinical supervision and evaluation. The activity enables members of the group to learn from one another and examine their own beliefs about the processes and standards of teacher supervision and evaluation. This is the first step toward creating common understanding and increasing the level of common practice.

Educational processes and standards of supervision and evaluation

Legal processes and standards of supervision and evaluation

Public relations (political) processes and standards of supervision and evaluation

Social–Emotional processes of supervision and evaluation

1. What are the educational processes and standards of teacher supervision and evaluation?

2. What are the legal processes and standards of teacher supervision and evaluation?

3. What are the public relations (political) processes and standards of teacher supervision and evaluation?

4. What are the social–emotional processes of teacher supervision and evaluation?

Steps of the Lesson

1. In your group, compare and contrast the definition of standard and the definition of process as found in the introduction to this book.

2. In your group, discuss the question (from preceding questions 1 through 4) assigned to your group. The leader should keep the discussion moving and ensure that everyone participates.

3. Your group's scribe should write the answers to your question on the chart paper and tape it to the wall.

4. When all the groups have hung up their papers, the groups will stand by their charts. The groups will then carousel clockwise around the room, reading the answers on each chart and adding any additional answers they may have for the questions on the chart papers.

5. When the groups have completed the carousel, the reporter from each group will report on the answers from the chart that was initially assigned to that group.

You will note that the design of the activity is to get the participants standing, moving and interacting soon after the start of the workshop. This sets the stage for a period of presentation by the trainer. It is important that the participants receive an overview of the educational, legal, public relations (political) and social–emotional dimensions in order to create a context for more in-depth learning about each area. It is recommended that any lecture period be kept to no more than thirty-six minutes. Provide two minutes at the end of each ten to twelve minutes of lecture for processing, questions and comments. The questions and comments will stimulate the group and enable the trainer to assess the group's level of understanding.

INCREASING INTER-RATER RELIABILITY USING YOUR DISTRICT'S PERFORMANCE AND CURRICULUM STANDARDS

The following activities are designed to increase inter-rater reliability in the district by focusing participants on the use of the district's performance standards and curriculum standards in their evaluations. Participants begin the process of discussing and defining which observable teaching practices represent each of the standards. They also develop their skills and willingness to talk with teachers about the "hard-to-hear" information. The assumption in the activities is that the participants have all been taught how to observe, script and write using claims, judgments, evidence and impact statements or some similar format that uses objective evidence to support inferred conclusions. (See chapter 3.) These skills should be fairly well internalized before moving to the more difficult task of teaching the participants to use the district's performance and curriculum standards. The next three activities focus on the use of the performance standards.

The first inter-rater reliability activity begins with the application of the standards to high-performing teachers. I have purposely started with high-performing teachers because this is psychologically easier for most evaluators. In many groups, the evaluators are uncomfortable admitting in front of their peers and/or supervisors that they have low-performing teachers in their buildings or departments until a certain level of trust has been established. They often feel guilty or embarrassed they haven't dealt with the low performer effectively up to this point.

The second inter-rater reliability activity uses the trainer's teaching to introduce the discussion of low performance. It sensitizes the participants to talking about less successful or unsuccessful performance in an environment that can be safer than talking about their own staff before they are ready. Activity 4 begins the discussion about the evaluator's own low performers. Be prepared for resistance from some during this activity for the reasons mentioned above.

INTER-RATER RELIABILITY ACTIVITY 2: HIGH-PERFORMING TEACHERS AND THE DISTRICT'S TEACHER PERFORMANCE STANDARDS

Visual Imagery

1. Close your eyes and take three deep, slow breaths. Picture your staff as a group (pause). Picture an excellent teacher . . . (pause), picture a teacher who is performing fine, but is one that you would like to move toward excellence . . . (pause), picture a marginal teacher . . . (pause), and, lastly, picture your lowest-performing teacher . . . (pause). First, we will focus on the excellent teacher.

2. Open your eyes and list the behaviors that make this teacher successful. Now connect one or more of these behaviors to the district's performance standards. Describe the behavior you have connected in the language of the district's performance standards and as much as possible in terms of observable behaviors. Write this description in paragraph form and be ready to share it with your group.

3. Each member of the group should share his/her example. While sharing, be sure to explain the following: Why is this example representative of the standard you chose? Does it demonstrate more than one standard? Can you determine this practice is successful from watching the students? If so, how? Why do you believe this practice is successful? How does this standard positively impact student learning?

4. Choose one of the examples from your group and be ready to share it with the larger group in a way that at least covers the five questions posed in number 3.

INTER-RATER RELIABILITY ACTIVITY 3: RECOMMENDATIONS FOR IMPROVEMENT ARE HARD TO HEAR! OR SAYING THE "HARD-TO-SAY STUFF" VERBALLY AND IN WRITING!

The following activity is designed to get evaluators to write about poor performance and to watch and/or participate in a post-conference in which the evaluator needs to talk about poor performance.[4] The activity uses the trainer as "the teacher" to provide practice in a safe yet authentic environment. Conferencing with teachers about performance that needs improvement and writing evaluation reports to teachers about this type of performance are two of the most difficult tasks for evaluators.

---

[4] As noted in chapter 4, it is important that the areas for improvement be stated orally to the teacher before putting them in writing. Saying the "hard to say stuff" before writing it is more respectful of the teacher. It enhances the school climate by increasing the respect the teachers feel and increasing the level of trust between the evaluator and the teacher he/she evaluates.

1. Think about the teaching you have observed thus far in this workshop. Apply one of the performance standards to what you have observed. Write an evaluation paragraph making a claim, judgment and interpretation, supported by evidence, about one aspect of the teaching that should be improved. (For help, see the description of these concepts in chapter 3.)

2. Write a recommendation for improving the teaching of that aspect of the workshop based on one of the performance standards.

3. Use the conference preparation sheet found on page 143 to prepare to give oral feedback to the trainer about an area of success and the area for improvement. You will give this information in a conference as you would to a teacher after a classroom observation.

> Always say the "hard to hear stuff" to the teacher before you give it to him/her in writing.

The trainer should bring one participant from each group to the front of the room to have a post-conference about something in the teaching the trainer should improve.

During and after the conferences, the following four points should be emphasized.

Important Rules for Giving Suggestions and Negative Feedback

1. Always say the "hard to hear stuff" to the teacher before you give it to him/her in writing.

2. Consider whether you are a mama bear, papa bear, or baby bear, and then be sure you give the feedback with the right balance of sensitivity and clarity. (See the explanation of the Goldilocks Effect on page 182 in chapter 6.)

3. Always begin with something positive.

4. Good questioning and good listening is as important or more important than good advice.

Chapter 4 (pages 137–149) discusses the use of good listening skills in difficult situations. It includes sample questions that evaluators can use in a post-conference to address the teacher's use of assessment. Similar questions can be applied to all areas of instruction.

ASSIGNING HOMEWORK

The following sample homework assignment uses work the participants have already completed or need to complete as part of their regular responsibilities prior to the next workshop. Busy administrators are reluctant to do homework that is not readily connected to their responsibilities.

There is also an implicit objective built into the assignment. The implicit objective is asking the administrators to begin to classify their teachers' performance as top third, middle third or bottom third. This is a new and often difficult concept for many evaluators to accept and implement. It is a summative, standards-based concept that measures teachers' performance against a district standard. Many administrators have become accustomed to and are more comfortable with solely formative supervision and evaluation that is devoid of judgments that in any way indicate that one teacher's performance on a standard may be better than that of another teacher's. You will note that the definitions of formative and summative are written on the homework sheet as a reminder to evaluators that both roles are important.

In my work with districts, I have found a significant disconnect between the way evaluators conduct evaluation conferences and write observation and evaluation reports and the language of the documents themselves on which they write their final evaluation reports. In many districts the conferences, observation write-ups and final evaluation narratives are solely formative. However, the districts' documents require that evaluators check one of three or more summative judgments of performance level. In these cases, the districts' evaluation processes often suffer from two big issues. The first is rampant grade inflation; the vast majority of teachers (as many as ninety-nine percent) receive the highest rating. The second is that when teachers do not receive the highest rating, they are justifiably shocked and angered at what appears to be a disconnect between what they have been hearing all year and the judgment checked-off on their evaluations.

SAMPLE HOMEWORK SHEET
HOMEWORK FOR THE NEXT WORKSHOP

Date: TBA
Time: TBA
Place: TBA

Formative supervision and evaluation is a positive, supportive and collaborative process designed to improve students' performance and attitudes by increasing the effectiveness and attitudes of a district's teachers.

Bring three observation write-ups you completed during the school year (or previous school year if this assignment is being done in the summer or early fall). One write-up should be for a teacher performing in the top third of your school/department, the second should be for a teacher performing in the middle third of your school/department and the third should be for your lowest-performing teacher. *Remember, this is your lowest-performing teacher. The teacher need not be considered a low-performing teacher in the district.*[5] You need not be self-conscious about the quality of the write-ups. We all come with different levels of skill attainment in this area and are here to learn how to improve our write-ups and other supervision and evaluation skills.

Be sure to use opaquing liquid or black marker to cover the names of the teachers. The write-ups will only be used in the privacy of the workshop. Covering the names and following the confidentiality instructions the trainer will give on the day of the workshop will ensure the teachers' privacy.

Summative supervision and evaluation is a process designed to measure the teachers' levels of success s as compared to the district's curriculum and performance standards.

INTER-RATER RELIABILITY ACTIVITY 4:
LOW-PERFORMING TEACHERS AND THE
DISTRICT'S TEACHER PERFORMANCE STANDARDS

1. Picture your staff again as a group. Picture the lowest-performing teacher in your building/department for whom you brought the write-up . . . List the behaviors that need to be improved and connect one of these behaviors to one of the district's performance standards. Identify the

---

5   Even though the directions ask participants to bring an evaluation for the lowest performer in your school/department, in every case in which I have given this assignment several administrators raise their hands and say they have no low-performing teachers. The trainer may need to repeat the directions several times and emphasize the fact that everyone has someone who is at the bottom of the school/department. Even if the administrator's lowest teacher is in the top third of the district, the teacher is still that administrator's bottom performer and warrants more time and attention than others in the building/department.

teaching technique using the language of the performance standard as much as possible (claim). Provide objective evidence supporting the claim, in terms of observable and or verifiable behaviors. Remember, verifiable behavior can come from many sources other than classroom observations. Indicate the impact of the teaching technique on student learning (interpretation). Finally, include a value judgment that indicates whether the teaching technique is below, barely meets, meets or exceeds the district's standard.

2. Write this description in paragraph form. If you have a good example in the write-up you brought, you may use it by rewriting the paragraph in the C.J.E.I. form. Make the claim in the language of one of the district's performance standards.

3. Write an evaluation recommendation for the teacher that is related to the behavior. To the extent possible, indicate the impact the recommendation will have on student learning.

4. Share the paragraph and recommendation with your partner and give and receive feedback using the peer-edit sheet found on page 95.

5. Each pair should choose one of their examples and share it with the group. Please do not use the teacher's name. While sharing, be sure to answer the following questions.

   a. Why is this example representative of the standard you chose?
   b. Does it demonstrate more than one standard?
   c. Can you determine that this practice is not successful from watching the students? If so, how?
   d. Why do you believe that this practice is not successful?
   e. How will your recommendation improve student learning?

INTER-RATER RELIABILITY ACTIVITY 5: THE WAY WE WANT SUPERVISION AND EVALUATION TO HAPPEN VERSUS THE WAY IT REALLY HAPPENS

The importance of contract and labor law increases exponentially when evaluating a low-performing teacher. Unfortunately, many administrators overestimate or underestimate the requirements of the law because they lack sufficient training in the standards and processes articulated in labor and contract law. When you combine this lack of knowledge with the administrators' varying predispositions toward addressing low performance (the Goldilocks effect), you often end up with one of two outcomes.

Some administrators act too quickly and skip steps because of their frustration with the time and effort needed to complete the process correctly.

Others act too slowly so they may avoid the final steps for a teacher who does not adequately improve (i.e., a "last chance year" or dismissal). As I often tell my workshop participants, typically there are only two mistakes an evaluator can make. The first is going too fast through the steps. The second is going too slowly through the steps.

This activity is intended to identify both the misconceptions and the accurate prior knowledge of the participants concerning the factors that increase the complexity of evaluating a low-performing teacher. It also begins the process of evaluators' identifying their own varied levels of willingness to address low-performing teachers. The participants' understanding of those differences is the first step toward district-wide amelioration of the differences in their supervision and evaluation of low-performing teachers.

1. Picture again the lowest-performing teacher in your building/department from the previous activity.

2. Imagine you are in a perfect world where you are not encumbered by factors such as time constraints, contract or labor law, the impact on other staff, emotional reactions, etc. List your goals for this teacher's improvement, and briefly develop a professional development or improvement plan and time line for achieving these goals. See pages 196–213 to refresh your knowledge about the structure of improvement plans.

3. Now look at your goals and time line in the context of the real world full of all of the educational, legal, public relations (political) and social–emotional challenges that come into play when you evaluate a below-standard, tenured teacher. List the factors that keep you from carrying out your perfect world plan for achieving your goals for this person. Be prepared to explain how these factors impede your ability to implement your goals from item 2.

4. When you finish, share the information with your partner and brainstorm strategies for overcoming the real life challenges faced by your plan. Please do not use the teacher's name.

5. Share with your group the goals, time line, list of challenges and any strategies you and your partner developed for overcoming the challenges.

6. The group recorder should list the challenges discussed that increase the complexity of evaluating a low-performing teacher and any corresponding strategies for overcoming these challenges.

INTER-RATER RELIABILITY ACTIVITY 6:
LEARNING FROM OUR MISTAKES AND OUR SUCCESSES

This activity is best used after the participants have completed the case study activity on pages 186–192 and learned the format for an improvement plan.

Think about a difficult evaluation you've done in the past. Now, think about the teacher in terms of the questions that appear on pages 191–192 after the Jeff Doe case study.[6] Be prepared to explain to your group your answers to the following questions:

1. What about the evaluation went well?

2. Why did that part go well?

3. What did not go well?

4. What would you do differently if you had the chance to do that evaluation again?

5. What supports would have been helpful for you when doing this evaluation?

Share your answers to questions 1 through 5 with a partner. What additional suggestions does your partner have for the next time you face a similar situation?

INTER-RATER RELIABILITY ACTIVITY 7:
DEVELOPING AN IMPROVEMENT PLAN

1. Skim chapter 6. (This chapter should have been read at an earlier point.)

2. Closely review the final evaluation and improvement plan for Karen Sullivan, beginning on page 205. Compare that improvement plan to the section that describes the components of an improvement plan on pages 210–212.

3. List those components that exist in Karen Sullivan's plan and those that are missing. Be prepared to share this list with your group.

---

[6] One of the most difficult areas for an evaluator to assess is the impact his/her intensive work with a low-performing teacher has on the other staff members and the school culture. One technique some evaluators use is to visualize each of their teachers individually. (This is best done in a quiet setting such as in the car during the commute to or from work.) They then do a brief assessment of each teacher's response to the evaluator's work with the low-performing teacher and try to place the teacher in one of the following categories: believes the evaluator is not addressing the issue sufficiently; is pleased that the issue is being addressed and fully supportive of the actions; is pleased that the issue is being addressed, but feels a bit threatened; believes that the evaluator is pushing too hard; believes that the evaluator is pushing too hard and feels threatened; believes that the evaluator's actions are inappropriate and unwarranted.

4. Think about how the components of the improvement plan apply to the lowest-performing teacher in your specific building/department. Remember, evaluation is a problem-solving process and one that requires situational leadership. Many of the strategies can be modified to match specific situations. Write an improvement plan for the lowest-performing teacher in your building/department. Use a pseudonym for the teacher when you share the plan with your working group.

5. Below, make a list of the questions that arose as you wrote the improvement plan. Be prepared to share these questions with your group.

6. Share the questions in the group and try together to answer as many as possible.

7. Make a group list of the questions that remain.

INTER-RATER RELIABILITY ACTIVITY 8: THE SOCIAL–EMOTIONAL COMPONENTS OF STONE SOUP

The workshop begins by asking participants to listen carefully to the story, *Stone Soup* (1993), published by Troll Associates and illustrated by Diane Paterson. *Stone Soup* is a French folktale that is excellent for starting discussions with children or adults about group dynamics. Other trainers may have other stories or discussion starters that work equally well.

It is recommended that the trainer have at least two copies of the big book version so the participants can follow the story while it is being read. If possible, it is good for each participant or group to have the small book version as well so they can refer to it during the activity. I usually have one of the participants read the story and two others hold the big books and show the pictures. This enables the trainer to quickly assess each participant's awareness of the impact of supervision and evaluation on a school's culture. The discussion about the questions below can then be tailored to the needs of the group. While the story is being read, the participants should think about the following questions.

1. In which ways are the social–emotional relationships in the story *Stone Soup* the same as those that occur between evaluators and teachers in their buildings/departments during the supervision and evaluation process?

2. In which ways are the social–emotional relationships in *Stone Soup* different from those between evaluators and teachers in their buildings/ departments during the supervision and evaluation process?

The trainer works to move the discussion toward an examination of the social–emotional factors in the story that are similar to supervision and evaluation. For example:

a. If an evaluator sees the villagers as the teachers and the soldiers as the supervisors and evaluators, the story indicates that you get more from teachers when you engage them as partners in the process and make evaluation something you do with teachers rather than to them. The story is a good example of how supervisors who use "expert power" (Hershey & Blanchard, 1982, p. 176) rather than "coercive power"[7] (Hershey & Blanchard, p.186) build a collaborative school culture in which the whole is greater than the sum of the parts.

b. Some evaluators initially see the villagers as the evaluators and the soldiers as the teachers protected by their union. These evaluators often verbalize that they are powerless to address low teacher performance because of coercive behavior by the union (see chapter 5). Trainers should remember that this response from evaluators may be caused by a union that uses strong-arm tactics, by the evaluators themselves who hide behind the "threat" of the union as the reason they don't address low performance or by both of these factors. In this scenario, the trainer should try to get more information from the senior administration and/or the union about the reason evaluators feel it is difficult to address low performance.

c. Reading the story initiates a discussion that allows the trainer to refer to many of the social–emotional components inherent in earlier activities.

EXTENSION ACTIVITIES

The movement away from homogeneous grouping by ability in classrooms has made them increasingly diverse academically. Academic diversity increases the difficulty of timing lessons so that all students remain productively on task and continue learning at their own levels throughout the work period. This challenge may be even greater when teachers use cooperative learning groups with different tasks assigned to each group. In these instances, some group's tasks may take less time than others. Therefore, it is essential that teachers plan lessons in ways that provide additional, relevant challenges for those students and/or groups who complete the primary task early. A way of doing this is to provide students with task-related extension activities.

Earlier in this chapter, I noted the importance of keeping the administrators interested and learning. The challenges discussed in the preceding paragraph are as important when teaching adults as they are when teaching

---

[7] Hershey and Blanchard define expert power as based on the leader's possession of expertise, skill and knowledge, which, through respect, influence others. They define coercive power as based on fear that a failure to comply will lead to punishment.

children. The following suggestions are for extension tasks for those individuals or groups who finish the primary tasks in this program early.

Extension 1: Review the teaching by the presenter in this workshop thus far. Write a paragraph for one of your performance standards on which you believe the presenter needs to improve. Be sure you identify the teaching in the language of the performance standard (claim), place a value judgment on the performance, interpret the impact on student learning and provide the evidence that supports these subjective conclusions. Write a recommendation for improvement. Be sure to specifically identify the impact of the recommendation on the administrators in the room.

Extension 2: Think about the recommendation you wrote in extension 1. Write one or more questions you can use in a post-conference that you should ask to be sure you have all the information to make the judgment leading to your recommendation. Remember, you can't read the presenter's mind, so he/she may have a well thought-out reason for the action taken that you don't yet understand.

Extension 3: Write a paragraph about a standard the presenter successfully met. Be sure you identify the teaching in the language of the performance standard, place a value judgment on the performance, identify the impact on student learning and provide the evidence that supports these subjective conclusions.

Extension 4: Go to the section in this book entitled "Where Do I Find the Time For All These Write-ups?" Describe any strategies, not on the list, that your group has used (or you have used) to save time or stay organized without diminishing quality. Your strategies can be added to the list and used to help other supervisors–evaluators in the future.

Extension 5: Put a check next to the performance standards you think are most important. Be prepared to explain why you chose those standards. Compare your answers with those of the other group members who are finished with the assignment. See if you can reach consensus.

Extension 6: Respond to the following statements and questions.
- Identify the ways in which teaching an effective lesson is the same as running an effective staff meeting.
- Identify the ways in which teaching an effective lesson is different from running an effective staff meeting.
- What are some techniques you have used or seen used for running effective staff meetings?

Extension 7: Answer the following questions.

- What is the most significant similarity between running an effective staff meeting and teaching a successful lesson? Why did you choose this similarity?
- What is the most significant difference between running an effective staff meeting and teaching a successful lesson? Why did you choose this difference?

Extension 8: Think about an upcoming staff meeting. Write a "lesson plan" for the meeting that utilizes the practices you identified as effective in the previous extension activities.

Extension 9: While you are waiting for the others, write a definition for the legal concepts of just cause (and/or progressive discipline, duty of fair representation or harassment) in your own words.

Extension 10: Write an improvement plan for the second lowest-performing teacher in your building/department.

Extension 11: Write your own extension activity to go along with one of the preceding lessons or one of the concepts taught in the book.

CHECKING FOR COMPETENCY AND UNDERSTANDING

Chapters 2 and 3 contain various instruments that can used to monitor evaluator competency on the concepts and skills taught in this book. These are structures designed to assist those assessing evaluators' work on the various skills and concepts. Below is an assessment that may be done once or twice a year with the training groups to refresh what has been learned and to identify the concepts that need re-teaching. It is fun, but effective.

"Hot Seat" Open Book Assessment

- Your group has thirty minutes to review the questions on the study guide below.
- After that, your group will be randomly given one of the four questions and have twenty minutes to prepare the answer to present to the class. You may use the book, your notes or any other materials from the workshop to prepare.
- Also in that twenty minutes, you must choose two members of your group (a.k.a. the "presenting pair") to come to the hot seat to present the information and two other group members (a.k.a. the "question answerers") to come to the hot seat after the presentation to answer questions from the trainer and the other groups about your question.
- Each group will be given two "life lines" that their two question answerers may pass to another group member who knows the answer when they are unable to answer one of the questions presented.

Study Guide for Open Book Test 1

1. Supervision and evaluation programs are designed to formatively assist teachers in their continuous improvement as it relates to their districts' educational standards and processes. Supervision and evaluation is also designed to summatively assess teachers' performance as measured against their districts' educational standards and processes.

   a. What educational standards do we use to supervise and evaluate teachers? (Think local, state and national.)

   b. How is supervision and evaluation effectively used by evaluators to assess performance as measured against those standards?

   c. How does your district's evaluation document create a process for this work?

   d. How do you assess your own knowledge of the educational standards and processes?

    e.   Where can an evaluator go for additional information and coaching related to your district's educational standards?

2. Supervision and evaluation programs are designed to formatively assist teachers in their continuous improvement as it relates to the districts' educational standards and processes. Supervision and evaluation programs are also designed to summatively assess teachers' performance against required legal standards and processes. It is important that evaluators have adequate knowledge of this body of legal information for all their evaluations. However, when an evaluator is working with a tenured teacher (other terms are used for tenure in some states) who barely meets or does not meet the standards, the typical outcomes are that the teacher improves sufficiently or that the teacher might be disciplined or terminated. These situations often shift the evaluation's context more heavily into the realm of labor law. In these cases, it is important that evaluators have comprehensive knowledge of the legal standards and processes.

    a.   Which legal standards and processes are important for an evaluator to be cognizant of during supervision and evaluation? (Think local, state and national.)

    b.   Which legal standards and processes must evaluators adhere to in their work with low-performing teachers?

    c.   Why is it important for evaluators to be cognizant of the legal standards and processes even when the evaluator is not working with a low performer?

    d.   How does your district's evaluation document create a process for following the required legal standards?

    e.   Where can an evaluator in your district go for help in following the legal standards and processes, particularly when involved in the evaluation of a low-performing teacher with tenure (professional teacher status)?

3. Supervision and evaluation programs are designed to formatively assist teachers in their continuous improvement as it relates to the district's educational standards. Supervision and evaluation is also designed to summatively assess a teacher's performance as it relates to the various public relations (political) standards and processes so schools can be accountable to the public.

    a.   Who are public educators' public relations (political) constituencies? Why is each of these constituencies important?

    b.   What are the public relations (political) impacts when a district ineffectively supervises and evaluates teachers?

    c.   What are the public relations (political) impacts when a district effectively supervises and evaluates teachers?

    d. What can teachers, building administrators, district administrators and support staff in our public schools do to build public support for public schools?

4. Supervision and evaluation programs are designed to formatively assist teachers in their continuous improvement as it relates to the district's educational standards and processes. Supervision and evaluation programs are impacted significantly by the various social–emotional standards and processes. It is our summative conclusions (particularly those we put in a written observation and/or evaluation) that can complicate and intensify the interpersonal and emotional climate during supervision and evaluation.

    a. In what circumstances does supervision and evaluation cause a strong emotional reaction in a teacher? (Think about average-performing and high-performing teachers as well as low-performing teachers.)

    b. In what circumstances does supervision and evaluation cause difficult interpersonal situations for evaluators?

5. How does supervision and evaluation impact a school's and/or a district's culture? What can an evaluator do maximize the positive impact and minimize the negative impact of supervision and evaluation on the school's/department's culture?

6. Where does an evaluator go for support/coaching/advice when involved in an evaluation that causes difficult emotional reactions in the teacher or the evaluator?

7. Where does an evaluator go for support/coaching/advice when involved in an evaluation that causes difficult social dynamics between the evaluator and the teacher and/or the evaluator and his/her staff?

8. In your group, choose a difficult social–emotional situation related to the supervision and evaluation of a teacher in which one of you was actually involved. Tell the class what skills and/or techniques the evaluator used in handling the situation and what the group learned from the chosen case.

9. How do you as an evaluator gauge the impact of your work as a supervisor and evaluator on the culture in your building/department or district?

CONCLUSION

The activities in this chapter are only a sample of the myriad of teaching strategies that can be used to teach the various concepts and skills in this book to evaluators. However, no amount of excellent teaching (training) ever eliminates the need for coaching, assessing and re-teaching. As illustrated in the cases noted in the Archaeological Dig on page 25, nearly all the impact of even the best training in supervision and evaluation will disappear in a relatively short time if there isn't continual coaching, assessing and re-teaching. The busy lives of evaluators inevitably make them focus on the "crisis du jour" and not on the time-consuming, emotionally challenging and less immediately compelling activities needed to successfully supervise and evaluate teachers.

The most effective way to monitor the continuous growth of your evaluators is through the file cabinet review. Continuous review of the evaluators' work, accompanied by specifically stated commendations and recommendations, keeps the district moving toward high quality teacher evaluation.

Yes, it is hard work for a district with low- or mediocre-functioning supervision and evaluation to transform its program. Yes, it does require a commitment of evaluators' and central administrators' time and resources to turn that system into a successful system.

Yes, it does take time, vigilance and a skilled central administrator to continuously coach, assess and re-teach, even in districts with successful supervision and evaluation programs.

However, once a district is operating a successful program of supervision and evaluation that attends to the educational, legal, public relations (political) and social–emotional dimensions, you can expect a school culture that provides:

- higher student achievement
- higher teacher morale
- higher public perception of the school's/department's performance.

Sources

Garmston, R. (1997). *The presenter's fieldbook: A practical guide.* Norwood, MA: Christopher Gordon Publishers.

Hershey, P. & Blanchard, K. (1982). *Management of organizational behavior: Utilizing human resources.* 4th ed. Englewood Cliffs, NJ: Prentice Hall, Inc.

Saphier, J. & Gower, R. (1997). *The skillful teacher: Building your teaching skills.* Acton, MA: Research for Better Teaching, Inc.

Stone Soup. Illustrated by Paterson, D. (1993). Troll Associates. ISBN 0-89375-479-1.

INDEX

Alternate data sources 1, chapter 4

Arbitration 69, 129, 166, 167, 171, 173, 174, 176, 218, 289, 315, 366, 367

Below standard tenured teachers (see unsatisfactory tenured teachers), chapter 6 and chapter 7, 445

Barely satisfactory tenured teachers (see mediocre tenured teachers) chapter 6 and chapter 7, 255, 280

Case studies 2, 176, 183–184, 186–192, 283, 284, 446

Charter Schools 9, 195

Claim 33, 39, 46, chapter 3, 180, 181, 185, 243, 251, 254, 255, 439

Classroom observations 5, 18, 19, 32, 39, 134, 137, 251
    Announced, chapter 3
    Unannounced chapter 3, 50

Clinical supervision and evaluation 97, 17, 18, 21, 66, 97, 438

Collective bargaining 170, 171, 282

Conduct unbecoming a teacher 169, 175, 226

Conferencing 19, 53, 139, 146–149, 173, 272
    pre-observation conferences 100, 137, 138, 139, 140, 288
    post-observation conferences 1, 74, 83, 100, 137, 139, 141, 143, 144, 146, 147, 236, 269, 288, 440
    final evaluation conferences 146

Constituencies 151, 237, 274, 275–279, 359, 451

Consulting teachers 113, 118, 119, 237, 245

Continuing contract teacher 275 (see also tenured teacher)

Contract negotiations 151 (see collective bargaining)

Corrective recommendation 216, 222, 226

Criteria for Effective Observation Write-ups 39, 43, 46, 54, 257, 263

Curriculum Frameworks 140, 356 (see also curriculum standards)

Curriculum standards 8, 20, 37, 62, 96, 97, 432, 439

Data 3, 4, 2, 18, 20, 35, 66, 67, 68, 73, 121, 131, 132–137, 142, 146, 173, 222, 236, 280, 315
    direct 67, 142
    indirect 67, 142, 175, 181

Dismissal 115, 119, 165, 166, 168, 169, 171, 173, 216, 223, 284, 319, 445

Domains of teaching (see performance standards and Texas Professional Development and Appraisal System (PDAS))

Due Process 8, 9, 14, 41, 42, 57, 154, 157, 165, 168–170 (see also just cause)

Duty of fair representation 9, 14, 41, 57

End of year evaluation report 184, 185, 198 (see also final evaluation write-up)

Eulogy observation write-up 235, 255

Evaluation reports 239, 241, 431 (see also observation write-ups, see final evaluation write-ups)

Evidence 20, 24, 25, 33, 40–44, 63–70, 131, 132, 135, 136, 146, 170, 173–179, 185, 240, 251, 252, 257, 258, 269, 369, 439

hearsay 174, 178, 195, 222

direct 174, 176, 178, 181, 222, 252

indirect 222, 252, 258, 264

circumstantial 175, 197

Expectation clarification memo 42, 57, 230, 231

File cabinet assessment 33, 38, 46, 237–267, 430

Final evaluation write-ups 101, 146, 205–209, 238, 240, 242, 246, 367, 442

Formative assessment of students 141

Formative assessment of teachers 165, 173, 177, 186, 215, 239, 274, 384, 442, 452

Ghost town effect 182

Goldilocks effect 182, 193, 441, 444

Harassment 9, 41, 56, 57, 179, 196, 226

Impact statement 39, 40, 41, 60, 64–70, 95, 121–129

Improvement plans 41, 56, 161, 166, 170, 196–212, 320, 366

Incompetency 41, 56, 69, 169

Inefficiency 41, 69, 169

Information 1, 132, 133, 142, 173–176, 179, 180, 181, 191, 230, (see also evidence)

Instructional standards (see performance standards)

Insubordination 42, 57, 169, 226

Interpretation 240, 252 (see also impact statement)

Inter-rater reliability 28, chapter 10

Investigations 219

Judgments 3, 5, 17, 18, 20, 33, 40, 42–50, 55, 60–70, 73, 84, 95, 123, 240, 312

Just cause 8, 9, 41, 42, 56–57, 168-170, 195, 215

Mediocre tenured teachers 196, 454

Needs assessment 34, 48, 50

Negotiations 151 (see also collective bargaining)

No Child Left Behind (NCLB) 3, 136, 368

Note Taking 51, 73, 83–94

literal notes 73, 95

analysis of notes 78–79, 83, 121

note-taking rubric 83–84

Non-professional teacher status teachers (see probationary teachers)

Non-tenured teachers (see probationary teachers)

Observation write-ups (see classroom observations, see walk throughs)

Parent data 180–181

Peer coaching for teachers 40, 53, 55, 116, 95, 103, 108, 109, 112, 113, 151, 274, 365

Peer coaching for administrators 180, 184

Performance standards 20, 22, 28, 29, 35, 38–40, 42–45, 47, 49, 53, 55, 57, 61, 62, 95, 97, 107, 108, 115, 116, 120, 280, 282

classroom teachers 294–302, 326–328, 369–424

school nurses 329–332

special education teachers 332–335

language arts specialists 335–339

psychologists 339–342

speech and language pathologists 342–345

library/media specialists 346–349

counselors 349–352

social workers 349–352

occupational therapists 352–355

curriculum leader 358–361

Permanent teacher (see tenured teacher)

Principles of Effective Teaching 282, 285, 294–302 (see also performance standards)

Probationary teacher 241, 275, 280

Professional teacher status 169, 275 (see tenured teacher)

Progressive Discipline 9, 14, 41, 42, 53, 56, 57, 170, 183, chapter 7

Reprimand 196
   Written 216, 217, 222, 225, 226
   Oral 216, 222, 226, 227, 229

Sample observation write-ups 71–72, 80–82, 126–128

Scripting (see note-taking)

Second evaluators 33, 41, 56, 184, 192

Stages of listening 146–149 (see conferencing)

Student survey data 303–306

Student performance data 270, 388–424 (see alternate data sources, see value-added)

Summative assessment of students 134, 384

Summative assessment of teachers 8, 112, 118, 120

Supervision 1, 2, 3, 5, 7, 17, 112, 113, 114

Supervision and evaluation documents 2, 8, 14, 20, 21, 22, 32, 40, 55, 120, 184, 197, 215, chapter 9
   developing documents 97
   sample documents 285–424

Supervision and evaluation procedures (see also supervision and evaluation documents)

Teacher performance standards (see performance standards)

Teachers associations 154, 167, 195 (see also unions)

Tenured teachers 8, 14, 104, 105, 112, 116, 117, 119, 153, 156, 160, 161, 162, 165, 168, 169, 179, 186, 219, 275, 452 (see also professional teacher status teachers and permanent teachers)

Texas Professional Development and Appraisal System (PDAS) 369–424 (see performance standards)

Time saving techniques 40, 53, 55, 98–113, 121, 123

Tom Sawyer effect

Track III teachers (see unsatisfactory tenured teacher)

Unions 9, 10, 13, 113, 118, 120, chapter 5, 171, 172, 195, 277

Unsatisfactory tenured teachers 41, 44, 53, 56, chapter 6, chapter 7

Value added 135, 136

Value judgments (see judgments)

Verbal reprimand (see reprimand, oral)

Vouchers 156, 159
Walk-throughs 19
Warnings (see reprimand)
Weingarten Right 41, 42, 56,
    172–173, 217

Written reprimand (see reprimand,
    written)

NOTES

NOTES

NOTES

NOTES